Culture and Gender in Leadership

Culture and Gender in Leadership

Perspectives from the Middle East and Asia

Edited by

James Rajasekar
Sultan Qaboos University, Sultanate of Oman

and

Loo-See Beh
University of Malaya, Malaysia

palgrave
macmillan

First published 2013 by
PALGRAVE MACMILLAN

Palgrave Macmillan in the UK is an imprint of Macmillan Publishers Limited, registered in England, company number 785998, of Houndmills, Basingstoke, Hampshire RG21 6XS.

Palgrave Macmillan in the US is a division of St Martin's Press LLC, 175 Fifth Avenue, New York, NY 10010.

Palgrave Macmillan is the global academic imprint of the above companies and has companies and representatives throughout the world.

Palgrave® and Macmillan® are registered trademarks in the United States, the United Kingdom, Europe and other countries.

ISBN 978–1–137–31156–6

This book is printed on paper suitable for recycling and made from fully managed and sustained forest sources. Logging, pulping and manufacturing processes are expected to conform to the environmental regulations of the country of origin.

A catalogue record for this book is available from the British Library.

A catalog record for this book is available from the Library of Congress.

To my wife, Viji, and children, Akhil and Talia

J.R.

To family and friends

L.-S.B.

Contents

Tables and Figures

Tables

Figures

Acknowledgements

We would like to thank, first and foremost, Virginia Thorp, senior commissioning editor, business and management, at Palgrave Macmillan, for approving this book. She was a solid supporter of this project from day one and whenever we wanted help she was always willing to help. We are indebted to her.

We are also thankful to Keri Dickens for her professional support during this project.

Our thanks also go out to the numerous contributors to this book.

Last, but not least, we would like to thank our friends for their timely advice and ideas, and our families for their patience, support and encouragement during the time-consuming process of preparing this book.

Contributors

Alan N. Aladano is the Assistant Regional Director for Operations of the Bureau of Fire Protection in Northern Mindanao, Philippines, with the officer rank of Fire Superintendent, and Professor of the Graduate School of Capitol University. He holds the following degrees: doctor of management, master in business management, master in public administration, bachelor of science in business administration, major in human resource development and bachelor of science in civil engineering. He is a prolific researcher and a lecturer of the Regional Training School of the Philippine Public Safety College. He also serves as a consultant of GH Research and Development Institute. Moreover, he is a member of the Philippine Association of Graduate Education and the Statistical Association of Region 10. E-mail: analadano@yahoo.com

Salem Al-Abri works as an assistant professor in the College of Economics and Political Science, Sultan Qaboos University, Sultanate of Oman. He was in the human resources management field in the oil industry prior to joining academia. He holds a PhD from the Australian National University, Australia. His research interests focus on leadership and various aspects of human resources management. He has conducted research on the interplay of culture and leadership styles in the Middle Eastern context, and he has taught at the undergraduate level as well as the postgraduate level on the MBA programme. E-mail: salemabri@squ.edu.om

Adil Al-Busaidi is a doctoral student in communication studies at Ohio University, US. His interests are in quantitative research methods and social network analysis. Organizational communication is his main focus in his doctoral programme with applied statistics as a minor. His current research interests are in the areas of small group communication, leadership communication, conflict and mediation, intercultural communication and the impact of computer-mediated communication on individuals, organizations and communities. He has served as a lecturer since 2007 at the College of Economics and Political Science, Sultan Qaboos University, Sultanate of Oman. He has taught courses including business communication, varieties of public and professional communication, and public speaking for business. Prior to teaching he worked as a computer network engineer in the telecommunications industry. His work has been published by the Institute of Electrical and Electronics Engineers on system sciences.

Sarah Alhaj holds an MBA from the University of Strathclyde Business School, UK. Her dissertation focuses on the development of Emirati leaders. She has worked in various human resources positions, including training, manpower and planning, and change management. Currently she is working as a human resource manager with the National Cyber Security Authority, United Arab Emirates. E-mail: sarah.ae@gmail.com

Alexandre A. Bachkirov is a faculty member of the Management Department, College of Economics and Political Science, Sultan Qaboos University, Sultanate of Oman. Previously he held a number of academic posts internationally, including at the University of New York in Tirana, Albania, and the University of Fortaleza, Brazil. Before joining academia, he provided export consulting, negotiation and cross-cultural enhancement support for small and medium-sized enterprises in the UK. His industrial and commercial experience is complemented by wide-ranging academic expertise in the area of management. His scholarly interests include cross-cultural leadership, managerial judgement and decision making, the effects of national culture on decision making and the effects of emotion on decision making. As an academic, he has an overarching goal of contributing to research capability building in the Sultanate of Oman through his research, lectureship, consultancy and community service. E-mail: alexbach@yahoo.com

David Beckett is an associate professor at the University of Melbourne, Australia. He is Associate Dean (Staffing) of Melbourne Graduate School of Education and Associate Dean (International) of Melbourne School of Graduate Research. He is a fellow of the Australian Council for Educational Leaders, a fellow of the Philosophy of Education Society of Australasia and a member of the Philosophy of Education Society of Great Britain. He has published extensively and his research interests include adult education, policy analysis and epistemological, ontological and ethical perspectives on practice. E-mail: d.beckett@unimel.edu.au

Loo-See Beh is an associate professor and Deputy Dean (International and Higher Degree) at the Faculty of Economics & Administration,

University of Malaya, Malaysia. She was previously a visiting academic at Griffith University, Australia. Her areas of interest include public administration, public policy, human resource management, communication, organizational behaviour, leadership and political economy. She has published in both local and international publications, and she sits on the board of reviewers for local and international journals, books and theses. She has many years of teaching and other professional experience, and consultancy work experience with public institutions and other international bodies. E-mail: lucybeh@gmail.com

Anna M. Danielewicz-Betz is an associate professor in the Centre for Language Research, University of Aizu, Japan. Her research interests include critical discourse analysis, pragmatics, interdisciplinary studies (e.g. forensic linguistics, corporate discourse), management of higher education and leadership. E-mail: adanielewicz_betz@yahoo.com

Francis Thaise A. Cimene is the Dean of the Graduate School of Capitol University, Philippines. She holds a PhD in educational management. She was appointed by the Commission on Higher Education as one of the assessors in the Philippines for the Institutional Monitoring and Evaluation for Quality Assurance. She is a member of the National Research Council of the Philippines, the Philippine Association for Graduate Education in Region 10, President of the Council of Deans of Graduate Schools Region 10, President of the Statistical Association of Region 10, Chairman of the Board of the Immanuel Mission International School and Co-Founder of Glorious Hope Christian Center, Inc. She also serves as the editor of *LAMDAG*, the official journal of the Graduate School and the Capitol University Research and Extension Office. She has lectured extensively on effective leadership, strategic management, educational leadership and methods of research for government and non-government organizations. E-mail: francisthaisec@yahoo.com

William R. Kennan is Professor of Communication at Radford University, US, and Vice Provost for Academic Affairs there. He was previously the Associate Dean and Chair of the Department of Communication at Radford University. His interests include communication effectiveness and organizational performance, leadership, organizational change and development, and public relations practice. He has served as a consultant and trainer for several organizations, including American Electric Power, Volvo, Virginia Police Chiefs Association and the various

Virginia State Departments. He has a keen interest in international and intercultural communication, especially with regard to Southeast Asia. E-mail: bill.kennan@gmail.com

Sami A. Khan is an associate professor in the Department of Human Resource Management, Faculty of Economics & Administration, King Abdul Aziz University, Jeddah, Saudi Arabia. Prior to that he was at Sultan Qaboos University, Sultanate of Oman. He is co-editor of *Human Resource Management: Emerging Perspectives in the New Era* (2000). He has also served as associate editor of *Management & Change* journal for four years. He is involved with Entrepreneurship Work in Organizations Requiring Leadership Development (E-WORLD), a global research project jointly run with faculty members of Missouri State University, US. His research interests lie in the areas of human resource strategy and interventions, performance management systems, leadership and teambuilding, and corporate social responsibilities. E-mail: khan.drsami@gmail.com

Hunmin Kim is a professor in the Department of Public Administration and Dean of Scranton College, Ewha University, Korea. She has a master's and a PhD from Harvard University, US. Her research interests are in women issues, local government innovation, urban development and related areas. She serves on several committees, including the Presidential Commission on Policy Planning and the Presidential Committee on Government Innovation and Decentralisation of the Government of Korea. E-mail: hmkim@ewha.ac.kr

Rajesh Kumar is an assistant professor at the Chandragupta Institute of Management, India. His research focuses on organizational behaviour. He has worked for seven years in various positions with development organizations in the areas of networking and programme evaluation of various developmental projects. E-mail: rajesh108r@gmail.com

Madhavi Harshadrai Mehta is an associate professor with more than 15 years of experience in teaching, research and consultancy with institutes such as the Social Development Centre Academy of Human Resources Development, K.J. Somaiya Institute of Management Studies and Research, Mumbai, non-governmental organizations and the Institute of Management Anand. She has published numerous articles in both local and international publications and is a reviewer both for the *International Journal of Rural Management* and for Oxford University Press in the areas of organizational behaviour and human resources. E-mail: madhavi@irma.ac.in

Edna Mitchell is Professor Emeritus at Mills College, US, where she was previously Head of the Department of Education, Director of Graduate Studies, Director of Alternative Programs for Working Women and Founding Director of the Mills College Women's Leadership Institute. She has worked as a consultant with the Ministry of Education in Afghanistan since 2004. She was a visiting professor and Acting Associate Dean in Family Studies at Zayed University in Dubai and Abu Dhabi in 2002, and a visiting Fulbright Professor at the Jozsef Attila University of Science and Technology in 1994. She was awarded a congressional fellowship from the Society for Research in Child Development to work as a senior fellow in the US Congress in 1980. Her research and writing have been largely on women's leadership and cultural issues in play and child development. E-mail: ednamitchell@yahoo.com

Unnikammu Moideenkutty is an associate professor in the Department of Management, College of Economics and Political Science, Sultan Qaboos University, Sultanate of Oman. He has a PhD in business administration from the Fox School of Business and Management, Temple University, US. His research interests include organizational citizenship behaviour, social exchange processes in organizations and strategic human resource management. His research papers have been published in international journals, including *Applied Psychology: An International Review*, *Organization Management Journal*, *Personnel Review* and *Asian Journal of Management Cases*. E-mail: moideenkutty@gmail.com

Brian T. O'Donoghue is Academic Director for NOESIS Ex Ed, one of the leading providers of adult professional education in Malaysia. He was formerly Acting Dean of the Faculty of Business for INTI College, Malaysia. He holds a master's in business studies from University College Dublin, Ireland. He is a member of the International Leadership Association and the Chartered Institute of Marketing. He has more than 20 years' leadership and management experience across various roles in industry and education in the UK, China and Malaysia, and he has spoken at various industry and academic conferences in those countries and the US. He has worked in management and consultancy roles for companies such as SPAR, Cadbury and Johnson & Johnson. He lectures on various MBA, professional and undergraduate business programmes. E-mail: brian@noesis.com.my

James Rajasekar is an assistant professor in the Management Department at the College of Economics and Political Science, Sultan Qaboos University, Sultanate of Oman. He specializes in the fields of strategic management and international business, and he has taught both undergraduate and postgraduate students in the US, the Middle East and the Indian subcontinent. He has been a consultant with several governmental agencies, and public and private sector organizations, and he has trained middle- and senior-level executives. He has contributed to institution-building and corporate governance by being on the board of the governing bodies of academic institutions. He was also one of the country coordinators for India for the GLOBE Project – Phase III between 2000 and 2003. E-mail: jrajas@gmail.com

Stuart M. Schmidt is Professor of Human Resource Management in the Fox School of Business and Management, Temple University, US, where he teaches postgraduate and undergraduate courses in management, and power and influence in organizations. His PhD in industrial relations was obtained at the University of Wisconsin-Madison, US. His research spans several fields, including leadership, organizational politics, dynamics of virtual authority relationships, cross-cultural team relationships and the power of wielding power. His research findings have been published in numerous journals, including the *Journal of Applied Psychology, Decision Sciences, Administration and Society, Human Relations, Organizational Dynamics, Administrative Science Quarterly, Psychology Today* and even the *National Enquirer*. He is also known for his training and assessment instruments, such as the Profiles of Organizational Influence Strategies instruments and training programmes. E-mail: schmidt@temple.edu

Xiao Ran Song is a marketing executive with Bupa International, in Shanghai, China, and a PhD candidate at the University of Melbourne, Australia, researching management and international communication. She has been working in two fields – business and education – in both China and Australia. She has been a manager and consultant for 11 years, with expertise in marketing and communication, management and training gained in the commercial and education sectors. She has a master's in commerce from Macquarie University, Australia, and has been working on managerial positions in multinational companies in China and Australia. She is also an experienced English language teacher, with a TESOL qualification from the University of Melbourne, Australia. E-mail: rebecca.song@bupa.com.cn

Yasser S. Tabouk is Head of Customer Care and Lease Management in Knowledge Oasis Muscat (KOM) Information Technology Park. He researches business development and case-study analysis in addition to managing key functions related to lease management. He graduated from the College of Economics & Political Sciences, Sultan Qaboos University, Sultanate of Oman, in 2004. He worked as a marketing specialist at the Ministry of Sports Affairs before joining KOM. He received an MBA from the same university in 2010. He is actively involved in research on technology issues and has presented papers at international conferences. E-mail: aziboon@yahoo.com

Constance Van Horne is Assistant Professor of Management at Zayed University in Abu Dhabi. She is extensively involved in student projects, including the Men's Business Association, the Men's Entrepreneurship Club and study abroad projects. She is the project leader for the 2011 UAE Global Entrepreneurship Monitor Report and has worked on several Middle East-based collaborative research projects with researchers from the MENA region, in particular North Africa, for several years. E-mail: constance.vanhorne@zu.ac.ae

Deepanjana Varshney is currently working as an assistant professor in the Human Resources Management Department at the Faculty of Economics & Administration, King Abdulaziz University, Saudi Arabia. She has 11 years' academic experience in teaching, research and consultancy work. She has a number of international publications to her credit. She has been associated academically with different universities and institutions in the past. Her areas of research include leadership, group dynamics and dysfunctional employee behaviour. E-mail: dvfaculty@yahoo.com

Susan Wardak is Director General of the Teacher Education Department of the Ministry of Education of Afghanistan, and is a special advisor to the minister. She is responsible for the training of teachers both pre-service and in-service through teacher education colleges and through in-service training workshops and courses for the nation's teachers. She was born in Afghanistan but went with her family as a young child to find refuge in Canada from the Taliban. She returned to Afghanistan in 2003. She received her master's in education leadership and research from Karlstad University, Sweden. Preceding her appointment to the Ministry of Education, she worked with UNESCO in Afghanistan revising the curricula and rewriting textbooks for elementary schools. She is one of the few women in a position of leadership in the government and is a strong voice for women's participation as leaders throughout all levels of society. She is the chair of a United Nations committee on gender equity and energetically promotes a variety of programmes through this group. E-mail: susanwardak2@hotmail.com

Emile Kok-Kheng Yeoh is Director and Associate Professor of the Institute of China Studies, University of Malaya, Malaysia. He acquired his PhD from the University of Bradford, UK, in 1998 and his research interests include institutional economics, China studies, decentralization and fiscal federalism, and socioracial diversity and the role of the state in economic development. His works have been published in journals including *The Copenhagen Journal of Asian Studies, GeoJournal: An International Journal on Human Geography and Environmental Sciences, Journal of Asian Public Policy, International Journal of China Studies, Malaysian Journal of Economic Studies* and the Copenhagen Discussion Paper series. Recent books, as both editor and contributor, include *Emerging Trading Nation in an Integrating World* (2007), *Facets of a Transforming China* (2008), *China in the World* (2008), *Regional Political Economy of China Ascendant* (2009) and *China-ASEAN Relations* (2009). E-mail: emileyeo@gmail.com

Introduction and Overview

James Rajasekar and Loo-See Beh

Aims and scope of this book

The overall aim of this book is to present the research carried out in the Middle East and Asia in the field of leadership, culture and gender, and hence to strengthen the development of theory and empirical research found in these regions. Through such collective efforts we hope to contribute to the body of knowledge and practice in this field.

We are witnessing enormous changes in the fabric of our organizations and in the various countries with regard to how, when, where and with whom we work. Furthermore, these changes pose considerable challenges to everyone where the understanding of global and local environments is intertwined and involves much complexity. These considerations range from cultural barriers and political barriers to local and international aspects where transformations constantly take place, and in managing all sociopolitical capital and collusions from within.

The scope of this book covers the themes of culture and gender in leadership where the study of behaviour in leadership emerges from organizational and societal influences. Here we extend our focus on leadership, factors and situations in explaining the meaningful variance in leadership styles and behaviours in the selected countries in the Middle East and Asia, which has not previously been made available. Many have long been interested in the diverse cultures of the Middle East and Asia, and the globalization and interconnectedness of issues have also caused an increase in interest and demand for factual information and research. The cultures and practices of these countries are hugely varied and this book brings together analyses of these themes in selected countries of the two regions. The detailed descriptions in and overview offered by the chapters provide for a good understanding of cultural relativism and gender in leadership. They enable a unique and comparative perspective that is drawn from the countries' own cultures as well as other cultures that don't share the same views as their own. We hope that readers will appreciate these circumstances and the need to know about others outside their own comfort zone, as well as inside the region where one is usually expected to adhere to strict sociobehavioural norms.

Section and chapter overviews

The chapters are written by leading and emerging academics and scholars guided by their respective fields to provide a retrospective account, which considers conceptual and methodological issues. In Section I ('Leadership') Chapter 1, Loo-See Beh and William R. Kennan deal with the tradition of situational leadership theory, which offers considerable promise for leaders attempting to adjust to particular situations. It offers an alternative view of leadership, which expands and makes more flexible situational leadership approaches in the East, particularly in East and Southeast Asia. Specifically, it reorients situational leadership to an awareness of the social capital properties of human relationships and how network connections can set the stage for appropriate and situated cooperative and collaborative leadership behaviour. The discussion includes reference to the current leadership environment characteristic of Southeast Asia and further suggests five touchstones for leadership action and effectiveness.

Chapter 2 by James Rajasekar, Salem Al-Abri and Yasser Tabouk investigates the nature and influence of three interrelated aspects of leadership in organizations in the Sultanate of Oman: providing vision, communicating effectively and responding to chaos. Some 140 individuals representing five different industry sectors were surveyed to explore these aspects of leadership in Oman, and to determine their interaction with, and effects upon, employees' outcomes of motivation and affective commitment. The study found that having a vision and communicating clearly positively contributed to employees' motivation and feelings of commitment, and visionary leaders had a positive attitude towards chaos.

In Chapter 3, Francis Thaise A. Cimene and Alan N. Aladano capture the different viewpoints on the practice of leadership in the Philippines and its implications for theory, research and practice. Their findings show that the leader respondents perceived leadership as an art, ability and process. It is a process because one never stops learning. As long as people continue to grow and society continues to change, it is inevitable that a leader will evolve with the organization and the society where they belong.

In Chapter 4, Xiao Ran Song and David Beckett elaborate on corporate settings in China and offer an evaluation where East meets West. They set out some traditional and contemporary scholarship about leadership in China, and contrast these with some key Western notions of leadership. They then give a brief account of semistructured interviews with Chinese and Western individuals who have been in management positions in China, thereby exploring the complexity and potential development of modern leadership in, and for, a globalizing China.

The process of social change typically involves a combination of four components: context, institutions, agents and events. Chapter 5 by Emile Kok-Kheng Yeoh analyses the nature and evolvement of political leadership in contemporary China across the political divide during critical junctures and at times of enforced stability, exemplified often by forms of societal expression and the corresponding state responses. It also looks at the crucial question of ultimately who gains at whose expense within this context and its impact on the changing nature of political leadership in the post-1989 Chinese social environment of increasingly pluralized conflicts, which has led to an increasingly complex structure of agent–institution interaction.

In Section II ('Culture') the reader will find that the majority of chapters are written from the perspective of management, and they fall within the purview of culture and how leadership is established in the particular social realm. Alexandre A. Bachkirov contributes to the literature in the field in Chapter 6 by synthesizing the extant scholarly work on the effects of Chinese national culture on leadership decision-making. Decision making is presented as the key activity in a leader's role, and the importance of understanding the impact of national cultures on decision-making processes is highlighted. The essential characteristics of modern Chinese societies are reviewed, including the paternalistic leadership style. The effects of Chinese national culture on cognitive processes of thinking and deciding are explored. Particular attention is paid to specific types of leadership decision: stock market buying/selling decisions, risky choice, reward allocation and ethical decision making.

When comparing the East and West (as in Chapter 4), in Chapter 7, Anna M. Danielewicz-Betz deals with the issue of glocalization and the extent of Westernization of Arab higher education in the Gulf region. This includes discussion of German and Saudi tertiary education where Islamic and Middle Eastern leadership style is compared with

German leadership style utilizing a qualitative method. Issues and cultural implications are discussed from glocalized and international perspectives.

Interestingly, the importance of 'face' in Asia has been acknowledged by many scholars. In Chapter 8, Brian T. O'Donoghue examines how 'face' impacts leadership, management and 'follower' behaviour in Malaysia. He also addresses relevant literature in the area of 'face', particularly that related to Chinese and Malay culture. This qualitative work is the first study of its kind in Malaysia. It introduces the concept of 'face' as a force, which is not felt equally by those in an organization, and provides guidelines on how certain Western management approaches should be adapted in the context of 'face'.

In India, leadership as a concept has culture, tradition and philosophy as its backdrop, providing context to the concept. Indian society has, for a long time, had religious or spiritual scriptures and beliefs, guiding leadership behaviour and actions. Chapter 9 by Rajesh Kumar and Madhavi Harshadrai Mehta attempts to understand the Indian leadership concept against the country's culture, traditions and philosophy. It addresses the cultural, philosophical and historical context in which the Indian concept of leadership has evolved, illustrating its unique features. The chapter is essentially a review of the existing literature from humanities and management, describing the concept of leadership and how it has been shaped and understood in India.

Moving to the Middle East, Sami A. Khan and Deepanjana Varshney illustrate transformational leadership in the Saudi Arabian cultural context in Chapter 10. They attempt to unravel the dynamics of transformation leadership and its relevance for Saudi managers, namely the deep-rooted values and the nature of the culture in which leadership qualities are found to be embedded. The subareas discussed focus on cultural values, organizational culture and the effect of Islam on leadership in the country. Successful cases of Saudi business and organization leaders reinforce learning about the dynamics of leadership, and provide a framework for understanding the emerging paradigms and challenges of leadership in Saudi Arabia.

Elaboration on Arab culture is provided in Chapter 11 by Stuart M. Schmidt, Unnikammu Moideenkutty and Adil Al Busaidi, who assess expatriate and Omani supervisor–subordinate dyadic workplace relationships and their respective individual workplace performance. Survey data were used from public and private sector organizations to assess the following workplace relationships between expatriates and Omanis: trust, affective relations, leader–member exchanges, supportive downward influence, supervisor effectiveness, organizational citizenship behaviour and individual performance. Counter to their expectations based on similarity-attraction theory, subordinates in dissimilar national status dyads were liked more by their supervisors than those in the same nationality status (Omani or expatriate) dyads. Additionally, expatriates appeared likely to be perceived as exhibiting more organizational citizenship behaviour towards their supervisors than did Omani subordinates. The authors conclude that organizational members may develop workplace relationships (trust, liking and quality exchanges) independent of nationality.

In Section III ('Gender and leadership'), Chapter 12 by Hunmin Kim shows that the glass fence is thicker than the glass ceiling. This study examines women's leadership in Korea focusing on four puzzling gaps: those gaps in women's leadership with economic growth and with human development, the leadership gap between government and business sectors, and the gap between social and household leaderships. These are explained by the exclusive division of gender roles separating the household from the society. The robust fence confining women's roles to those within the house, reinforced by institutional barriers, keep Korean women from actively pursuing careers and reaching leadership positions. Comparisons with Organisation for Economic Co-operation and Development and Asian countries are made. Having the first female president in 2012 breaks the highest glass ceiling in a hugely male-dominated nation, which is a great achievement. However, for many Korean women, the glass fence has yet to be hurdled.

Interestingly it is common knowledge that the role of women in many aspects of life in countries such as Afghanistan remains a huge challenge given the cultural setting. Susan Wardak and Edna Mitchell's Chapter 13 elaborates on why women's roles are missing and, in particular, in the field of education, which forms the backbone of a country's development. According to the authors, women are barely visible in positions of public leadership in Afghanistan despite the new constitution that declares equity in every sphere, and despite efforts of the government and international agencies to educate and promote women. Providing a theoretical, historical and cultural setting for discussion about women's leadership in Afghanistan, the chapter describes the current barriers, lack of education and restrictions posed by cultural traditions. A brief history of Afghan women leaders is followed by an analysis of conditions today, with suggestions for future directions.

Finally, in Chapter 14, Sarah Alhaj and Constance Van Horne similarly look at the roles of lived experiences in developing these leaders, as opposed to formal interventions, and this Emirati perspective seeks to explore the underlying factors that enable women to learn how to lead. The findings are illustrated in a leader apprenticeship framework, which consists of experiencing influential encounters, dealing with and learning from difficult events, and transforming through a formal training programme. The findings support proposals to treat leadership learning as a form of apprenticeship where learning is embedded in the social fabric in which it transpires, calling for contextualizing leader development as supported by situational learning theory.

Section I

Leadership

1
Leadership in the East: A Social Capital Perspective

Loo-See Beh and William R. Kennan

Introduction

Considerable effort has been devoted to understanding leadership in a cross-cultural context and a fair amount of work has focused on Asia. A significant part of the dialogue has focused on whether Western-oriented theories and concepts apply to the Asian experience, with considerable conversation devoted to understanding the hegemonic nature of Western leadership approaches. This chapter suggests an alternative focus rooted in social capital theory and grounded in a description of how leaders could operate rather than focusing on prescriptive formulations that might or might not be relevant to dynamic and constantly changing contexts. It reviews selected portions of the literature on situational leadership; it considers the applicability of Western theories and practices in state–society relationships and social capital creation as an approach to understanding how leadership works in context; and it concludes by offering touchstones for leader awareness and action. At a broader level, the chapter focuses on leadership conceived broadly as an activity designed to produce movement towards desirable goals and outcomes that benefit all stakeholders. It argues that effective leadership involves the creation, retention and utilization of social capital resources that provide the potential for sustainable and competitive goal attainment while recognizing that all leadership is fundamentally contextual in nature.

There is absolutely no doubt that one of the barriers to economic, political and social growth in Southeast Asia has to do with the ability of leadership to accumulate, retain and use the collective social resources that lie as potential in their spheres of influence. For example, in Southeast Asia, Singapore stands as an example of what happens when those resources are managed, while other nations continue to struggle with social, cultural, religious and political divisions. This chapter seeks an approach to leadership and learning that is grounded in the connections that naturally emerge through human interaction and that can be cultivated in ethical, productive and responsible ways.

Leadership theory, leadership research and theoretic utility

The applicability of Western perspectives

The key issue is whether Western-oriented theories of leadership can be productively, or even ethically, applied to the case of Asian leadership. The critical theorists, especially those operating from a post-colonial perspective, would argue that such use imposes a set of destructive categories that ignores and devalues the essential characteristics of the culture under consideration. Theories, they would argue with some justification, should be organic and should emanate from the cultural ground where they are to be applied, arguing essentially for a subjective approach to leadership that illuminates and empowers as they seek effectiveness and success.

While there is much to be sympathetic about in this scholarly tradition, there is also a very practical reality that is emerging quite independently. The reality is that the world is quickly globalizing and because of the rapid and pervasive influence of new communication technologies there is constant interaction and mutual influence in ways and with effects that no one would have anticipated just a few years ago. This process is frequently turbulent and even chaotic, and adaptation is driven in large measure by stark economic realities that privilege political and social realities. The fact is that governments as well as organizations look for what works, and in the looking they often turn to the West with its well-developed and widely distributed thinking on leadership. The resulting situation is a mash-up of perspectives on leadership that evolves through a discussion and analysis of best practices.

With regard to whether contextually (culturally) specific theories are relevant to Asian leadership, all human interaction is essentially and fundamentally contextual/situational and is therefore influenced by a number of factors, including but not limited to culture, religion, ethnicity/cultural membership/minority membership, gender and political orientation.[1] This does not deny or render useless the idea that some Western approaches are useful. It does provide an important caution that assumptions drawn from outside the real context of human interaction may be unwarranted and potentially dangerous (Pye, 1985, 1999). What is possible is the creation of a framework for a discussion of what works, which allows a contextual/situation consideration while looking for broader unifying touchstones that are sensitive to cultures and traditions.

Leadership research focused on (East and Southeast) Asia

The literature on situational leadership is vast, and with that vastness comes an almost endless supply of theories and perspectives. That same breadth is to be seen in leadership research focusing on Asian nations and the institutions in that region. East Asian nations reflect considerable differences in their political orientations, establishing a situation and context for leadership. For example, China, the Republic of Korea and Japan are often identified as traditional societies where people believe that power emanates from above, and as such results in single supreme rulers and deference to authority. China embraces an increasingly dynamic and capitalistic communist ideology while Japan seems closest to a Western-style liberal democracy with the Republic of Korea in between.[2] Southeast Asian nations tend to be semidemocracies in contrast to Western pro-democracy ideology. Collectively, these national contexts produce unique cultural attitudes towards leadership, both internally and externally. This in turn has produced a cross-cultural leadership literature that has attempted to describe various contexts.

In Southeast Asia it is crucial to realize the relationship between political liberalization and leadership, and social media, being censored or self-imposed censorship: for instance, Indonesia and Malaysia have a higher degree of censorship and less political liberalization in contrast to the Philippines and Thailand. Countries such as the Philippines, Thailand and Indonesia have experienced breakdown of authoritarian regimes more often through violent clashes following military-engineered unseating of leaders and internal bickering. In transitions, leaders as key players may be forced to negotiate selective and piecemeal amendments and reforms. The role of leaders in political decision making will only be clear when we examine the way in which situations emerge that shape groups and society and, consequently, the web of network connections that create social capital. This phenomenon is representative of Southeast Asia where institutional mechanisms for development take a backseat to dominant leadership politics.

Situational leadership theory

Mainstream leadership literature has undergone four phases: i) the 1930s to the 1950s – great man and traits; ii) the 1960s – behavioural approaches (transactional); iii) situational (transformational) perspectives; and iv) integration of transformational and transactional models (van Mart, 2003). Generalization of leadership effectiveness has long been indicated as a situational mediating variable that affects leader action and follower response. Context is often embedded in theories linking situation to leadership style (Fiedler, 1967; Hersey & Blanchard, 1969; House, 1971). According to Hunter, Bedell-Avers and Mumford (2007), what seems to be noticeably absent from the typical leadership study is a consideration of the context in which leader behaviours are occurring as well as the intervening variables that may be operating within that context. By saying that context is 'out there' underplays how leadership is 'situated' (Grint, 2005). As we often observe, leaders proactively 'read the situation', interpreting the context and constantly shaping the contextual factors that can be manipulated, and giving feedback regarding their consequences resulting from their actions within the context (Mowday & Sutton, 1993).

In the intercultural communication context, the adaptation of leaders, at least in terms of traditional theory, is largely based on general categories of follower behaviour that are likely to be based in Western cultural relations and traditions. What follows is a discussion of Western leadership theories that advocate situational adaptation but provide little advice when situations are complicated by culture and the many other variables that have become increasingly important in an increasingly global world.

Fiedler's (1967) theory of situation leadership was among the first to advance leadership behaviour as a contextually grounded activity. Other well-known formulations, such as Taylor's scientific management (1911), Mayo's human relations theory (2003) and Chester Barnard's (1968) analyses of managerial functions all promoted a single best way to manage and, hence, to lead.[3] Fiedler argued that leadership consisted of two issues that were interrelated: leadership style and situational favourableness. He measured leadership using the least preferred co-worker scale (LPC), which asked individuals to rate the person with whom they worked least well. He assumed that people-oriented leaders would rate least preferred co-workers more favourably than would someone who is task oriented. The LPC approach recognizes that both high people-oriented and high task-oriented individuals are capable of exerting effective leadership depending on the situation defined by the characteristics of followers. Fiedler identified the situational characteristics in which those leadership styles could be operative: leader member relations, task structure and leader position power. The key element is the match between the leader and the situation. According to him, situations must be matched to the styles of leaders since personality type remains relatively unchanged across time.

Hersey and Blanchard (1969) recognize that one model of leadership is not appropriate for all situations and, consequently, they advanced two situational dimensions: the structure of the task and the nature of employee relations. Task-oriented behaviour involves communication to organizational members about how activities are to be performed. Highly task-oriented leaders are typically control oriented. The socioemotional piece of this approach deals with leader communicative behaviours focused on relational climate. Such behaviours tend to foster cooperation, dialogue and a positive socioemotional climate. This approach then looks at these two dimensions in terms of follower willingness and ability to comply with requests. The key issue in this regard is identified as 'maturity' – that is, whether individuals are willing, confident and able to comply with requests. This leads to a four-stage model. In this the organizational member is:

- unable and unwilling to comply in first stage;
- unable but willing in the second stage;
- able but unwilling in the third stage;
- able and willing in the fourth stage.

The job of the leader is to adapt to the maturity (ability and willingness) of the individual, and this is done in four ways: telling, selling, participating and delegating:

- When people are unwilling and unable, the leader 'tells' them how to perform, taking control of the context through directive leader communication behaviour.
- When people are unable but willing to comply, a 'selling' approach to convince them is attempted to enact new behaviour.
- When people are able but unwilling, a 'participation' approach is used where they are put in situations where they must make decisions and take actions.
- When people are willing and able, a 'delegation' model is used where task responsibilities are given to them to complete.

The central idea of the Hersey and Blanchard (1977) approach is that there is no one best leadership approach and that leaders must adapt their leadership style to the situations they confront, and those situations are defined by followers with particular characteristics. The model also makes it clear that situations change and as those changes occur, leaders must also adapt their behaviour.

Vroom and Yetton (1973) consider the quality of decisions as emerging from particular situations that are connected to how much followers understand about the problem. For example, the leader takes known information and makes the decision alone; the leader gets information from followers and then decides alone; the leader shares a problem with followers, listens to input and then decides alone; the leader shares information with a group, listens to input and then decides alone; and the leader shares a problem with a group, then seeks and accepts a consensus-based decision. This model then specifies the situation characteristics that would then determine which approach would be most appropriate. These situational factors include when decision quality is important and followers possess useful information; when the leader sees decision quality as important but followers don't; when decision quality is important, the problem is unstructured and the leader lacks information; when decision acceptance is important and followers are not likely to accept an individually made decision; when decision acceptance is important and followers may disagree with each other; when decision quality is unimportant but the need for acceptance is great; and when decision quality is important, all agree that it is important and the decision is unlikely to be autocratically made.

The theory goes on to specify which leadership approach is best in each of the situations described above. Again, the purpose is to match leader style with situational conditions, creating a flexibility and adaptability that lead to high decision quality and high acceptance. Goleman's (1998) emotional intelligence (EI) theory provides another way of describing leadership characteristics, which can be linked to situational factors. He argues that it is the emotional makeup of the leader and how that makeup manifests in leader actions that are of particular interest. He argues that there are five components of EI: self-awareness, self-regulation, motivation, empathy and social skill:

- 'Self-awareness' reflects the degree to which a leader can recognize and understand their own emotional makeup and how that makeup impacts others.
- 'Self-regulation' is the ability of a leader to control disruptive behaviour, suspend judgement and think before acting.
- 'Motivation' refers to the drive to achieve.

- 'Empathy' involves taking and understanding the situations and constraints of followers.
- 'Social skill' is the ability to enact appropriate behaviour in particular situations.

Goleman argues that EI is highly correlated with successful leadership but he also cautions that different situations require different leadership approaches. EI serves as the basis for the flexibility and ability required to adapt to a variety of situations.

The social identity theory of leadership (Haslam, 2001; Hogg, 2001; Reicher, Haslam & Hopkins, 2005) argues that people who are perceived to match their group's social identity are more likely to be endorsed as leaders. Reicher et al. (2005) explore the way in which a shared sense of identity could make leadership possible, and the ways in which leaders act as entrepreneurs of identity in order to make particular forms of identity and their own leadership viable. The analysis also focuses on the way in which leaders' identity projects are constrained by social identity, and on the manner in which effective leadership contributes to the transformation of reality that mobilizes and redirects a group's identity-based social power. In order to be influential and effective, leaders need to represent and define social identity in *context*. This approach opens the way to an analysis of the active role of leaders in shaping groups and shaping society, and of how the leaders or politicians create an image of themselves that matches their image of the category. This is very much a group process of group cohesion, social attraction and sometimes group polarization.

This situation can be observed in Southeast Asia where actors sometimes display greater in-group loyalty and ethnocentrism, behaving in a more group-serving manner (e.g. Malaysia, Thailand and Indonesia). A leader who acts as 'one of us' by showing in-group support is more socially attractive and accrues legitimacy (Hogg, 2001). Social identity research shows that groups often interact and communicate with one another through their leaders; indeed, most intergroup bargaining and negotiation are via group leaders.

Collectively, these models recognize what is obvious in Elliot's Mishler's (1978) *Meaning in Context: Is There Any Other Kind* – that leadership always occurs, as does any human activity, in a particular situation that includes rules, boundaries and limitations for leaders and followers. Each of these theories, in its own way, seeks to identify how leaders can approach the complexity presented by situations. What they leave unaccounted for is situational dynamism and complexity that characterize cultural, social, political and global interaction. It is quite daunting to list the relevant leadership contingencies and to recommend relevant strategies for each one, and, in addition, to specify how a leader is to adapt to those contingencies and what resources facilitate adaptation and adjustment given the complexity of contexts. How does a leader, for example, who is a people-oriented leader, navigate a negative climate, loosely structured task, with a prior history of poor leader–member relations, and involving people from different cultures? What, for example, is the first thing that a leader does or says? How are those strategies to play out in the lived world of social work relationships? While these theories add immeasurably to our understanding of leadership in context, they also remain largely silent as to the interactive mechanisms required for leadership.

Social capital perspective

A thorough review of the social capital tradition and all of its variations and derivations is well beyond the scope of this chapter even though these have been carefully studied by, among others, Portes (1998), Adam and Roncevic, (2002), Woolcock (1998) and Woolcock and Narayan (2000). The social capital perspective is highly interdisciplinary in nature, drawing from work in economics, science, sociology, business, education, communication and so on. The topics addressed by this literature are diverse and deal with a variety of theoretical and practical issues (e.g. job advancement and gender, educational attainment, managerial effectiveness, community development, economic development and health care). What follows draws from the social capital literature to create a framework for analysis and an understanding of the complexity that confronts Southeast Asian leadership.

Bourdieu's (1986) perspective emanates from a social critique of the fabric of society in which he emphasizes that social groups seek domination over others. His thought is broad and complex, but it is his notions of social capital and symbolic violence that are of interest here. He defines social capital as 'the sum of the resources, actual or virtual, that accrue to an individual or a group by virtue of possessing a durable network of more or less institutionalized relationships of mutual acquaintance and recognition' (Bourdieu & Wacquant, 1992:119). Bourdieu recognizes that power and influence are exercised through connections with others and that where these networks are regular and durable, they offer an entry point through which individuals can access social and cultural power.

His focus is primarily on the education context (Bourdieu & Passeron, 1990), where education gives individuals and families access to networks that provide information and expertise, as well as entry into professional networks where power and influence can be acquired. In this regard he identifies four kinds of capital: economic, cultural, social and symbolic. Of special interest here is symbolic capital, which provides the means through which economic, cultural and social capitals acquire meaning through symbols and through which their influence spreads.

Education provides a setting in which those who participate learn information and skills but, more importantly, gain access to the networks that represent that knowledge and skill. An education in business, for example, provides the learner with knowledge and skill but also connects them to networks represented by faculty, businesses, politicians and so on. It is these connections that give students the opportunity to access the potential rewards embedded in various networks. In this way, societies constantly reproduce themselves by educating and embedding individuals in networks. In essence, the value of an educated person lies in their various connections because it is the resources embedded in networks that confer power and influence. Educated people have those connections; others often don't. Consequently, a family's investment in education for their children is an investment in potential future social capital returns.

Coleman (1988) defines social capital functionally as 'a variety of entities with two elements in common: They consist of some aspect of social structures, and they facilitate certain actions of actors – whether persons or corporate actors – within the structure' (Coleman, 1988: s98). It is the emergence of the forms of social capital in various contexts that produces social capital (Baker, 1990, Coleman, 1988). Social capital emerges through the rich, varied and textured communicative exchanges that occur among various organizational actors who are embedded in various network contexts. These exchanges involve individuals, groups, organizations, cultures and nations producing a shifting sea of relational creation, maintenance and dissolution that forms that framework for successful human activity.

Coleman's metaphor is economic and he describes social capital as a network resource that can be acquired and stored in a kind of bank account. The accumulated resources in an individual's account can be expended to produce desirable outcomes. Coleman (1988) describes the essential components of the relationship and its basic components by making two distinctions: obligations and expectations. Both are created through the social exchange and both contain actor beliefs about past and future exchanges. Coleman (1988: S102) notes:

> If A does something for B and assumes that B will reciprocate in the future, an expectation is established in A and an obligation incurred on the part of B. This obligation can be conceived as a credit slip held by A for the fulfillment of an obligation by B. These credit slips constitute a relational deposit that has a value that A can spend to accomplish various goals and objectives – unless, of course, the actor who has the obligation defaults on the debt.

Some clarification is necessary at this point. A financial obligation is fungible (exchangeable with others) while a social capital obligation isn't. For example, a debt can be sold or passed on to another individual or organization. Unlike financial or economic obligations, social capital is rooted in, and constrained by, the particular context in which it emerges. One could not tell Fred that he ought to buy John lunch because John had bought Sam lunch last Tuesday. The relationship and the social capital exist only between John and Sam and within a particular context.

Like Bourdieu (1986), Coleman's (1988) interest in social capital has much to do with his interest in education. Basically, social capital deposits allow individuals to access networks and network resources, and in so doing actors are able to accomplish activities that are not possible without their embeddedness in social networks that brings them into contact with those possessing valuable resources. According to Coleman, closed networks where there are historically close connections among individuals produce high levels of social capital, including trust and established norms of reciprocity, but they also limit the amount of new information that is available (Lin, 2002).

Robert Putnam's perspective (2000) has had considerable scholarly and political influence. His argument is as follows. American society, via Tocqueville, has been founded in close association with individuals working in close concert with one another to produce desirable societal outcomes. The emergence of a number of factors, among them the rise of new technologies and social media, has resulted in a society whose members spend less time with each other and more time in isolation, often interacting online. This shift has reduced the amount of civic participation, and hence the amount of civic engagement and community action. Putnam's use of bowling as a metaphor fits into this model and, of course, serves as part of the title of his work on social capital. At the time the book was written, more people than ever were bowling but fewer were participating in bowling leagues. Putnam notes that there is less participation in a variety of civically oriented activities, including churches, political parties, parent–teacher associations, town and city meetings, and so on. Consequently, the US is confronted by a decline in the amount of social capital and there is, accordingly, less trust and involvement among citizens. This pattern, according to Putnam, is to be observed in a variety of contexts.

Putnam is responsible for the definition of two kinds of social capital: bonding and bridging. Bonding social capital occurs where networks of association are close and continue unabated over time. In these relationships, trust can emerge along with norms of reciprocity and cooperation that facilitate civic and societal action. However, bonding capital and the networks that support it typically do not produce much new information as the same information content circulates within a relatively closed network. To account for this problem, actors seek connections with those outside their relatively closed networks as a mechanism for securing new information and resources. Both kinds of social capital are necessary for social and civic development and both are in decline in the US according to Putnam's basic argument.

Burt's (1992; 1997; 2004; 2005) perspective is primarily organizational and outcome oriented. He is responsible for the structural hole concept,and the application of bridging and bonding social capital to structural holes. All actors are embedded in various networks that provide them with information. The nature of their network connections has the potential to produce new information of benefit to the actor or limited information access based on closed networks. In terms of new information, actors are best served when they are located adjacent to structural holes. Bridging structure holes establishes new networks with possible access to new resources, which can be utilized to achieve goals and objectives. A structure hole is a network gap where there is no connection between actors. Part of Burt's programme is teaching organizational members to detect structural holes and to strategically determine which ones should be bridged (Burt & Ronchi, 2007).

Hazleton and Kennan (2000) and Kennan and Hazleton (2006: 322) build on these traditions to define social capital as the 'ability that organizations have of creating, maintaining, and using relationships to achieve desirable organizational goals'. Theirs is a synthetic perspective, drawing from a number of theorists but uniquely identifying communicative behaviour as central to the process of social capital creation, maintenance and utilization. It is this perspective that provides the necessary means of describing and analysing leader behaviour in particular contexts, including cultural ones. As a perspective, it is not context dependent but rather metacontextual as it posits basic concepts relevant to all contexts, which can help to illuminate the nature of connectivity among a variety of actors at different times and locations, and in different circumstances.

According to this perspective, individuals and groups acquire, retain and expend social capital through communication, the basis of relationships, which in turn becomes the foundation of social capital. Hazleton and Kennan (2000) emphasize the multidimensional nature of social capital beginning with the work of Nahapiet and Ghoshal (1998). They adopt their structural and relational dimensions proposed by Nahapiet and Ghoshal but omit their cognitive dimension in favour of a communication dimension.

The structural dimension refers to the web of network connections that create the potential for social capital. Individuals are constrained by networks but are also capable of expanding, organizing and reorienting their networks. Burt (1992) proposes three components of networks: access, referral and timing. Hazleton and Kennan (2000) draw from Coleman's (1988) work to add a fourth component: appropriability, which means the following:

- 'Access' refers to the ability to send and receive messages as well as to gain entry to networks.
- 'Referral' indicates the degree to which individuals can access networks through their associations with others.
- 'Timing' encompasses the availability of messages in a timeframe useful to individuals, groups and organizations.

The relational dimension of social capital focuses on the nature and character of connections among individuals (Hazleton & Kennan, 2000). Hazleton and Kennan identify three relational components: trust, identification and tie strength (Granovetter, 1973):

- 'Trust' refers to anticipated cooperation (Burt & Knez, 1995).
- 'Identification' refers to the degree to which individuals see themselves as being connected to others in a network (Portes, 1998).
- 'Tie strength' refers to the frequency and intimacy of the connection among actors.

Seibert, Kraimer and Liden (2001) found that relational connections can increase access to information and resources, as well as career sponsorship, which can in turn increase both career success and satisfaction.

The communication dimension centralizes the essential mechanism through which social capital is created, maintained and expended. Essential to the communication dimension is the role of messaging in forming and maintaining relationships (Fussell, Harrison-Rexrode, Kennan & Hazleton, 2006). Communication becomes essential to accessing and expending social capital through basic communication activities, such as exchanging information, identifying problems and solutions, regulating behaviour and managing conflict (Hazleton & Kennan, 2000).

Within these three dimensions it must be understood that actors create, maintain and utilize social capital. Social actors engage others in the creation of obligations and expectations (Coleman, 1988) that create network connections that, in turn, create deposits and potential for goal attainment. Creation often occurs through the day-to-day reality of social exchange but it can also be an intentional activity (Burt, 1992; 1997; 2004; 2005), where strategic decisions lead to the development of connections that increase the potential for positive outcomes. Maintenance refers to the fact that all network connections and the relationships that they support have a shelf life. Over time those connections, without attention, degrade to the point where they no longer have the potential for action. Successful actors must invest time and energy into keeping social capital fresh so that it is available when needed. Finally, when the time comes, social capital is expended, hopefully in ways that produce desirable outcomes. However, it should be noted that like any other form of capital, social capital can be expended wisely or unwisely, effectively or ineffectively, or for ethical or unethical purposes. The use of social capital to produce desirable outcomes requires knowledge, skill and motivation, along with a strong ethical and moral purpose.

The picture that emerges from this discussion is that the history of situational leadership is a focus on matching leadership to situations in contexts that are relatively stable. The description of those situations is limited, as are the possible responses. For example, in that scholarly tradition, much has been made of the distinction between task- and people-oriented leadership. When considering much more complex leadership contexts one has to wonder if the only two options are task- and people-oriented. And, through what mechanism might a leader diagnose and appropriately respond where culture is at issue? Underdeveloped in the situational leadership literature is the manner in which leaders must continually adapt to a cultural context that is unfamiliar to them, and where the application of their own cultural framework sets the stage for contemporary concerns with unrestrained globalization and cultural destruction.

Pye's (1985; 1999) work at this point is relevant. This looks at Asian cultures along three dimensions: civility, social capital and orientations toward aggression. His description of these with regard to various Asian cultures is instructive as it illuminates the foundational and traditional elements that influence present-day interactions. There are two challenges. First, those cultures are described as unitary societies where traditional rules are fundamental influences on all interactions. This, of course, leaves underplayed the idea that diverse cultural orientations (e.g. Bumiputra and native Chinese Malaysians) give rise to variations in day-to-day practice that mediate the influence of traditional concepts.[4] Second, and of particular relevance from a leadership perspective, is how these various orientations play out in social interactions where those differences are present. Communication scholars are quick to argue that human communication is a process and fundamentally transactional in nature. They argue that relationships and their outcomes are evolutionary and that what emerges is a new state of affairs co-created and constantly renegotiated by the actors themselves. It is the necessity of a dynamic and transactional response that is underdeveloped in much of the literature.

There is work that deals, in part, with these concerns. However, no single publication directly addresses the decisions that leaders must make, in context and often in very difficult circumstances. For example, the literature on expatriation considers adaptation to cultural situation but primarily from the perspective of the culture of the leader or manager, and here cross-cultural communication training is provided pre-departure as an attempt to provide situational adjustment. But it must be admitted that the focus of expatriate training is on an idealized vision of culture and relationships rather than on the mechanism of how, for example, social capital is created and recreated through day-to-day interaction. It is the daily struggle to accommodate actions in all their diversity that is so challenging for expatriates and their families.

Accomodation theory recognizes that communication is necessarily an activity dedicated to an ongoing adjustment between actors. This literature has often focused on the level of conversation where micro-communicative activities provide the mechanism for adjustment in all situations. While this literature does not focus directly on leadership or cultural concerns it does clearly indicate that for communication (through which leadership occurs) to be successful requires accommodative behaviours on the part of all participating actors.

The learning organization is one additional perspective worth consideration as it has a bearing on both situational leadership and social capital theory. The literature on the learning organization (Senge, 2006) makes the argument that the success of organizations of all sorts hinges on two factors. First, the human capital that is available to the organization, and second, its subsequent capacity to adapt, alter and maintain in its environment. In this view, organizations are seen as organic systems that reside in environments. Key to this ability to transform and survive in an environment is the ability to learn and grow. Senge argues that systems theory's emphasis on holism and interdependence sets the stage for a highly interconnected organization where formal and informal learning, which build tacit and explicit knowledge, produce the knowledge and insight that are required for change and innovation.

The one element that gets less attention in these formulations describing the 'ideal' learning organization is the manner in which knowledge and insight are transformed into change and innovation. Basically, knowing and learning is one element, and an important one, but that does not guarantee that they can be used in any meaningful way to actually create change and innovation. This is where the notion of social capital, as described above, becomes relevant because it offers a conceptual framework for understanding how situations and interdependence emerge and re-emerge dynamically.

Given this review of relevant literature, the following section offers a discussion of leadership in Asia. Several themes emerge here. First, Asian nations are highly diverse and that diversity is manifest in very different social capitals. Second, changes in social capital occur in short timeframes as political and social realities change. Third, considering the work of scholars such as Pye (1985; 1999) and the discussion provided above, social capital is a dynamic affair that challenges contemporary leaders to adapt surely and quickly in dynamic and often chaotic environments. Finally, social capital creation, maintenance and use are increasingly driven through new technologies that centralize social media as a force for change to social capital. The overall theme of this section is that leadership requires a clear understanding of the nature of social capital and an intentional, strategic and dynamic response to its character and development.

Leadership in the East: East and Southeast Asia

Too often today's leaders remain self-serving and demonstrate little regard for anything unrelated to improving their personal wealth and power (Pye, 1999), and few are altruistic except in the most pragmatic of ways. It is important to note that nation-building and state consolidation remain ongoing processes in many Asian nations. For instance, Vietnam is still relatively new as a consequence of the dual processes of colonization and decolonization. Indonesia has been challenged by the secession of East Timor and, in particular, the continuing influence of a politicoeconomic system that was constructed to ensure that the family of the former president, Suharto, utilized political power to advance its economic status and control. Ethnic tensions and resentment about the control of political power by dominant ethnic groups in Malaysia, Indonesia and, to a lesser extent, Singapore, for example, restrict the emergence of civility and social capital. Similarly, in China, as it experiences a transition from socialism to a more open economy, while retaining its socialist heritage, leaders seek to create stronger ties between elite policy-makers and beneficiaries, many of whom emerged from within the party-state system. Japan appears to be the most liberal in Asia in that it looks like a Western democratic system, which includes doubt regarding its 'traditional' understandings of democratization (Breslin, 2002). A key element in understanding the connection between social capital and leadership is evidenced in the writings of Chalmers Johnson (1999). He opines that the autonomy of elite bureaucrats who plan economic strategy (albeit in market-conforming actions) is critical for the success of a developmental state where politicians reign but bureaucrats rule. Irrespective of the result of democratic elections, an elite group of professional bureaucrats makes economic policy based on their conceptions of national interest, unconstrained by considerations of electoral popularity and insulated from the demands of social interest groups.

The Japanese occupation of Korea resulted in weak social capital in the current South Korea. In Taiwan, various groups were eliminated following the Kuomintang's takeover, resulting in the party-state control of society and the economy. As evidenced in these East Asian states – Japan, South Korea, China and Taiwan – the nation-building process by the leaders used proclaimed strategies of national renewal and national mobilization to defend their new position. Naturally, in the Cold-War context or post-Cold War, for these states, being authoritarian was often enough to qualify for considerable US economic aid and Western tolerance of the lack of democratic forms (Breslin, 2002). These circumstances provided the framework of Bourdieu's social capital theory.

Even though the great transformation of industrialization in Europe in the 19th century marked the institutional separation of society into an economic and a political sphere, for large parts of the world – not necessarily just in Asia – such transformation has not taken place or is at best incomplete. Lack of separation is evident not only in communist party states, where there is state control over society and economy, but also in other states in Asia that might appear to be Western-type democracies. This being so, is the ability of the leaders to influence through political processes and economic policy-making that impinges on the lives of society especially through the structure of domestic political economies.

The widespread impression of China is that the leader of the Chinese Communist Party maintains a monopoly of power. Values of traditional Chinese culture have inclined to the ideology of Mao Zedong with many scholars pointing to the consistency and continuity of Confucianism and Chinese communist ideology after the founding of the People's Republic of China (Pye, 1985). In contrast to democratic governance, Confucianism and Maoism have exercised control over information and so have prevented and undermined the manifestation of democratic values. Mouffe (1993; 2000) argues that every society is the product of a series of practices attempting to establish order in a context of contingency and she refers to the struggle for hegemony as 'agonism': the symbolic context over the constitution of society, the institution of an order in which a potentially intercommunal conflict is represented as communal (politics). It is in this context that we argue that despite authoritarianism, each leader plays a decisive role, popularizing the function of reforms as witnessed by Deng Xiaoping, who changed China's socioeconomic system and international status whilst undermining the communist ideology to a certain extent. China's leaders have depended on both ancient wisdom and communist doctrine as guides to action, as in those of Mao Zedong, Deng Xiaoping, Jiang Zemin and Hu Jintao. Each leader's ideology combines their own formulations with particular elements strategically selected from previous leaders' guiding thoughts. Hu's political demeanour seems to suggest a Confucian style of leadership, one that governs by virtuous example, but old Maoist structures remain with traditional-sounding rhetoric about harmony and peace. Hu advocates the principle of Confucianism where the interests of rulers and people are closely related, and in describing state–society relations, the leader or government is always the head, the thinker, and is hence less contingent on the situation of the society's demands resulting in the diminishing or weakening of public decision making (Beh, 2008).

In contrast, in South Korea, there is a diminishing role of the leader or head of state. The president's role is certainly decreasing, as also its military services (except during the recent threat from North Korea's artillery attack on South Korea's Yeonpyeong Island near the disputed Yellow Sea border, the first involving a civilian area since the Korean War).

The Southeast Asian nations, as in Malaysia, Singapore, Thailand and Indonesia, typically seem to be constructed to ensure that an elite group of insiders utilizes a linkage between political power, economic policy-making and state or family control over major sectors of the economy, deliberately self-rewarding at most times in the nation-building processes. Even in East Asian states, as in Japan, being the closest match to the Western political democratic system, the national interest is defined by a group of leaders comprising bureaucrats, business groups and leaders of the Liberal Democratic Party (LDP), the hegemonic party until the 1990s. Evidently the retired bureaucrats enjoyed second careers within either the business world or the LDP, while the bureau of the Ministry of International Trade and Industry provided the formal framework within which business interests could influence the national economic planning and subsequently national interest. Remarkably, this scenario is deployed as well in Malaysia since its implementation of Look East policy. It is from within these countries that many of the pressures for change now emanate in Thailand, Indonesia and Malaysia, with leaders' actions in particular ensuring the under-representation (or even over-representation or manipulation by the leaders/elites in each country) of pressure groups and civil society organizations in some issues, recently observed at a time when the society in question needs it more than ever as an important element of true democratic politics. Nevertheless, many Asian states do not have transparent policy-making processes from a Western perspective. Hence this also means that leaders' actions largely do not reflect Western practices and interests. It is false universalism that conflicts over the allocation of resources that could be resolved with effective state machinery or legalistic judgement, as practised more in the West. Most often, within Eastern culture, leaders deal with conflicts or opportunities through informal community channels before going to the next level of formal and legal channels. It goes to show that such informal leadership style and amount of control are much witnessed in the countries of Southeast Asia specifically and to a limited extent in East Asia in contrast with Western practices.

Nation-building in Indonesia has been hindered by a multitude of political parties rooted in a variety of traditions, ideologies and beliefs. Leaders often appear indecisive and overly cautious when faced with political opposition and lobbying from all directions, resulting in a tendency to seek compromise while maintaining the status quo and slowing reform. Political exploitation of tensions between groups and within the 48 registered political parties tends to polarize and jeopardize leadership coalitions and policy-related collaborations. Widespread disillusionment with post-Suharto leadership has been exacerbated by perceptions of ineffective economic reforms, increasing unemployment and inept anti-corruption campaigns. To a similar or lesser degree, the increasing separatism in Malaysia did not demonstrate the increased accountability of legislators to their constituents, thus further limiting unity and the region's ability to reduce maladministration excesses. Independence from the Dutch for Indonesia in 1945 led to the presidency of Sukarno, who ended liberal democracy and mobilized nationalist slogans for his political survival and authoritarian rule. His leadership was undermined following an attempted coup, which paved the way for the second president, Suharto, in 1966. He ruled for the next 32 years, known as the New Order era, which was also characterized by authoritarian rule and strong leadership. Despite economic and social growth, the region suffered epidemic problems of corruption, elections that were neither free nor representative, poor political accountability, and the use of the military as an agent of enforcement of social policy marred further by security issues from communal violence, terrorism and lawlessness (Emmerson, 200; Tan, 2002). Suharto only allowed three political parties, including his own Golkar Party, which had close associations with the widely criticized military apparatus. Widespread disillusionment of his leadership precipitated by the Asian financial crisis led to his regime's collapse, constitutional reforms and eventually bringing Abdurrahman Wahid to power in 1999. Wahid was a proponent of liberal democracy, and he benefited from the situational politics of public expectations, the era of democratization and growing religious tolerance. However, within two years he was forced to resign due to claims of ill health and impeachment charges, paving the way for Megawati Sukarnoputri, daughter of Indonesia's first president, Sukarno, in 2001. In the 2004 general elections, Megawati formed a coalition of four major parties but lost to Susilo Bambang Yudhoyono from the Democratic Party and his vice-presidential candidate, Jusuf Kalla, from the Golkar Party. Indonesia's leadership has left an authoritarian legacy transmitted by an elite group with a history of collaboration with political parties, allowing loci of authority to shift from one clique of leadership to another.

Strong and effective leadership was an advantage of authoritarian rule even though it sacrificed democratic principles and fair elections – despite consisting independent monitoring commissions – and many contentious issues remain. The Indonesian experience is also similar to the reign of Mahathir Mohamed in Malaysia, who impressed and engendered awe in economic development, which became his political lexicon, and established a legacy that tended to the national interest, encouraged Bumiputra Malays in all sectors, especially business, which may have led to the pursuit of wealth untempered by ethics or even fear of the law, but was seemingly tolerated (Wain, 2009: 150, 230). Mahathir was able to gain attraction both domestically and, at times, internationally, and utilized various political situations as instruments in securing his post for more than 22 years, almost as long as his three predecessors combined. He ensured that religion became an even more vital part of Malay identity, making controversial claims which led to significant numbers of Malay Muslims to question many aspects of Malaysian society (Wain, 2009: 217–218). While sometimes he preferred to persuade and implore to enforce his policies and norms, he did not hesitate to threaten or use coercion when he deemed it necessary, imposing government ownership and control of the media but also, paradoxically, creating much animus within the diplomatic etiquette of international relations. The culture was that of subdued society in a leader–followers relationship, allowing the tyrannical leader to impose his views, typical of Eastern philosophy, which were constantly reiterated by the Mahathir administration to seemingly champion the disgruntlement of a privileged segment of society and the interests of the East in contrast to the Western culture to further boost his political career. Despite his contributions, controversial issues remain, such as his family's business operations and involvement when he was in office, which prompted critics to compare his administration with Suharto's corrupt regime in Indonesia (Wain, 2009: 323). This may be difficult to redress politically, economically and socially.

This form of leadership is utilized by many leaders in Southeast Asia in negotiated relationships that individuals have with other individuals, or with society, in addition to the cultural factor that changes across social and political situations. As such, elements of leadership are contingent on situations, sentiments and complexity, of which feudalism is still the norm in the East. This is in contrast to the Western emphasis on capacity-building, transformation and transparent governance, though we may be being oversimplistic. The situation here demonstrates the use of Fiedler's theory, which suggests that leaders must learn to manipulate or influence the leadership situation in order to create a match between their leadership style and the amount of control within the situation at hand.

In the West, as well as in Asia Pacific, the role of party leaders has assumed greater prominence as it is common practice for governments to be named after their leaders rather than after the party that holds office. The Howard government and the Obama administration are just two examples of this trend towards the personalization of politics. Hence leaders communicate with voters and seek to convert the audience by dominating the dissemination of political information through the media providing visual and oral information. This trend is catching up in the East where social media are popularly used to define the leaders and, paradoxically perhaps, determine how they act and manipulate social communication media in different situations. The outcome often lacks professionalism, resulting in public cynicism about leaders and politicians in Southeast Asia.

Leaders ought to understand the context (political and wider environment) and the processes necessary to bring about strategic change, as well as how change can be instigated. Leaders in these countries in Southeast Asia often fail to recognize that they must show the capacity to effect public purposes and accountability to the polity to the acceptable level of leaders' good governance in East Asia, if not the West. Considering the capacity of leaders to deal with new ideas and changes, from concentrated power to diffused power, hierarchy to heterarchy, it has to be pointed out that new challenges are constantly arising, which leaders need to face in the politics of situational development . These challenges can be daunting, given conflicts that arise between leaders' actions and citizens in many countries, and especially so in developing countries in East and Southeast Asia, before they achieve full democratic governance.

Touchstones for leadership in the East

The preceding discussion allows the derivation of the following touchstones for effective leadership behaviour with specific emphasis on Southeast Asian concerns.

First, leadership can be profitably conceived as an activity dedicated to creating, maintaining and utilizing social capital in order to achieve ethical and responsible goals and outcomes whether at the national, regional, local or even individual level. Implicit within this is the notion that what can emerge when social capital comes into existence is a sense of community and identification, which fosters the potential for action. Leadership is unfortunately too often seen as a kind of control mechanism of the self-serving sort where leader behaviour is cognizant of situation and context but where the behavioural options are relatively few. Thus leaders, in trying to produce desirable outcomes for their institutions, attempt to provide a control mechanism whereby appropriate behaviours are cultivated while others are discouraged. In what is presented above, context and situation are central to the recognition that successful leadership begins with a moment-to-moment dynamic adjustment to the incredible complexity that more accurately characterizes the ebb and flow of human activity.

Second, the availability of social capital, where managed effectively and appropriately, creates the potential for action. However, as the literature on the dark side of social capital makes clear, the 'expenditure' of social capital can be made wisely or unwisely, effectively or ineffectively, or for noble or base outcomes (Portes & Landolt, 1996). One author explores the nature of social capital in Russian crime and concludes that it can be utilized for illegal activities in much the same manner as it can for positive outcomes (Gilbert, 2009a; 2009b). In Thailand, for example, one has to wonder how the 'Red Shirts' coordinated their activities and included outsiders as key actors in their violent protests without sufficient network connections, which would allow highly orchestrated cooperative action. Only through social capital use for unethical and dangerous purposes can such activities occur.

Third, there is also a skill dimension to leadership seen from a social capital perspective, and for this we turn to the communication competence literature (Spitzberg & Cupach, 1984), which explains that the essence of expenditure is the selection of the appropriate communication behaviours in context. In particular, Spitzberg and Cupach suggest three components of communication competence: knowledge, skill and motivation. Kennan and Hazleton (2006) argue for a communication dimension to social capital, suggesting that it is through human interaction that connections are formed, kept and used. Actors who do not have a sophisticated knowledge of the communication process as it relates to social capital, and hence leadership, may choose tactics that do not maximize the use of deposits of social capital that exist. Leaders not skilled as communicators may squander social capital in an effort to achieve goals and objectives through the selfish and self-serving kinds of actions described in the previous section. Finally, some leaders are simply not motivated as communicators and may miss opportunities to use social capital for positive gain. In sum, leadership involves social capital seen as a mechanism that allows the achievement of goals and objectives. Ultimately, leader effectiveness depends on effectively managed communication leveraged on behalf of ethical and responsible motives, which, in turn, create a strong sense of solidarity and identity in often turbulent and chaotic contexts. A deep understanding of communication as a leadership and social capital creation, use and maintenance mechanism is fundamental to a sure-footed response to the almost infinite and contextually driven litany of challenges that confront contemporary leaders.

To add a fifth point to the discussion, leader behaviour can be seen as a conscious and intentional effort to cultivate, use and retain the connections that can serve as potential resources for goal attainment. Among the many other topics that could be discussed, at this point it is important to acknowledge the importance of new communication technologies for the creation of social capital and to suggest that effective leader behaviour must now consist in leveraging a variety of opportunities, including social media.[5] *Facebook*, as one prime example of this type of technology, is rapidly expanding among users in Southeast Asia. In Indonesia, for example, its use has grown to 30 million users and other Southeast Asian nations have shown similar growth. *Facebook* allows families and friends to connect, and to maintain and even intensify their connectedness, sometimes turning weak or previously unknown connections (Granovetter, 1973) into stronger ones.[6] It also creates an opportunity for leader action in making new connections, keeping them fresh, and using them when and where needed. In Malaysia, for example, there are more than 500,000 friends of the McDonald's fan *Facebook* page. It should be noted that in addition to the emerging potential inherent in social media there remains, among Southeast Asian governments, a tendency to not use social media and to not engage in leadership via connection but to restrict technological impact through what one commentator identifies as a kind of 'Chinese-style' intervention. So while technology affords the opportunity for social capital creation and the generation of broad-based support for action, Southeast Asian nations have often limited the potential of connections in favour of fostering isolation and, in some quarters, resentment.

As mentioned, morals and ethics are imperative for leaders to create new forms of social capital (Putnam, 2001). The discussion regarding the leadership environment in Asia is pointed in its recognition that social capital is unevenly distributed, creating vast cultural and political inequalities. Even if this idea of a just distribution of social capital, and hence the ability to achieve goals and exert influence, is Western, the moral and ethical implications of empowering individuals and groups must be universal. The central issue for contemporary leaders is not simply social capital creation but social capital that is distributed evenly and fairly across all of the many and diverse groups and organizations, which provides access to network resources in a timely fashion.

The enumeration of touchstones for leader behaviour could easily continue. However, the evolution of the impact of social capital as a leadership reality in Asia must continue in an effort to document the manner in which deposits of social capital come into being and are used for appropriate and inappropriate means, and how those connections are maintained or altered across time. However, this discussion concludes with one final observation. Leadership in Southeast Asia is complex, as it is in other contexts. Traditional situational leadership theories point in the right direction but are limited in their scope and understanding of the nearly infinite number of factors that must be entered into the leadership equation. Social capital spans cultures and situations by focusing on what people do as they seek collective action. It avoids issues of control in favour of connection, it emphasizes cooperation and collaboration, and it identifies community as a valuable asset for effective leadership. It recognizes the negative potential inherent in the social capital perspective, and it takes for granted the fact that situations and contexts demand continuous re-evaluation and adjustment. These are valuable considerations for leaders in any context and at any time.

Conclusion

This chapter's contribution lies in the application of a social capital perspective in the approach to the relationship between leadership and cultural contexts in East and Southeast Asia. First, the discussion suggests that leadership is inherently contextual/situational and cultural/national, although the search for best practices sets the stage for the integration of various culturally grounded formulations. Second, it argues that leaders can benefit from envisioning leadership as the creation, maintenance and use of social capital to produce social equity, political stability and economic development. Leaders who can exercise good judgement, who are capable of synthesizing the enormous numbers of contradictory forces and can respond to the politics of situations via consultative forms of citizen engagement and trust-building will develop a competitive advantage that will benefit them and their institutions in an increasingly turbulent future.

Notes

1. The list of factors is, in fact, almost endless, with new factors and concerns emerging as societies change and adapt.
2. See Hofstede (2001); Hofstede (1984); Hofstede and Hofstede (1997), Trompenaars and Hampden-Turner (1998) for detailed discussions of cultural dimensions as they relate to Southeast Asia.
3. In fact, Taylor's biographer titled his work *The One Best Way: Frederick Winslow Taylor and the Enigma of Efficiency* (Kanigel, 2005).
4. Only a short walk through the streets of Kuala Lumpur demonstrates the incredible diversity of orientation towards the models of civility, social capital and attitudes toward aggression that Pye describes.
5. The controversy over whether technology reduces the availability of social capital (Putnam) or builds it is discussed.
6. One of the remarkable social capital outcomes of the Arab Spring uprisings is the impact of social media in helping likeminded individuals to discover common goals and objectives, and to create productive network connections that produce remarkably sophisticated and coordinated action. In this case, leadership emerges in a dynamic process of networked relationships that form and re-form as context and circumstance dictate. This reality should cause a reconsideration of what leadership is and how it is effectively wielded.

References

Adam, F. & Roncevic, B. (2002). Social capital as a useful scientific metaphor. In N. Genov (Ed.), *Advances in Sociological Knowledge Over Half a Century* (pp. 207–234). Paris: International Social Science Council.

Ailon, G. (2008). Mirror, mirror on the wall: *Culture's consequences* in a value-test of its own design. *Academy of Management Review*, 33(4), 885–904.

Baker, W. (1990). Market networks and corporate behavior. *American Journal of Sociology*, 96, 589–625.

Barnard, C.I. (1968). *The Functions of the Executive*. Boston, MA: Harvard University Press.

Bass, B.M. (1985). *Leadership and Performance beyond Expectations*. New York: Free Press.

Bass, B.M. (1997). Does the transactional-transformational leadership paradigm transcend organizational and national boundaries. *American Psychologist*, 52,130–139.

Bean, C. & Mughan, A. (1989). Leadership effects in parliamentary elections in Australia and Britain. *American Political Science Review*, 83(4), 1165–79.

Beh, L.S. (2008). Reinventing administrative prescriptions: Spirituality in China? *The Copenhagen Journal of Asian Studies*, 26(2), 11–25.

Bennis, W., & Nanus, B. (1985). *Leaders: Strategies for Taking Charge*. New York: Harper & Row.

Breslin, S. (2002). East Asia. In P. Burnell (Ed.), *Democratization Through the Looking Glass* (pp. 169–187). Manchester and New York: Manchester University Press.

Burt, R.S. (1992). *Structural Holes: The Social Structure of Competition*. Cambridge, MA: Harvard University Press.

Burt, R.S. (1997). The contingent value of social capital. *Administrative Science Quarterly*, 42(2), 339–365.
Burt, R.S. (2004). Structural holes and good ideas. *American Journal of Sociology*, 110(2), 344–399.
Burt, R.S. (2005). *Brokerage and Closure: An Introduction to Social Capital*. New York: Oxford University Press.
Burt, R.S. & Knez, M. (1995). Kinds of third-party effects on trust. *Rationality and Society*, 7(3), 255–292.
Burt, R.S. & Ronchi, D. (2007). Teaching executives to see social capital: Results from a field experiment. *Social Science Research*, 36, 1156–1183.
Bourdieu, P. (1986). The forms of capital. In J.G. Richardson (Ed.), *Handbook of Theory and Research for the Sociology of Education* (pp. 241–258). New York: Greenwood.
Bourdieu, P. & Passeron, J.C. (1990). *Reproduction in Education, Society and Culture*. London: Sage Publications Ltd.
Bourdieu, P. & Thompson, J.B. (1991). *Language and Symbolic Power*. Cambridge, MA: Harvard University Press.
Bourdieu, P. & Wacquant, L.J.D. (1992). *An Invitation to Reflexive Sociology*. Chicago, IL: University of Chicago Press.
Bryman, A. (1996). Leadership in organizations. In S.R. Clegg, C. Hardy, & W.R. Nord (Eds.), *Handbook of Organization Studies* (pp. 276–292). Thousand Oaks, CA: Sage.
Chapman, R.A. & O'Toole, B.J. (2010). Leadership in the British civil service: An interpretation. *Public Policy and Administration*, 25(2), 123–136.
Chondroleou, G., Elcock, H., Liddle, J. & Oikonomopoulos, I. (2005). A comparison of local management of regeneration in England and Greece. *International Journal of Public Sector Management*, 18(2), 114–127.
Coleman, J.S. (1986). Social theory, social research, and a theory of action. *American Journal of Sociology*, 91(6), 1309–1335.
Coleman, J.S. (1988). Social capital in the creation of human capital. *American Journal of Sociology*, 94(1), 95–120.
Emmerson, D.K. (2002). Indonesia: A violent culture? *Asian Survey*, 42(4), 582–605.
Fiedler, F.E. (1967). *A Theory of Leadership Effectiveness*. New York: McGraw-Hill.
Fiedler, F.E. (1996). Research on leadership selection and training: One view of the future. *Administrative Science Quarterly*, 41, 241–250.
freedomhouse.org: Map of Freedom in the World. (n.d.). Retrieved from http://www.freedomhouse.org/template.cfm?page=363&year=2010.
Fussell, H., Harrison-Rexrode, J., Kennan, W.R, & Hazleton, V. (2006). The relationship between social capital, transaction costs, and organizational outcomes: A case study. *Corporate Communications: An International Journal*, 11(2), 148–161.
Gilbert, L.E. (2009a). Civil society and social capital in Russia. In H.K. Anheier & S. Toepler (Eds.), *International Encyclopedia of Civil Society*, Retrieved from http://www.springer.com/sociology/book/978-0-387-93997-1.
Gilbert, L.E. (2009b). Analyzing the dark side of social capital. In M. Cox (Ed.), *Social Capital and Peace-Building: Creating and Resolving Conflict with Trust and Social Networks* (p. 57). New York: Routledge.

Goleman, D. (1998). *Working with Emotional Intelligence*. New York: Bantam.
Graeff, C.L. (1983). The situational leadership theory: A critical review. *Academy of Management Review*, 8(2), 285–291.
Granovetter, M. (1973). The strength of weak ties. *American Journal of Sociology*, 78(6), 1360–1380.
Grint, K. (2005). Problems, problems, problems: The social construction of leadership. *Human Relations*, 58(11), 1467–94.
Haslam, S.A. (2001). *Psychology in Organizations: The Social Identity Approach*. London: Sage.
Hatch, J.H. (2006). *Organization Theory*, 2nd edition. Oxford: Oxford University Press.
Hazleton, V. & Kennan, W. (2000). Social capital: Reconceptualizing the bottom line. *Corporate Communications: An International Journal*, 5(2), 81–86.
Hersey, P. & Blanchard, K. (1969). *Management of Organizational Behavior: Utilizing Human Resources*. Englewood Cliffs, NJ: Prentice Hall.
Hersey, P. & Blanchard, K. (1977). *Management of Organizational Behavior: Utilizing Human Resources*, 3rd edition. Englewood Cliffs, NJ: Prentice Hall.
Hofstede, G. (2001). *Culture's Consequences: Comparing Values, Behaviors, Institutions, and Organizations Across Nations*. London: Sage Publications.
Hofstede, G. & Hofstede, G.J. (1997). *Cultures and Organizations: Software of the Mind*. London: McGraw-Hill.
Hofstede, G.H. (1984). *Culture's Consequences: International Differences in Work-Related Values*. London: Sage Publications.
Hogg, M.A. (2001). A social identity theory of leadership. *Personality and Social Psychology Review*, 5, 184–200.
House, R.J. (1971). A path-goal theory of leader effectiveness. *Administrative Science Quarterly*, 16, 321–339.
House, R.J. Hanges, P.J. Javidan, M. Dorfman, P.W. & Gupta, V. (Eds.) (2004). *Leadership, Culture and Organizations: The GLOBE Study of 62 Societies*. London: Sage.
Hunter, S.T. Bedell-Avers, K.E. & Mumford, M.D. (2007). The typical leadership study: Assumptions, implications and potential remedies. *The Leadership Quarterly*, 18(5), 435–446.
Jepson, D. (2009). Studying leadership at cross-country level: A critical analysis. *Leadership* 5(1), 61–80.
Johnson, C. (1999). The developmental state: Odyssey of a concept. In M. Woo-Cumings (Ed.), *The Developmental State* (pp. 32–60). Ithaca and London: Cornell University Press.
Kanigel, R. (2005). *The One Best Way: Frederick Winslow Taylor and the Enigma of Efficiency*. Cambridge, MA: MIT Press Books.
Kennan, W.R. & Hazleton, V. (2006). Internal public relations, social capital, and the role of effective organizational communication. In C.H. Botan & V. Hazleton (Eds.), *Public Relations Theory II* (pp. 311–338). Mahwah (NJ): Lawrence Erlbaum Associates.
Lin, N. (2002). *Social Capital: A Theory of Social Structure and Action*. Cambridge, New York: Cambridge University Press.
Mayo, E. (2003). *The Human Problems of An Industrial Civilization*. New York: Routledge.

Mishler, E.G. (1978). Meaning in context: Is there any other kind. Paper presented at the 62nd Annual Meeting of the American Educational Research Association, Toronto, Ontario, Canada, March 27–31.
Mouffe, C. (1993). *The Return of the Political*. London: Verso.
Mouffe, C. (2000). *The Democratic Paradox*. London: Verso.
Mowday, R. & Sutton, R. (1993). Organizational behavior: Linking individuals and groups to organizational context. *Annual Review of Psychology*, 44,195–220.
Nahapiet, J. & Ghoshal, S. (1998). Social capital, intellectual capital, and the organizational advantage. *Academy of Management Review*, 23, 242–266.
Osborne, S. (2009). Delivering public services: Are we asking the right questions? *Public Money & Management*, 29(1), 5–7.
Prince, L. (2005). Eating the Menu rather than the Dinner: Tao and Leadership. *Leadership*, 1(1), 105–126.
Portes, A. (1998). Social capital: Its origins and applications in modern sociology. *Annual Review of Sociology*, 24, 1–24.
Putnam, R. (2000). *Bowling Alone: The Collapse and Revival of American Community*. New York: Simon and Schuster.
Pye, L. (1985). *Asian Power and Politics: The Cultural Dimensions of Authority*. Cambridge: Belknap Press.
Pye, L.W. (1999). Civility, social capital, and civil society: Three powerful concepts for explaining Asia. *Journal of Interdisciplinary History*, 29(4), 763–782.
Reicher, S., Haslam, S.A. & Hopkins, N. (2005). Social identity and the dynamics of leadership: Leaders and followers as collaborative agents in the transformation of social reality. *The Leadership Quarterly*, 16, 547–568.
Seibert, S.E., Kraimer, M.L. & Liden, R.C. (2001). A social capital theory of career success. *Academy of Management Journal*, 44(2), 219–237.
Senge, P.M. (2006). *The Fifth Discipline: The Art and Practice of the Learning Organization*. London: Random House.
Spitzberg, B.H. & Cupach, W.R. (1984). *Interpersonal Communication Competence*. London: Sage.
Trompenaars, A. & Hampden-Turner, C. (1998). *Riding the Waves of Culture: Understanding Cultural Diversity in Global Business*. New York: McGraw Hill.
van Mart, M. (2003). Public sector leadership theory: An assessment. *Public Administration Review*, 63(2), 214–228.
Vroom, V.H. & Yetton, P.W. (1973). *Leadership and Decision Making*. Pittsburg, CA: University of Pittsburg Press.
Wain, B. (2009). *Malaysian Maverick – Mahathir Mohamad in Turbulent Times*. Basingstoke: Palgrave Macmillan.
Woolcock, M. (1998). Social capital and economic development: Toward a theoretical synthesis and policy framework. *Theory and Society*, 27(2), 151–208.
Woolcock, M. (2002). Social capital in theory and practice: Where do we stand? In J. Isham, T.Kelly, & S. Ramaswamy (Eds.), *Social Capital and Economic Development: Well-Being in Developing Countries*. Cheltenham: Edward Elgar Publishing, pp. 18–39
Woolcock, M. & Narayan, D. (2000). Social capital: Implications for development theory, research, and policy. *World Bank Research Observer*, 15(2), 225–249.

2

Visionary Leadership in the Arab World: Its Nature and Outcomes in the Omani Workplace

James Rajasekar, Salem Al Abri and Yasser S. Tabouk

Introduction

Despite recent interest in exploring leadership practices in the Middle East, still little is known about this important part of the world (Common, 2011; Pellegrini & Scandura, 2006; Scandura, von Glinow, & Lowe, 1999). This dearth in research has been attributed largely to the difficulty in gathering data (Dorfman & House, 2004; Scandura et al., 1999). Despite this challenge, however, and as the region is increasingly becoming a hub for foreign investments (Pellegrini & Scandura, 2006), more research is needed to explore effective leadership practices. The need for such research is becoming even more significant as the region is currently undergoing considerable transformation fuelled by the public uprisings that have swept the Arab World recently. Thus, by conducting the current research in Oman, we intended to make a contribution to the leadership literature by increasing our understanding of visionary leadership.

The majority of research conducted on leadership in the Middle East has focused primarily on the influence of the local culture and societal structures on leadership practices. For instance, Neal, Finlay, and Tansey (2005) examined the influence of tradition and tribal elements in modern management in the Arab Gulf, including Oman. Similarly, Ali (1995; 1989) identified key cultural prototypes of Arab leadership, particularly the traditional relationship between the tribal leader (or *sheik*) and the tribe. A more recent study by Almoharby (2010) has refined this work by highlighting another key influence on modern Arab leadership and management – a traditional form of highly consultative, or *shuratic*, decision making. Looking at gender differences, Al-Lamky (2007) and Al-Lamki (1999) highlighted the experience of women in the Arab Gulf workplace and identified the challenges they face as they rise into leadership positions. Rajasekar and Moideenkutty (2007) more specifically investigated how the dynamic leadership at Oman Air turned round this once struggling airline. Although these studies provide some valuable feedback about leadership in Oman, they have not given enough emphasis to one of the important leadership behaviours – visionary leadership.

The economic and political changes that are currently shaping the region, including Oman, have created a highly unstable environment for business organizations. Such transformations require leaders to adopt more effective leadership practices to handle such environments and eventually lead the organization to a land of safety. Transformational/charismatic leadership behaviours become more appropriate in situations characterized by change and uncertainty (Northouse, 2010; Shamir, House, Arthur, & 1993). Although Neal and Finlay (2008) and Neal et al. (2005) have analysed the nature and importance of charismatic and transformational leadership in Arab organizations and society, there has been no research to date on something related, but distinct, in Arab leadership – vision. Therefore the aim of this chapter is to investigate two important activities of charismatic leadership: visioning and responding to chaos as practised in Oman, a highly traditional but rapidly developing country in the Arabian Peninsula. The following section reviews the literature pertinent to the nature of visionary leadership.

Literature review

Visionary leadership and followers outcomes

A visionary leader is one who communicates a compelling vision, or a picture, of where a group of people should be going (Manning & Robertson, 2002). A vision can be defined as 'a general transcendent ideal that represents shared values' (Kirkpatrick & Locke, 1996). Such a vision is general and broad enough to allow for alternative approaches to accomplish it (Choi, 2007). Hence there is a consensus that visioning or visionary leadership is considered one of the top leadership attributes for effective leaders (Den Hartog, Hanges, Ruiz-Quintanilla, & Dorfman, 1999). Specifically, Ehrhart & Klein's (2001) review of the literature of charismatic leadership identified articulating a vision of the future as one of the four charismatic leadership behaviours.

Visionary leadership is important because of its significant effects on followers (Northouse, 2010; Shamir et al., 1993). When successful, this abstract picture is transformed by followers into actions, ideas, and, ultimately, reality. This effect is achieved because visionary leaders are dreamers, who win the hearts and minds of the audience and take the organization into a new – and sometimes discontinuous – phase of development (Nwankwo & Richardson, 1996). In this regard, the leader motivates others to understand and share the vision, and energizes and empowers them to make decisions, achieve goals, and initiate actions to achieve it. In doing this, visionary leaders stress core values, empowering relationships and creative action. When one or more of these aspects is missing, the vision becomes less convincing, and the leader is correspondingly less influential (Manning & Robertson, 2002). Moreover, the effect of visionary leadership is also explained by the shared sense of purpose that visionary leadership develops among followers: 'Their eyes are on the horizon, not just on the near at hand. They are social innovators and change agents, seeing the big picture and thinking strategically' (Groves, 2005).

As to outcomes, Bono and Judge (2003) found that followers of visionary leaders had greater satisfaction and organizational commitment. That is because when a company's vision is successfully formulated and assimilated, it increases their identification and emotional bond with the organization and hence their affective commitment (Dvir, Kass, & Shamir, 2004). In light of the previous discussion, we draw the following hypothesis:

> Hypothesis 1: visionary leadership is positively related to employees' level of motivation and affective commitment.

Vision communication and outcomes

The aforementioned followers' outcomes are only achieved when the leader communicates the vision to the followers. That is because the development of a vision – no matter how coherent – is not enough for visionary leadership to take effect. Visionary leaders 'articulate, express and share organizational missions and goals in a simply, easily understood and tangible vision statement.' (Ahmad & Chopra, 2004). Specifically, effective communication is one of the skilful competences that separate superior from average leaders (Sorenson & Savage, 1989). However, it is not merely generic 'communication' that influences subordinates but a complex co-arising of disparate messages' contents, and their relational dimensions. Sorenson and Savage (1989) observed that 'Relational communication consists primarily of nonverbal signals and provides information about how the communicators perceive each other in a relationship. Of significance for participation in decision-making, relational messages also control who can talk when about what.'

By endowing content with relational qualities, leaders communicate not just information but their preferences, their fears, their suspicions, their hopes, and ultimately their vision with their colleagues. In this way, sensitive and skilled communication is a crucial aspect of leading organizations. Communication between the leader and team members 'produces outcomes such as increased employee satisfaction, the opportunity for increased socialization in the workplace, increased autonomy, opportunity to learn new skills, and other aspects such as reduced absenteeism and turnover and increased performance and inspiration' (Elloy, 2008). Based on the above discussion about the positive effect of the effective communication of vision on followers' outcomes, we draw the following hypothesis:

> Hypothesis 2: Effective communication of the vision is positively related to employee's motivation and affective commitment.

Leadership, order and disorder

These days 'new breed of companies are emerging that seems to thrive on chaos. These companies – which I call 'quantum organizations' – operate on an organic model that closely mirrors the functions of natural systems' (Youngblood, 1997). It is widely recognized today that to achieve and sustain competitive advantage, organizations need to respond to rapid change, and survive in the emerging political and economic realities: 'Survivors will have the ability to react, constantly improve, and continuously implement change. Excellent firms of tomorrow will cherish impermanence – and thrive on chaos' (Peters & Waterman, 1982). Visscher and Rip (2003) discuss the same issues but from a more circumspect position, pointing out the limitations of leadership when faced with unpredictability and risk: 'In their effort to change organizations, managers and change consultants are time and again confronted with the limited controllability of organizations, the complexity and indeterminacy of change process and the uncertain and ambiguous effects of their actions. In short, they are confronted with chaos' (Visscher & Rip, 2003).

In their attempt to deal with chaos, some managers hope to enhance their control over their organizations by trying to reducing chaos. Others adopt a more positive approach towards it by embracing it, and they base their decisions on recognition of it. Leaders, by definition, consider themselves to be agents of change, while they often have limited control over the uncertain and unpredictable effects of their actions. To cope with these changes and problems, some leaders 'embrace the chaos, advise modesty and help in different ways to change their organizations' (Visscher & Rip, 2003). Chaos is thus seen by some leaders as an opportunity for restructuring organizations and moving to a better position within the sector. Based on this, we have developed the following hypothesis:

> Hypothesis 3: Visionary leaders will have a positive orientation towards chaos.

Methodology

Sample and procedure

The sample of this study was drawn from a Middle Eastern country, Oman. We chose to conduct our study there as the Middle East is culturally different and has been increasingly attracting foreign investment in recent years, and hence more research is needed to understand leadership practices in this part of the world (Pellegrini & Scandura, 2006; Scandura et al., 1999). As mentioned earlier, to date only very limited leadership research has been conducted in Middle Eastern countries (Pellegrini & Scandura, 2006; Scandura et al., 1999). Participants in this study represented various sectors, both public and private. Figure 2.1 shows the main industries from which the data were collected. As shown, 49% of the respondents were from government sectors. With the assistance of the human resources department and using systematic sampling, respondents were selected randomly. They were assured of the confidentiality of responses. Out of 260 surveys, 140 usable questionnaires were returned yielding a response rate of 46%. This was unexpectedly high compared with similar studies which had a lower response rate. Of the 140 respondents, 66% were men. The majority of respondents (39%) were between 30 and 34 years of age with the same percentage of respondents having an average organizational tenure of ten years or over, representing diverse occupational backgrounds.

Measures

A survey instrument was developed to test the above hypotheses in Omani organizations. As this study was conducted in a culturally different context from the Western context, it was important to make

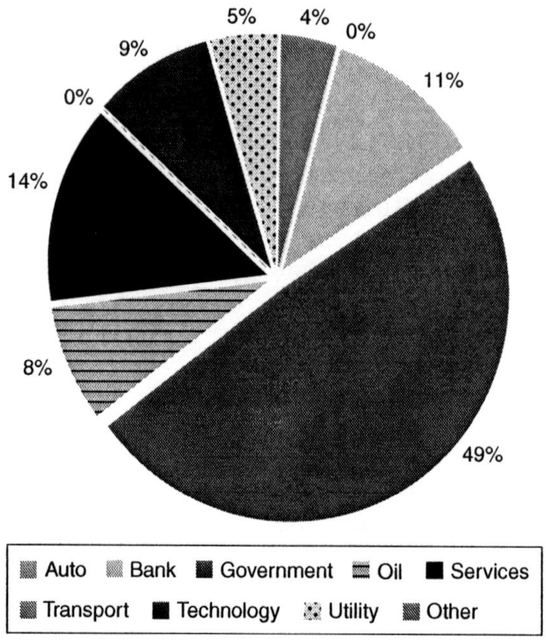

Figure 2.1 Representation of industries

sure that the measurement tool was also culturally consistent. This is because already established measures are tailored to Western contexts and hence using these measures in a different cultural context might produce invalid results. Hence a measure that better captures the local interpretations of these variables might provide more meaningful results. The instrument was first pilot-tested for further refinement. Based on feedback from respondents and management scholars, it underwent subsequent refinement. All items were scaled on a five-point Likert-type scale ranging from 'strongly disagree' to 'strongly agree'. Reliability alphas for the different variables are reported in Table 2.1. We controlled for demographic variables of age, gender, tenure and industry sector. Previous studies found that some of these variables had significant effects on outcome variables.

Data analysis and results

We used regression analysis using *SPSS 18* to analyse the data. The correlated results are presented in Table 2.1. Correlations among the variables

Table 2.1 Means, standard deviations, reliabilities and correlations among study variables

Variables	Mean	SD	1	2	3	4	5
Visionary leadership	3.41	0.67	(0.71)				
Motivation	3.26	0.48	0.43*	(0.77)			
Affective commitment	3.12	0.52	0.39**	0.63*	(0.79)		
Effective communication	3.10	0.53	0.61**	0.52*	0.51**	(0.80)	
Chaos	3.30	0.70	0.65*	0.39**	0.59**	28*	(0.84)

Notes: **Correlation is significant at the 0.01 level (two-tailed).
*Correlation is significant at the 0.05 level (two-tailed).
Values between parentheses refer to reliability alphas.

show initial support for the proposed hypotheses. Visionary leadership had a significant positive relationship with the outcome variables of motivation and affective commitment, hence providing preliminary support for Hypothesis 1. In addition, effective communication was positively correlated with the above outcomes too, providing preliminary support for Hypothesis 2.

Hypothesis 1 proposes that visionary leadership will positively relate to employees' motivation and affective commitment. The results revealed that visionary leadership positively influences the dependent variables of motivation and affective commitment ($\beta = 0.29$, $p < 0.01$ and $\beta = 0.21$, $p < 0.05$, respectively). Visionary leadership explains 23% of variance in both motivation and affective commitment.

Hypothesis 2 predicts that effective communication of the vision will positively relate to employees' motivation and affective commitment. The results show that effective communication of the vision has a positive impact on employees' motivation and affective commitment ($\beta = 0.33$, $p < 0.01$ and $\beta = 0.19$, $p < 0.01$, respectively). Effective communication explained 17% of change in both motivation and affective commitment.

Hypothesis 3 relates to the relation between visionary leadership and perception of chaos. The results indicate that visionary leaders has a positive orientation towards chaos ($\beta = 0.27$, $p < 0.05$).

Discussion and implications

As discussed earlier, the purpose of this study is to shed more light on leadership practice in the Middle East in general and specifically in Oman. As the Middle East is currently witnessing a transformational phase, the need for transformational leaders who can envision a better future for their followers is greater than ever been before. As stated earlier, this chapter examines the nature and influence of visionary leadership on employees' level of motivation and commitment in Oman. It also looks at the relationship between visionary leadership and chaos. Consistent with the aforementioned theorization and discussion, the results reveal that visionary leaders have a significant positive impact on their followers. This is accomplished by developing a sense of shared purpose and empowering employees in crafting their own future. The results further reveal that such employees' outcomes are only achieved through effective communication of the vision. Hence one implication of this is that the mission of a visionary leader is not limited to the formulation of the vision. Rather, it goes beyond this to include communicating the vision to followers in a way that is engaging and stimulating. Another implication of this study relates to the position that leaders take towards chaos – visionary leadership is especially needed during times of chaos and uncertainty. This is reflected by the results, which show a positive relationship between visionary leadership and chaos.

Overall, the findings of this study provide insights into key aspects of leadership in Oman, which appear to influence organizations and employees in differing, but often complementary, ways. The importance of vision is apparent, and this fits in well with the prototypical aspects of Omani culture discussed by Ali (1995) and Almoharby (2010). The current systems of communication can be seen to be embedded in the consultative, *shuratic*, networked forms of leadership and decision making typical of Omani leadership through the centuries. With the increase in change, the ongoing indigenization of the workforce and the restructuring of the public and private sectors, the importance of 'thriving on chaos' is increasing in Oman. Those with clear, transcendent visions of the future are thus increasingly necessary, as turbulence in the labour markets, and markets generally, increases.

What we see from this research is both complex and clear. The results highlight the complex interrelationships between communications, relationship-building and managing disorder and risk, enabling us to see how these aspects of Omani leadership are embedded in traditional prototypical social systems. It is clear that to harness this complexity, visionary leadership is vital for the sustained development of the country, and indeed the Arab Gulf region as a whole.

Future research and limitations

Since the study employed a cross-sectional research design, causality cannot be interpreted from its findings. For example, it is plausible to argue that employees who scored higher in terms of motivation and commitment were perceived so by their managers and hence their managers communicated better with them. Future research might utilize a longitudinal design to assess the impact of visionary leadership on employees' levels of motivation and commitment over a period of time. Moreover, common method bias might be a concern here as all variables were reported by a single source. However, since motivation and affective commitment are attitudinal variables that relate to one's personal feelings, it might be more appropriate to obtain self-reports rather than reports by peers or supervisors.

Finally, the context in which the study took place might limit the generalizability of the results. This work was conducted using an Omani sample so cultural aspects specific to Middle Eastern or Omani cultures might have influenced the results. Thus the results may not be generalizable to other cultures and so caution should be taken with regard to their generalizability.

References

Ahmad, A., & Chopra, O.P. (2004). *Passion to Win*. New Delhi: Excel Books.

Ali, A.J. (1989). Decision style and work satisfaction of Arab Gulf executives: A cross-national study. *International Studies of Management and Organization*, 19(2), 22–28.

Ali, A.J. (1995). Cultural discontinuity and Arab management thought. *International Studies of Management and Organization*, 5(3), 7–30.

Al-Ali, J. (2008). Emiratisation: Drawing UAE nationals into their surging economy. *International Journal of Sociology and Social Policy*, 28(9/10), 365–379.

Al-Lamki, S. (1999). Paradigm shift: A perspective on Omani women in management in the Sultanate of Oman. *Advancing Women in Leadership*, 5, Spring.

Al-Lamky, A. (2007). Feminizing leadership in Arab societies: The perspectives of Omani female leaders. *Women in Management Review*, 22(1), 49–67.

Almoharby, D. (2010). Shuratic decision-making practice, a case of the Sultanate of Oman. *Humanomics*, 26(1), 4–17.

Bono, J.E., & Judge, T.A. (2003). Self-concordance at work: Understanding the motivational effects of transformational leaders. *Academy of Management Journal*, 46, 554–571.

Choi, J.N. 2007. Change-oriented organizational citizenship behavior: Effects of work environment characteristics and intervening psychological processes. *Journal of Organizational Behaviour*, 28, 467–484.

Common, R.K. (2011). Barriers to developing 'leadership' in the Sultanate of Oman. *International Journal of Leadership Studies*, 6(2), 215–228.

Den Hartog, D.N., House, R.J., Hanges, P.J., Ruiz-Quintanilla, S.A., & Dorfman, P.W. (1999). Culture specific and cross-culturally generalizable implicit leadership theories: Are attributes of charismatic/transformational leadership universally endorsed? *Leadership Quarterly*, 10, 219–256.

Dorfman, P., & House, R. (2004). Cultural influences on organizational leadership. In R. House, P. Hanges, M. Javidan, P. Dorfman, & V. Gupta (Eds.), *Culture, Leadership and Organizations, the GLOBE Study of 62 Societies*. Thousand Oaks, CA: Sage.

Dvir, T., Kass, N., & Shamir, B. (2004). The emotional bond: Vision and organizational commitment among high-tech employees. *Journal of Organizational Change Management*, 17, 126–143.

Ehrhart, M.G., & Klein, K.J. (2001). Predicting followers' preferences for charismatic leadership: The influence of follower values and personality. *Leadership Quarterly*, 12, 153–179.

Elloy, D.F. (2008). The relationship between self leadership behaviors and organization variables in a self managed work team environment. *Management Research News*. 31(11), 801–810.

Groves, S.K. (2005). Leader emotional expressivity, visionary leadership, and organizational change. *College of Business and Economics*, 27(7), 566–583.

Kirkpatrick, S.A., & Locke, E.A. (1996). Direct and indirect effects of three core charismatic leadership components on performance and attitudes. *Journal of Applied Psychology*, 81, 36–51.

Manning, T., & Robertson, B. (2002). The dynamic leader -leadership development beyond the visionary leader. *Industrial and Commercial Training*, 34(4/5), 138–139.

Neal, M., & Finlay, J.L. (2008). American hegemony and business education in the Arab world. *Journal of Management Education*. 32(1) 38–83.

Neal, M., Finlay, J., & Tansey, R. (2005). 'My father knows the minister': A comparative study of Arab women's attitudes towards leadership authority. *Women in Management Review*, 20(7/8), 478–498.

Northouse, P.G. (2010). *Leadership: Theory and Practice*, 5th edition. Thousand Oaks, CA: Sage.

Nwankwo, S., & Richardson, B. (1996). Quality management through visionary leadership. *Managing Service Quality*, 6(4), 44–47.

Pellegrini, E.K., & Scandura, T.A. (2006). Leader-member exchange (LMX), paternalism, and delegation in the Turkish business culture: An empirical investigation. *Journal of International Business Studies*, 37, 264–279.

Peters, T.J., & Waterman, R.H. (1982). *In Search of Excellence: Lessons from Americas Best Run Companies*. New York: Warner Books.

Rajasekar, J., & Moideenkutty, U. (2007). Oman Air: Challenges of repositioning through business level strategy. *Asian Journal of Management Cases*, December 4, 117–141.

Scandura, T.A., Von Glinow, M.A., & Lowe, K.B. (1999). When east meet west: Leadership best practices in the US and the Middle East. In W.H. Mobley (Ed.), *Advances in Global Leadership* (pp. 235–249). Greenwich, CT: JAI Press.

Shamir, B., House, R.J., & Arthur, M.B. (1993). The motivational effects of charismatic leadership: A self-concept based theory. *Organization Science*, 4(4), 577–594.

Sorenson, R. & Savage, G.T. (1989). Signaling participation through relational communication: A test of the leader. *Group & Organization Studies*, 14(3), 325–336.

Visscher, K., & Rip, A. (2003). Coping with chaos in change processes. *Creativity & Innovation Management*, 12(2), 35–37.

Youngblood, M.D. (1997). Leadership at the edge of chaos: From control to creativity. *Strategy & Leadership*, 25(5), 8–13.

3

Leadership Perspective from the Philippines: Its Implications for Theory, Research and Practice

Francis Thaise A. Cimene and Alan N. Aladano

Introduction

Classic leadership literature is replete with examples of leaders' attempts to predict, categorize, classify, and control for every variable imaginable within organizations. Most research in academia defines leadership as a behaviour, a relationship, and in some cases an activity. Leadership traits and styles also dominate in establishing leadership perspectives. But what if organizations were unpredictable and impossible to control? More and more, organizational scholars are looking to theoretical constructs that paint a picture of leadership as fluid, emergent, or connected, and the result is concepts of chaos theory.

Over the years, leadership has been viewed from various angles and in different dimensions. It has gained the interests of graduate faculty and students, and business and government leaders to conduct and support research on leadership. The teaching about and research on leadership have surged, with many students majoring in the field. Indeed, it has been an intriguing topic for centuries during which academicians have formulated many definitions and theories of leadership. Many scholars and practitioners alike are convinced that effective leadership is required to meet most organizational challenges. Hence many curricula in leadership and management schools now emphasize the development of such skills.

Munro (2008:xvi) writes about the interface of person-as-leader, place, and participants, otherwise known as situated leadership, in her recent book entitled *Organizational Leadership*. This is a departure from other publications on leadership, which focus solely on the person as leader. The selected readings deal with organizational leadership issues from multiple perspectives, believing that there is no single correct answer to any of the questions raised. She emphasizes that from the perspective of situated leadership, the best answer is "it depends." She goes on to say that "Firm and fast rules or tried and true principles are less reliable when the focus shifts from solitary leader to interaction of key leadership factors." According to situational leadership theories, leaders work in complex settings where rules, players, problems, and objectives can change from hour to hour. It is unlikely that any one strategy or style will fit all of these changing conditions. That is why the principle behind situational theories is that "There is no one best way." Rather, the best way is contingent on the situation.

Leadership in the Philippines even from the grassroots point of view is full of challenges considering that crisis penetrates all sectors of society. Political and educational crises are the most publicized because they affect the economy. It is common knowledge that the country's economy is primarily supported by remittances from overseas foreign workers. However, this condition has resulted in the disintegration of families in particular and society in general. The greatest leadership challenge for the government then is to provide employment for its people so that they don't have to work abroad.

Moreover, the education sector has been characterized by yearly budget cuts, soaring tuition and other fee hikes, the highest dropout rate in recent years, unbridled and still unresolved cases of graft and corruption, and systematic government neglect of the education sector. Whether the qualitative standards are equally high is another issue. It is a difficult question to answer since there is little concordance between the aims and accomplishments of education in the Philippines.

Since the entire world's most prosperous industrial countries have a rather high proportion of educated citizens, it might be assumed that when this is the case a country will be prosperous. Unfortunately there is no guarantee that an expansion of schools will produce economic prosperity. The Philippines ranks much higher in education than in the income of its people. For instance, the percentage of literacy is practically the same as in Singapore, but the Philippine per capita income is only one-eighth that of Singapore. This is just one of the many challenges that the country's leaders are facing today.

In the Philippines, establishing leadership perspectives means understanding the culture and subcultures of the people. The manifestations of culture in the everyday socioeconomic and political life of the people are very evident. For instance, because the Filipinos are family-centred, organizational leaders and those who are led are looking for a work environment that they can call home. This explains why they value smooth interpersonal relationships pakikisama and social acceptance at work. However, when we speak of certain values as being characteristic of Philippine society, we do not mean that these conceptions of the desirable are found only in the Philippines. On the contrary, it will be seen that almost all of the values explained in the following pages feature in the value systems of other nations in Asia.

Objectives of the study

This study aims to capture the different viewpoints about the practice of leadership in organizations for a deeper understanding of personal leadership in the Philippines and its implications on theory, research, and practice. It is anchored in grounded theory (Glaser & Strauss, 1967; Strauss & Corbin, 1990) described as a qualitative research method in which theoretical explanations of participants' subjective experiences and situational meanings are generated. Because of its focus on social processes, grounded theory is particularly suited to this study.

The term "grounded" refers to the idea that the theory developed is based upon, or grounded in, participants' reality rather than on theoretical speculation. Grounded theory is best used to study social processes and structures, hence the focus on links and interactions among ideas or categories. Grounded theory methods often incorporate time into the study, because the focus is usually on processes or change. The method itself, however, does not specify any particular timing for the data collection and analysis process. As with all qualitative methods, grounded theory has as a goal of avoiding placing limits or external controls on the processes being studied because the function of the method is to ground theory in reality.

Limitations of the study

It was expected that cultural stereotypes would emerge in this study. Nevertheless, it assumes that no generalization or stereotype regarding cultural characteristics can apply to every member of a cultural group. We can only have predominant cultural traits. For instance, in the Philippines, the people place a high value on being, which emphasizes the intrinsic quality of the individual, hence the value of self-esteem (amor propio) among the Filipinos.

Also, the researchers did not attempt to determine whether leadership perspectives obtained from the respondents are right or wrong, good or bad. Such efforts are of little use in the process of establishing leadership perspectives considering that one cannot transplant one leadership style indiscriminately into the local context and expect it to work as it does in the other context. Also, what is most effective in one environment does not guarantee its effectiveness in a different environment.

Lastly, the leadership perspectives established in this study emanate from the leaders themselves and not from those who are being led. These perspectives are based on how leaders make sense of their experiences under challenging circumstances.

Method research

Research design

According to Merriam (1991:6), as cited by Brooks (2006)

> A research design is similar to an architectural blueprint. It is a plan for assembling, organizing, and integrating information (data), and it results in a specific end product (research findings). The selection of a particular design is determined by how the problem is shaped, by the questions it raises, and by the type of end product desired.

Hence this study made use of the descriptive method of research, specifically the qualitative approach. Data were gathered primarily through a series of in-depth interviews with the key informants. The researchers chose this method because the nature of the research demanded a comprehensive examination of multiple perspectives.

Though it is said that in studies like this one might be subjective or prejudiced, the researchers ensured that objectivity was maintained at all times in every part of the procedure. The study was based on in-depth interviews, so it was almost inevitable that the value judgements of the interviews would infiltrate the text to some degree. The researchers thus made every effort to eliminate or neutralize them where they appeared.

Key informants in the study

Respondents and key informants were identified through purposive sampling using a predetermined set of criteria, as follows:

- they must be in the top and middle management positions;
- the institution must be a private or public sector situated in Northern Mindanao, Philippines;

- they must be considered successful leaders as evidenced by local, national, and international awards.

There were a total of 71 respondents comprising a university president, a congressman, a governor, 9 mayors, and 59 regional and provincial directors; 19 had received international awards, aside from the local and national awards, 43 had national awards, and all had received at least 10 local awards in recognition of their exemplary leadership. Their identities are kept confidential in this study for ethical reasons.

Data analysis

The data management in this study included careful reading and listening to interviews that had been transcribed to ensure that the transcription was accurate and complete. Organizing and synthesizing the subjective responses gathered from the participants is the heart of the research method of this study. In fact, the data were analysed throughout the study process, and the results of this analysis were then used to guide additional data collection. Hence data analysis requires understanding, digesting, synthesizing, conceptualizing, and reconceptualizing descriptions of feelings, behaviours, experiences, and ideas. In other words, the study involved content analysis.

The aim of content analysis is to categorize and understand the data and the relationships among the categories to eventually categorize the data into themes. It starts by breaking down the data into units that are meaningful and then develops a categorization scheme. Categories are developed through analysis and are then used to collect additional data, which are then coded and categorized further. The process ends when data saturation (the point at which all new data collected become redundant) occurs.

Findings

The findings reveal the following perspectives on leadership:

- It is the art of leading followers effectively and efficiently without fear or intimidation, and inspiring the latter to perform given tasks, which involves gaining loyalty and sympathy from people.
- It is the ability to make people work with enthusiasm for the attainment of the organization's vision, mission, goals, and objectives without undermining their own growth and development.
- It is the process of establishing discipline, integrity, and creativity.

Leadership as an art

Leadership as an art entails leaders getting things done despite opposition, setbacks, and limited resources. All respondents experienced opposition in various directions and from different sources – from authorities above them or even the motivations and behaviour people below them. Some opposition and setbacks emanate from the organizational culture. The term 'culture' was for many years the domain of anthropologists and sociologists, but now leaders and managers are well aware of culture as a powerful force that could make or break organizations.

Common to the respondents is the perception that leadership provides the "glue" to hold all parts of the organization together, and this significantly shapes the culture of the organization. Understanding then the existing culture, and having the ability to engender support for a shared vision, become a major leadership challenge. The key is for leaders to use the ingrained values and beliefs as the bases for building positive organizational improvement.

The leader in these circumstances, according to the respondents, needs to be a strategic leader in order to orchestrate strategies to achieve objectives. However, they say that "this is never easy." They believe that one has to have enough experience in leadership with regard to the following: the number of years in leadership position; the type of opportunities and challenges faced as a leader; the number of people led; and the nature of the organization, particularly the organizational culture. That is why leadership is an art according to them because they have to study the surrounding circumstances, including the tasks at hand, the people who will make them happen, and the resources available. These factors do not always stay the same –the task may vary, and people and circumstances change. The leader in this case must be able to discern in depth how they can put all of these factors together to efficiently and effectively attain the organizational objectives.

This implies that effective leadership contributes to coordination and control in ways that formal mechanisms cannot. This is because the traditional family is still the foundation of Filipino society. Family takes precedence over work and all other aspects of life. As one executive respondent said, "our family is our first priority because it is the reason for striving hard in the workplace." However, one person noted that in the Philippine context the family is also one reason why some leaders are involved in corruption. In general, family members are dependent on each other such that leaders use their position to accommodate family members in the organization. What is worse, according to this individual, is when the said family member is not qualified for the position and so their appointment has a negative impact on the organization's performance, particularly if the position requires them to make major decisions.

One executive respondent said that to be an effective leader is to be a "father" of the organization. He said that one can hardly say that they have to maintain formality because people will always look for relationships. According to him, "We Filipinos are relational people and we value relationships so much. This explains why we always look for belongingness in the organization. Once we feel that we belong, we give our utmost cooperation and loyalty to achieve organizational goals." Indeed, leadership in the Philippines is an art of building relationships with people with whom leaders work.

Moreover, all respondents revealed that experience taught them how to lead with limited resources, particularly with regard to the financial aspects. Financial constraints also limit human resources and activities. One strategy that they found to be effective is networking. They realized that networking too is an art because there is no hard-and-fast rule about how to tap other organizations in order to share resources. One respondent shared that being in the organization for several years with accomplishments recognized by the community work to his advantage. He was able to establish a name because of what his organization had accomplished over the years under his leadership. With this name, he now easily gets the support of the community whenever it is needed. He added:

> There is a choice you have to make in everything that you do—either you settle for the mediocre or drive for excellence. For government executives who are confronted with great demand to innovate, I should say that they are engaged in the most challenging and ever-demanding world of work that cannot afford to settle for less despite shrinking budgets and increasing expectations and rigorous ethical standards.

Hence, leadership is an art.

Not all respondents, however, shared the same view. School leaders who were interviewed, though they were new to their organization and hadn't yet established a name, said that sincerity and diligence are the key ingredients to successful networking. One respondent who leads an educational organization with very limited finances was able to acquire facilities by writing to people about the financial needs of the institution. Though it took months and countless follow-ups to get a positive response, the effort paid off because hers become a success story shared with other school leaders. She learned that if a leader is sincere about their work and really believes that what they want to accomplish is for the greater good, they will avoid getting tired and frustrated while trying to achieve their goal.

Moreover, respondents perceived communication and interpersonal skills as crucial. These are referred to as an art because a leader should be able to adjust to different personalities, know how to bring out the best in people and advance their growth, and be able to deliver more than what is required given limited resources. It is worth noting at this point that Filipinos really value a smooth-interpersonal relationship (*pakik-isama*), whether in a formal or informal organization. The respondents shared that to lead successfully in the Filipino context, a leader must be able to get along well with their staff without being controlling or abusive. This is the way to gain people's loyalty. They have found that people who are loyal to their leaders and their organizations tend to achieve optimum performance and even go beyond the call of duty. Nevertheless, they are aware that there are also leaders who feign *pakik-isama* and are not really sincere. People, they said, are smart enough to detect this and they detest it because they feel that their leaders just want to manipulate them.

Respondents also noted that there are many leaders they know of who do not really care about adjusting to the personalities of their staff. They say that they don't have time for that and all they care about is for employees to perform their tasks efficiently and effectively. The respondents stressed that this is one reason why they failed to succeed in leadership.

Leadership as an ability

Respondents also perceive leadership as ability particularly in generating cooperation, trust, and goodwill of staff. They need ensure the employees' clear understanding of the vision and direction of the organization and to appreciate what is in it for them. Staff must be convinced that the organization is looking after their welfare as evidenced by a competitive compensation package, opportunities for growth and advancement.

Since this study was conducted in the Philippines, where organizational leaders cannot really promise their people a competitive compensation package owing to it being a developing country, the challenge is great for a leader in trying to get the cooperation, trust, and goodwill of those who work for them. A lot has been written about employees who take something from the office, justifying the act as just getting even with the organization that did not pay them reasonably. In other cases, some people use office hours to engage in other gainful activities to augment their income. Of course, these people know that these are forms of corruption, and these are some of the challenges that the leader respondents have to deal with.

For employees to be motivated, they must receive rewards that they value. Rewards matched to one's greatest needs will be perceived as valuable. Since most companies have difficulty in increasing these rewards (because they cannot afford it or they simply do not want to give them) to satisfy people's needs, they are now perceived as less valuable than they were in the past.

Based on the leader respondents' experience, people are able to get the cooperation and trust of staff once they are able to connect with them. This is why most agree that an effective leader needs to spend time with their people both in and outside the organization. One area of Filipino culture that reinforces this thrust is a fondness for celebrations. Respondents said that they always set aside time to celebrate birthdays, fiestas, Christmas, and other special occasions with their staff. Celebrations are opportunities to build relationships and to show to the members of the organization that their leaders care about them.

Leaders are also able to connect with their people when they collaborate to accomplish important projects. Hence they ensure their presence when big tasks are at hand. This implies that leadership is a partnership, and Sergiovanni (1997) called this leadership by bonding where the leader and the led develop a set of shared values and commitments that bond them together in a common cause.

One leader who was interviewed emphasized that they must have the ability to inspire their people to get their cooperation, trust, and goodwill. This respondent leads an organization with many competent and highly qualified people. He said that equipping his people to do the work is not much of a problem because of their competence. Given this kind of organization, he observes that how well the organization performs can be attributed to the skills of his people. Hence he realized that his role is mainly to inspire them to continue to perform and even do better, since they are self-directed and motivated. He concluded that getting the right people into the organization and investing in their professional development simplified the leader's role.

Another executive respondent stressed the importance of the ability of the leader to ensure that the organization is one of learning. He said that having a degree and prior experience in leadership is not enough.

As well as the business climate changing, so do people, organizations, and society. A leader must therefore be able to strategically mobilize the organization and its people to tackle change. He said that from time to time his organization faces new demands and expectations. This requires him to reflect and understand in depth what kind of change is needed, to determine how to implement such a change while knowing that there will be people who resist it. According to him, the answer is in becoming a learning organization.

The idea of the learning organization has been around for some time. It derives from Argyris' work in organizational learning (Argyris & Schon, 1978) and is indebted to Revans' (1983) studies of action learning. It has roots in organization development (especially action research methodology) and organizational theory (most notably, Burns and Stalker's work on organic organizations). Its conceptual foundations are firmly based on systems theory (Senge, 1990) and its practical application to managing a business has evolved from strategic planning and strategic management (Fiol & Lyles, 1985; Hosley, Lau, Levy, & Tan, 1994), which have recognized that organizational learning is the underlying source of strategic change (DeGeus, 1988; Jashapara, 1993). Much of the quality improvement movement of recent years, with its emphasis on continuous improvement, represented the first widespread application of learning organization concepts (Senge, 1990; Stata, 1989).

Leadership as a process

For leadership as a process, all respondents perceived integrity as the key to staying longer in power. This requires transparency in an organization. Members' loyalty is affected by integrity, as well as love and humility. Most respondents stressed that in the organization, every member is expected to perform his duties with diligence, integrity, dedication, honesty, dignity and honour. One respondent said that "accepting money or gifts in exchange for services is a form of corruption and dishonours the organization." The respondents are aware that, as leaders, they are "living in a fish bowl." Even a little indiscretion or misdemeanour could be blown out of proportion and sensationalized by the media because of this.

Regarding love, one respondent, who holds a key position in one of the uniformed agencies of the Department of the Interior Local Government (DILG) and a Dangal ng Bayan (a national award for exemplary leadership and an untarnished integrity) awardee, stressed that "A leader must have love for God so that he can love his work (no matter what the job demands) and the people he is leading (no matter what their personalities are)." He added that "love keeps you going when the going gets tough in leading people." Only a few respondents expressed freely about love as one of the most important ingredients of leadership. For most respondents, they found it emotional for leaders to even discuss the part of love in leadership. Some considered it as a point of weakness and vulnerability. They would rather call it "commitment."

They saw rewarding good, if not the best, performance as one of the components of a leader's integrity. All respondents considered the process of establishing integrity as fundamental to leadership. Giving people what they need and what they deserve is one way of establishing integrity, they said. Considering that, by nature, Filipinos crave importance, love, respect, recognition, dignity, and financial security, leaders should be able to provide their people with these. In this way, people would not feel that they are not merely tools for the attainment of organizational objectives.

Furthermore, the respondents perceived leadership as a continuous learning process. For them there are no shortcuts to effective leadership – it requires discipline and creativity. To maintain discipline, one must stay focused on the goal and stay true to one's values. The respondents saw the temptation of being a leader especially in a government institution. There are people who will really challenge their integrity just to get what they want. They said that there are many who get sidetracked away from their goal because of corruption, but in the end they lose not only their leadership position but also the respect of their people. They strongly conclude that to succeed in leadership, accountability is key.

Creativity is also needed because if a leader discovers an effective strategy in running an organization, they don't have an assurance that it will continue to work in the future. Having stayed in the leadership position for several years, they realize that work demands never stay the same. Hence they must continue to learn in several ways. These include where they want to take their people and organization according to their mandate, and how they will get there. Periodically they have to determine where they are now and to ascertain whether the way they do things will take them to their destination. This creativity requires further study. These leaders take time off to pursue formal and informal training. For others this is a luxury, so they must be creative enough to extract learning from their daily activities at work. This they called "embedded learning." For them, all it takes is intelligent reflection and action. This is a process wherein leaders learn by reflecting on day-to-day activities and then acting on them. This is continuously repeated until the lessons learned are established in the individual's leadership behaviour. They also found out that creativity facilitates solving problems in the organization.

Implications

In summary, the respondents perceived leadership as an art, ability, and process. These factors, however, are not independent of each other. They are perceived to operate dynamically in an interlocking mode. It is worth noting that the respondents admitted that they have their less pleasant attributes as leaders. They believe that it is difficult to find a perfect leader, only real leaders. The good qualities of leader must be traded off with negative ones. For instance, relational skills could perhaps balanced against operational efficiency.

The findings of the study illustrate the alternative approaches to leadership theory development. Theories are explanations of events and their interrelations and they are believed to approximate reality. From the late 1800s to roughly the 1920s, great social science theorists and theories emerged. The 1930s were a period of testing and verifying theories, believing that there were already plenty of theories. Schlegel (1974) pointed out the need to test theories against data gathered from real situations. The data should then be analysed to determine whether the theories should be confirmed, negated, or altered.

Leadership theories that apply in one context may not necessarily be applicable in another. Based on the findings of this study, this is primarily due to organizational culture. In the Philippine context, organizational culture cannot be ignored because it is critical to leadership performance. It is a system of shared values held by members of the organization. According to Schein's model (1985), most corporate cultures operate on several levels simultaneously. The first level consists of material, symbolic, and behavioural artifacts that are easily observed but hard to interpret without access to deeper levels. The second level puts more emphasis on values, or the way things ought to be, in contrasted with the way they are. The third level consists of basic assumptions and beliefs that guide and construct social reality and the interpretation of "objective" environmental realities. In the Philippine setting, the impact of organizational culture on leadership is governed by the basic assumptions found at this third level.

Since all leaders included in the study have earned their graduate education in management and leadership, this has implications for the kind of leadership models discussed in the Philippine graduate schools. It is true that most of these models are Western in origin simply because more work is published by the West. When these leaders are sent for training and seminars, Western theories and concepts are the ones being taught. This is not to discredit Western theories but it is important to adopt an appropriate approach when applying Western models in the Philippine context. Andres (1985) cited four roles that a leader can adopt to contextualize these approaches:

- A *syncretizer* tries to harmonize the Western management system with Filipino culture.
- An *accommodator* selects good ideas and practices from other management systems and adapts them for Philippine purposes.
- A *situationist* seeks to contextualize Western management systems in relation to the living situation of the Filipino people at a crucial time.
- An *orienter* relates management systems to the actual issues that Filipino management practitioners are facing today in the Philippines.

Of these four, Andres (1985) recommends the fourth.

This implies that leadership in the Philippines must be indigenized, taking into consideration two subcultures: the organization and the community where the employees come from. It must be noted also that Filipinos have a rich Eastern and Western heritage that influences their mental models of leadership. Hence it is expected that indigenized leadership models will be an integration of both.

Furthermore, the findings of this study imply the need for grounded research with the aim of developing dynamic grounded theories of organizational leadership. Grounded research encourages researchers to build a theory on the assumption that social theory is nothing more than an explanation which is based on the phenomenon being studied. It highlights the importance of doing analysis based on the data at hand, and not on any predetermined ideas or concepts. These leadership theories must be developed in the context of the culture, values, mores, and peculiarities of the people where it is applied and practiced. Although generalizations about culture might be difficult to achieve, they are imperative if these research studies are to be of practical value. The aim is not to analyse and dissect culture but to observe as objectively as possible how it is embodied in, and influences, leadership behaviour. Generalizations, though superficial in some sense, provide a valuable tool for understanding why leaders behave the way they do in an organization.

Conclusions

Successful leaders do not have complicated perspectives on leadership. They simply categorize it as an art, ability, and process. It is an art because one is leading people with unique personalities to perform organizational tasks. It is an ability since one is faced with various challenges from different sources. It is a process because one never stops learning. As long as people continue to grow and society continues to change, it is inevitable that a leader will evolve with the organization and the society where they belong.

In understanding leadership, to describe its underlying concepts and principles is not enough. Due to the changing dynamics of organizations, one has to analyse in depth the interactions of these concepts and principles to show how and why they interact as they do.

Despite studies conducted about leadership, researchers still get caught out by the following questions. What are all of these leadership theories and research good for? And how do we really go about the job of leading, particularly in exercising influence that can be used to enhance organizational performance. These have surfaced in the context of a number of leaders identified and awarded in their fields, yet society, in general, is still waiting for genuine leaders who will make a difference and bring the country to a state of progress and development that every Filipino aspires to and deserves. This is what Maxwell (1993) meant when he said that everything rises and falls with leadership.

Recommendations

From the foregoing findings and conclusions, this study recommends the following:

- Munro (2008) emphasizes that an organization's viability is being determined by its ability to make such systemic, organization-wide change happen, and happen fast. In fact, many authors would agree that the organization's capacity to learn, as it confronts unpredictable and uncertain internal and external conditions, may be the only true source of competitive advantage. Hence, there is a need for organizations to be learning organizations.
- There is a need to pursue other research that would venture into any of the following: i) understanding leadership from the perspective of the members of the organization other than the leaders; ii) determining the impact of organizational culture on leadership

and organizational effectiveness with an emphasis on organizational tasks and individual relations; iii) investigating how the culture of the organization affects many administrative processes from the perspective of practitioners (among these are not only motivation and leadership but also decision making, communication and change; iv) understanding a Filipino as a worker and as a leader; and v) undertaking grounded researches that would build more grounded theories and thereby enhance the integration of theory, research, and practice in the discipline.

- If leadership is a process, an investigation must be made into the unfolding of leadership over time, rather than just capturing particular moments of success or failure. Also, what features of the organization and community contribute to effective leadership must be examined as part of this endeavour.
- There is a need to further stimulate research that sharply focuses on practical leadership concepts and models. These could be from the West but should at least modified to suit the Philippine conditions and the Filipinos' given behaviour, sentiments, and values. It is high time for Filipinos to stop borrowing leadership perspectives from the West and to try to develop a homegrown leadership perspective.
- Moreover, there is a need to have more publishers who will publish research-based books that will help both students and practitioners understand Asian leadership. Despite the abundance of research studies conducted in the field, there is a dearth of Asian leadership books that can be used in the graduate schools where we train current and future leaders and managers.

References

Andres, T. (1985). *Management by Filipino Values.* Quezon City: New Day Publishers.

Argyris, C., & Schon, D. (1978). *Organizational Learning: A Theory of Action Perspective.* Boston, MA: Addison-Wesley.

DeGeus, A. (1988). Planning as learning. *Harvard Business Review*, 66 (2), 70–74.

Fiol, C., & Lyles, M. (1985). Organizational learning. *Academy of Management Review*, 10(4), 803–813.

Glaser, B., & Strauss, A. (1967). *The Discovery of Grounded Theory.* London: Aldin Transaction.

Hosley, S., Lau, A., Levy, F., & Tan, D. (1994). The quest for the competitive learning organization. *Management Decision*, 32(6), 5–15.

Jashapara, A. (1993). The quest for the competitive learning organization. *Management Decision*, 31(8), 52–62.

Maxwell, J. (1993). *Developing the Leader within You.* India: Injoy, Inc.

Merriam, S.B. (1991). *Case Study Research in Education: A Qualitative Approach.* San Francisco, CA: Jossey-Bass.
Munro, J. (2008). *Organizational Leadership.* McGraw-Hill Contemporary Learning Series. Dubuque, IA: McGraw-Hill.
Revans, R. (1983). *The ABC of Action Learning.* Bromley: Chartwell-Bratt.
Schein, E. (1985). *Organizational Culture and Leadership.* San Francisco, CA: Jossey-Bass.
Schlegel, S. (1974). *Grounded Research in the Social Sciences.* Darussalam, Banda Aceh: Pusat Penelitian Ilmu-Ilmu Sosial.
Senge, P. (1990). *The Fifth Discipline: The Art and Practice of the Learning Organization.* New York: Doubleday/Currency.
Sergiovanni, T. (1997). Value-Added Leadership: How to Get Extraordinary Performance. In *Schools,* 2nd edition. New York: Harcourt Brace.
Stata, R. (1989). Organizational learning – The key to management innovation. *Sloan Management Review,* 30(3), 63–74.
Strauss, A., & Corbin, J. (1990). *Basics of Qualitative Research: Grounded Theory, Procedures and Techniques.* Thousand Oaks, CA: Sage Publications.

4

Conceptualizing Leadership for a Globalizing China

Xiao Ran Song and David Beckett

Introduction: Modern China – and the Past

Since the 1978 reforms, China has undergone dramatic social and economic changes and now it has become one of the major international economic and political powers. In its move towards internationalism and modernization (which we can call "globalization"), its deeply rooted old cultural traditions, its encounter with Western thought and behaviour, and the need to upgrade on all levels of civil and business practice and to adapt to the global economy, have generated a new China within a dynamic and ever-changing social and cultural environment. This "evolution" (Louie, 2008: 2–3) of Chinese culture and its impact on different aspects of the country, from society and people, to organizations and business practices, is being widely discussed and studied.

This chapter explores leadership as a particular manifestation of such an evolution, and argues for its relational significance. By this we mean that leadership in (and for) a globalizing China is best conceptualized through flexibility, fluidity and dynamism. There has never been a "one-size-fits-all" model of traditional Chinese leadership; neither does contemporary globalization generate any ideal model of the "leader". Rather, we claim that it is in the relationality of leadership that more helpful characteristics of leadership can be identified.

This claim is embedded in more extensive scholarship that establishes that lifelong learning, for adults, is relational: it emerges from the practical experiences of daily work and life, and it builds to expertise (Beckett, 2012). There are three universally acknowledged adult learning principles. In brief, adults, anywhere – but especially at work – learn best when they have a strong sense of self-direction, when they are able to involve their (w)holistic experiences, and when they have an immediate need to know something (Beckett, 2011). Leadership, we will argue, emerges from such experiences, in particular East–West management contexts.

Yet we first look backwards, because the Chinese past is so instructive. Despite constant changes at all levels in China's strive towards globalization, as suggested by Louie (2008: 5), "China continued to be "Chinese", and despite the increasing modernization..., many core traditions continued to characterize the landscape". As one of the world's oldest existing civilizations, many of China's values are still preserved and are still important. This mode of adapting Western to traditional cultural values results in a combination of complexity and challenges. Transformation between old and new presents complexity when one tries to understand leadership in China; and adaptation of the Chinese to globalization generates challenges and confusion for management and leadership at all levels. As Björn Bjerke (1999: 129) suggests,

> China is an ancient civilization. During the Chou Dynasty (1122–256 BC) the wheel, wire saw, diamond drill, and the crossbow were developed. In mathematics and astronomy, the Chinese were at times ahead of the Western civilization.
>
> (Harris and Moran, 1979: 309)

> China survived when other civilizations vanished. After many years of isolation, stagnation and internal turmoil, China is once again asserting its importance in the international community and the urge to understand the Chinese has gained a new impetus.... Western management principles must certainly be challenged to do business in Asia in general and with the Chinese in particular.
>
> (Lasserre & Schütte, 1995: xvi–xvii)

Chinese leadership philosophy

"Everyone in China is at least half philosopher", states Chu (1991: 187). Chinese religion, people's daily conduct, management practices and business strategies are all related to the country's ancient philosophy, which people frequently refer to when they confront obstacles, challenges, or even achieve success. Bjerke (1999: 139) suggests to business leaders that for the Chinese, "faith and philosophy are lived every day as a way of life. To understand the Chinese... it is important to understand the principle by which they live and to what extent the teachings of their philosophers are still applicable today."

Philosophically, Confucianism, Buddhism, and Taoism are major influences in China. Among them, Confucianism is most influential ideologically in both political and social life. It has also attracted Western interest, especially among business management practitioners, who try to understand specific cultural elements that make such a unique business environment in China, and to look for ways to make adjustments to Western leadership and management. Confucianism "for some 2,000 years" has "played an essential role in making China what it is" (Chan, Ko, & Yu, 2000: 180). Since the rise of the Chinese economy, this subject has been studied by researchers and practitioners in seeking a management and leadership model suitable for Chinese culture, as well as Eastern culture more broadly.

Confucianism

Confucius (孔子, September 28, 551 BC–479 BC) was a Chinese thinker and philosopher of the Spring and Autumn Period. His thoughts have been developed into a system of philosophy known as Confucianism (儒家), which constitutes the core ideology of feudal China. His main words and thoughts are preserved and presented in the *Analects of Confucius* (論語). The core of Confucius' philosophy is benevolence (仁), based on which the notions of harmony and rites were developed to promote and maintain social and spiritual coherence, as follows:

Benevolence (仁): "To return to the observance of the rites through overcoming the self constitutes benevolence. If for a single day a man could return to the observance of the rites through overcoming himself, then the whole Empire would consider benevolence to be his. However, the practice of benevolence depends on oneself alone, and not on others" (Lun Yu, XII: 1. in Nolan, 2004: 157).

Rites (禮): The Confucian theory of ethics as exemplified in *Lǐ* (禮) establishes conceptual aspects of life: ceremonies associated with sacrifice to ancestors and deities of various types, social and political institutions, and the etiquette of daily behaviour (http://en.wikipedia.org/wiki/Confucius).

Harmony (和): "Of the things brought about by the rites, harmony is the most valuable. Of the ways of former kings, this is the most beautiful, and is followed alike in matters great and small ... " (Lun Yu. I: 2. in Nolan, 2004: 161).

Confucius' political thoughts are based on his ethical thoughts. He argues that the best government is one that rules through rites and people's natural morality, rather than by using bribery and coercion (http://en.wikipedia.org/wiki/Confucius). Such notions "laid down principles for a hierarchical political system culminating in the emperor" (Bjerke, 1999: 140).

Confucius' value system contributes to the fundamental principles of Chinese leadership: "the primacy of order and stability, of co-operative human harmony, of accepting one's place in the social hierarchy, of social integration" (Feuerwerker, 1976: 15) and "ideology is the key to the system's long-term stability and cohesion" (Nolan, 2004: 124).

Taoism

Born in 571 BC, Lao Zi (老子) is one of the most famous philosophers in ancient China. His main thoughts were written in the book *Dao De Jing* (道德經). Taoism emphasizes themes such as naturalness, vitality, peace, "non-action" (*Wu Wei* or "effortless effort"), emptiness (refinement), detachment, flexibility, receptiveness, spontaneity, and the relativism of human ways of life, including ways of speaking and guiding behaviour. The central concept of Taoism is *Wu Wei* (无为/無爲) which is directly translated as "without action". Its meaning is often expressed as "action without action", implicating the universe works harmoniously in its own ways and that human beings should not act against it. The symbol *Taijitu* (太极图), reflects the balance between yin and yang, and the harmony and tranquillity of the universe (http://en.wikipedia.org/wiki/Taoism).

Taoist thoughts and principles have been adopted by the Chinese throughout the ages and its influence can be seen in Chinese management and leadership strategies, especially its ideas about flexibility, spontaneity, and relativism. Bjerke (1999: 145) comments that

> One characteristic of the Chinese business leaders is that their power rests on high flexibility, adaptability (Jansson, 1987: 28) and political pragmatism (Seagrave, 1996: 17). In general, the Chinese have a pragmatic view of how to get things done by considering each situation on its own merits, not following general guidelines.

Similar strategies and practices can be found among contemporary Chinese leaders – for example, in Deng Xiaoping's famous 1962 aphorism: "No matter if the cat is white or black, as long as it can catch the rat, it is a good cat" (邓小平在深圳的讲话 Deng Xiaoping's Speech in Shenzhen, http://wenwen.soso.com/z/q123375845.htm).

There are other philosophical thoughts in Chinese history but Confucianism and Taoism are considered fundamental in constituting Chinese leadership philosophy and its social and political ideology.

One Chinese leader

Starting from about 2852 BC, China has gone through different kingdoms and dynasties, from Ancient China (ca. 2852–221 BC) through Imperial China (221 BC–1912) to Modern China (1912 – present).

It is not the purpose of this paper to discuss each Chinese ruler. We want to look at one famous and controversial leader in Chinese history to see if we can identify some particularities. We understand that we cannot make generalization by studying one single case, yet, as Stake (1995: xi) suggests, "Case study is the study of the particularity of and complexity of a single case, coming to understand its activity within important circumstances." Our exploration of the relationality of leadership in a globalizing China is an example of "important circumstances".

Mao Ze Dong

毛泽东统一了中国, 给予人民一套新的道德观, 提高了工农的地位, 并在中国建立了一个廉洁的政府O
(加拿大记者马克·盖恩)

Mao unified China, gave people a new set of moral values, improved the status of workers and peasants, and a clean government in China. (Canadian reporter Mark Gein,

http://bbs1.people.com.cn/postDetail.do?id= 110044378&boardId= 60)

他有很好的教养, 内部是钢, 有坚强的抵抗力。毛从来不是教条主义者。

他是灵活的, 愿意变革和学习, 而最重要的, 是忍耐——, 一直到那个转折点上。
他等待着那个最低点, 然后在车轮向上转动时采取行动, 不太早,
也不太晚。他跟着历史来引导历史。

(美国记者海伦·斯诺)

He is well cultivated, the interior is steel, has a tough resistance. Mao is never doctrinaire.

He is flexible, willing to change and learn, most importantly, he sustains (is patient) – until that turning point. He waits for the lowest

> point, and then takes action as the wheels turn up, not too early and not too late. He follows history to guide the history, states
>
> (American journalist Helen Snow, http://www.mzdthought.com/pingjiaweiren/200808/22-9300.html)

Regarded by most as a heroic Chinese leader, Mao was also a pragmatic one. He united and built a socialist China, improved the status of common people ("Serve the People", 为人民服务), departed from the Soviet Marxism ideology and initiated the "Chinese Way", as well as starting the Cultural Revolution.

According to Schram (2005), from 1912 (when Mao was 18 years old) to 1949 (when he united China and became a leader with a name and real authority), the development of Mao's thoughts was a reflection of the constant and comprehensive political, social, and cultural evolution: "We claim his leadership emerged from the relationality of the times as they changed around him." In Mao's earlier life, he had a different experience. This formed his views about Chinese issues and their solutions. His thoughts changed not only every ten years but, under some circumstances, every year (Schram, 2005: 13).

Mao was not a firm supporter of Confucianism but many of his thoughts were deeply rooted in the traditional Chinese ideology/culture, and he liked to use the past to guide the present and the future. "Although Mao was fiercely opposed to Confucianism, the organizational model prescribed by him was not, in fact, very different from that of Confucius. The major difference was that Mao emphasized egalitarianism instead of a benevolent bureaucratic elite", states Hoon-Halbauer (1994: 90 in Bjerke, 1999: 140).

Culture and change

Leaders like Mao obviously shape the culture of their environment. Indeed, culture has become a concept that is found to be useful in many management and leadership studies, especially at a time of globalization. Often, to understand a country and the practices of its people, the first step is to understand the culture. This was made explicit, for example, almost 20 years ago, in the Preface to the Australian Language and Literacy Council (1994) report, with reference to the international business of Australia:

> World industry operates across political, linguistic and cultural frontiers. If Australian industry is to be successful in this global market,

> it must be able to move and operate across frontiers. Cultural understanding must permeate the company in Australia and overseas.
>
> (ALLC, 1994: viii)

Leadership and culture are thus quite central, but complex, concepts. Both are relational – that is, they exist in the very dynamism of life and work, right amid change. There have been various ways of defining culture. Kluckhohn states:

> Culture consists in patterned ways of thinking, feeling and reacting, acquired and transmitted mainly by symbols, constituting the distinctive achievements of human groups, including their embodiments in artifacts; the essential core of culture consists of tranditional (i.e. historically derived and selected) ideas and especially their attached values.
>
> (Kluckhohn, 1951: 86, n.5)

Drawing on Kluckhohn's (1951) definition, another well-known definition of culture is by Hofstede (2001: 10), who defines it as

> the collective programming of the mind that distinguishes the members of one group or category of people from another ... the "mind" stands for the head, heart, and hands – that is, for thinking, feeling, and acting, with consequences for beliefs, attitudes, and skills ... systems of values are a core element of culture.

He then develops (in Figure 4.1) some manifestations of culture with value (invisible) as the core, and other visible elements: rituals, heroes and symbols. In this diagram, "symbols, heroes and rituals are subsumed under the term practice. As such, they are visible to an outside oberver; their cultural meanings, however are invisible and lie precisely and only in the ways these practices are interpreted by insiders" (Hofstede, 2001: 10–11). Based on this notion of cultural practices (very relevant to our interest in the relational), Hofstede further develops the 'Dimensions of Culture', which will be elaborated on when we discuss differences in Western and Chinese cultural values.

We claim that Confucian philosophy constitutes the core value of Chinese culture. It formed the norms of traditional Chinese society. Taoism functions mainly in strategy, change, and flexibility. Both philosophies constitute the Chinese pattern of thinking and doing,

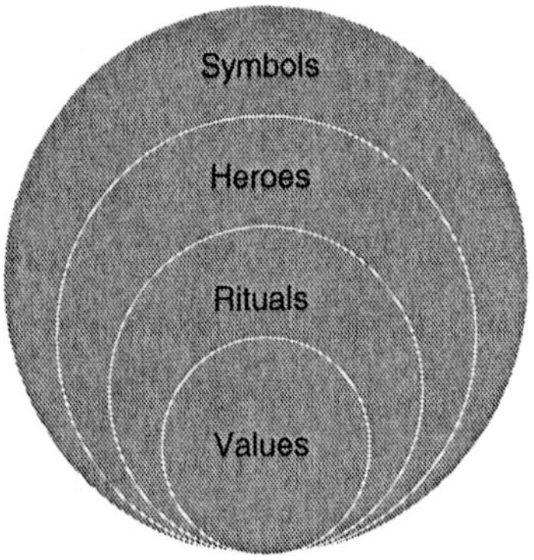

Figure 4.1 The "onion diagram": manifestations of culture at different levels of depth (Hofstede, 2001: 11)

and it is amid this thinking and doing that the relationality of leadership, and other learning and management practices, is made manifest (cf. Beckett, 2012).

So, as a complex and elusive construct, culture has a dynamic that varies throughout time and space. Throughout 140 years of Western history, there have been radically different approaches to defining culture as a concept. And in Chinese history, the concept of 文 or 文化 ("culture") has also been in constant evolution. There is some similarity between East and West. For example, Arnold's (1869) famously normative notion views culture as "personal improvement via encounter with the civilizing arts" and connects culture to "perfection", "beauty" and "intelligence". A similar notion can be found in Chinese traditions. At a time of globalization, cultures are involved in an endless self-evolution and in a constant encounter with others. New hybridities emerge, as our empirical examples, below, will show.

Lo Bianco (2003: 25, emphasis added) summarized the relationality of culture, as follows:

> Some characteristics of culture are universal (it is learned and shared, meaning that culture is always a collective activity). But culture is also moving, unstable, and variable. It is challenged from within and modified from without...culture is not random, or idiosyncratic, or wholly personal, but that however we define culture, the entity we are defining refers to behaviour that is patterned, learned, and social, but also changing, and constructed, sometimes

"in the moment" as hybrid compromises of values are produced, such as interaction between people of widely varying backgrounds interacting with each other.

Culture and individuals

If culture is at one point regarded as the "programming of mankind" (Hofstede, 2001: 10) then, at an individual level, we cannot deny the uniqueness of this programming and the significance of differences between each other. Being individuals in our own community, it requires no more than common sense for us to understand that there is a lot we share with others that creates our sense of belonging. At the same time, however, there are personal factors which can be attributed to the uniqueness of individuals – that is, individual variations generated from personal experience. If we recognize individuals as self-reflective and self-directed (cf. Beckett, 2011), then individual selves may evolve more or less from the integrative community framework of settings and values, of which they are members.

Accordingly, one cannot seek explanations for every single individual behaviour from within the integrative framework of that community. Based on this view, Bargiela-Chiappini and Harris (1997: 5, emphasis added) suggest an understanding of culture as a setting "derived not from the accounts of the individuals operating in that setting but from the observation and/or reconstruction of their relational work in an attempt to map both distinctive and universal values".

So it is the individual readings of personal character, political preference, leadership style, as these are performed differently in different historical situations, where we must look for insights into leadership. Mao ZeDong, for example, did not overtly support and adopt the mainstream Chinese philosophy. He made his version for his own leadership within a situation. Yet, with the benefit of hindsight, one should not ignore traditional Chinese philosophies because these are core values that Mao lived within and acted out.

Similarly, current research into Chinese "local" leadership, especially the new breed of entrepreneurial elites, is showing how family and political relationships intertwine across marriages and across generations (Goodman, forthcoming). In these ways, local power emerges from particularistic social constructions and re-constructions of traditions over time (pre-Mao, Mao, and post-Mao).

So from the highest to the most local experiences of leadership and cultures(s), we believe that what is important is attention to particular mouldings and perceptions of leadership, as these are apparent in what people actually do – their actual cultural practices. We turn to this in detail now.

Some fieldwork

We interviewed Westerners and Chinese senior managers working (or who have worked) in China for their views about cultural differences and management/leadership in China. We interviewed, separately, three individuals (A, B, and C). To explore the relationality of their leadership, we asked each of them about their perceptions of leadership and culture, as well as their workplace experience of managing people in China. Below is a summary of their answers.

A: a Chinese general manager

> Chinese people have their unique culture, which is very different from the West. Chinese management strategies are rooted deeply in its traditional cultural value. Confucian philosophy is important in shaping Chinese leadership. Culture plays a big role in our daily management practice.

B: a British managing director who has worked in China

> Cultural awareness is necessary but within organizations the leader plays the biggest role. They can shape the organizational culture and guide the subordinates even when they come from different culture background. My experience working worldwide is that it might be different at the surface – artifacts and cultural manifestations – but down to the core of leadership strategies, culture is not the most important. Working in management positions in China does not make much difference for me compared with working elsewhere.

C: a Westerner who is now head of an international company in China

An intensive interview was conducted with subject C, the chief representative of an international company in China. He is a Westerner who has lived and worked in China for more than ten years and speaks fluent Chinese. He elaborated on much that is relational.

> *Geography*: The differences, if you look at China first, the differences between cities, it is very different managing a team in Beijing from managing a team in Shanghai. It's not a question of Beijing

> or Shanghai culture, but in Shanghai the costs are higher, the costs of living are higher, [although the] standards of living are not really that much higher for the same type of position, it is pretty much the same. So there is a lot more pressure on people in Shanghai. You can feel that. Also they are more say, mixed, who is from Shanghai, who is from outside. There is more migration into Shanghai than into Beijing, at least of the staff pool that you hire from, from international companies. So that's one part.
>
> *Age*: The next part is generational. Working in China with people, I'd say I've had staff all the way from just graduated up to 60 plus. Working with someone who is 50–60, working with someone in their 30–40s, working for something in their 20–30s is very, very different.
>
> *Gender*: Then you also have the gender issue. There are very different work ethics and work styles between men and women in China and it becomes very clear I think, especially in foreign companies, where you very often will see a higher proportion of female mid-level and top-level managers than you will see in Chinese companies. Not because foreign companies hire differently but because foreign companies look at performance in a different way.
>
> *Chinese management*: When traditional Chinese managers reach a certain level it is very much a networking position. They have the driver of the car, the secretaries, they basically sit back, they do lunches, they do dinners, they do cigarettes, they do drinking, but they don't do a lot of work, and that doesn't really work in a foreign-owned company.

C further summarized the complexity of management and workplace culture, as well as individual differences with examples. He further pointed out that this complexity exists in all cultures, and the risk of generalization and differentiating according to East and West.

> You have workplace politics, you have organizational internal issues in all cultures. It is very easy to generalize and say that maybe foreigners do one thing. Probably it is more a question of, if you look at Europeans now, I mainly work with Northern Europeans and it's very different if you go to Southern Europe. I have worked with Scandinavians, with Germans, Dutch, Belgium, this area, so North-Western Europe. But it's very different when you go to France or Italy for example. Now Northern Europe is very individual, people are

more – and it's a question of the way its education is built up, more pro-active, more individual. So they are much stronger at realizing, okay this has to be done, thinking of a solution, going into any – and more willing to take risks. So, "Okay, I try it, I mess up, but I tried, I did my best so no one will be angry for that. I will still be appreciated because I did my best in trying to solve this." And people use the group to evaluate after: "Could we have done this better in any way? That is a very Northern European way of working, whereas in Southern Europe it's much more hierarchical, and much more like I think the way I see traditional Chinese companies, and very often in literature on management in China you will see Chinese doing it. They are not individual, individualistic, they're not risk-takers ... [yet] if you look at the way China has developed, if you look at the way private Chinese entrepreneurs work, if you look at the way that in general even the state-owned companies work, there are a lot of risk-takers, there are a lot of individual people out there doing crazy stuff and trying out things. I mean, lot of it is people trying first and they see how it goes, so I think it is very dangerous to try to generalize."

There are a lot of cultural issues, but again I wouldn't say there is one Chinese cultural issue. Again, it depends on age, where people are from, gender. There is a very big difference between how a stated-owned enterprise is managed, as to how are some of the young, new Chinese companies, whether large or small, are being managed. I mean, I had lunch a few weeks ago [with] ... a large private company in Shanghai. [The CEO] ... is a couple of years younger than me – a billionaire. He started that company together with a group of people that he studied with at Fudan University. There are the entrepreneurs, they are self-taught, but then they have done all the MBAs, they have done all the things, and they are very structured. So you have these kind of companies in China, you have the old traditional state-owned companies, you have people with no education starting their own companies. If you go back a little bit to the early part of the reform period, the people who jumped ship basically and went out and set up small companies ... they were the people who had the least to lose ... So whereas when you are looking at the early 80s when the reform started a lot of people who secured state sector jobs, they were not the ones who went out and started up private companies and private business, it was the people with nothing to lose. It was the people who had no education, out of prison, and then they became rich of course.

> If you look at China and compare it to Europe, it is pretty much the same size, with as diverse a population... if you are in Europe you talk about Italian management style, French management style, general management style, you will have lots of people already defining the differences there. So there would be equally big differences in China.
>
> If there is one thing that I think is common in, not just China, but maybe East Asian management cultures, at least the Confucian inspired areas...one thing there maybe is, is the kind of the protection of the CEO. So you will very often [find that] number one, in a meeting, will not really articulate anything but it will be the subordinates if something wrong is said, if a wrong decision is made [and] the subordinate would be sacrificed, and sometimes that's kind of a ritual sacrifice. But if it is a success the subordinate is rewarded and elevated. But I think it... if you look at a Western corporate organization, it is exactly the same. I mean, the CEO always can wipe the blame off on middle-level management and get rid of that and survive until it becomes really biggish.

We learn in these accounts from A, B, and especially C, that leadership is situated in, and emerges from, the context of a culture – for example, Chinese culture. But culture is a fluid concept, in constant with interaction, especially at a time of globalization, as we stated at the beginning, and here we find that East and West managers "read" their experiences in a way which is just as paradoxical as how we "read" great Chinese leaders, such as Mao: tradition is essential but so is innovation. Also, as suggested by C, there are issues like geography, gender, generation, age, individual differences, and differences in business. These exist in all cultures. Globalization brings with it the need for exchange, adaptation, mutual influence, and blurred boundaries between traditions and emergent values. All of these are, we claim, relational – and all of them contribute to leadership.

In the business world, we can claim that culture is relationally emergent in that it is dynamic, hybrid and never static. There are interactions within different members of a culture as well as interactions between cultures. Therefore strategic leadership in a globalizing world (which includes China) involves understanding and managing collectives, which share core values among their members as well as individualized variations from that norm. Here we make these three concepts and their relationship clearer:

Collective: A context has core components (values, beliefs, and philosophies) which are interrelated and, through interaction, contribute to the norms of a community, and which are therefore learned about and shared by people within the community. There are shared patterns and norms which are comparatively stable that form the uniqueness of each cultural community.

Individualized: Each individual is self-reflexive and creative given their personal experience, and is in constant interaction with the broader community. "There are similarities between culture and personality as well as differences", notes Bjerke (1999: 19).

Dynamic, never static, and always hybrid: Changes come from both inside and outside; dynamism is created by the interaction inside, and between the inside and outside. As suggested by Bjerk (1999: 249), "from the international perspective of today, people are influenced by other cultures almost no matter what they do. It is becoming harder for people to isolate themselves."

How do these three relate? The challenge for cultural leadership is in harnessing the dynamism, amid the blurring of boundaries between collectives, and between collectives and individuals, as Figure 4.2 makes plain.

Conclusion: Leadership in a globalizing China

Our attention to the significance of emergent hybridities, at both the individualistic and the collective levels of practical work life, is the basis of conceptualizing leadership for a globalizing China. This is seriously relational in nature: it requires the unpacking of the details of daily workplace experiences and their reassembly in viable models of leadership, situation-by-situation, as Mao was able to show during his lifetime.

While Western theorists are debating the difference between two words – "leader" and "leadership" – or "decoupling 'leader as a person' from 'leadership as a process'" (Parry & Hansen, 2007: 282), in Chinese there is only one word, 领导 (Ling Dao), for both leader and leadership. 领导 is both a noun and a verb, and its meaning varies according to the context: from a person (leader), to a position (leadership) and then to an action/process (to lead or leadership).

To many Chinese, 领导 has a combined meaning: a person, in a leading position, through their action, performing leadership roles/functions

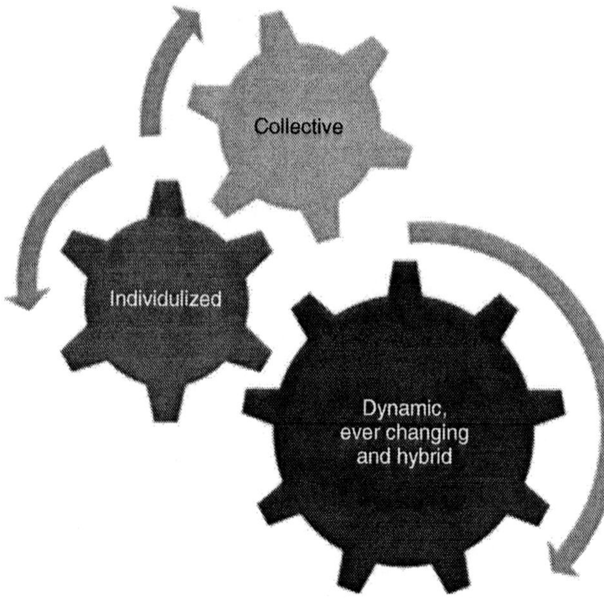

Figure 4.2 The gear diagram of strategic leadership

in the leading process. Differences in language and understanding of leadership between the East and the West have originated from their different cultural and philosophical value systems. Developed over thousands of years of history, the core of Chinese traditional values continues to make the Chinese how and who they are, but both East and West need to "read" these in a more dynamic environment – that of globalizing business (which includes China).

This is best described by the founding prime minister of Singapore (one of the world's most dynamic Eastern economies), Lee Kuan Yew (1978):

> 也许我英语比华语好，因为我早年学会英语；但是即使再过一千个世代，我也不会变成英国人
> 我心中所信守的不是西方的价値体系，而是东方价値体系

> Maybe my English is better than my Chinese, but that is because I learned English when I was young. But even after one thousand years, I will not become British. What I believe in my heart is the Eastern value system, not the Western one. (世界遗产名录)

The China of the past was a different context. Along with economic growth, as discussed in the previous sections, modern China and Chinese society are characterized by their dynamism and never-static transformation in a continued "adaptation and re-adaptation" (Lo Bianco, 2009) into the rest of the world.

In fact, we acknowledge that "foreign" and/or "Chinese" is now becoming a vague concept as the East and West merge into each other socially and culturally (as an old Chinese term describing interpersonal relationships: "You have yours in mine and I have mine in yours": 你中有我, 我中有你). Recognizing Chinese leadership and philosophy as discussed in previous sections, but in a more dynamic international environment, we claim that flexibility, fluidity, and dynamism are themselves now features of Chinese culture and philosophy. Originating from traditional Chinese culture, these features will more or less capture the emergent style of Chinese leadership, especially at a time of globalization when the world is in constant flux.

Accordingly, no matter how China and the Chinese change, a knowledge and appreciation of Chinese culture is always important for any leadership in a Chinese context. With reference to business management, Bjerke (1999: 258) suggests that in the internationalized world, culturally sensitive business leaders should "understand what a culture means and how it is to be used. They appreciate the manifestations of culture in daily life, look at themselves as players in the cultural drama and have a definite understanding of the importance of culture to the long-term survival of its carriers as well".

We argue that, in a globalizing world, successful leadership requires cultural knowledge (often shown in "practical wisdom"; see Beckett & Hager, 2002) as well as strategy. This chapter encourages a more flexible and fluid view of (at least business) leadership in a globalizing world. As indicated by Hickman (2010: x),

> The fast pace and rapidly changing environment in which new era or postindustrial organizations function require leadership that is substantially different from Max Weber's solitary executive at the top of a bureaucratic hierarchy. Organizations require leadership that is fluid, not simply positional, dispersed rather than centralized, and agile not inflexible.

The Chinese are standing at a crossroads – itself a dangerous place, with a lot happening, very fast. We have argued that there is no single best way to lead. Instead, leaders should try to analyse and understand different situations, by being flexible and adopting dynamic strategies, to find the most effective solutions. Recall the saying of Deng: "No matter if the cat is white or black, as long as it can catch the rat, it is a good cat."

References

ALLC (Australian Language and Literacy Council) (1994). *Speaking of Business: The Needs of Business and Industry for Language Skills*. Canberra: Australian Government Publishing.

Arnold, M. (1869). *Culture and Anarchy*. Oxford: Oxford World's Classics.

Bargiela-Chiappini, F. & Harris, S. (1997). *Managing Language: The Discourse of Corporate Meetings*. Amsterdam: John Benjamins.

Beckett, D. (2011). Adult learning: Philosophical issues. In K. Rubenson (Ed.), *Adult Learning and Education*. Oxford: Elsevier.

Beckett, D. (2012). Of maestros and muscles: Expertise and practices at work. In D. Aspin & J. Chapman (Eds.), *Second International Handbook of Lifelong Learning*. The Netherlands: Springer.

Beckett, D. & Hager, P. (2002) *Life, Work and Learning: Practice in Postmodernity*. London: Routledge

Bjerke, B. (1999). *Business Leadership and Culture: National Management Styles in the Global Economy*. Cheltenham: Edward Elgar.

Chan, H.L., Ko, A. & Yu, E. (2000). Confucianism and management. In O.H.M. Yau & H.C. Steele (Eds.), *China Business: Challenges in the 21st Century* (pp. 179–192). Hong Kong: Chinese University of Hong Kong.

Chu, C.-N. (1991). *The Asian Mind Game*. New York: Macmillan.

Feuerwerker, A. (1976). *State and Society in Eighteenth-Century China: The Ch'ing Empire in All Its Glory*. Ann Arbor, MI: Center for Chinese Studies.

Goodman, D. (2013). (forthcoming) New economic elites: The social basis of local power. In Z. Xiaowei (Ed.), *Elites in the People's Republic of China*. London: Routledge.

Harris, P.R. & Moran, R.I. (1979). *Managing Cultural Differences*. Houston, TX: Gulf Publishing Company.

Hickman, G.R. (2010). Introduction. In G.R. Hickman (Ed.), *Leading Organizations: Perspectives for a New Era* (pp. x–xii). Thousand Oaks, CA: Sage.

Hofstede, G. (2001). *Culture's Consequences: Comparing Values, Behaviors, Institutions, and Organizations Across Nations,* 2nd edition. Thousand Oaks, CA: Sage.

Hoon-Halbauer, S.K. (1994). *Management of Sino-Foreign Joint Ventures*. Lund: Lund University Press.

Jansson, H. (1987). *Affärskulturer och relationer i Sydöstasien* (Business Cultures and Relations in Southeast Asia). Stockholm: Marknadstekniskt Centrum, No. 29.

Kluckhohn, C. (1951). The study of culture. In D. Lerner, & H.D. Lasswell (Eds.), *The Policy Sciences* (pp. 86–101). Stanford, CA: Stanford University Press.

Lasserre, P. & Schütte, H. (1995). *Strategies for Asia Pacific*. London: Macmillan.

Lo Bianco, J. (2003). Preface. In J. Lo Bianco, & C. Crozet (Eds.), *Teaching Invisible Culture: Classroom Practice and Theory* (pp. 3–6). Melbourne: Language Australia Ltd.

Lo Bianco, J. (2009). Intercultural encounters and deep cultural beliefs. In J. Lo Bianco & Y.H. Gao (Eds.), *China and English: Globalization and the Dilemmas of Identity* (pp. 23–55). Bristol: Multilingual Matters.

Louie, K. (2008). Defining modern Chinese culture. In K. Louie (Ed.), *The Cambridge Companion to Modern Chinese Culture* (pp. 1–19). Cambridge: Cambridge University Press.

Nolan, P. (2004). *China at the Crossroads*. Cambridge: Polity Press.

Parry, K.W. & Hansen, H. (2007). The organizational story on leadership. *Leadership, 3*, 281–300.

Schram, S.R. (2005). *The Thought of Mao Tse-tung*. Beijing: China Renmin University Press.

Seagrave, S. (1996). *Lords of the Rim*. London: Corgi Books.

Stake, R. (1995). *The Art of Case Study Research*. Thousand Oaks, CA: Sage.

Wikipedia. Confucius. Retrieved from http://en.wikipedia.org/wiki/Confucius.

Wikipedia. Taoism. Retrieved from http://en.wikipedia.org/wiki/Taoism.

邓小平在深圳的讲话. Retrieved from http://wenwen.soso.com/z/q123375845.htm.

晶牛毛泽东思想网. Retrieved from http://www.mzdthought.com/pingjiaweiren/200808/22-9300.html.

人民网.. Retrieved from http://bbs1.people.com.cn/postDetail.do?id= 110044378 &boardId= 60.

世界遗产名录. Retrieved from http://baike.soso.com/v94484.htm?pid= baike.box.

5

Evolving Agencies amid Rapid Social Change: Political Leadership and State–Civil Society Relations in China

Emile Kok-Kheng Yeoh

Introduction: Leadership, structure and agency amid social change

Causes of social change can usually be categorized into three groups: economic, political and cultural factors. Economic factors, especially the impact of industrial capitalism, form the core of the Marxist approach to social change. Such a Marxist emphasis on economic factors, whether for ideological reasons or for the convenience of power maintenance, still forms the basis of the Chinese Communist Party's (CCP) fundamental definition of human rights as the people's rights to be fed, to be sheltered, to be educated and to be employed. Nevertheless, straying from this orthodox Marxist tenet is the neo-Marxist expansion of sources of social contradictions, which are inherent in social structures, to the political, religious, ethnic and ideological factors of conflicts and also the importance of culture not least as a marker for political mobilization. Adapting Buckley's (1967: 58–59) concepts of morphostasis referring to 'those processes in complex system-environment exchanges that tend to preserve or maintain a system's given form, organization or state' and morphogenesis referring to 'those processes which tend to elaborate or change a system's given form, structure or state', Archer (1995), on the other hand, posited that humanity had entered the stage of the morphogenetic society and spoke of the central importance of the role of the human agency that generates the social segments' morphostatic and morphogenetic relationships which, in turn, are not able to exert causal powers without working through human agents. Nevertheless, the cautious but pragmatic approach to reform, whether economic or political, of post-Mao Zedong and post-Deng Xiaoping China seems to reflect the neo-Marxist view that total system or revolutionary change is not inevitable and a stalemate or Reeler's (2007) cold stuckness could be the preferred outcome of social conflicts. Such stance of 'stability above all else' (*wending yadao yiqie*) tends to reaffirm dominance maintained by gradualism in reform and piecemeal changes.

Pluralized conflicts, one of the possible major patterns of conflict from the point of view of neo-Marxists, help in such maintenance of dominance, characterized by the distinctive feature of 'fragmentation and absence of a feeling of commonality' of current Chinese extra-party politics (Benton, 2010: 322). This is partly a result of the relentless crackdown on generalist dissent that the CCP regime perceived as most threatening, which has lately escalated into a wider crackdown on civil rights defenders and whistle-blowers. However, in comparison with the different waves of almost a century of Chinese dissent, as pointed out by both Benton and Wasserstrom, today's dissent in China lacks a unifying thread that connects the actions of different disgruntled groups (Wasserstrom, 2009). This is partly due to the actions of the regime and partly as 'a result of the increasing complexity, differentiation, and individualization of Chinese society, which is no longer monochrome and predictable but as diverse as other contemporary societies, and geographically even more diverse' (Benton, 2010: 322). This increased diversity has inevitably impacted on the increasingly complex structure of the agent–institution interface (for Green's model of social change as applied to the Chinese case, see Green, 2008; Yeoh, 2010: 271) at the core of the circles of social transformation. Green's model basically shows that the process of social change typically involves a combination of four different components:

- context (the environment within which changes take place, thus crucial in determining the nature and direction of change);
- institutions (the organizations and rules, both formal and informal, that establish the 'rules of the game' governing the behaviour of agents – including culture, family structure, civil service, private sector, governmental system and patron–client network);
- agents (organizations and individuals actively involved in promoting or blocking change, e.g. ruling party, social movements, political and business elite, military and police, inspirational leaders and social entrepreneurs);

- and events (one-off events triggering wider change and being key catalysts to social and political changes, e.g. wars, pandemics (AIDS, SARS, A(H1N1), etc.), civil conflicts ('mass incidents', ethnic or ethnoregional riots, demonstrations and crackdowns, natural disasters, economic crisis, etc)).

And, as Eisenstadt (1992: 416) noted, any setting of social interaction involves a plurality of actors, including elites who 'continuously struggle over the control, ownership, and the possibility of using [natural and social] resources, generating ubiquitous conflicts on all levels of social interaction'.

The categories listed above may, however, overlap – for example, the CCP is both an institution and an agent in blocking or promoting different kinds of change. Green's inner circle consists of active citizens as agents and the effective state – here the CCP's party-state – as the most important institution, in terms of change components. This inner circle is surrounded by an outer circle of context consisting of wider components of change, which in a way are less susceptible to political or public action, such as events. While the contextual factors (outer circle) are having an immediate and crucial impact on the institutions and agents of change, these institutions and agents are also having certain, though limited, control over these contextual factors.

On the other hand, Archer's double morphogenesis sees both such structure and agency as cojoint products of interaction in which agency is both shaped by and reshapes structure (Archer, 1995; 1996; 2000; 2003). Operating structures and purposely acting human agencies (combinations of acting individuals) in combination form the praxis and interface of social interaction that effects social change. Within these the agencies are both creating and being limited by the structures, exemplified no doubt by the voicing of dissent and the corresponding crackdowns justified by the notion of 'stability above all else'. However, social control, as ironically seen by Dahrendorf (1959), could be the broadest basis of social conflicts. In a sense, such coercion to extract conformity is normal, as all social systems exhibit an association of roles and statuses that embody power relationships which tend to be institutionalized as authority, sometimes self-perpetuated, that gives political leadership normative rights to dominate.

Leadership at critical junctures

On the macrosociological level, while conflict is an inevitable part of social life and not necessarily negative as it is the engine for social change from both Marxian and Weberian perspectives, the key question is ultimately who gains at whose expense. This is a question of equity, which leads in turn to the actions of the rights-defending activists. Indeed, from the interpretive perspective, social reality is ultimately a construction by people and interactions among them so that patterns and standards of behaviour emerge – be they the ruling political elite or the increasingly persecuted civil rights lawyers and activists. Many of the latter are the survivors of the 1989 Beijing-Tiananmen massacre, who unlike the also persecuted democracy movement organizers, such as Liu Xiaobo and Xie Changfa, seek instead 'to protect and improve the rights of citizens within China's constitutional constraints and legal framework with minimal political requests, yet not totally apolitical' (Hung, 2010: 333–334).

It is a well-recognized fact that leadership's decisions at critical junctures often have far-reaching implications for the subsequent long years of economic and political development of a country. As a comparison we go back to before the beginning of China's reforms, just a year prior to Mao's passing. On the other side of the globe in 1975, in Spain, which constitutes 85% of the Iberian Peninsula, Generalísimo Francisco Franco y Bahamonde[1] (the *Caudillo*) died. While repeatedly expressing confidence that he would leave Spain *atado, y bien atado* ('tied-up, well tied-up'),[2] his death was followed within two years by the dismantling of the structure of the whole Franquist regime, and the first free parliamentary elections in more than 40 years were held on 15 June 1977. One of the most remarkable developments under the democratic transition had been the political decentralization of the state. Nevertheless, the controversy and confusion over the regional picture and the fear for the loss of Spain's national identity, as well as the continued attacks by the Basque separatist group ETA, continued to fuel right-wing discontent. This had led to a series of conspiracies against the democratic government and culminated in the almost successful military coup of 23 February 1981. However, the result has not been to roll back reforms but to push the ethnoregional question even more firmly to the top of the political agenda.

Hence, going back to the 1970s, what we see is that at their respective critical structural junctures, in 1975 and 1976, fascist Spain and Marxist-Leninist China embraced different paths of reforms. To hold the country together against potentially separatist ethnoregional conflicts, post-Franco Spain spurned overnight its fascist-corporatist past and embraced multiparty democracy and federalism, taking the risk of the disappearance of the central state. Meanwhile, post-Mao China has followed a more cautious path that was to evolve later into an institutionalized relationship between the central state and the localities some would call 'selective centralization' (Zheng, 1999).

Moving away from the Spanish scene of the post-Franco determined reform and change, across the globe in China, since the demise of Mao, another critical juncture arrived in 1989, with the 100-day peaceful Tiananmen demonstrations and hunger strikes that received global sympathy. However, political leaders behind the high walls of Zhongnanhai, after three long months of indecision amid intra-politburo ideological and power struggle, finally fell back on the usual Leninist-Maoist defensive feedback mechanism for dealing with such 'deviation-amplification'[3] that could trigger systemic change, namely armed repression against state-defined 'counter-revolutionary riots'. The poignancy of the 1989 tragedy resulted, from an Archerian perspective (Archer, 1988), from the disjunction between the system segments' relations of contradictions and complementarity and those between human agents in terms of conflict and cooperation. Shocking it might have been, but it was not surprising that the 1989 Beijing Spring had ended in the tragic Rape of Beijing[4] when the system segments' relations did not mesh with those of the human agents. This is the same mismatch that is still manifesting itself today where the political elite in the life-world is adamant in holding ground against the masses' demand for transformative political change amid lively debate and consensus on universal values at the general level of the cultural system. This has served to nip morphogenesis in the bud, leading to the subsequent protracted morphostasis. Distinctively, Archer's critical realism grants causal powers to the human agency that are indeducible from or irreducible to the causal powers of society (Archer, 2000). Such endowment of causal powers must be crucial for the Bourdievian human agents who are being transformed into Tourainean corporate agents who now set out as social actors to transform society, personalizing the latter as per their ultimate concerns (Bourdieu, 1974; Touraine, 1969, 1973, 1978). This is due to their gaining cognizance of their class members' common interests, being agents involuntarily occupying social positions that define their life-chances (*ibid.*). It is in this context that, according to Archer, the existing system itself would shape the life-world practices geared towards reproducing, reshaping or transmuting the system. Its result, not really incompatible with Deng's 'river-crossing' dictum[5] or Mao's 'perpetual revolution', is poised to be contested and modified in the subsequent phase of the series of endless morphogenetic cycles of sociopolitical and sociocultural interaction and systemic conditioning and elaboration. Looking at the stand-off in 1989 between the state leadership and the student-led demonstrators that ended in the 4 June tragedy, such causal powers of human agency across the political divide cannot be underestimated.

From the perspective of interpretivism, change in the forms of interaction, process and negotiation is primal, while structure is a by-product and temporary. In this context, be it in 1989 or today, both the pro-democracy and civil rights activists, and members of the ruling political elite, are human agents engaged in the constant creation, negotiation and re-creation of the social order. Within this process of social change there exists a negotiated consensus about what constitutes objective social reality. At the level of the individual human agent, Archer (2003) described the integration of subjective projects and objective circumstances in a viable *modus vivendi* linking structure with agency (p. 133). This is achieved through constantly examining one's social contexts, asking and answering oneself in a trial-and-error manner about how one can best realize the concerns that one can determine, in circumstances that were not one's own choosing (*ibid.*).[6]

Leadership change and post-crisis social ramifications

Spain's 1981 failed coup had placed greater urgency on the decentralization plan by highlighting the peril in the management of decentralization, the threat from conservative forces and the threat from regional reformers and secessionists. On the contrary, the Tiananmen demonstrations had instead ended in the spill of innocent blood and arrested the maturing of the political system with the purge of Zhao Ziyang, the arrest of Bao Tong and the exile of other chief reformists and intellectuals who advocated democratization, such as Yan Jiaqi and Fang Lizhi, and the student leaders in the forefront of the mass protest.

The 1989 Beijing-Tiananmen upheaval and tragedy also saw the purge of Zhao Ziyang and the obliteration of the one and only political reform package in the history of the CCP which attempted to introduce the most far-reaching political structural reforms, such as the separation of power between party and state, proposed by Zhao earlier at the 13th Party Congress in October 1987. Such events undeniably formed the watershed that serves to define subsequent state–civil society interactions and the concomitant development in China's political and socioeconomic structure, as well as central state–ethnic regional relations (Yeoh, 2010: 278–280). In the aftermath of the hot crisis (see Reeler, 2007) of 1989, continued survival of one-party rule became the paramount concern. This occurred in an environment wherein the prime directive of 'stability above all else' and the ruthless 'dissent-harmonizing' maintenance of a 'harmonious society' delineated a safe zone wherein the political elite are parading administrative innovations as political reforms and political fudge (*zhengzhi huyou*) as visionary leadership. Meanwhile, having been disillusioned by the once-revolutionary vision of socialist transformation while still maintaining the monopoly of political power, as Womack (2011: 161) observed, the party now 'attracts risk-avoiding careerists rather than risk-taking revolutionaries'. Such a 'post-revolutionary syndrome' may not afflict only new recruits, when instead of statesmen with conscience and prescience, holding the helm are visionless, overcautious political careerists resplendent in hollow, sentimental rhetoric and showmanship. They are both the products and the survivors of the yesteryear of Maoist horror and still reeling from the shock of the perceived political debacle of 1989. Political reform that had hardly begun during the Hu Yaobang-Zhao Ziyang administration inevitably entered a stage of cold stuckness (see Reeler, 2007). Meanwhile, as Émile Durkheim (1895) said, 'The air does not cease to have weight, although we no longer feel that weight', brewing social forces bringing along subliminal emergent changes continue to threaten to subvert the stability of well-laid-out projectable changes envisaged by the ruling regime (Yeoh, 2010: 241–245), aided in no small measure by the advent of the Internet Age. Indeed, in an increasingly globalized world, as Lee (2011) observed, no authoritarian regime or leader, who rules not only by fear but also in fear, is capable of imposing absolute control without challenge and compromise amid the current global electronic network transformation. This is evident in the astounding 'jasmine revolutions' that have been sweeping the Arab world and reverberating in the nightmares of the Chinese leaders.

Leadership amid social instability

While aspects of political reform have since been either rolled back or stalled after the hot crisis of 1989, the tragic end of the Tiananmen protests and democracy movement of June 1989 was a disaster for democratic pluralist development and ethnoregional accommodation. This is so especially in view of the close link between political decentralization and democratization. The post-4 June robust, even miraculous, economic growth has been used time and again rather successfully by the CCP for the *ex post* justification of the Tiananmen crackdown of 1989. The suggestion is that this brutal suppression was necessary to preserve China's stability and economic progress. However, if the blood-chilling words attributed to Deng Xiaoping[7] – that it was worth killing 20 *wan* (i.e. 200,000) people to ensure 20 years of stability for China – in ordering the massacre of June 1989 were truly his, then the continuing, even recently escalating, social unrest (including those more alarming incidents with ethnic or ethnoregional flavour) that culminated in Xinjiang's 5 July deadly riots of 2009, just a month past that year's 20th anniversary of the Beijing[8] tragedy, look somehow like an omen that time might be running out. The student movement which snowballed into social protests of unprecedented scale is in many ways a return of the May Fourth Movement. The May Fourth Movement 1919 eventually led to the triumph of Maoism-Leninism, which in a way hijacked the early socialism of Ch'en Tu-hsiu (Chen Duxiu).[9] The violent suppression of the 1989 mass protests, on the other hand, represented a prelude to the subsequent hijacking of the Hu Yaobang-Zhao Ziyang administration's initiative for politicoeconomic liberalization[10] by the strengthening of one-party authoritarian state corporatism preferred by Deng Xiaoping, who once and again felt wary of and threatened by his protégés' 'bourgeois liberalism'. The conservative backlash had since worsened the uneasy coexistence of a highly decentralized economic structure with a highly centralized intolerant political regime, which has, among other ramifications, stalled the more rational accommodation of ethnic and ethnoregional aspirations and precipitated the horrific events of 14 March 2008 and 5 July 2009.

Yet the 1989 Beijing-Tiananmen massacre could be seen as a wake-up call for the CCP to embark rigorously on a path of continuing economic reform while rolling back the Hu Yaobang-Zhao Ziyang era of limited politicocultural liberalization. The subsequent collapse of Communist Party rule in the USSR and Eastern Europe from the end of 1989 to early 1990[11] had seemed to reaffirm the correctness of such a decision to crack down on part of the CCP to ensure the survival of its one-party rule. One could also view 4 June as a catalyst for the single-minded determination to deliver on the economic front after Deng Xiaoping's 'southern tour' (*nanxun*) later in 1992 to reaffirm the party's policy of moving forward with economic reform and liberalization, coupled with more determined repression of political dissent.

There are indeed many similarities between the May Fourth Movement 1919 and the student movement 70 years later (which culminated in the 4 June tragedy) – the passion for social reform and national rejuvenation; the resentment against contemporary sociopoliticoeconomic injustice; the call for democracy, science, human rights and modernization; and the forlorn challenge against the overwhelming power of a ruthless state. The May Fourth Movement 1919, while inclusive of the liberal tradition, eventually turned Chinese intellectuals away from Western liberalism to Bolshevism, and planted the seeds of Mao's ascending the Tiananmen on 1 October 1949[12] and of the contradictions between national rejuvenation, modernization and radicalism. Coinciding with the 200th anniversary of the French Revolution, the 70th anniversary of the May Fourth Movement and the 40th anniversary of CCP rule, 4 June 1989[13] in a way also sowed the seeds of escalating internal contradictions and tension in subsequent policy orientation.

Even not seen in ethnic and ethnoterritorial terms, such social contradictions have manifested themselves in the alarmingly widening income gap, deteriorating socioeconomic inequalities and proliferating social unrest. The state's neurosis towards the meaning of May, which was supposed to be a day of national pride, and its link to the spirit of 4 June, for instance, was manifest in the quiet passing of the recent 92nd anniversary of the May Fourth Movement in Beijing and at Peking University, the birthplace of the movement. Besides the suppression of free thought and dissent, and the ubiquitous 'thought police' on campus, Peking University's economics professor, Xia Yeliang, attributed the dire atmosphere to the government's denial of the universal value of liberal democracy, freedom of expression and political choice.[14] In contrast with the students who participated and led the 1989 democracy movement who dared to turn ideals into action, according to Professor Xia Yeliang, today's students tend to heed their parents' advice to beware of the political minefield given the memory of the 1989 Beijing massacre and the subsequent two decades of relentless repression of dissidents and, increasingly, even civil rights activists and lawyers. This has been getting worse recently partly due to the CCP regime's fear of the spread of the tantalizing 'jasmine revolutions' from the Arab North Africa and West Asia into this East Asian giant.

Leadership and regime legitimacy

Meanwhile, building upon the foundation set by the Hu-Zhao administration's audacious reformist programmes, Deng Xiaoping moved forwards from where his purged former protégés had left by reinvigorating the post-Tiananmen chilling politicoeconomic milieu through his *nanxun* in 1992. This culminated recently in China first superseding Germany to become the world's third largest economy in early 2008, ranked only after the US and Japan, and then overtaking Japan in mid-2010 to become the world's number 2.[15]

According to Wang Qinfeng, the deputy head of CCP's Central Committee Organization Department, from the 4.48 million party member in 1949 at the founding of the People's Republic of China, the CCP has grown to have more than 80 million members by the end of 2010, of whom a quarter were less than 35 years old. In fact, about 80% of those who applied to join the party in 2010 were less than 35 years old, with the party members with university or other high academic qualifications continuing to increase in number.[16] The CCP has also been intensively recruiting professionals in private enterprises as party members. For instance, of the 200 employees of Beijing company Hengtai Shida, about 10%, mainly from the middle and higher echelons, are now CCP members.[17] On the other hand, Chen Xiqing, the deputy head of CCP's Central Committee United Front Department, declared at a recent press conference that China's 'multiparty' system was already perfect, hence there was no need to establish new political parties.[18] The CCP, according to Chen, has been absorbing workers, peasants and soldiers, as well as members of the intelligentsia, as party members, while the eight existing 'democratic parties' (*minzhu dangpai*) are focusing mainly on recruiting people from the middle and upper social strata, including those in the fields of technology, culture and sports. In China's so-called 'multiparty cooperation' (*duodang hezuo*) system, these 'democratic parties' are neither 'non-ruling parties' (*zaiyedang*) nor 'opposition parties' (*fanduidang*), but 'participating parties' (*canzhengdang*). Besides that, according to Chen, there are also 'party-less' (*wu dangpai*) people in the system, comprising those who are not members of these nine political parties.

However, the situation in 2011 shows that the nomination of independent candidates for the county- and village-level elections has apparently been blocked on the grounds that the nomination of such independent candidates has no legal basis, while official media are accusing these independent candidates of learning from the Western opposition, creating confrontation, being irresponsible and causing political hazards in Chinese society. These independent candidates are also warned not to touch the government's 'red line'.[19] According to China's electoral law, only the 'official representative candidates' are legal candidates for the county and village elections, being nominated and recommended by the political parties, civil organizations and the electorate. Thus, 'independent' candidates are considered illegal. For instance, a female *xiagang* worker in Jiangxi Province, Liu Ping, was placed under tight police surveillance after she declared her intention to stand in Xinyu City's Yushui District elections. A labour-rights activist, she has been arrested before for her *shangfang-weiquan*[20] activity and she believed that she would be arrested again in the government's attempt to stop her from standing in the coming elections.[21]

Hence, while many authors inside and outside China have been lauding the country's 'grassroots democratization' and intraparty reforms as pointing to a promising path of de-authoritarian evolvement, the perception that China is moving out from the 'politically closed authoritarian' category of regime type (see taxonomy in Diamond, 2002: 30–31, table 2) could prove to be as misleadingly whimsical as it is empirically unfounded. Furthermore, the past record of mismanagement and repressive, often violent, response to dissent, including the excesses during the Cultural Revolution both in China proper and in the ethnic regions, like Tibet and Xinjiang, and the 4 June atrocities, may not be encouraging for many.

While not denying that much progress is required before China becomes democratic, Bo (2010) argued against the accusation that the CCP's rule is illegitimate. According to him, CCP faces no crisis of legitimacy because to assess the legitimacy of a political regime one needs 'to see whether such a regime is receptive to the governed', and it is 'wrong to evaluate the legitimacy of the CCP rule by relying solely on "expert" opinions of the Western academia and media because they are in no position to judge whether the CCP has right to rule or not' (Bo, 2010: 117).

Yet, according to Arthur Stinchcombe, legitimacy depends little on abstract principle or assent of the governed for the 'person *over whom power is exercised* is not usually as important as *other power-holders*' (Stinchcombe, 1968: 150, original emphasis),[22] the probability of whose confirmation of the decisions of a given authority constitutes the latter's legitimacy. These other authorities, said Tilly (1985: 171–172), 'are much more likely to confirm the decisions of a challenged authority that controls substantial force; not only fear of retaliation, but also desire to maintain a stable environment recommend that general rule [which] underscores the importance of the authority's monopoly of force'. It is in this way that these 'other power-holders', be they societal pressure groups and professionals, or academics and the intelligentsia, 'have been co-opted into the decision-making process, rewarded with perks and privileges, and are no longer available as a source of inspiration [for the dissident activists]...retreating from "politically engaged and intellectually oppositional topics" to inquiries reconcilable with the prevailing order and designed to legitimate the hegemonic order' (Benton, 2010: 321–322).[23] This is "hegemonic order" of a regime claiming credit for the economic successes that brought heightened international stature and diplomatic prowess and propounding existing stability as the key to continued economic prosperity. Such prosperity is in fact the unfailing characteristic of the Chinese and Chinese diaspora worldwide – achievement which could have come naturally for the people once the Maoist yoke, both in the forms of the suppression of free entrepreneurial spirit and the political horrors, was lifted by the same regime that had foisted that yoke upon the Chinese people for three decades since 1949. Anyhow, according to Tilly, a tendency to monopolize the means of violence 'makes a government's claim to provide protection, in either the comforting or the ominous sense of the word, more credible and more difficult to resist' (Tilly, 1985: 172).

With the carrot-and-stick approach to maintain its survival, the once-brutal-dictatorship-turned-benevolent-*dictablanda* (*à la* O'Donnell & Schmitter, 1986) has managed to preserve the *status quo* of its own rule as well as the interests of the 'other power-holders'. This was achieved by selling the credit it claimed on behalf the industrious, enterprising and persevering masses, whose newly freed entrepreneurial spirit, long-recognized in the communities of their brethren worldwide, resulted from the party's repudiation of the Maoist policies, has doubtlessly led to the country's economic success during the economic reform decades since 1979. It was also accomplished by extracting the support of those 'other power-holders', who are willing to abdicate their opportunity to rule in exchange for other kinds of protection by the ensuing strong state run by the present regime (Stepan, 1985), in a *faute de mieux* deal much like Karl Marx's description of the Bonapartist regime in *The Eighteenth Brumaire of Louis Napoleon* (1852). Marx's classic analysis of Bonapartism as a basis of state autonomy rests mainly in the sharing of common interests between the state and the dominant group, which in the case of contemporary China, the ruling CCP regime and the dominant social elite, and groups whose inability to overcome the present state's monopoly of violence to force a regime change has given the party-state the opportunity to use the leverage gained both to preserve the *status quo* and to propound its claim as the protector of stability and prosperity in exchange for the acceptance of its legitimacy. For even when 'a government's use of force imposes a large cost, some people may well decide that the government's other services outbalance the costs of acceding to its monopoly of violence' (Tilly, 1985: 172), though it could turn out to be a Faustian bargain that these social elite and groups might live to rue. In the stylized representation of Yeoh (2010: 254, Figure 8), proscription of even the slightest manifestation of dissent against the one-party rule has managed to contain societal political action to the routine intraparty politics at the far bottom right-hand corner, despite the sporadic outbursts of people power usually stemming from localized grievances which have always been quickly suppressed. Amid all of this, individual political actors are playing a central role in giving existence to the obduracy of the system, for the causal powers of systems and structures cannot exist without the mediation through the human agency, as Archer (2003) admitted, despite her rejection of the theorem of the duality of agency and structure.

Leadership in times of calamities

The ultimate project of a self-seeking state is also manifest in the single-mindedness in pursuing greater economic prosperity, sometimes dubbed 'GDPism',[24] a crazed quest that has increasingly been unfolding in recent years to be at a terrible social cost, epitomized recently by the horrible train mishap in Wenzhou on 23 July 2011 – the very Wenzhou that has long found its place in modern Chinese history in the typonym of the 'Wenzhou model'. The scandalous nature of the disaster lies neither in the derailment itself, which is not an uncommon phenomenon in China, nor the scale of the human casualties, nor the unfolding or imminent clampdown on media reportage and civil rights activists and lawyers, which has been quite a routine from the Sichuan earthquake's 'tofu dregs' schoolhouse scandal to the Sanlu milk contamination disaster, but rather in the scale of the disregard for the dignity of human life. However, the uniqueness of this event, the unusual uproar it has led to stems from the open urban setting of the occurrence that renders surreptitiousness of scandalous actions impossible. This is unlike, for instance, the case of a similar mishap in Jiangxi on 23 May 2010, in which the similarly alleged immediate destruction of train wreckage with utter disregard for the victims trapped therein, whom the authorities had hurriedly presumed dead, had also been carried out both to avoid publicity and to speed up the return to normal operation. In the Jiangxi case, the efficient returning to operation of the rail segment where the accident had occurred took even shorter time – merely 16 hours compared with Wenzhou's 34 hours, which is already considered reckless by international standards in the handling of such disasters.[25] Wen Jiabao's late appearance in Wenzhou six days after the disaster, while being jeered at by some who did not believe his excuse of illness[26] and rationalized by others in terms of the power struggle between the Hu-Wen and Jiang Zemin factions,[27] followed exactly the now routine format of Wen showing onsite the caring, human face of the party-state, while the latter began to clamp down on media coverage and social activism stemming from the incident. Wen's pronouncements at the site of the disaster were apparently, as had become routine in past calamities, to project the impression of a benevolent central court ruling an impossibly vast country, struggling to keep a rein on the sometimes wayward, corrupt and uncaring local officials.

Nevertheless, as a paramount figure within the gargantuan party-military-industrial complex that has metamorphosed during the reform years into an incredible modern Leviathan[28] whose state-capital-collusion reach has since permeated into every corner of Chinese society, Wen's routine calamity-site pronouncements tend to sound hollow if not pretentious After all, while the perpetuation of one-party rule has depended upon the monopoly of violence and ruthless suppression of dissent ever since the June 1989 massacre, its legitimacy ultimately lies in the ability to maintain the miraculous gross domestic product (GDP) growth that has brought the country from poverty to prosperityand catapulted the nation to the second place in the world in terms of economic size. Such achievements have given back the Chinese people the long-lost pride, at least in material terms, in the nostalgia for the formidable Han and Tang dynasties which had been reduced by the early part of the 20th century to the shameful fate of the 'sick man of Asia' and the *bainian guochi* (hundred years of national humiliation), in a partial redemption for the unspeakable atrocities committed by the party during the Mao years. While riding the wave of the miraculous economic performance that its reborn self has given to the long-suffering Chinese people by lifting the Maoist yoke, the party has demanded the same gratefulness and reverence long demanded by ancient imperial China's Sons of Heaven for the very economic prosperity that the newly freed, long-suppressed Chinese entrepreneurial spirit has brought to fruition with incredible speed and force.

Nevertheless, the party's ultimate concern is never disguised in the pronouncements of its leaders in party congresses, namely the perpetuation of the anachronistic one-party rule, while rejecting the 'bourgeois liberal' practices of multiparty elections and *trias politica* separation of powers. This depends very much, however, on its continued ability to deliver on the economic front as well as to curb social ills resulting from economic transformation, including the rampant corruption and increasing income inequality before they lead to uncontrollable, large-scale system-threatening social protests. This also has to be supported by the ruthless suppression of dissent and nipping any sign of 'deviation-amplification' in the bud before it can take the first step towards triggering systemic change, all under the façade of territorial unity, political stability and a 'harmonious society' (*hexie shehui*), the key conceptual cornerstone since the Sixth Plenary Session of the 16th Central Committee of the Communist Party of China in October 2006 passed the 'Resolution on Major Issues Regarding the Building of a Harmonious Socialist Society'.

While rumours in cyberspace that the order for the alleged Wenzhou cover-up attempt immediately after the derailment had in fact come from the central state at a level beyond the Ministry of Railways could probably never be confirmed or refuted in a governing environment of lies and deceptions, the central party-state's paramount priority of maintaining a 'harmonious society' and the 'stability above all else' prime directive would have had a primary impact on local-tier decision-makers' policy choices. Take the case of the famous Weng'an incident of 2008 that shocked the nation, when tens of thousands of people walked the streets of Weng'an, Guizhou Province, on 28 June 2008, attacking police and burning law-enforcement vehicles and government offices after the suspicious death of a beautiful young schoolgirl, Li Shufen, discovered at 1.00 a.m. on 22 June 2008, drowned at the Daan Bridge on the Ximen River. Three people were present at the scene: Li's female schoolmate, Wang Jiao, and two male brick factory workers, Chen Guangquan and Liu Yanchao. Li's family members believed that she was brutally raped and murdered, and Wang, Chen and Liu were the prime suspects. There were even rumours that thugs were hired to rape and murder Li to punish her for refusing to submit to plagiarism demands during a school examination, and that the perpetrators of this hideous crime had kinship relations with the county's party secretary, Wang, and the provincial public security department head, Jiang. Official autopsy results, however, stated that Li had committed suicide and drowned, and Wang, Chen and Liu were released before the first autopsy even began. It is a social fact that rapid economic transformation during the reform era has brought about an overall rise in crime. The *2010 Blue Book of China's Society* (edited by Ru, Lu & Li, December 2009) reported 12,000 cases of homicide (an increase of 0.4% from the previous year), 28,000 cases of rape (11.4% increase), 6064 cases of arson (26.4% increase), 1,045 cases of planting dangerous material (37.5% increase) and 237,000 cases of robbery (6.7% rise) in the first 10 months of 2009 (Fan, Song, & Yan, 2009: 86).[29] It is also a fact that acute social contradictions, deteriorating social order and state–civil society relations, out-of-control crime, worsening income and wealth disparity in Weng'an, a mining county with a highly mixed ethnic minority and Han Chinese population of 460,000, have often been blamed for the June 2008 riots, the standard official 'black box' approach, as in so many other cases throughout the country, had served to accentuate the people's distrust of the state and government leadership and fed further the rumour mill and pushed the situation to boiling point.

Covering up and news blackouts have become standard procedure. In the Li Shufen case, for instance, the government moved swiftly to impose *si feng* (four blockades) – that is, *feng wang* (blocking the Internet), *feng cheng* (blocking the town), *feng tongxin* (blocking mails) and *feng jizhe* (blocking reporters). As a result, the mainstream media simply reflected the standardized version from the local government officials, Internet postings were severely cut, people involved were kept out of reach of the press and many family members of the victim disappeared for many days before reappearing to tell the press about their full support for *hexie*[30] (harmony). In the parlance of the sarcastic Chinese netizens, they had already been 'harmonized' (*bei hexie*) while Li Shufen had been 'suicided' (*bei zisha*).[31] Just like in the case of the Wenzhou derailment and many other cases, while such state responses can be blamed on the local governments and their officials, what lies behind is ultimately the central party-state's paramount concern regarding any perceived threat to a 'harmonious society' and the 'stability above all else' bottom line that it sees as a cornerstone, besides economic prosperity and the monopoly of violence, of the perpetuation of its one-party rule.

However, the ultimate question remains: Can social harmony be imposed top-down by state coercion and relentless suppression of dissent in a legal system devoid of judicial independence? Such a question is indeed futile as there has never been any pretension in the party leaders' pronouncements that the fundamental concern represents anything other than the ultimate aim of perpetuating the one-party rule of the CCP, which looks upon itself as the only political organization in modern Chinese history that has been proven able to advance the livelihood of the Chinese people and make China a great and proud nation. Such a leadership mentality was recently described by China's well-known writer Han Han in his weblog after the Wenzhou derailment as follows:

> They feel that, from a larger perspective, 'We've organized the Olympics, we've abolished the agricultural tax, yet you're not applauding but instead always making a great fuss about trivialities – What are you up to? Originally we could be tighter in politics than

North Korea, poorer in economy than Sudan, more ruthless in governing than the Khmer Rouge, because we have a much larger army than they do, but we aren't. Yet you do not show your gratitude, but want us to apologize.'[32]

Leadership at a crossroads

'Infidelity', said Thomas Paine, 'does not consist in believing, or in disbelieving, it consists in professing to believe what one does not believe.'[33] Among members of the political elite, without the pressures from emerging critical junctures (Katznelson, 1971), critical decisions like those coming from Zhao Ziyang and Deng Xiaoping in 1989 are no longer forthcoming. Political decision makers tend to lapse, for career security, into the safe zone behind the veil of ignorance – postponing critical decisions on the pretext of maintaining stability in the hope that problems would not come to a head so soon or would fade into the background with increasing prosperity – and come to be, to use a Shakespearean term, political 'seemers'[34] characterized by rhetoric barrages of nationalistic rhapsodies and what Steven Poole called 'unspeak'.[35] As a case in point, Premier Wen Jiabao is increasingly being accused by the disillusioned masses of not matching any action to his frequent verbal outbursts advocating political reform, the details of which have been noted by observers to be similar to those advocated in Charter 08, which landed its proponent, Liu Xiaobo, with an 11-year imprisonment.[36]

Postponing critical decisions on the last leg of reform – that in the political sphere – can only be postponing the inevitable. It is in fact accentuating the existing social contradictions, for both the speed and volatility brought about by the country's breakneck economic transformation under increasing morphogenesis are making whatever state-sanctioned system with the bottom line of one-party rule short-lived in viability when all state-guided *modi vivendi* as such could be at best *pro tem*. Such considerations could be behind the recently alleged repeated attempts by Premier Wen to push the long-overdue political reform to the top of the politburo's agenda, though it could just be reflecting his feeling of urgency to leave behind a reputation, before he steps down in March 2013, as a top reformer taking on the mantle of Zhao Ziyang.[37] Otherwise, the inability to face up to the rapidly changing reality and shifting social context, and keep their meta-reflexivity (Archer, 1995) constantly on call to realistically assess their existing *modus vivendi* and to be receptive to a transformative change (Yeoh,

2010: 285, Figure 21), has trapped the ruling elite, for political survival, in the unwavering upholding of a prolonged stage of morphostasis. This is because they constitute the agency and most powerful institution that is best positioned to block or promote (Yeoh, 2010: 271–272, Figure 19) the path of morphogenesis, which according to Archer (1995), like morphostasis, is both generated and only exerting causal powers by working through social agents.

Indeed, the political reform much hoped for by China watchers when Hu Jintao and Wen Jiabao took over the presidency and premiership respectively has never materialized. They were both colleagues and subordinates of the former reformist premier Zhao Ziyang, who was disgraced in 1989 in a power struggle with hardliner Li Peng, who subsequently executed Deng Xiaoping's decision for a brutal crackdown on the Beijing-Tiananmen protesters. Hence, Hu and Wen's absence at the memorial service for Zhao ('the conscience of China', placed under house arrest for 16 long years for his refusal to repent his decision to oppose the 1989 Beijing-Tiananmen crackdown and to urge for the accommodation of the hunger-striking students' demands) when he passed away in 2005 has added to the doubt regarding the degree of their political power in the central politburo.[38] While the utter cold-heartedness that Wen Jiabao exhibited towards the plight of Zhao Ziyang has long puzzled observers of Chinese politics and Zhao's family and relatives have long found chilling, the necessity for political survival could probably explain much of his behaviour. Having survived through both purges of Hu Yaobang and Zhao Ziyang, Wen Jiabao has indeed acted with good political sense as a rational human agent interfacing with the harsh political realities of his time. Nevertheless, revelations by political analysts based on internal party sources have shown that, as in the case of Wen Jiabao, the personal allegiance and political orientation of individual political players who were highly visible during those critical junctures like June 1989 might have been greatly misread (see e.g. Liu, 2010).

After all, the real 'ruminating self' that intervenes in between the field and the habitus (*à la* Bourdieu, 1990; 2008) through those soul-trying months of passion and anguish at that critical juncture in 1989 and in the aftermath of the massacre, which constitutes the intercessor that connects the structure's causal powers to agency, may be fully understood only by the particular human agents themselves. This is because the actuation of social structures' causal powers through constraints and enablements has to be contingent upon the existential projects that these human agents construct *in foro interno* (Archer, 2003).

It is in this context that human agents act to mediate their own social conditionings as well as effectuate the reproduction or transformation of society. 'It is not an accident that Premier Wen Jiabao once called himself "grandpa Wen" (*Wen yeye*) in front of the people', noted Hung (2011). In a sense, the role of Wen, long cultivated as the loving grand patriarch who is at every scene of disaster to offer moral care for his 'children', is orchestrated to be an onsite projection of the central party-state as the modern successor to the caring, benevolent emperor who was always there to *zuozhu* (enforce justice) for his downtrodden subjects and punish his abusive officials, in a system that survives today in the form of *shangfang* (travelling to the capital for petitioning) by the abused people suffering in the hands of corrupt local officials. Such an image is crucial to the survival of the party-state, as any self-seeking dynasty-builder has long understood, for the mandate of heaven would be lost if that image is shattered – ever since Mencius emphasized 2,300 years ago the people's satisfaction as an indicator of a ruler's moral right to power, and justified the overthrow of an unworthy ruler.[39]

Conclusion

This chapter has discussed various key issues underlying the nature and role of the political elite and leadership in the context of the relationship between structure and agency within the overall political milieu in contemporary China, where social change is moving apace amid astounding economic transformation. Ironically, some factors which at first seem to be system-threatening may instead work for the state leadership's advantage. According to Perry (2002), for instance, social protests in today's China constitute one of the major components of social stability, as they serve as checks against the leaders' abuse of power and as mechanisms ensuring the accountability of the government, thereby 'undergirding rather than undermining the political system' in China's authoritarian polity where multiparty competitive elections do not exist to provide an effective check on the misbehaviour of state authorities.[40] In addition, Tong & Lei (2010: 499–500) considered large-scale mass incidents driven by economic grievances, which were due to 'the misconduct of local officials or the process of socioeconomic transformation when there was a lack of experience in handling these problems or the lack of proper regulations', as not regime-threatening. This is because by asking the government and political leaders to *zuozhu*, the protests had in fact endorsed the legitimacy of the regime and political leadership. Seen from this perspective, as long as the regime had plenty of financial resources to satisfy the protesters' demands – hence the significance of GDPism as a cornerstone of regime maintenance – it further consolidates its legitimacy. On the other hand, in the case of inequality, Friedman (2009) argued that the beneficiaries of economic growth were able to find their own individual solutions to their problems and resigned themselves to an authoritarian government with leaders not popularly elected, as a defence against the threat from potentially vengeful losers in the market economy, thereby rendering social polarization inconducive to democratic sentiment among them.[41]

Finally, it needs to be noted that amid the dynamic interplay of such an array of critical socioeconomic factors that underlie the surging currents of social change, be they the overt or subliminal emergent changes that tend to act to subvert the stability of well-laid-out projectable changes envisaged by the ruling regime (Yeoh, 2010) or an illusive transformative change biding its time prior to a critical point of bifurcation as pointed out by the chaos theory (Yeoh, 2010; Prigogine, Stengers, 1984), the role of the individual in the context of political leadership, whether within the state apparatus or the community of dissidents as a catalyst for change, cannot be underestimated. This is true even if the long-term impact of the individual's action is not immediately explicit and the lone crusade involved does not receive adequate sympathy from the wider public. Such is the tragedy of the commons (*à la* Hardin, 1968) resulted from incomplete feedback loops, among others.

On the other hand, the duality of structure and agency as pointed out by structuration theory implies that there exists a symbiotic relationship between structures that shape agencies' motives into practices and agencies whose routine practices in turn create structures. One cannot exist without the other. For instance, while the brutal crushing of the democracy movement of 1989 was of such magnitude that it continues 'to reverberate in people's imagination and the collective memory – and in the sleep of party leaders and officials, as a nightmare', as Benton (2010: 322) noted – the experience of facing down the government 'created a generation no longer prepared to act as an off-stage army for party factions, an attitude passed on to the protestors' children'. In fact, in the current harsh political environment, some among the 1989 generation continue to shoulder leadership responsibilities within the dissident community in China as well as keep alive the democracy movement in exile in working for political and social change. After all, individuals, who together form social movements and who as individuals provide indispensable leadership to such movements, are at the very foundations of all socioeconomic and sociopolitical changes.

Notes

1. Born Francisco Paulino Hermenegildo Teódulo Franco Bahamonde in 1892 in the northwestern Iberian coastal town of El Ferrol.
2. *'Atado, y bien atado'* ('Tied-up, well tied-up'), ruminated Generalísimo Francisco Franco (*El Caudillo*), prior to his death on 20 November 1975 (cited in Gunther, 1980: 285).
3. See Buckley (1967).
4. 'The Rape of Peking' (editorial), *Asiaweek*, 16 June 1989.
5. Referring to Deng's well-known gradualist dictum 'Cross the river by groping the stones' (*Mo zhe shitou guo he*).
6. While Archer's theorizing has sometimes been criticized as focusing too much on internal conversation, conceptualized as a causal power that transforms both human agents and society, at the expense of intersubjective communication, which is crucial to understanding the morphogenesis of structure through collective action and social movements – her emphasis that 'Were we humans not reflexive beings there could be no such thing as society' (Archer, 2003: 19) – it would be unfair not to take into consideration the relevance of her theorizing to the latter and the great potential of extracting a theory of collective action from her work. Her 'metareflexives' for instance, while (true to her assertion that private life is an essential prerequisite for social life) being idealists seeking self-knowledge and practising self-critique for self-realization, are also driven by their personal missions to criticize their environment – Habermasian Meadian *wertrationale* social utopians constantly judging themselves and their societies in a critical manner from the point of view of the 'generalized other' and the alternative 'rational society' (Habermas, 1987; 1992; Mead, 1934), showing concern for social injustice and refusing morphostasis or 'cold stuckness' (Reeler, 2007) in the name of some cultural or political ideal or the preference for stability. Mead's 'generalized other', after all, is the 'organized community or social group which gives to the individual his unity of self' (Mead, 1934: 154), enabling the human agent to raise questions of justice and rights.
7. The twice-purged pragmatist and reformist Deng Xiaoping is today one of the most enigmatic figures in the history of China who is remembered both as the pragmatist saviour of modern China who dealt the *coup de grâce* to Mao's failed autarkic collectivist utopia in 1978 and the butcher of Beijing who unleashed his deadly wrath upon the 'ungrateful' students and other denizens of the ancient capital in 1989.
8. 'Beijing' or 'Beijing-Tiananmen' is a more appropriate appellation for the massacre than just 'Tiananmen', as most civilian casualties occurred not in Tiananmen Square but on Beijing streets leading to the square, especially Chang'an Avenue, when the People's Liberation Army clashed with residents and workers trying to protect the student demonstrators in Tiananmen Square during that fateful night of 3–4 June 1989.
9. In a way analogous to the French Revolution being hijacked by Maximilien Robespierre's Reign of Terror. Ch'en Tu-hsiu's socialism was but one of the twin manifestations of the spirit of the May Fourth Movement, the other being liberalism represented by Hu Shih.

10. While still rudimentary, the rehabilitation and other *de facto* de-Mao (i.e., refudiating Maoism) programmes, or even the liquidation of the research office of the central secretariat, and the closing-down of left-wing magazines, such as *Red Flag*, led the way to further internal structural reform of the CCP in the coming days (MacFarquhar, 2009: xxi).
11. The 1989 Tiananmen demonstrations being the first uprising in a the whole series of similar events that led to the demise of authoritarian rule in Eastern European countries and Mongolia, the fact that most of these countries were Soviet satellite states with Communist Party rule virtually planted by the USSR rather the result of, in the main, a part homegrown (though foreign-inspired) mass revolutionary movement, and that their 1989–1890 protest movements came after the shocking Beijing massacre, all apparently played a role in the diverse state responses between China and these states, perhaps with the exception of Romania, which took a popularly supported palace and army coup to overthrow the hated communist dictator Nicolae Ceauşescu.
12. Spontaneous as the 1989 Tiananmen protests were, the 'demonstrations that erupted on 4th May 1919 developed into a loose nationalist political movement that was one of the antecedents of the Communist Party's own official foundation in 1921' (Hutton, 2006: 7).
13. Notably, too, this was just less than a year after the anniversary of the posting by Wei Jingsheng of his manifesto, 'The Fifth Modernization', on the 'Democracy Wall' on the morning of 5 December 1978. The state responded by sentencing him to 15 years in prison. (Wei Jingsheng was the earlier vanguard of China's democracy movement and an electrician like the Polish labour union activist Lech Wałesa, who was later elected president of Poland after the fall of the Communist Party dictatorship.)
14. *Oriental Daily News* (*ODN*, Malaysia), 5 May 2011.
15. According to a report published on China's National Bureau of Statistics website on 14 January 2009, the confirmed 2007 GDP of China at current prices amounted to ¥25.7306 trillion, an increase of 13% from the previous year (*ODN*, 16 January 2009). While observed to be still short of a third of the US's GDP, analysts predicted China's GDP to overtake Japan's in three to four years, just as it overtook those of the UK and France in 2005 and Germany in 2008. Nevertheless, according to an announcement by Yi Gang, the director of the State Administration of Foreign Exchange and the deputy governor of China's central bank, the People's Bank of China, on 30 July 2010, China had already superseded Japan to become the world's second largest economy in 2010. However, in terms of GDP per capita, Japan's (US$37,800) was more than ten times that of China (US$3600) in 2009, and Japan's GDP per capita ranking, while having dropped from the world's number 2 in 1993 to number 23 by 2008, was still far ahead of China's, which ranked more than 100 (*ODN* , 9 August 2010).
16. *ODN*, 1 July 2011.
17. Ibid.
18. Ibid.
19. *ODN*, 11 June 2011.

20. *Weiquan* refers to the quest to protect and defend the civil rights of the citizenry by non-state actors. *Shangfang*, a centuries-old tradition in China, refers to the action of people with grievances who take the last resort of going to Beijing, the capital, to attempt to get their complaints heard against local injustice.
21. *ODN*, 11 June 2011.
22. Cited in Tilly (1985: 171).
23. Citing Lewis and Xue (2003: 933); Ma (2007); Xu (1999: 1, 168).
24. See e.g. Qi (2010: 420).
25. *ODN*, 27 July 2011 and 1 August 2011.
26. *ODN*, 30 July 2011.
27. *Apple Daily* (Hong Kong), 1 August 2011.
28. The June 1989 tragedy can be seen as the catalyst of the subsequent authoritarian corporatist evolution and reaffirmation of the path of economic reform (after Deng's *nanxun*) and economic success as realization of the root causes of the tragedy had served to spur the CCP into attempting to reinvent itself as a strong, benevolent and enlightened ruler (i.e. a *dictablanda*), or, as Thomas Hobbes wrote in his 1651 treatise, 'the generation of that great Leviathan':

    > The only way to erect such a common power, as may be able to defend them from the invasion of foreigners, and the injuries of one another...is, to confer all their power and strength upon one man, or upon one assembly of men, that may reduce all their wills, by plurality of voices, unto one will...This is the generation of that great Leviathan.

29. On the current crime trend in China, see also Yeoh (2010: 246–249).
30. Often ridiculed by the Chinese netizens with its homonym *hexie* (river crab).
31. *Yazhou Zhoukan*, 22(27), 13 July 2008, p. 4; see also Liu (2009).
32. *ODN*, 28 July 2011.
33. Thomas Paine, *The Age of Reason, Part First* (1794).
34. 'Hence shall we see,/If power change purpose, what our seemers be.' (William Shakespeare, *Measure for Measure*, Act I, Scene IV)
35. Defined as a 'mode of speech that persuades by stealth' (see Steven Poole's *Unspeak*™ (2006), which begins with a description of Confucius' 'Rectification of Names').
36. For instance, see Yu (2010) and Lin Chuo-shui, '*Liu Siaopo he Wen Chiapao te minchu lu*' ('The democracy road of Liu Xiaobo and Wen Jiabao'), at http://gb.udn.com/gb/blog.udn.com/baogon/4499978. Lin is a former legislator of Taiwan's Democratic Progressive Party.
37. *ODN*, 23 March 2012; *Apple Daily*, 22 March 2012, 23 March 2012, 26 March 2012.
38. See, for example, the 2005interview of the exiled dissident Yan Jiaqi, Zhao's advisor when he was premier at http://www.epochtimes.com/gb/5/1/30/n798431.htm
39. *Mencius*, edited and translated with an introduction by D.C. Lau, London: Penguin Books, 2005 (Penguin Classics first published in 1970).
40. Cited in Tong and Lei (2010: 499).
41. Cited in Benton (2010: 321).

References

Archer, M. S. (1988). *Culture and Agency: The Place of Culture in Social Theory*. Cambridge: Cambridge University Press.

Archer, M. S. (1995). *Realist Social Theory: The Morphogenetic Approach*. Cambridge: Cambridge University Press.

Archer, M. S. (1996). *Culture and Agency: The Place of Culture in Social Theory*, 2nd (revised) edition. Cambridge: Cambridge University Press.

Archer, M. S. (2000). *Being Human: The Problem of Agency*. Cambridge: Cambridge University Press.

Archer, M. S. (2003). *Structure, Agency and the Internal Conversation*. Cambridge: Cambridge University Press.

Benton, G. (2010). Dissent and the Chinese communists before and since the post-Mao reforms. *International Journal of China Studies*, 1(2), 239–308.

Bo, Z. (2010). China's model of democracy. *International Journal of China Studies*, 1(1), 102–124.

Bourdieu, P. (1974). Avenir de classe et causalité du probable. *Revue Française De Sociologie*, 15(1), 3–42.

Bourdieu, P. (1990). *In Other Words: Essays towards a Reflexive Sociology*. Stanford, CA: Stanford University Press.

Bourdieu, P. (2008), *Political Interventions: Social Science and Political Action*. London: Verso.

Buckley, W. (1967). *Sociology and Modern Systems Theory*. Englewood Cliffs, NJ: Prentice-Hall.

Dahrendorf, R. (1959). *Class and Class Conflict in Industrial Societies*. Stanford, CA: Stanford University Press.

Diamond, L. (2002). Elections without democracy: Thinking about hybrid regimes. *Journal of Democracy*, 13(2), 21–35.

Durkheim, É. (1895; translation 1938). *The Rules of Sociological Method*. Edited with introduction by S. Lukes (1982). New York: The Free Press.

Eisenstadt, S. N. (1992). A reappraisal of theories of social change and modernization. In H. Haferkamp, & N. J. Smelser (Eds.), *Social Change and Modernity* (pp. 412–429). Berkeley, CA: University of California Press.

Fan, Z., Song, E., & Yan, C. (2009, December). 2009 nian shehui zhi'an zhuangkuang fenxi (Analysis of the public security of China's society in 2009). In X. Ru, X. Lu, & P. Li (Eds.), *2010 nian Zhongguo shehui xingshi fenxi yu yuce* (Society of China: analysis and forecast (2010)] (*Shehui lan pi shu/Blue Book of China's Society*) (pp. 85–97). Beijing: Shehuikexue Wenxian Chubanshe (Social Science Academic Press, China).

Friedman, E. (2009). China: A threat to or threatened by democracy? *Dissent* (2009, winter). Retrieved from http://www.dissentmagazine.org/article/?article=1318.

Green, D. (2008). *From Poverty to Power: How Active Citizens and Effective States Can Change the World*. Washington, DC: Oxfam International.

Gunther, R. (1980). *Public Policy in a No-Party State: Spanish Planning and Budgeting in the Twilight of the Franquist Era*. Berkeley, CA: University of California Press.

Habermas, J. (1987). *Theory of Communicative Action, Vol. II: Lifeworld and System: A Critique of Functionalist Reason*. Boston, MA: Beacon Press.

Habermas, J. (1992). Individuation through socialization: On George Herbert Mead's theory of subjectivity. In W.M. Hohengarten (Trans.), *Postmetaphysical Thinking: Philosophical Essays*. Cambridge: MIT Press, 149–204.

Hardin, G. (1968). The tragedy of the commons. *Science*, 162(3859), 1243–1248.

Hobbes, T. (1651). *Leviathan, The Matter, Forme and Power of a Common Wealth Ecclesiasticall and Civil*, published by Andrew Crooke/Leviathan (Oxford World's Classics) (2009). New York: Oxford University Press.

Hung, C.-F. (2010). The politics of China's *Wei-Quan* movement in the internet age. *International Journal of China Studies*, 1(2), 331–349.

Hung, H.-F. (2011). Confucianism and political dissent in China. *East Asia Forum* (2011, July 26). Retrieved from http://www.eastasiaforum.org/2011/07/26/confucianism-and-political-dissent-in-china/.

Hutton, W. (2006). *The Writing on the Wall: China and the West in the 21st Century*. London: Little, Brown.

Katznelson, I. (1971). Power in the reformulation of race research. In P. Orleans, & W. R. Ellis, Jr (Eds.), *Race, Change, and Urban Society* (*Urban Affairs Annual Reviews*, 5). Beverly Hills, CA: Sage.

Lee, J.T.-H. (2011). Media and dissent in China: A review. *International Journal of China Studies*, 2(2), 525–529.

Lewis, J.W., & Xue L. (2003). Social change and political reform in China: Meeting the challenge of success. *The China Quarterly*, 176, 926–942.

Liu, Y.-S. (2010). *Chungkuo Tsui Chü Chengyi Te Jen: Wen Chiapao Ch'üanchuan* (China's Most Controversial Person: The Full Biography of Wen Jiabao). Hong Kong: Mingching Ch'upanshe (Mirror Books).

Liu, Z. (2009). *Xin qunti shijian guan: Guizhou Weng'an '6 • 28' shijian de qishi* (A new view on mass incidents: Implications of the 28 June (2008) Guizhou's Weng'an incident). Beijing: Xinhua Chubanshe.

Ma, Y. (2007). China's stubborn anti-democracy. *Policy Review*, 141, February–March. Retrieved from http://www.hoover.org/publications/policyreview/5513661.html.

MacFarquhar, R. (2009). Foreword. In Z. Zhao (posthumously), P. Bao, R. Chiang, & A. Ignatius (Eds., Trans.), *Prisoner of the State: The Secret Journal of Zhao Ziyang* (pp. xvii–xxv). New York: Simon & Schuster.

Marx, K. (1852). *The Eighteenth Brumaire of Louis Bonaparte*. Original version published in the first number of the monthly *Die Revolution* in 1852 (excerpts included in Karl Marx and Friedrich Engels: Basic writings on politics and philosophy, edited with introduction by L.S. Feuer. New York: Doubleday/Anchor Books, 1989).

Mead, G.H. (1934). *Mind, Self, and Society from the Standpoint of a Social Behaviorist* C.W. Morris (Eds.). Chicago, IL: University of Chicago Press.

O'Donnell, G., & Schmitter, P.C. (1986). *Transitions from Authoritarian rule: Tentative Conclusions about Uncertain Democracies*. Baltimore, MD: Johns Hopkins University Press.

Paine, T. (1776). *Common Sense*, Issued at Philadelphia (Edited with Introduction by I. Kramnick, Published by Penguin Books Ltd., Harmondsworth, Middlesex, England, 1976, reprinted 1986 (included in *The Life and Major Writings of Thomas Paine*, collected, edited and annotated by P.S. Foner. New York: Carol Publishing Group/Citadel Press, 1993).

Paine, T. (1794–1807). *The Age of Reason, Part First* (1794), *Part II* (1795) and *Part III* (1807) (included in *The Life and Major writings of Thomas Paine*, collected, edited and annotated by P.S. Foner. New York: Carol Publishing Group/Citadel Press, 1993).

Perry, E.J. (2002). *Challenging the Mandate of Heaven: Social Protest and State Power in China*. New York: M.E. Sharpe.

Poole, S. (2006). *Unspeak™*. London: Little, Brown.

Prigogine, I., & Stengers, I. (1984). *Order Out of Chaos: Man's New Dialogue with Nature*. New York: Bantam Books.

Qi, D. (2010). Chinese working class and trade unions in the post-Mao era: Progress and predicament. *International Journal of China Studies*, 1(2), 413–433.

Reeler, D. (2007). *A Three-Fold Theory of Social Change and Implications for Practice, Planning, Monitoring and Evaluation*. Woodstock: CDRA.

Stepan, A. (1985). State power and the strength of civil society in the Southern Cone of Latin America. In P.B. Evans, D. Rueschemeyer, & T. Skocpol (Eds.), *Bringing the State Back in* (pp. 317–343). Cambridge: Cambridge University Press.

Stinchcombe, A.L. (1968). *Constructing Social Theories*. Chicago, IL: University of Chicago Press.

Tilly, C. (1985). War making and state making as organized crime. In P.B. Evans, D. Rueschemeyer, & T. Skocpol (Eds.), *Bringing the State Back in* (pp. 169–191). Cambridge: Cambridge University Press.

Tong, Y., & Lei, S. (2010). Large-scale mass incidents and government responses in China. *International Journal of China Studies*, 1(2), 487–508.

Touraine, A. (1969). *La société post-industrielle: Naissance d'une société*. Paris: Éditions du Seuil.

Touraine, A. (1973). *Production de la société*. Paris: Éditions du Seuil.

Touraine, A. (1978). *La Voix Et Le Regard*. Paris: Éditions du Seuil. (Translated as *The Voice and the Eye: An Analysis of Social Movements*. Cambridge: Cambridge University Press, & Paris: Éditions de La Maison des Sciences de l'Homme (1981)).

Wasserstrom, J. (2009). Two decades after the fall: Patterns of Chinese protest – 1919, 1989, 2009. *Dissent* (2009, September 29). Retrieved from http://www.dissentmagazine.org/online.php?id=291.

Womack, B. (2011). Modernization and the Sino-Vietnamese model. *International Journal of China Studies*, 2(2), 157–175.

Xu, B. (1999). *Disenchanted Democracy: Chinese Cultural Criticism after 1989*. Ann Arbor, MI: University of Michigan Press.

Yeoh, E.K.-K. (2010). Changing China: Three decades of social transformation. *International Journal of China Studies*, 1(2), 239–308.

Yu, J. (2010). *Chungkuo yingti Wen Chiapao* (China's best actor Wen Jiabao). Hong Kong: Hsin Shihchi Ch'upanshe (New Century Press).

Zheng, Y. (1999). *Zhu Rongji xinzheng: Zhongguo gaige de xin moshi* (Zhu Rongji's new deal: A new model for reforming China). Singapore: World Scientific.

Section II

Culture

6
Organizational Leadership Decision Making in Asia: The Chinese Ways

Alexandre A. Bachkirov

Introduction

Decision making constitutes the essence of leadership. Whether it is related to strategy formulation, corporate policies on sustainability, a product range review, a budget approval, or the agenda of a meeting, the leader's role is fundamentally about making decisions. The outcomes of good leadership decisions are numerous and important: strong follower commitment, smooth teamwork, strong employee motivation and job satisfaction, enhanced performance, sustained competitive advantage and, ultimately, superior value creation for customers and shareholders. Not surprisingly, organizational decision processes in general have been persistently investigated and discussed (Bazerman & Moore, 2008; Beach & Connolly, 2005; Shapira, 1997), and decision making as the primary leadership activity has been continuously emphasized (Kotter, 1990; Mintzberg, Ahlstrand & Lampel, 1998; Yukl, 2002). As a distinct research domain, leadership decision making has remained in the focus of scholarly attention for decades (Aldag, 2012; Guerra-Lopez & Blake, 2011; Lipshitz & Mann, 2005; Paul & Ebadi, 1989; Simon, 1997; Vroom & Yetton, 1973; Westaby, Probst & Lee, 2010).

In organizational science, decision making is defined in many ways. The definitions range from very concise, such as "a commitment to action" (Mintzberg, 1983:188), to more extended, such as "a moment, in an ongoing process of evaluating alternatives for meeting an objective, at which expectations about a particular course of action impel the decision maker to select that course of action most likely to result in attaining the object" (Harrison, 1995:4). For our purposes, leadership decision making is defined as a cognitive-emotional activity involving information processing, which leads to the selection of, and a commitment to, a course of action aimed at achieving desirable organizational outcomes. This definition will focus the discussion presented in this chapter.

One direction in recent decision research stands out as being particularly critical for leadership theory and practice at the beginning of the 21st century: the impact of national cultures on decision making. The assumption that decision making has characteristics that are universal across national cultures has proved to be unsustainable (Peterson, Miranda, Smith & Haskell, 2003). There is now ample and growing evidence to suggest that national cultures cause significant dissimilarities in this cognitive process (Atran, Medin & Ross, 2005; Brooks, 1994; Carr & Harris, 2004; Chu, Spires & Sueyoshi, 1999; Güss & Dörner, 2011; Rouzies, Segalla & Weitz, 2003; Schramm-Nielsen, 2001; Tse, Lee, Vertinsky & Wehrung, 1988).

While Chinese decision making has already received some research attention (Yates & Lee, 1996), the focus on Chinese organizational decision making is motivated by the country's growing global presence (Arora & Vamvakidis, 2011). An understanding of how Chinese organizational leaders arrive at a choice is increasingly becoming a matter of strategic wisdom (Olson, Bao & Parayitam, 2007). This chapter takes stock of what has been achieved in the field so far and is organized as follows. To set the scene, the sources of Chinese culture are briefly reviewed, and the aspects which are most relevant to organizational leadership are emphasized. An important consequence of the Chinese cultural tradition is a paternalistic leadership style, which is discussed next. After that, a description of the general thinking pattern of Chinese decision makers is presented, and the research on decision modes is reviewed. This is followed by an examination of specific types of leadership decision. First, stock market decisions, risk perceptions, and risk preferences of Chinese decision makers are described, and their implications for leadership decision making are discussed. Then compensation decisions by Chinese organizational leaders are examined, given the critical role which reward allocation decisions play in employee motivation and, ultimately, in organizational performance. Finally, the effects of Chinese national culture on the ethical dimensions of leadership decision making are described. The chapter concludes with a sketch of the Chinese organizational decision maker, and emphasizes the need for clear and accurate contextualization of future research.

Chinese culture

Chinese culture is a complex amalgam of diverse traditions, and this complexity is evident at various levels. Historically the Chinese cultural landscape has been formed by Confucianism, Taoism, Buddhism, Legalism, and the Art of War (Pan, Rowney & Peterson, 2011). By and large, the teachings of Confucius are a major component of Chinese culture structure. The core of this worldview comprises a set of moral virtues – for example, societal harmony and stability through a hierarchy of unequal social relationships, dedication to collective interests, filial piety, respect, humanness, reciprocity, and long-term orientation[1] (Hill, 2006; Ip, 2009; Xing, 1995). Leaders embracing Confucian tradition would be expected to promote group harmony, teamwork, and concern for followers. They would also exhibit a self-sacrificial attitude, build cordial relationships, and execute the leadership authority with kindness (Rarick, 2009). Another major Chinese cultural tradition is Taoism. This is based on the belief that the universe is ruled by two equally powerful forces, yin and yang, which are also manifested in human societies and organizations (Bai & Roberts, 2011; Fang, 2010). When these forces are in a harmonious balance, goodness ensues; if the balance is broken, evil surges (Rarick, 2009). Therefore, Taoist leaders who would have such traits as flexibility and humility would embrace multiple perspectives when making decisions, seek consensus in conflict situations, avoid actively exerting influence on followers and would generally keep a low profile (Johnson, 2000). Following a recent study by Pan et al. (2011), who conducted an analysis of the structure of Chinese culture, it can be reasonably assumed that the decisions of Chinese organizational leaders would reflect such cultural values as harmony, hierarchy, and reciprocity (Confucianism); simplicity and non-strife (Taoism); mercy and restraint (Buddhism); keeping potential, manipulation, and concealing weakness (Legalism); planning, strategizing, non-fight, and deceit (Art of War). It must be strongly emphasized that because of a diverse cultural heritage, some native Chinese can be expected to be influenced by one particular tradition, whereas others will follow a different set of principles (Pan et al., 2011).

Modern oriental Chinese societies

Geographically, modern oriental Chinese societies include the People's Republic of China (PRC), also known as mainland China, Taiwan, and Hong Kong. The historically recent influences experienced by these societies have been diverse (Li, Fu, Chow & Peng, 2002), which has resulted in a certain differentness between their modern cultures. Because cross-national studies, including those on leadership and decision-making, have been conducted with Chinese participants of different cultural origins, it is helpful briefly to review the salient characteristics of modern oriental Chinese societies.

The People's Republic of China

In the second half of the 20th century, the PRC experienced the powerful economic and political influence of the former USSR. Chinese cultural heritage suffered a devastating blow during a series of state-sponsored initiatives, including the Cultural Revolution (1966–1976). The Marxist-Leninist ideology of Mao Zedong (Ladany, 1988), Maoism, attempted to remove Confucianism by indoctrinating people with the ideology of the Chinese Communist Party and to create a society based on the principles of collective ownership and collective identity, conformity, self-sacrifice in favour of the state's interests, and complete social equality with no class distinctions (Vohra, 2000). The societal reality into which this ideology materialized was a highly centralized command and control system stimulating the survivalist pursuit of personal bureaucratic power (Inglehart, 1997).

Economic revival, which started in 1978, has turned the PRC into a global trade player and has caused deep sociocultural changes. Despite the decades of supremacy of Maoist ideology, the country is now described as "network capitalism" (Boisot & Child, 1996), with a unique blend of revived Confucian values (Ip, 2009), and growing materialistic and individualistic trends in thinking, attitudes, and behaviours among the younger population (Rosen, 1990). This observation was confirmed by Fang (2010), who noted that in the PRC, traditional values coexist with their recently emerging opposites – for example, family/group orientation and individualization, aversion to the law and respect for legal practices, importance of face and directness, age/hierarchy and competence. From an organizational perspective, the most important perceived goals of business leaders in the PRC include respecting ethical norms, being a patriot, power, honour, reputation (face), and responsibility, whereas the least important goals, among others, are personal wealth and staying within the law (Hofstede, Van Deusen, Mueller, Charles & the Business Goals Network, 2002). A recent study (Fernandez, Carlson, Stepina & Nicholson, 1997) across the four classic cultural dimensions found that business professionals in the PRC score high on power distance, uncertainty avoidance, and masculinity, but score below the mean on individualism – that is, they can be considered a collectivistic society.[2] In management contexts specifically, it was shown that organizational leaders in the PRC have comparatively lower tolerance of uncertainty (Cragin, 1986; Leong, Bond & Fu, 2006), rely heavily on rules, procedures, colleagues, and subordinates (Smith, Peterson & Wang, 1996), are status conscious, and have pronounced autocratic tendencies (Li et al., 2002). At the same time, Wang (2011), revealing the changing nature of organizational leadership in the PRC, found that the new Chinese are "supportive, caring, engaging, self-disciplined, unselfish, responsible, and knowledgeable" (p. 16) and involve subordinates in decision-making processes rather than simply exercising power and control.

Taiwan

In contrast to the PRC, in contemporary Taiwan, which was deeply impacted by the Japanese and the Americans, the societally sanctioned cultural values encompass progressiveness, democratic attitude, self-reliance, and independence (Yang, 1991). It was also demonstrated that Taiwanese leaders are highly diplomatic and procedural (Li et al., 2002), and that Taiwanese entrepreneurs score lower levels of uncertainty avoidance and power distance in comparison with the respondents from the PRC (McGrath, Macmillan, Yang & Tsai, 1992).

Hong Kong

The economic and sociocultural environment of this society was shaped by more than 150 years of British rule, which promoted an entrepreneurial spirit, a proactive and self-reliant stance, and risk-taking behaviours. However, living "in a borrowed place and on borrowed time" (Hughes, 1968) encouraged a preference for short-term orientation. An analysis of data obtained from the Global Leadership and Organizational Behavior Effectiveness Project (House et al., 1999) revealed further variations in leaders' characteristics in modern oriental Chinese societies – for example, organizational leaders in Hong Kong were found to be highly autonomous whereas in the PRC and Taiwan they tend to value collectivism, and they have pronounced and collaborative team orientation.

Such heterogeneity of cultural roots and leadership behaviour profiles could make it challenging to identify factors shaping the "Chinese ways" of making decisions in organizations. Yet despite the noted dissimilarities, modern oriental Chinese societies do possess a number of important cultural commonalities. To begin with, a deeply rooted Chinese notion of *guanxi* – the practice of developing networks and maintaining personal connections in order to secure reciprocal exchange of favours in personal, organizational, or business relationships (Fan, Woodbine & Scully, 2012; Park & Luo, 2001; Yen, Barnes & Wang, 2011) – is probably a common underlying cultural phenomenon for all Chinese societies. According to Yen, Barnes, & Wang (2011), the quality of *guanxi* is measured by the related concepts of *ganqing* (emotional connectedness, the sharing of feelings, social bonding, loyalty), *renqing* (empathy, reciprocity-based obligation, and an ongoing exchange of favours), and *xinren* (trust, confidence in and dependence on an associate). An important organizational implication of *guanxi* is that it can make it difficult to identify one sole "real" decision maker. As Davies, Leung, Luk, & Wong (1995) suggested, this is because, in all probability, the actual decision maker is the *guanxi* network itself.

Within the Western conceptual frameworks, Chinese culture has been demonstrated to be high in power distance and in collectivism (Bond, 1996; Chinese Culture Connection, 1987; Cragin, 1986; Hofstede, 2007; Hofstede & Hofstede, 2005; Schwartz, 1994). In addition, paternalism, personalism, and insecurity/defensiveness (Redding & Hsiao, 1990) constitute another set of common underlying cultural aspects. Here, paternalism is conceptualized as a social force which maintains order in a society through basic societal units like families rather than a legislative system and law-enforcing institutions. Personalism is based on mutual interpersonal obligations and entails establishing, developing, and maintaining connections for the purposes of everyday transactions. Finally, insecurity/defensiveness, as a cultural pattern, is said to stem from the age-old exploitative nature of Chinese social structures. In terms of leadership behaviours, the GLOBE project data revealed important similarities in leadership styles across the PRC, Taiwan, and Hong Kong: some of the most preferred leadership characteristics were shown to be performance orientation, administrative competence, decisiveness, and integrity, while some of the common least preferred leadership characteristics include being malevolent and self-centred (Li et al., 2002). These characteristics shared by the Chinese of diverse cultural backgrounds encourage the quest to find the essence of Chinese organizational decision making. Therefore, in order to avoid a reductionist approach, it is judicious to consider empirical findings generated by research in all modern oriental Chinese societies.

Chinese personality

This introductory discussion would not be complete without brief reference to Chinese personality. While there is an association between cultural dimensions and personality traits, the debate about the causal direction of this relationship has not been settled. One stance suggests that culture explains personality; the opposite viewpoint maintains that culture is a product of personality structure – that is, aggregates of nation-level personality traits (Hofstede & McCrae, 2004). Without taking either side in this debate, it is worth acknowledging a growing body of relevant work. For instance, Schmitt, Allik, McCrae, & Benet-Martinez (2007) discovered that, out of ten world regions, East Asians score the lowest on extraversion, agreeableness, conscientiousness, and openness, while they score the highest on neuroticism. As regards the Chinese personality specifically, Dong & Liu (2010), summarizing previous research, noted that the Chinese score high on straightforwardness, compliance, dogmatism, and external locus of control, but they score low on altruism and Machiavellianism. An additional Chinese personality trait which has not been captured by models developed in the West is interpersonal relatedness (Cheung, Leung, Zhang, Sun, Gan, Song & Xie, 2001).

An important organizational consequence of the Chinese cultural tradition is the paternalistic leadership style (Aycan, 2006; Cheng, Chou, Wu, Huang & Farh, 2004; Farh & Cheng, 2000; Redding, 1990; Silin, 1976; Westwood, 1997). The characteristics of Chinese organizational paternalism and its consequences for leadership decision making are discussed next.

Paternalistic leadership

The roots of Chinese paternalistic leadership can be traced back to Confucian philosophy (Kao, Sek-Hong & Kwan, 1990). A comprehensive model of this concept was developed by Westwood (1997) and included three components: general structural context (centralization, low/selective formalization, and non-complexity), general relational context (harmony-building, relationship maintenance, and moral leadership), and personalism. These are crystallized into specific stylistic elements: didactic leadership, non-specific intentions, reputation-building, protection of dominance, political manipulation, patronage and nepotism, conflict diffusion, aloofness and social distance, and dialogue ideal. More recent research identified three dimensions of paternalistic leadership in China: benevolence, authoritarianism, and morality (Cheng, Chou & Farh, 2000; Cheng et al., 2004; Farh & Cheng, 2000). These underlie the decisions of Chinese organizational leaders and are conceptualized as follows:

Benevolence refers to a holistic concern for the well-being of followers and their families; benevolent leaders provide individualized care, grant favours, understand, and forgive; they establish and maintain a family-type environment in the work setting and nurture an informal personalized relationship with subordinates.

Authoritarianism is defined as a behavioural tendency to assert unquestionable authority over the group members while, at the same time, to expect their absolute obedience, complete subordination, and compliance without dissent. Specific behaviours comprise establishing absolute power and control, powerfully subduing followers, hiding intentions, maintaining rigorous standards, and upholding a doctrine.

Moral leadership is manifested in superior personal moral virtues of paternalistic leaders, their unselfishness, and self-discipline, and it is visible through such behaviours as showing integrity, being "a selfless paragon", fulfilling one's duties, and not taking advantage of others.

To better understand the effects of Chinese paternalism on leadership decision making, it is important to consider the responses of followers. According to Cheng et al. (2004), these are mostly positive. Chinese paternalistic leadership elicits in followers a feeling of gratitude and a desire to repay the leaders.[3] In addition, the followers experience affection for their leaders and want to depend on, identify with, and imitate them. All of this prompts the followers completely to obey the leader's instructions and comply with their decisions, even though the followers themselves may have a different view on the subject matter at hand (Niu, Wang & Cheng, 2009). The attitudes underlying such behaviours are revealed by the followers' belief that their leaders are always right in the decisions that they make (Cheng et al., 2004). Within this paternalistic context, Chinese organizational leaders may obtain opinions of trusted associates before making important choices but, ultimately, they make decisions by themselves and do not reveal their personal intentions and action policy in order to maintain their decision-making space (Hsieh & Chen, 2011). Interestingly, it was argued that a hidden agenda in the decisions of powerful organizational members results in such leadership outcomes as a reduction in the control costs, lower staff turnover, enhanced organizational commitment, loyalty, and improved teamwork (for a review, see Aycan, 2006).

As a final comment on paternalistic leadership, it is worth noting that this style is typical of high power distance cultures, including China (House, Hanges, Javidan, Dorfman & Gupta, 2004). Because in high power distance contexts the delegation of decision-making authority tends to be perceived as leadership inadequacy (Offermann, 2004), it can be reasonably speculated that Chinese organizational leaders will be unlikely to entrust responsibilities to followers and engage in such practices as participative leadership and empowerment.

Decision making of Chinese organizational leaders: A psychological perspective

This section begins by reflecting on the general thinking style of East Asians. The subsequent discussion is focused on the areas which have recently been at the centre of scholarly attention and produced stimulating empirical results. It reviews the findings on decision modes and integrates research on how culturally shaped thought processes impact specific categories of leadership decisions, including stock-market decisions, risky choice, reward allocation decisions, and ethical decision making.

Holistic thinking of Chinese decision makers

The thinking style of East Asians, including the Chinese, is influenced by Confucian culture and is often referred to as holistic thinking[4] (Peng & Nisbett, 1999). The characteristics of cognitive holism include field-centredness,[5] expectation of change in the *status quo*, and tolerance of contradictions (Choi, Dalal, Kim-Prieto & Park, 2003; Nisbett, Peng, Choi & Norenzayan, 2001; Spencer-Rodgers, Williams & Peng, 2010). Decision-making consequences of holism are that Chinese leaders can be expected to consider a significantly greater amount of information than their Western colleagues (cf. Choi, Dalal, Kim-Prieto & Park, 2003), associate a situation with more causes, contemplate more consequences (cf. Maddux & Yuki, 2006), and seek integrative compromising solutions rather than pursue only one possible "correct" decision (Spencer-Rodgers et al., 2010). Importantly, such a holistic approach would cause Chinese leaders to be more tolerant of contradictory cues in the environment and view inconsistency as normal and acceptable behaviour. Conceptually, holistic thinking is associated with what is known as *Zhong Yong* (or *Chung Yung*) – the Doctrine of the Mean (Chan, 1963) – rooted in the teachings of Confucius. Here, "the mean" refers to a state characterized by equilibrium or harmony, with no "inclination to either side". The Doctrine of the Mean also suggests that a single truth does not exist and that it is multiple truths that make up reality; the inevitable paradoxes generated by this view prompt a synthesis-based reasoning process attempting to resolve the apparent contradictions.

Decision modes

Recent research further unveiled distinctive features of decision-making behaviour typical of this part of Asia. For instance, it was demonstrated that in comparison with Americans, the Chinese tend to use more recognition-based decision making (role-, case-, and rule-based decision-processing), arrive at a decision in a less analytical fashion, exhibit a more pronounced orientation towards locomotion (i.e. making a decision and moving on) and they are inclined to favour decisions which are less prevention focused (Weber, Ames & Blais, 2005). To elaborate, in role-based decision making it is a role-predetermined behavioural code that automatically and implicitly shapes the decision; the evaluative processes to assess advantages and disadvantages of alternative courses of action are not engaged at all. The underlying mechanism of role-based decision processes is rooted in the collectivistic culture of the Chinese: leaders feel discouraged from making self-serving decisions when such self-centredness is contrary to the interests of their in-group. In respect of rule-based choice, this mode of decision making derives from a set of situation-specific and explicit rules of conduct which have been learned, acquired, assimilated, or otherwise internalized by the person. Given that a salient characteristic of Chinese national culture is *guanxi*, Chinese leadership decisions are likely to be determined by a sense of social obligation to engage in a specific course of action. In other words, due to the great value which the culture places on interconnectedness, Chinese leadership decision-making will be driven by socially sanctioned rules. As regards the case-based decision mode, it is associated with the processes of recognizing similarities between the current situation and a past situation in which a decision problem was successfully solved. Therefore, effective decision making by a Chinese leader would, in the first place, necessitate a substantial number of past dilemmas and their effective resolution being stored in his/her memory. A second requirement is the person's well-developed ability to classify past experiences in order accurately and rapidly to identify which one of these experiences can be used as a precedent in the solution of the analogous situation at hand.

The prevalence of role-, rule-, and case-based decision modes may suggest that Chinese decision makers can be expected to be less prone to analytical, calculation-based decision-processing. In other words,

Chinese decision processes would not typically involve decomposing alternatives and weighing up their pros and cons, conducting a cost–benefit analysis of available options, or trying to identify the final choice of alternatives which have the best value for the decision maker. Indeed, it was demonstrated (Weber et al., 2005) that in this part of Asia, decisions are made less analytically. One implication is that, for instance, the calculation of the best alternative would be a comparatively less frequent strategy used in Chinese leadership decision making. This is in agreement with earlier work (Nisbett, 2003; Nisbett et al., 2001) suggesting that the Chinese mind embraces holistic thought, rather than analytical reasoning, and views paradoxes as interdependent rather than exclusive opposites (Chen, 2002).

Leadership decisions: stock market and risky choice

When deliberating, Chinese decision makers attend not only to a comparatively larger breadth of context-relevant information but also to its greater historical depth (Ji, Guo, Messervey & Zhang, 2009). In addition, while Westerners tend to believe that the current state of events and objects will continue into the future, the Chinese mind predicts a constant change – for example, an activity will lead to stagnation, a standstill will turn into a motion, what moves fast will slow down, and so on. In other words, change is emphasized more than stability (Ji, Nisbett & Su, 2001). These characteristics of the Chinese national culture have been empirically detected in research on stock market decisions to buy or sell. For instance, Ji, Zhang, and Guo (2008) demonstrated that in comparison with Westerners, the Chinese do not make linear predictions; they expect change rather than stability. In practical terms this means that if, for example, Canadians would buy when the latest trend for stock prices is to rise but sell when the stock prices are falling, Chinese investment decision makers would follow the opposite predictions: they would buy when the stock trend is down and sell when it is up. These observations of investment decisions reveal how the Chinese relate to time. In contrast with Westerners, who construct the future as being similar to and a continuation of the immediate past and/or present, the Chinese perception is that the past, present, and future create a non-linear cycle (Ji et al., 2001; 2008). These findings suggest that an important consequence of Chinese national culture for organizational leadership decisions is that these are unlikely to be ultimately determined by instant information, immediate trends, or recent events. It is the consideration of preceding occurrences, foregoing situations, and earlier experiences, on the one hand, and the expectation of change, fluidity, and reversals, on the other hand, that will drive Chinese organizational leaders in their decision making.

Interesting effects of national culture have been found for risk perceptions (Weber & Milliman, 1997), which, in turn, influence choice-related risk preferences in financial decision making. A series of studies demonstrated that the Chinese are more risk-seeking (Hsee & Weber, 1999; Weber, Hsee & Sokolowska, 1998; Weber & Morris, 2010) and perceive uncertain financial prospects as less risky in comparison with Americans (Weber & Hsee, 1998; Weber & Hsee, 1999). These results were interpreted in the light of a "cushion effect" hypothesis. According to this, the tendency for the Chinese to be less risk averse can be explained by the high level of collectivism within Chinese culture. Specifically, it was argued that in collectivistic societies like China, individuals have access to comparatively larger economic support networks (families and other in-groups), which provide assistance in a worst-case scenario – for example, ruinous financial loss following a risky choice. In other words, it is a cultural expectation that if the worst comes to the worst, the decision maker will not be left alone to absorb losses. It is a feeling of being protected by their in-groups that influences the risk preferences of Chinese decision makers and prompts them to be less risk averse. Additional evidence of risk-seeking behaviour of Chinese decision makers comes from a study by Brumagim and Wu (2005), who examined the attitude towards risk by testing the prospect theory (Kahneman & Tversky, 1979). According to this, decision makers perceive potential losses more acutely than potential gains and, as a consequence, are more risk-seeking in situations that are perceived as leading to losses and more risk-avoiding in situations that are perceived as associated with potential gains. Prospect theory has been shown to predict a wide range of decision behaviours across many different domains, such as consumer behaviour, marketing, finance, management, health care and medicine, politics, international relations, sociology, law, and communication (Maule & Villejoubert, 2007). However, contrary to the predictions of prospect theory, risk-seeking behaviour is preponderant in China not only in loss situations but also in gain situations. Importantly, the pattern of risk-seeking behaviour was evident across different scenarios – for example, financial, medical, and family decision making (Brumagim & Wu, 2005).

It is important to acknowledge, however, that the postulations of the "cushion effect" hypothesis and the findings on the risk-seeking behaviour of Chinese decision makers are inconsistent with the Doctrine of the Mean. According to this traditional cultural value, the

Chinese can be expected to pursue non-extreme outcomes in a choice situation, which implies risk-averse rather than risk-seeking preferences and behaviours. Indeed, several studies demonstrated the risk aversion of Chinese decision makers (Bian & Keller, 1999; Feng, Keller & Zheng, 2011; Gong, 2003). Interestingly, Li, Bi, and Zhang (2009) directly tested the "cushion effect" hypothesis and found no support for it: participants in the family decision-making condition were not more risk-seeking than those involved in individual decision making. Advancing a counterargument, Li et al. (2009) suggested that, rather than being a "cushion" which could potentially absorb negative consequences of a poor decision, a tight social network, or family, acts in the capacity of a "restrainer". The awareness of being an integral part of a tight social network and feeling responsible for the well-being of its members holds the decision maker back because a poor decision can implicate everybody and set them back financially. Thus, the collectivistic nature of Chinese society still has an effect on risk preferences and attitudes, yet the prediction is in the opposite direction. Rather than promoting risk-seeking, the collectivistic orientation causes Chinese decision makers to avoid risks.

By way of concluding this section, it may be pertinent to stress that organizational leaders are increasingly required effectively to deal with a variety of risks related to technology, instabilities, and uncertainties in the financial sector, as well as natural and man-made disasters, terrorist activities, flu pandemics and so on. Importantly, risks are intrinsically related to crises and catastrophes, and many become borderless in nature (Smith & Fischbacher, 2009). Are Chinese organizational leaders risk-seeking or risk-averse? It appears that the current empirical findings are inconclusive. Given the growing impact of the Chinese world on the global economy, further research is urgently required to answer this important question.

Leadership decisions: Reward allocation

Particularly sensitive and critically important for employee motivation and performance are leadership decisions related to reward allocation – for example, salary increases and bonuses. These decisions have great potential either to stimulate the performance of team members if made correctly, or utterly to dispirit them if the leader makes fundamentally wrong decisions. The four distributive principles which can be employed to allocate rewards – equity, equality, need, and seniority or tenure (Fischer, 2004; Fischer & Smith, 2003) – are likely to be differentially favoured by different national cultures.[6]

Preliminary findings on the influence of culture on reward allocation decisions are inconsistent. Some work (Erez, 1997; Leung, 1997) suggests that it is the cultural dimension of collectivism-individualism that exerts a defining influence on reward-allocation decisions. Specifically, individualistic cultures tend to rely on the equity-based reward allocation principle, whereas collectivistic societies employ the needs, seniority, and equality rules for in-group members and the equity rule for out-group members (James, 1993; Smith & Bond, 1998). In addition to the collectivism-individualism cultural syndrome, Hofstede's dimension of masculinity–femininity (Hofstede, 1983; Hofstede & Hofstede, 2005) was speculated to induce a reliance on the equity principle in compensation decisions (Kim, Park & Suzuki, 1990).

Initial research into Chinese approaches to distribution of awards confirmed the proposition that collectivism-individualism plays a defining role in this type of leadership decision. Zhou and Martocchio (2001) showed that when deciding on monetary rewards – for example, bonus allocation – Chinese decision makers de-emphasize employees' work performance while being sensitive to their needs. Such a pattern is suggestive of a blend of egalitarian and needs-based approaches rather than an equitable solution. However, other studies (e.g. Fischer & Smith, 2003) conclude that hierarchical cultural dimensions (Schwartz, 1994), not collectivism, can better explain differences in reward-allocation decisions. A related argument holds that the dimension of collectivism needs to be refined in order to be a more accurate predictor (Chen, Meindl & Hunt, 1997). To achieve this, Chen et al. (1997) used the constructs of vertical and horizontal collectivism[7] (Triandis, 1995; Triandis & Gelfand, 1998) and demonstrated that in the PRC, these dimensions have differing effects on the attitude towards reforms of the egalitarian compensation system: while vertical collectivists were supportive of reforms, horizontal collectivists were against them. Further research confirmed these findings. The study by He, Chen, and Zhang (2004) found that vertical collectivism is associated with preferences for the principle of differential allocation of rewards, whereas horizontal collectivism is linked with the principle of equalitarian allocation. Overall, it appears that in the PRC, organizational leaders use multiple approaches to ensure the acceptance of their reward-allocation decisions by followers in the context of the country's transition from a centralized egalitarian command-and-control system to a free-market, contribution-oriented economy. Where the organization embraces traditional collectivistic values, the extent of monetary rewards will be unaffected by the individual's outstanding skills and performance, while consideration of needs will be given a priority. In contrast, firms open to capitalist ideology and to methods of compensation based on individual contribution will expect their leaders to employ the equity principle in their reward-allocation decisions.

Ethical decision making

This final section is devoted to ethical decision making. In the West, recent high-profile scandals ensuing from unethical behaviour by business leaders highlighted the extent to which the disregard for morality can be devastating for people, organizations, and society as whole (Carson, 2003). Increasing realization of the criticality of ethical behaviour for business success triggered intensive research into ethical decision making (Ford & Richardson, 1994). However, it is important to acknowledge that it may be very difficult directly to translate the notions of right and wrong from one culture into another (Cherry, 2006; Weltzien Hovik, 2007). For instance, *guanxi* is perceived to be ethical by Chinese people (Lovett, Simmons & Kali, 1999), yet it was shown to be negatively correlated with the Western notion of social corporate responsibility (Ang & Leong, 2000). Similarly, Hooker (2009) argues that what is perceived as natural and acceptable in the West – for example, litigation and lawsuits – is rejected as corrupting ways of life by East Asian societies which value harmony, humility, and conflict avoidance. The reverse is also true: what in the West is viewed as corruption – for example, cronyism and nepotism – is a legitimate practice, the foundation for trust, and a way to increase efficiency and effectiveness elsewhere.

Reflecting this proposition, research on Chinese ethical decision-making so far has yielded inconsistent results and the most likely reason for this is probably related to the different frame of reference used. On the one hand, it is argued that the principal source of Chinese business ethics is Confucian paternalism (Cheng et al., 2000). In a Confucian context, for example, the decision of a Chinese leader to employ a relative rather than a non-family member may represent a utility-maximizing choice. The first-hand and intimate knowledge of the job-relevant strengths and weaknesses of this relative will enable the leader "to extract" more work out of this employee (Hooker, 2009). Similarly, Resick, Martin, Keating, Dickson, Kwan, and Peng (2011) put forward the importance of Confucianism in shaping the ethical dimension of leadership in Chinese oriental societies. For instance, in the PRC, ethical decisions would be driven by principles of consideration and respect for others, fairness, and non-discriminatory treatment, while decisions of unethical leadership would entail acting in self-interest and misusing power. In Hong Kong, ethical decisions would emphasize collective orientation, and consideration and respect for others, whereas unethical leaders would make decisions based on dishonesty and deceit. Finally, in Taiwan, accountability would be an underlying principle of ethical decisions, whereas a dominant characteristic of unethical decision making would be acting in self-interest and misusing power.

Despite a clear emphasis on ethical values in leadership decisions (Resick et al., 2011), some research findings point in the opposite direction. For instance, Li and Persons (2011) looked into how such cultural characteristics as power distance, collectivism-individualism, socioeconomic values (e.g. distinction between privately owned versus collectively owned assets), and rule of law versus rule of men affect decision making in corporate contexts. Li and Persons (2011) showed that Chinese decision makers tend to make comparatively fewer ethical decisions in various areas of the corporate business ethics code, including compliance with laws, proper use of company assets, and reporting of unethical behaviour – that is, whistle-blowing. Yet, although from a Western perspective the identified decision-making behaviours are viewed as unethical, these can be interpreted as congruent with the culturally shaped Chinese moral values. The ensuing discussion illustrates this point.

To begin with, the study by Li and Persons (2011) is based on a corporate code of ethics which, in essence, is a collection of formalized rules to be followed by organizational members. Yet in a Chinese context it is not rules but relationships, and particularly long-term relationships of mutual obligation, which create a background against which the ethicality of decisions is established (Hooker, 2009). Therefore, it can be expected that in a context in which impersonal rules are divorced from personalized relationships, Chinese organizational leadership decisions will be influenced by the latter rather than the former.

As regards proper use of company assets, it may be helpful to explore how Chinese organizational leaders would form causal judgements about fraudulent[8] behaviour. For example, the study by Wong-On-Wing and Lui (2007) revealed that the Chinese are comparatively more sensitive to the characteristics of the surrounding context when making judgements about whether or not the behaviour of the person involved in a fraudulent act is moral or immoral.[9] The consequences of two aspects of the situational context on moral attributions were investigated: conditions of low choice versus high choice, and whether a fraudulent act is committed for a collective rationale or for an individual rationale. The findings revealed that Chinese decision makers imply that the person is less immoral under conditions of low choice to be involved in a fraudulent act, and in situations when the fraudulent behaviour is driven by a collective rationale. These results were explained within the approach of holistic causality (Choi et al., 2003). That is, in the world around, everything is related to everything else; therefore, if the causality and its direction need to be ascertained, one should scrutinize the interaction between the object and the field in which it is embedded (Choi & Nisbett, 2000).

Finally, the research on whistle-blowing in Chinese organizations has not yielded conclusive results. While it was shown that the practice of reporting unethical behaviour is sensitive to the cultural syndrome of collectivism, the effects were shown to be inconsistent. For instance, Zhuang, Thomas, and Miller (2005) found that, in comparison with Westerners, Chinese employees are more likely to report unethical acts; they are also more likely to report unethical behaviours of peers than those of supervisors. The argument employed to explain these findings stems from an assumption that Chinese employees perceive the whole organization as their natural in-group, rather than a collection of separate individuals who happen to be in the same place at the same time. Being loyal to the organization prompts them to report unethical acts as they strive to protect "the good of the organization". However, differing conclusions were reached by Brody, Coulter, and Lin (1999), who demonstrated that Chinese decision makers refrain from whistle-blowing. To explain their findings, Brody et al. (1999) argued that collectivistic cultures not only emphasize loyalty, protection of in-groups, and emotional dependency between employees and their immediate supervisors, but also discourage assertion of individual opinions and disclosure of problems due to the fear of losing social status. Importantly, the organization in its entirety is not perceived as one's in-group. Therefore, the greater the commitment, loyalty, and responsibility are towards the immediate colleagues in a working group rather than towards some distant higher managers to whom unethical acts would have to be reported. This, together with the importance of "saving face" for the members of one's current team, discourages Chinese decision makers from whistle-blowing.

In sum, Confucian tradition clearly requires that leadership decisions adhere to the principles of morality (Lam, 2003). However, from the perspective of the Chinese, the evaluation of the ethicality of any particular course of action necessitates a comprehensive and holistic consideration of all the interconnected factors and issues present in the decision-making context.

Conclusion

It may be fitting to conclude this chapter by offering a sketch of the Chinese organizational decision maker. Empirical findings, reviewed in this chapter, provide some pointers. For instance, Chinese organizational leaders are likely to have a holistic mindset, be sensitive to the contextual cues in the environment, and avoid extreme choices; their decisions can be expected to be congruent with the leader's paternalistic role, meet the requirements of socially sanctioned rules (e.g. *guanxi*), and be based on past good solutions.

It is important to stress, however, that this is merely a sketch, rather than a photograph, or even a portrait. The sheer vastness of the Chinese world and the marked diversity of cultural influences preclude any definite claims on precise generalizations. When looking into the cultural antecedents of leadership actions, meaningful social research into modern oriental Chinese societies demands consideration of the perspectives of time, place, and social position. These are particularly consequential in the context of the PRC. It may indeed be tempting to interpret current organizational processes, including leadership decision making, through the lens of Confucian values. However, contemporary popular Confucianism in mainland China may also be viewed as a nostalgic attempt to rationalize the rapidly changing society. A more accurate approach perhaps would be to seek immediate cultural triggers of leadership decision making in the last 100 tumultuous years of mainland China's history, including the era of the Cultural Revolution, which has led to deep national trauma. The geographic immensity of the PRC also compels avoidance of generalizations. In the same way as Europe and the US are intricate mosaics of multiple diverse cultural clusters, there are many different "Chinas" in China. It can be reasonably anticipated, therefore, that organizational leaders in Shanghai would perceive themselves to be culturally quite dissimilar from those in Beijing, much in the same way as New Yorkers see themselves as distinct from those living in Los Angeles. Finally, it is imperative to regard the social position of the research participants: having a Communist Party affiliation, being employed by the government, or working in the private sector are likely to exert significant and differing effects on organizational decision making. In sum, given the historically determined cultural heterogeneity of Chinese oriental societies, it is critical that future research on the cultural antecedents of Chinese organizational leadership decision making is thoroughly, explicitly, and comprehensively contextualized.

Acknowledgements

The author thanks Dr Peter Ditmanson, Institute of Oriental Studies, University of Oxford, for helpful comments on an earlier version of this chapter, and Ms Mandy Engelsma, Handfast Point, Translation and Proofreading Agency, for careful proofreading and suggestions on the manuscript.

Notes

1. Xing (1995) reminds us that Confucius' ethical code includes the Three Cardinal Guides (the ruler guides the subject, the father guides the son, and the husband guides the wife) and the Five Constant Virtues (wisdom, righteousness, benevolence, fidelity, and propriety).
2. Hofstede defines power distance as "the extent to which members of a society accept that power in institutions and organizations is distributed unequally"; uncertainty avoidance as "the level of anxiety within the members of a society in the face of unstructured or ambiguous situations"; masculinity as characteristic of a society in which "social sex roles are sharply differentiated and the masculine role is characterized by need for achievement, assertiveness, sympathy for the strong, and importance attached to material success"; and collectivism as "a preference for a tightly knit social framework in which individuals are emotionally integrated into an extended family, clan, or other in-group which will protect them in exchange for unquestioning loyalty" (Hofstede, 1983: 295, 296).
3. It should be noted that the issue of reciprocity – for example, repaying favours – may need further investigation. While it is clear that repaying the paternalistic leader with loyalty is expected and practised (Farh & Cheng, 2000), other forms of repayment may not be as welcome. It has been argued, for instance, that denial of reciprocity is one of the features of paternalistic leadership (Aycan, 2006). This is evident when a generous giver of some sort of benefit (the leader) makes sure that the receiver (the follower) is unable to reciprocate (cf. Goodell, 1985). Whether or not this would be typical for Chinese paternalism may require further research, although aloofness and social distance, discussed by Westwood (1997), suggest the possibility.
4. In contrast with East Asians, Westerners are believed to be analytical thinkers. This type of thinking is object-centred and is directed at extracting an item from its context in order to have it scrutinized (Nisbett, Peng, Choi & Norenzayan, 2001).
5. Field-centredness refers to a wider attentional scope which involves examining the context or the situation as a whole and accentuating a broader picture rather than narrowly focusing on one object.
6. The equity principle is based on the concept of social exchange and denotes a reward-allocation system tied to individual inputs – for example, contribution. The equality principle suggests that organizational members are entitled to equal rewards regardless of their performance or contribution. According to the need principle, the distribution of benefits is determined by individual

needs of organizational members. Finally, the principle of seniority mandates that more generous compensation be allocated to older employees or those with longer tenure in their jobs.

7. Several researchers (e.g. Kim, Triandis, Kagitcibasi, Choi & Yoon, 1994; Triandis, 1995, 1996; Triandis, Bontempo, Villareal, Asaim & Lucca, 1988; Triandis & Gelfand, 1998) proposed that collectivism-individualism should be viewed not as a bipolar but as a bivariate model, in which both constructs are essentially multidimensional and can coexist. The vertical dimension describes the relationship between the group member and the group, while the horizontal dimension refers to the relationship of group members to each other. Within this model, vertical individualism emphasizes competitiveness and the desire to be superior to others; horizontal individualism accentuates uniqueness, self-reliance, and independence from others yet de-emphasizes hierarchical differentiation (superiority). Vertical collectivism promotes submission to authorities and conformity to the established norms and accepted standards; horizontal collectivism encourages cooperation, sociability, and empathy.
8. Fraud is a crime against property and can be defined as "the intentional use of deceit, a trick or some dishonest means to deprive another of his/her/its money, property or a legal right" (www.law.com) accessed 9 May 2012.
9. Greater sensitivity of Chinese organizational leaders to contextual aspects was also found in dispute-resolution situations. Brett, Tinsley, Shapiro, and Okumura (2007) showed that decision-related behaviours of Chinese managers were predicted by contextual cues in the environment.

References

Aldag, R.J. (2012). Distinguished Scholar Invited Essay. Behavioral decision making: Implications for leadership and organizations. *Journal of Leadership & Organizational Studies*, 19(2), 133–141.

Ang, S., & Leong, S. (2000). Out of the mouths of babes: Business ethics and youths in Asia. *Journal of Business Ethics*, 28, 129–144.

Arora, V., & Vamvakidis, A. (2011). China's economic growth: International spillovers. *China & World Economy*, 19(5), 31–46.

Atran, S., Medin, D.L., & Ross, N.O. (2005). The cultural mind: Environmental decision making and cultural modeling within and across populations. *Psychological Review*, 112(4), 744–776.

Aycan, Z. (2006). Paternalism: Towards conceptual refinement and operationalization. In K.S. Yang, K.K. Hwang, & U. Kim (Eds.), *Scientific Advances in Indigenous Psychologies: Empirical, Philosophical, and Cultural Contributions* (pp. 445–466). London: Cambridge University Press.

Bai, X., & Roberts, W. (2011). Taoism and its model of traits of successful leaders. *Journal of Management Development*, 30(7), 724 – 739.

Bazerman, M.H., & Moore, D. (2008). *Judgment in Managerial Decision Making*, 7th edition. New York: John Wiley & Sons, Inc.

Beach, L.R., & Connolly, T. (2005). *The Psychology of Decision Making: People in Organizations*, 2nd edition. Thousand Oaks, CA: Sage.

Bian, W.Q., & Keller, L.R. (1999). Chinese and Americans agree on what is fair, but disagree on what is best in societal decisions affecting health and safety risks. *Risk Analysis*, 19(3), 439–452.

Boisot, M., & Child, J. (1996). From fiefs to clans and network capitalism: Explaining China's emerging economic order. *Administrative Science Quarterly*, 41, 600–628.

Bond, M.H. (1996). Chinese values. In M.H. Bond (Ed.), *The Handbook of Chinese Psychology* (pp. 208–226). Hong Kong: Oxford University Press.

Brett, J.M., Tinsley, C.H., Shapiro, D.L., & Okumura, T. (2007). Intervening in employees' disputes: How and when will managers from China, Japan, and the USA act differently? *Management and Organization Review*, 3(2), 183–204.

Brody, R.G., Coulter, J.M., & Lin, S. (1999). The effect of national culture on whistle-blowing perceptions. *Teaching Business Ethics*, 3, 385–400.

Brooks, I. (1994). Managerial problem solving: A cultural perspective. *Management Decision*, 32(7), 53–59.

Brumagim, & Wu (2005). An examination of cross-cultural differences in attitudes towards risk: Testing prospect theory in the People's Republic of China, *Multinational Business Review*, 13, 67–86.

Carr, C., & Harris, S. (2004). The impact of diverse national values on strategic investment decisions in the context of globalization. *International Journal of Cross Cultural Management*, 4(1), 77–99.

Carson, T.L. (2003). Self-interest and business ethics: Some lessons of the recent corporate scandals. *Journal of Business Ethics*, 43(4), 389–394.

Chan, W. (1963). The doctrine of the mean "Zhong Yong Chung Yung", attribute to Confucius. In: *A Sourcebook in Chinese Philosophy* (pp. 95–115). Princeton, NJ: Princeton University Press.

Chen, C.C., Meindl, J.R., & Hunt, R.G. (1997). Testing the effects of vertical and horizontal collectivism: A study of reward allocation preferences in China. *Journal of Cross-Cultural Psychology*, 28, 44–70.

Chen, M.-J. (2002). Transcending paradox: The Chinese "middle way" perspective. *Asian Pacific Journal of Management*, 19(2/3), 179–199.

Cheng, B.S., Chou, L.F., & Farh, J.L. (2000). A triad model of paternalistic leadership: The constructs and measurement. *Indigenous Psychological Research in Chinese Societies*, 14, 3–64.

Cheng, B.S., Chou, L.F., Wu, T.U., Huang, M.P., & Farh, J.L. (2004). Paternalistic leadership and subordinate responses: Establishing a leadership model in Chinese organizations. *Asian Journal of Social Psychology*, 7, 89–117.

Cherry, J. (2006). The impact of normative influence and locus of control on ethical judgments and intentions: A cross cultural comparison. *Journal of Business Ethics*, 68, 113–132.

Cheung, F.M., Leung, K., Zhang, J.X., Sun, H.F., Gan, Y.Q., Song, W.Z., & Xie, D. (2001). Indigenous Chinese personality constructs: Is the Five-Factor Model complete? *Journal of Cross-Cultural Psychology*, 32(4), 407–433.

Chinese Culture Connection (1987). Chinese values and the search for culture-free dimensions of culture. *Journal of Cross-Cultural Psychology*, 18(2), 143–164.

Choi, I., Dalal, R., Kim-Prieto, C., & Park, H. (2003). Culture and judgment of causal relevance. *Journal of Personality and Social Psychology*, 84(1), 46–59.

Choi, I., & Nisbett, R. (2000). Cultural psychology of surprise: Holistic theories and recognition of contradiction. *Journal of Personality and Social Psychology*, 79(5), 890–905.

Chu, P.C., Spires, E.E., & Sueyoshi, T. (1999). Cross-cultural differences in choice behavior and use of decision aids: A comparison of Japan and the United States. *Organizational Behavior and Human Decision Processes*, 77(2), 147–170.

Cragin, J.P. (1986). Management technology absorption. In S.R. Clegg, D.C. Dunphy, & S.G. Redding (Eds.), *The Enterprise and Management in East Asia* (pp. 327–340). Hong Kong: Centre of Asian Studies, University of Hong Kong.

Davies, L., & Luk, W. (1995). The benefits of "Guanxi": The value of relationships in developing the Chinese market. *Industrial Marketing Management* 24(3), 207–214.

Dong, K., & Liu, Y. (2010). Cross-cultural management in China. *Cross-Cultural Management: An International Journal*, 17(3), 223–243.

Erez, M. (1997). A culture based model of work motivation. In P.C. Earley, & M. Erez (Eds.), *New Perspectives on International Industrial/Organizational Psychology* (pp. 193–242). San Francisco, CA: New Lexington.

Fan, Y.H., Woodbine, G., & Scully, G. (2012). *Guanxi* and its influence on the judgments of Chinese auditors. *Asia Pacific Business Review*, 18(1), 83–97.

Fang, T. (2010). Asian management research needs more self-confidence: Reflection on Hofstede (2007) and beyond. *Asia Pacific Journal of Management*, 27(1), 155–170.

Farh, J.L., & Cheng, B.S. (2000). A cultural analysis of paternalistic leadership in Chinese organizations. In J.T. Li, A.S. Tsui, & E. Weldon (Eds.), *Management and Organizations in the Chinese Context* (pp. 84–127). London: Macmillan.

Feng, T., Keller, L.R., & Zheng, X. (2011). Decision making in the newsvendor problem: A cross-national laboratory study. *Omega*, 39, 41–50.

Fernandez, D.R. Carlson, D.S., Stepina, L.P., & Nicholson, J.D. (1997). Hofstede's country classification 25 years later. *The Journal of Social Psychology*, 137(1), 43–54.

Fischer, R. (2004). Organizational reward allocation: A comparison of British and German organizations. *International Journal of Intercultural Relations*, 28, 151–164.

Fischer, R., & Smith, P.B. (2003). Reward allocation and culture: A meta-analysis. *Journal of Cross-Cultural Psychology*, 34(3), 251–268.

Ford, R.C., & Richardson, W.D. (1994). Ethical decision making: A review of the empirical literature, *Journal of Business Ethics*, 13, 205–221.

Gong, W. (2003). Chinese consumer behavior: A cultural framework and implications. *Journal of American Academy of Business*, 3(1/2), 373–380.

Goodell, G.E. (1985). Paternalism, patronage, and potlatch: The dynamics of giving and being given to. *Current Anthropology*, 26(2), 247–257.

Guerra-Lopez, I., & Blake, A.M. (2011). Leadership decision making and the use of data. *Performance Improvement Quarterly*, 24(2), 89–104.

Güss, D.C., & Dörner, D. (2011). Cultural differences in dynamic decision-making strategies in a non-linear, time-delayed task. *Cognitive Systems Research*. doi:10.1016/j.cogsys.2010.12.003

Harrison, E.F. (1995). *The Managerial Decision Making Process*, 4th edition. Boston, MA: Houghton Mifflin.

He, W., Chen, C.C., & Zhang, L. (2004). Rewards-allocation preferences of Chinese employees in the new millennium: The effects of ownership reform, collectivism, and goal priority. *Organization Science*, 15(2), 221–231.

Hill, J.S. (2006). Confucianism and the art of Chinese management. *Journal of Asian Business Studies*, 1, 1–9.

Hofstede, G. (1983). National cultures revisited. *Cross-Cultural Research*, 18(4), 285–305.

Hofstede, G. (2007). Asian management in the 21st century. *Asia Pacific Journal of Management*, 24(4), 411–420.

Hofstede, G., & Hofstede, G.J. (2005). *Cultures and Organizations: Software of the Mind*. New York: McGraw-Hill.

Hofstede, G., & McCrae, R.R. (2004). Personality and culture revisited: Linking traits and dimensions of culture. *Cross-Cultural Research*, 38(1), 52–88.

Hofstede, G., Van Deusen, C.A., Mueller, C.B., Charles, T.A., & the Business Goals Network. (2002). What goals do business leaders pursue? A study in fifteen countries. *Journal of International Business Studies*, 33, 785–803.

Hooker, J. (2009). Corruption from a cross-cultural perspective. *Cross-Cultural Management*, 16(3), 251–267.

House, R.J. Hanges, P.J. Javidan, M. Dorfman, P.W. & Gupta, V. (Eds.). (2004). *Culture, Leadership and Organizations: The GLOBE Study of 62 Societies*. Thousand Oaks, CA: Sage.

House, R.J., Hanges, P.J., Ruiz-Quintanilla, S.A., Dorfman, P.W., Javidan, M., Dickson, M.W. Gupta, et al. (1999). Cultural influences on leadership and organizations: Project GLOBE. In W.H. Mobley, M.J. Gessner, & V. Arnold. (Eds.), *Advances in Global Leadership* (pp. 171–233). Stamford, CN: JAI.

Hsee, C.K., & Weber, E.U. (1999). Cross-national differences in risk preference and lay predictions. *Journal of Behavioral Decision Making*, 12, 165–1 79.

Hsie, K.C., & Chen, Y.C. (2011). Development and significance of paternalistic leadership behavior scale. *Asian Social Science*, 7(2), 45–54.

Hughes, R. (1968). *Hong Kong: A Borrowed Place – Borrowed Time*. London: Andre Deutsch.

Inglehart, R. (1997). *Modernization and Postmodernization: Cultural, Economic, and Political Change in 43 Societies*. Princeton, NJ: Princeton University Press.

Ip, P.K. (2009). Is Confucianism good for business ethics in China? *Journal of Business Ethics*, 88, 463–476.

James, K. (1993). The social context of organizational justice: Cultural, intergroup, and structural effects on justice behaviors and perceptions. In R. Cropanzano (Ed.), *Justice in the Workplace: Approaching Fairness in HRM* (pp. 21–50). Hillsdale, NJ: Lawrence Erlbaum.

Ji, L.J., Guo, T., Messervey, D., & Zhang, Z. (2009). Looking into the past: Cultural differences in perception and representation of past information. *Journal of Personality and Social Psychology*, 96(4), 761–769

Ji, L.J., Nisbett, R.E., & Su, Y. (2001). Culture, change, and prediction. *Psychological Science*, 12(6), 450–456.

Ji, L.J., Zhang, Z., & Guo, T. (2008). To buy or to sell: Cultural differences in stock market decisions based on price trends. *Journal of Behavioral Decision Making*, 21, 399–413.

Johnson, C. (2000). Taoist leadership ethics. *Journal of Leadership & Organizational Studies*, 7(1), 82–91.

Kahneman, D., & Tversky, A. (1979). Prospect theory: An analysis of decision making under risk. *Econometrica*, 47, 263–291.
Kao, H.S.R., Sek-Hong, N., & Kwan, C. (1990). Cultural adaptations and diffusion for managerial strategies and responses in Hong Kong. *International Journal of Psychology*, 25(5/6), 657–674.
Kim, I.K., Park, H-J., & Suzuki, N. (1990). Reward allocation in the United States, Japan, and Korea: A comparison of individualistic and collectivistic cultures. *Academy of Management Journal*, 33(1), 188–198.
Kim, U., Triandis, H.C., Kagitcibasi, C., Choi, S.C., & Yoon, G. (1994). Introduction. In U. Kim, H.C. Triandis, C. Kagitcibasi, S.C. Choi, & G. Yoon (Eds.), *Individualism and Collectivism: Theory, Method, and Applications*, Thousand Oaks, CA: Sage.
Kotter, J.P. (1990). What leaders really do. *Harvard Business Review*, 68(3), 103–111.
Ladany, L. (1988). *The Communist Party of China and Marxism (1921–1985)*. Hong Kong: Hong Kong University Press.
Lam, K-C.J. (2003). Confucian business ethics and the economy. *Journal of Business Ethics*, 43, 153–162.
Leung, K. (1997). Negotiation and reward allocation across cultures. In P.C. Earley, & M. Erez (Eds.), *New Perspectives on International Industrial/ Organizational Psychology* (pp. 640–675). San Francisco, CA: New Lexington.
Leong, J.L.T., Bond, M.H., & Fu, P.P. (2006). Perceived effectiveness of influence strategies in the United States and three Chinese societies. *International Journal of Cross-Cultural Management*, 6(1), 101–120.
Li, J., Fu, P.P., Chow, I, & Peng, T.K. (2002). Societal development and the change of leadership style in oriental Chinese societies. *Journal of Developing Societies*, 18(1), 46–63.
Li, S., Bi, Y-L., & Zhang Y. (2009). Asian risk seeking and overconfidence. *Journal of Applied Social Psychology*, 39(11), 2706–2736.
Li, S.F., & Persons, O.S. (2011). Cultural effects on business students' ethical decisions: A Chinese versus American Comparison. *Journal of Education for Business*, 86, 10–16.
Lipshitz, R., & Mann, L. (2005). Leadership and decision making: William R. Ruckelshaus and the Environmental Protection Agency. *Journal of Leadership and Organizational Studies*, 11(4), 41–53.
Lovett, S., Simmons, L.C., & Kali, R. (1999). *Guanxi* versus the market: Ethics and efficiency. *Journal of International Business Studies*, 30, 231–247.
Maddux, W.W., & Yuki, M. (2006). The "ripple effect": Cultural differences in perceptions of the consequences of events. *Personality and Social Psychology Bulletin*, 32(5), 669–683.
Maule, J., & Villejoubert, G. (2007). What lies beneath: Reframing framing effects. *Thinking and Reasoning*, 13, 25–44.
McGrath, R., Macmillan, R.L., Yang, E., & Tsai, W. (1992). Does culture endure, or is it malleable? Issues for entrepreneurial economic development. *Journal of Business Venturing*, 7, 441–458.
Mintzberg, H. (1983). *Power in and around Organizations*. Englewood Cliffs, NJ: Prentice Hall.
Mintzberg, H., Ahlstrand, B., & Lampel, J. (1998). *Strategy Safari: A Guided Tour through the Wilds of Strategic Management*. New York: Free Press.

Nisbett, R.E. (2003). *The Geography of Thought*. New York: The Free Press.

Nisbett, R., Peng, K., Choi, I., & Norenzayan, A. (2001). Culture and systems of thought: Holistic versus analytic cognition. *Psychological Review*, 108, 291–310.

Niu, C.P., Wang, A.C., & Cheng, B.S. (2009). Effectiveness of a moral and benevolent leader: Probing the interactions of the dimensions of paternalistic leadership. *Asian Journal of Social Psychology*, 12, 32–39.

Offermann, L.R. (2004). Empowerment. In J.M. Burns, G.R. Goethals, & G. Sorenson (Eds.), *Encyclopedia of leadership*. Thousand Oaks, CA: Sage.

Olson, B., J. Bao, Y. & Parayitam, S. (2007). Strategic decision making within Chinese firms: The effects of cognitive diversity and trust on decision outcomes. *Journal of World Business*, 42, 35–46.

Pan, Y., Rowney, J.A., & Peterson, M.F. (2011). The structure of Chinese cultural traditions: An empirical study of business employees in China. *Management and Organization Review*, 8(1), 77–95.

Park, S.H., & Luo, Y. (2001). Guanxi and organizational dynamics: Organizational networking in Chinese firms. *Strategic Management Journal*, 22, 455–477.

Paul, J.R., & Ebadi, Y.M. (1989). Leadership decision making in a service organization: A field test of the Vroom-Yetton model. *Journal of Occupational Psychology*, 62, 201–211.

Peng, K., & Nisbett, R.E. (1999). Culture, dialectics, and reasoning about contradiction. *American Psychologist*, 54(9), 741–754.

Peterson, M.F., Miranda, S.M., Smith, P.B., & Haskell, V.M. (2003). The sociocultural contexts of decision making in organizations. In S.L. Schneider, & J. Shanteau (Eds.), *Emerging Perspectives on Judgment and Decision Research* (pp. 512–555). Cambridge: Cambridge University Press.

Rarick, C.A. (2009). The historical roots of Chinese cultural values and managerial practices. *Journal of International Business Research*, 8(2), 59–66.

Redding, S.G. (1990). *The Spirit of Chinese Capitalism*. Berlin: Walter de Gruyter.

Redding, S.G., & Hsiao, M. (1990). An empirical study of overseas Chinese managerial ideology. *International Journal of Psychology*, 25, 629–641.

Resick, C.J., Martin, G.S., Keating, M.A. Dickson, M.W., Kwan, H.K., & Peng, C. (2011). What ethical leadership means to me: Asian, American, and European perspectives. *Journal of Business Ethics*, 101(3), 435–457.

Rosen, S. (1990). The impact of reform policies on youth attitudes. In D. Davis, & E.F. Vogel (Eds.), *Chinese Society on the Eve of Tiananmen: The Impact of Reform* (pp. 283–374). Cambridge, MA: Harvard University Press.

Rouzies, D., Segalla, M., & Weitz, B.A. (2003). Cultural impact on European staffing decisions in sales management. *International Journal or Research in Marketing*, 20, 67–85.

Schmitt, D.P., Allik, J., McCrae, R.R., & Benet-Martinez, V. (2007). The geographic distribution of big five personality traits: Patterns and profiles of human self-description across 56 nations. *Journal of Cross-Cultural Psychology*, 38(2), 173–212.

Schramm-Nielsen, J. (2001). Cultural dimensions of decision making: Denmark and France Compared. *Journal of Managerial Psychology*, 16(5/6), 404–424.

Schwartz, S.H. (1994). Beyond individualism-collectivism: New cultural dimensions of values. In U. Kim, H.C. Triandis, C. Kagitcibasi, S.C. Choi, & G. Yoon (Eds.), *Individualism and Collectivism: Theory, Method and Applications*. Thousand Oaks, CA: Sage.

Shapira, Z. (Ed.) (1997). *Organizational Decision Making*. Cambridge: Cambridge University Press.
Silin, R.F. (1976). *Leadership and Values*. Cambridge, MA: Harvard University Press.
Simon, H.A. (1997). *Administrative Behavior: A Study of Decision Making Processes in Administrative Organizations*, 4th edition. New York: The Free Press.
Smith, D., & Fischbacher, M. (2009). The changing nature of risk and risk management: The challenge of borders, uncertainty and resilience. *Risk Management*, 11(1), 1–12.
Smith, P.B., & Bond, M.H. (1998). *Social Psychology across Cultures*, 2nd edition. Hemel Hempstead: Prentice Hall.
Smith, P.B., Peterson, M.F., & Wang, Z.M. (1996). The manager as mediator of alternative meanings: A pilot study from China, the USA, and UK. *Journal of International Business Studies*, 27(1), 115–137.
Spencer-Rodgers, J., Williams, M.J., & Peng, K. (2010). Cultural differences in expectation of change and tolerance for contradiction: A decade of empirical research. *Personality and Social Psychology Review*, 14(3), 296–312.
Triandis, H.C. (1995). *Individualism and Collectivism*. Boulder, CO: Westview Press.
Triandis, H.C. (1996). The psychological measurement of cultural syndromes. *American Psychologist*, 51(4), 407–415.
Triandis, H.C., Bontempo, R., Villareal, M.J., Asaim, M., & Lucca, N. (1988). Individualism and collectivism: Cross-cultural perspectives of self-in-group relationships. *Journal of Personality and Social Psychology*, 54, 323–338.
Triandis, H.C., & Gelfand, M.J. (1998). Converging measurement of horizontal and vertical individualism and collectivism. *Journal of Personality and Social Psychology*, 74(1), 118–128.
Tse, D.K., Lee, K.-H., Vertinsky, I., & Wehrung, D. (1988). Does culture matter? A cross-cultural study of executives' choice, decisiveness, and risk adjustment in international marketing. *Journal of Marketing*, 52(4), 81–95.
Vohra, R. (2000). *China's Path to Modernization: A Historical Review From 1800 to the Present*. Upper Saddle River, NJ: Prentice-Hall.
Vroom, V.H., & Yetton, P.W. (1973). *Leadership and Decision Making*. Pittsburg, PA: University of Pittsburg Press.
Wang, J. (2011). Understanding managerial effectiveness: A Chinese perspective. *Journal of European Industrial Training*, 35(1), 6–23.
Weber, E.U., Ames, D., & Blais, A.-R. (2005). "How do I choose thee? Let me count the ways:" A textual analysis of similarities and differences in modes of decision making in China and the United States. *Management and Organization Review*, 1, 87–118.
Weber, E.U., & Hsee, C.K. (1998). Cross-cultural differences in risk perception but cross-cultural similarities in attitudes towards risk, *Management Science*, 44, 205–1217.
Weber E.U., & Hsee, C.K. (1999). Models and mosaics: Investigating cross-cultural differences in risk perception and risk preference. *Psychonomic Bulletin & Review*, 6(4), 611–617.
Weber, E.U., Hsee, C.K., & Sokolowska, J. (1998). What folklore tells about risk and risk taking: Cross-cultural comparisons of American, German and Chinese proverbs. *Organizational Behavior and Human Decision Processes*, 75(2), 170–186.
Weber, E.U., & Milliman, R.A. (1997). Perceived risk attitudes: Relating risk perception to risky choice. *Management Science*, 43, 122–143.

Weber, E.U., & Morris, M.W. (2010). Culture and judgment and decision making: The constructivist turn. *Perspectives on Psychological Science*, 5(4), 410–419.

Weltzien Hovik, V.H. (2007). East meets West: Tacit messages about business ethics in stories told by Chinese managers. *Journal of Business Ethics*, 67, 457–469.

Westaby, J.D., Probst, T.M., & Lee, B.C. (2010). Leadership decision making: A behavioral reasoning theory analysis. *The Leadership Quarterly*, 21, 481–495.

Westwood, R.I. (1997). Harmony and patriarchy: The cultural basis for paternalistic headship among the overseas Chinese. *Organization Studies*, 18, 445–480.

Wong-On-Wing, B., & Lui, G. (2007). Culture, implicit theories, and the attribution of morality. *Behavioral Research in Accounting*, 19, 231–246.

Xing, F. (1995). The Chinese cultural system: Implications for cross-cultural management. *S.A.M. Advanced Management Journal*, 60(1), 14–20.

Yen, D.A., Barnes, B.R., & Wang, C.L. (2011). The measurement of *guanxi*: Introducing the GRX scale. *Industrial Marketing Management*, 40, 97–108.

Yang, K.S. (1991). "Will traditional and modern values co-exist?" Paper presented at *International Conference on Values in Chinese Societies: Retrospect and Prospect*, May, Taipei, Taiwan.

Yates, J., & Lee, J. (1996). Chinese decision-making. In M. Bond (Ed.), *Handbook of Chinese Psychology* (pp. 338–351). Hong Kong: Oxford University Press.

Yukl, G. (2002). *Leadership in Organizations*. Englewood Cliffs, NJ: Prentice Hall.

Zhou, J., & Martocchio, J.J. (2001). Chinese and American manager's compensation award decisions: A comparative policy-capturing study. *Personnel Psychology*, 54(1), 115–145.

Zhuang, J., Thomas, S., & Miller, D.L. (2005). Examining culture's effect on whistle- blowing and peer reporting. *Business and Society*, 44(4), 462–486.

7
Glocalization of Leadership and Cultural Implications for Higher Education: A German-Saudi Case

Anna M. Danielewicz-Betz

Introduction

The aim of this chapter is to present some Western leadership styles and employers' expectations regarding future leaders in contrast with the Arab style, in particular Saudi Arabian. This is done in line with Liu's (2010) suggestion to reach beyond the primarily US model of leadership. Internalization and globalization of higher education constitute a focal point of the chapter, as linked to the issue of sustaining quality of higher education in general and in the Gulf Cooperation Council (GCC) countries, and especially in the Kingdom of Saudi Arabia (KSA), where standards still fail to match expected levels. Moreover, German and Saudi tertiary education will be presented and evaluated, based on my first-hand experience, as well as the qualitative survey results, which, however, were limited to a reduced number of submitted questionnaires due to the fact that many potential respondents decided against participation (Germans supposedly not willing to invest the time and Saudis reluctant to express their own opinion, since their culture fosters criticism avoidance). The final section of the chapter will deal with the issue of glocalization and the question regarding to what extent the Arab higher education programmes should be Westernized, and whether uncritical application of US models of education and leadership should be recommended in the Gulf region.

With regard to general limitations of this chapter, the discussion of executive competences, for instance, had to be shortened owing to the chapter size guideline. As for the sources on Arab leadership and education quoted, in particular concerning the KSA, these were limited to the more objective ones. These topics, on the whole, have not been addressed much in the (non-Arabic) literature available.

Culture-specific leadership: Middle-Eastern and German styles

There seems to exist a (US) bias towards the pursuit of a universal model of leadership. According to Liu (2010) the challenges in departing from the US model include:

- finding one's own best way of management or leadership, the one that suits one's cultural context;
- leading in a cross-cultural context;
- making a cultural "paradigm shift" in leadership – that is, absorbing leadership wisdom from other cultures and integrating it into one's own.

The US model of leadership, which has dominated the world both as a school of thought and as a guide for practice for the past several decades, should be upgraded as a result of learning from other cultures. Asian leadership serves as an example of leadership embedded in the cultural context of the Confucian principles (cf. Hasegawa & Noronha, 2009). The Japanese leadership style, for instance, has evolved around such core categories as a liberal approach, trust, punctuality, networking, support, provision of direction, and protection, as well as those of participative, achievement-oriented, and "after-five" leadership (cf. Fukushige & Spicer, 2007: 521–522).

Turning to culture as one of the key executive competences, one may say that the learning curve of global executives is long and requires hands-on on-site experience (cf. McCall & Hollenbeck, 2002). The cultural context of business has a profound effect on the learning curve: culture affects how business is done; and the impact of cultural differences can be very powerful. Theoretical training prior to a placement abroad may not be sufficient for business operations, and therefore is less predictable in an international setting. Learning to work across cultures is an essential competency of the global executive, both emotionally and intellectually. Moreover, there exists a danger of so-called "cultures of similarity". It has been proved that "similar cultures" can present an even greater challenge for expatriate adjustment – for example, for the British in France.

Smith, Saslow, and Thomas (1999) have found that one of the key issues of global executive development is the ability to influence people from other cultures. It appears that expatriate assignments, external networking, and internal mentoring are the most effective methods for developing global executives.

Islamic leadership model and Middle-Eastern leadership style

As Beekun and Badawi (2005) point out, leadership in Islam is based on trust (*amanah*), which is also one of the values of Asian leadership. It represents a psychological agreement between a leader and those to be guided, protected, and treated fairly and with justice. Hence the focus of leadership in Islam is on doing good. Murad (1996) indicates that leadership is the ability to see beyond assumed boundaries, and to come up with solutions or paths that few can visualize. The leader must then project this vision for everyone to see and pursue. Leadership is depicted as the process by which the leader seeks the voluntary participation of followers in an effort to reach organizational objectives. Whoever wishes to become a leader should educate themselves before educating others and preaching. One who improves their own morals is superior to those who try to teach and train others. Kuwaiti entrepreneur, Islamic author, and speaker, Dr Tareq Al Suwaidan, successfully trains leaders in his "Leaders' Training Academy". They all share the vision of raising the Islamic nation to its lost place in the world. The training sessions draw on two main sources: Western leadership knowledge, and leadership envisaged in Mohammad's and his followers' lives (personal communication with a participant).

All in all, the conduct of Muslim leaders is seen in a rather idealistic way as related closely to their religious values. They should, first of all, excel in self-awareness, which involves thankfulness and respect for Allah and His creation (the Quaranic concept of *at-taqwá)*; exhibit purity (*taharat*), patient perseverance, and steadfastness (*sabr*). A prominent model leader in Islamic history was, naturally, the Holy Prophet Muhammad (for leadership development in the Arab world, see also Al-Dabbagh & Assaad, 2010).The above description of Islamic leadership clashes with the Western perception of Middle-Eastern leadership style as reported by Workman (2008b) and Arnold (2009), and supported by my first-hand experience in the KSA. The Middle-Eastern style of management is seen by Westerners as highly authoritarian. Most Middle-Eastern managers believe that their employees are lazy by nature. Therefore coercion is often needed to get them to perform. Consequently, a strong work-centred approach is taken to ensure that subordinates complete their tasks. This includes virtually no delegation of responsibilities or empowerment, as workers have little ambition, try to avoid responsibility, and prefer to follow directions from their leaders; accompanied by control and threats of punishment to ensure the attainment of organizational objectives.

Arnold (2009: 276–278) stresses the importance of image (public face), the reason for shame avoidance, religion, tribal, and extensive family relations (paired up with *wasta* – connections, influence, clout), as well as Arab cultural pride as core factors in understanding how leadership assessment and development are practised in the Middle East. To avoid shame and personal conflict (loss of face), leaders give mainly positive feedback, if any. It is assumed that subordinates share the same motives to perform with their bosses and therefore leaders usually fail to differentiate between the employees (hence low popularity of assessment centres and individual bonus/commission systems).

Another point made by Arnold (2009: 278), which I can corroborate, is that of an "external locus of control" influencing both leaders and followers. According to a strong Muslim belief, one's destiny is in the hands of Allah. Although one is expected to do one's best, due to the fact that deictic will is ultimately required to "make things happen" (*Inshallah*), Islamic leaders often lack the willingness and ability to demand accountability and to demonstrate power to affect their environment and the people whom they lead. Additionally, shame avoidance is linked to mistake avoidance at any price. The Middle-Eastern work culture promotes following policy and procedure, since questioning orders and policies is considered a mistake. Consequently it is difficult to get things done until the boss explicitly says to do so.

Unfortunately, the same norms and measures tend to be applied to foreign employees, disregarding the cultural background. Middle-Eastern managers clearly contrast with those from North America, Europe, Japan, and China, for example, who believe that their employees will work hard and seek greater challenge and responsibility, depending on the rewards associated with task achievement. In those regions, employees learn not only to accept but also to seek responsibility. And since employees are committed to the goals, workers will exercise self-control and self-direction, with no threats of punishment required. Therefore expatriates in the KSA, for instance, often feel that they are not trusted, nor sufficiently empowered, and, in fact, frequently overcontrolled and mismanaged.

Managers from the Middle East also differ considerably from leaders in Japan who generally follow the more participatory approach. Japanese managers assume that subordinates are motivated by a strong sense of commitment to being part of the organization in which they work. Furthermore, Middle-Eastern organizations are characterized by a one-way top-down flow of information and influence from authoritarian leader to subordinates. Consequently, decisions are made only at the highest levels. Performance evaluation and control are informal, with routine checks on performance. This is due in part to the fact that personnel policies depend on personal relationships. Contacts and social networks are more important than finding the strongest candidate through more formal channels. The tone of communication used in a Middle-Eastern company depends on the speaker's social position and power. In view of what has been said above, the question arises as to how Saudi or Middle-Eastern graduates in general can/should be prepared for leadership roles and management tasks, considering the fact that the Western (US) models of (business) education dominate in the region.

German leadership style

As far as German leadership style is concerned, according to Workman (2008a), and again supported by my first-hand experience, it has to be approached by applying the "German filter", which reflects Germany's nationalistic management methods. Germany's rule-oriented, hierarchical focus on task accomplishment is an example of so-called "Eiffel Tower" management style. German subordinates rarely disobey or openly question orders from higher-level authority. Germany is famous for its more deliberate, stodgy process of management by consensus. Jobs are well defined while assignments are fixed and limited. With the corporate culture being hierarchical, orders come down from the top with very little bottom-up communication.

German organizations rely heavily on formal qualifications in deciding what slots personnel ought to fill. Companies typically manage their human resources through assessment centres, appraisal systems, training, development programmes and job rotation. Generally, German managers are slow to accept change partly because of the country's strong aversion to risk. Germany's superiority complex sometimes leads to an ethnocentric style of management in which strong nationalism compels German headquarters to maintain control of key international management positions. A more global management approach that relies on selection of the best-qualified applicants regardless of the country of origin often fails to be implemented strategically in German companies. Moreover, Germans like to be directed, they are committed to goals, and they exercise strong self-control. Consequently, no threats of punishment are required to ensure task completion. In view of this the Saudi leadership style of close control, threats, and punishment may be met with opposition, criticism, and, eventually, lack of cooperation by German subordinates. As a result, the potential of a German employee will not be utilized, thus motivation, efficiency, and productivity will decrease.

Brodbeck and Frese (2007), in their discussion of post-reunification, say that the "competence first" principle (cf. Glunk, Wilderom & Ogilvie, 1997) still prevails, as reported by Hammer (1990) more than a decade earlier. Emphasis is on the technical expertise of leaders and the bureaucratic rule-setting role of management rather than on the communicative and interactive process of people-oriented leadership. Furthermore, depersonalized participative leadership (cf. Martin, Keating & Brodbeck, 2004) is fostered, based on the subordinates' expectation to be consulted about decisions (cf. Bass, 1990; Reber et al., 2000; Szabo et al. 2000). According to Brodbeck and Frese (2007: 177), referring to the GLOBE study results, middle managers perceive outstanding leadership as high in performance orientation and autonomy, as well as high in participation and team orientation.

Internationalization versus globalization

Internationalization is concerned with the standardization of goals and content of education; administration and management of educational institutions in terms of internationally accepted criteria; and international cooperation, communication, and exchanges between higher-education institutions. It implies recognition of cultural difference, diversity, and identity, accompanied by adaptation of a multidisciplinary and multicultural approach. At the same time, it seeks to recognize a relation to the other, and difference between nations despite a globalized capitalism seeking to replace national cultures with a global consumerism. Numerous questions arise in relation to the internalization of higher education, such as those of profit orientation, other than economic values, and relation to globalization.

According to Harris (2008), the idea of global culture is empty and difficult to identify with, despite global trends and increasingly homogeneous tastes: it is not embedded in people's everyday lives. Instead, local cultures and traditions still persevere but are driven by global capitalism.

Generally speaking, global trends in tertiary education certainly exist. Nevertheless, local cultures and traditions influence and differentiate between the individual curricula and regulations, starting at the pre-university educational levels.

One way of fostering global leadership talent is by providing the so-called liberal education model. "College Learning for the new global century – A report for the National Leadership Council for Liberal Education and America's Promise" (2009) specifies liberal education as an approach to learning that empowers individuals and prepares them to deal with complexity, diversity, and change. It provides students with broad knowledge of the science, culture, and society, as well as in-depth study of a specific area of interest. Such education helps students to develop a sense of social responsibility, as well as strong and transferable intellectual and practical skills, such as communication, analytical and problem-solving skills, and a demonstrated ability to apply knowledge and skills in real-world settings. Liberal education seems to be the key in ensuring that students accept the internalization process at their universities and prepare for the challenges of global leadership.

China serves as a good example of a country that seeks to find its own local solution to internationalization issues in education. Positive signs of internalization of Chinese universities comprise affiliation with universities around the world, international academic exchanges, international studies, degree and non-degree programmes in Chinese language and culture, and recruitment of foreign students into other departments, such as Chinese medicine. According to Ma and Vermaak (2010), the quality of education in China is to some degree in line with internationally accepted standards. In many areas, their universities perform even better than most other universities around the world. There are still numerous obstacles, however, on the path to internalization, such as the fact that students of Chinese in Confucius Institutes are not exposed to the Chinese language intensively enough. There are also virtually no courses offered in English, so foreign students have to study in Chinese. Courses in English would, however, allow foreign students both to pursue the study of Chinese language and culture, and keep up with their own field of academic study. The dilemma remains whether the priority ought to be attracting international students to study and do research in China and so enrich Chinese academic life, or whether Chinese universities should remain "Chinese" – that is, attractive only to Chinese students.

By contrast, the European Master in Business Studies (EMBS) is an example of a truly international programme offering a master's degree in management. It is officially integrated into the new European Bologna system of higher education and is composed of four semesters in for different European countries – Italy, France, Germany, and Spain – representing a total of 120 European Credit Transfer and Accumulation System (ECTS) points. Small groups of students of various nationalities learn to work and study together over a two-year period. All courses are taught in English, both by qualified faculty members and managers directly involved in developing syllabi for lectures, seminars, and workshops.

Munich Business School also offers an international programme, which is presented in a practical and interactive way. The curriculum is based on a solid scientific foundation, geared towards the current needs of the economy and subject to continuous quality control. The practical approach is reflected in three mandatory internships, with one integrated semester abroad at a renowned partner university. Additionally, frequent workshops, guest lectures, and field trips allow for direct dialogue with businesses.

Sustaining quality of higher education: The case of the Gulf countries

The issue of quality is crucial to a discussion of international education and glocalization models. According to Lenn (2000), the global marketplace stresses the need for cross-border movement of professionals. The most quickly growing areas for transnational education appear to be IT and MBA. The most rapidly globalizing professions are engineering, construction (including architecture), and accounting, followed closely by medicine, specialized nursing, and international law. There are, however, numerous quality questions and problem areas with the "export" of higher education, such as questionable alliances with the mission of the host institution; questionable control over the programme (teaching staff, key operations) by the exporting institution; and language of instruction and instructor qualifications.

Further issues comprise appropriate and sufficient learning resources, students' proficiency in the language of instruction, student services, physical resources and facilities, and financial resources. Cross-border education providers also face difficulties in translating degrees into national equivalents by qualifications authorities, custom regulations limiting movement of education and training materials, telecommunications laws, limited movement of persons due to barriers such as visas and work permits, and disregard for intellectual property rights (cf. Lenn, 2000).

With respect to the Middle East, state education in the GCC countries, in particular, has long been criticized for being rigidly academic and for failing to promote creative thinking. Hence the Gulf states have recently made improving education standards a major priority for investment. Governments have realized the need for school systems that produce well-educated, ambitious students who are capable of contributing to the growth of their countries. An exclusive survey of business professionals conducted by Middle East News, Data and Analysis (MEED) in 2010 revealed the areas in which GCC local school leavers are strongest/weakest. Strong emphasis is clearly placed on religious studies and Arabic. Knowledge of foreign languages and problem-solving, by contrast, are inadequate. It appears that many school leavers still lack basic skills, including timekeeping and a strong work ethic. When it comes to ambition, the results were slightly better, but still only 34.4% marked this area as good or excellent, with 30.1% rating school leavers' ambition as poor. Arabic students are not familiar with the basic workplace requirements, such as meeting deadlines. Moreover, there is no incentive for students to undertake vocational training because it is regarded as low in status. The old-style system of memorization of information still dominates, and time-management, work ethic, and creativity are not taught. More emphasis should be placed on verbal communication skills, stricter enforcement of school attendance, and greater investment in educational facilities.

The above survey also revealed that graduate employees from Jordan and Lebanon are considered to be the strongest. In the GCC, graduates from Bahrain are the best (46.3% rated them as good or excellent), followed by the United Arab Emirates (41.1%). Graduates from the KSA, by contrast, were ranked the weakest, with only 25.9% considered to be of high calibre and 41.1% described as poor. Not surprisingly, the KSA is heavily investing in the creation of new universities. It is hard to expand so rapidly, however, and to improve quality at the same time.

The Saudi system of education is particularly criticized by Kamal and Palmer (2009), who claim that it entirely suppresses critical thinking and is dominated by the religious curriculum, coupled with rote memorization of texts and uncritical acceptance of tribal practices. Consequently, such a system cannot prepare students for professional opportunities in the modern world. The main argument is that investing billions of oil money into public education will not replace radical educational reforms. Saudi students consistently score among the worst in maths and science because these subjects are much neglected in school curricula. An impressive investment in the infrastructure of higher education has not yet yielded positive returns. Moreover, it appears that each year thousands of students graduate from universities with degrees in Shariah (Islamic law) or Arabic literature, which predominantly render them unemployed, underemployed, or employed in the bloated government sector.

German university education – A qualitative survey

A small-scale (due to the low number of respondents) qualitative survey study was conducted among ten German (both female and male) graduates from German universities, eliciting responses to the questions discussed belowI (see Appendix 1). The main purpose of the survey was to find out the respondents' opinions regarding internationalization of German universities and to what extent they prepare graduates for future leadership/managerial roles. As for the characteristics perceived as negative by the respondents, the most frequently mentioned ones were the following:

- insufficient public relations and lack of external relations, especially in comparison with foreign, private universities;
- lack of educational placement offices is of low priority (this does not count for influential rankings);
- low practical orientation;
- women mostly employed in administration, human resources, and supporting positions, while professors are predominantly male (except in languages);
- confusion related to the new bachelor's/master's system and tuition fees (introduced a few years ago);
- overcrowded lecture halls (especially in social sciences, law, and management schools);
- virtually no personal contact with professors (anonymous students);
- lectures are offered predominantly in German.

Regarding the internationalization/globalization of German universities, the internationalization process is seen as dependent on the strategies employed by individual universities and their faculty. In particular, technical universities in Germany typically collaborate with partners and affiliates in countries across the world and "franchise" their teaching methods (see e.g. the activities of Deutscher Akademischer Austauschdienst (DAAD)). Another option is to increase the share of non-German speaking students. An important step is to make the German postgraduate studies more lucrative for top candidates from other countries. However, this requires some structural changes in terms of how doctorate students are embedded into the system and how supervision is administered. Due to the fact that German dominates as the instruction medium, English for Specific Purposes courses tend to be popular with students. Many also interact with foreign students and participate in international exchange programmes. Foreign exchange students, in particular, are dissatisfied with the scarce offer of business courses in English.

The survey also dealt with the question of whether German universities prepare students for managerial/leadership roles. Apparently, a typically German understanding of management tends to be promoted. The German notion of *Betriebswirtschaftslehre* (BWL; "business administration") does not, however, correspond with any English-speaking university programmes/majors, where management is distinct from specialized degrees in accounting and finance. Furthermore, it is claimed that students are not offered sufficient preparation for leadership roles. The curricula focus primarily on the "technical" aspects of organizations like finance, production, control, and statistics, with no room for leadership. Consequently, the "soft" side of management is not granted the status it has in professional settings. This is therefore perceived as a weakness of business education in Germany. In non-business majors there exists even less preparation for leadership roles. Students never properly learn how to manage or delegate tasks. Nevertheless, they are given options, such as joining the world's largest student-driven organization, AIESEC. Alternatively, there is the TopBWL programme in Munich that targets the top 10% of students in Munich's School of Management, with frequent company contacts, business breakfasts, and workshops with partner companies offering first-hand corporate insight.

The final part of the German survey referred to the question of whether a degree from a German university secured a competitive advantage in the international job market. It was observed that German students/graduates do have a good standing internationally. Given the weaknesses of the German system mentioned above, many students tend to structure their degree programme in such a way so that they can gain at least some of the skills expected by future employers, as well as practical experience, by working on the side and completing as many internships/exchange programmes as possible. Often, "made in Germany" is an internationally recognized "label" in education, carrying a strong reputation and competitive edge without questioning whether German graduates actually exhibit the skills required to compete internationally.

Saudi university education – A qualitative survey

A survey was also carried out with 15 (primarily Saudi, but also Palestinian) respondents (female and male), both graduates and senior students relaying their experience of Saudi education (see Appendix 2). The first question dealt with the measures aimed at the localization of Saudi education. According to the majority of respondents, the country's social values and strong religious tradition should be respected. Changes should be introduced by means of gradual, achievable steps, and not by accepting foreign solutions without the appropriate feasibility studies and strategic planning.

In other respects, Saudi education is considered very local – that is, Arab/Islamic. It was noted that it is only at the higher-education level that the study material goes beyond local reference, and this not in all cases either. This is perceived as a negative point, however. Moreover, Saudi schools are still traditionally Arab/Islamic, especially with regard to the dress code, local holidays, and Islamic restrictions. Nevertheless, there are certain aspects that could easily undergo localization, such as curricula, which have to meet international standards. According to the respondents, English is useful as a medium of instruction at universities, but Arabic should not be neglected. Hence teaching the curriculum material in Arabic should also be encouraged at college level, with curricula being created by Arab educational authorities that will not depend solely on Western resources. One should also make sure that the materials provided are culturally and ethically sensitive. The respondents maintained that Arab educators ought to face "with courage" Western criticism of Arabic and Islamic culture and teaching. What suits the West does not necessarily suit Arab societies. Instead of emulating Western patterns uncritically, the focus should be on drawing on the Arabic and Islamic legacy. Furthermore, local research should be encouraged and supported financially. Most importantly, Arab teachers' qualifications have to match those of Western teachers so that the quality of teaching does not suffer in the process. Localization is perceived as an important factor and can be achieved by offering more courses related to work in the Arab world.

Another survey question elicited the respondents' opinions regarding the current model of Saudi (higher) education. The opinions varied to the degree that some perceived higher education as being of a high international standard, with modern facilities, equipment, and study materials (including library resources) being readily available. By contrast, others were very negative. Some respondents claimed that Saudi education did not prepare students for real life and they could not think of any positive aspects to mention. Others were convinced that there were many positive aspects but some required enormous changes. Many believe that Saudi educational institutions are incapable of measuring up to the latest in the market because course materials are outdated, and they lack topicality and local relevance. Matching international standards of foreign education programmes is seen as priority. This can be achieved by engaging staff with hands-on industry experience and by introducing extensive cooperation with international institutions.

Other critical views on Saudi higher education included such points as the fact that educational policy-makers wasted money, time, and effort on futile projects that had not been thoroughly thought through, such as creating the biggest university campus in the world (i.e. Prince Nurah University). Moreover, numerous new majors have been introduced, especially for women, without taking into consideration the job market needs, and the cultural and religious restrictions (gender segregation, professional limitations for women, etc.). On a more positive note, it is worth mentioning that the Ministry of Higher Education has recently established a scholarship programme for Saudi students, although it is said to be more "foreign" than "Saudi", since it offers Saudi citizens the opportunity to study abroad rather than taking care of local needs.

With reference to the question concerning the Americanization of Saudi universities, most respondents disagreed. Even though numerous universities in the KSA operate in English and use the US/UK published study materials, in the respondents' opinion the educational system in the KSA is not much affected by the US models. They believe that Saudi universities devote enough attention to Arabic and Islamic studies. Many admitted, however, that it was difficult for them to make a comparison given the lack of first-hand information about US education. Those who were in a position to compare admitted, for instance, that the science majors are too American, and almost all Saudi postgraduates tend to study in the US. Some respondents raised the concern that if Americanization went beyond the mere use of US titles, job descriptions, standards, activities, and the like and resulted in graduating "Americanized" students, this would raise serious concerns.

Paradoxically enough, all of the respondents seemed to be convinced that if one wishes to obtain the best education, one ought to study at a US university. Some also strongly believed that other countries, such as Germany, France, China, and Japan, have a great deal to offer in terms of education provision. Moreover, some respondents recommend a thorough revision and upgrade of educational models and resources.

Two further questions were as follows. Does Saudi university education prepare the graduates for challenges of the global job market? Are the necessary skills to become successful leaders of the future acquired? Overall, the respondents were rather sceptical about appropriate university preparation for jobs in the global environment. Many believe that educational institutions in the KSA do not offer sufficient preparation for market challenges. College courses mainly focus on spoon-feeding students with knowledge rather than on teaching professional skills. It was suggested that skills such as public speaking, strategic planning, and debating could be improved by participating in extracurricular activities and community involvement.

The main point of criticism is that students are incapable of delivering professional presentations or writing term research papers, which mainly implies plagiarism, for which they are not penalized. In general, the quality of preparation for job challenges was said to vary from university to university and even from department to department. It was also observed that many students lack the necessary motivation and do not appear to have any professional goals, but rather study for the sake of it.

In most respondents' opinions, leadership is not nurtured at all. Students are generally reluctant to take initiative and participate in extracurricular events, not to mention voluntary work. They seem to be unaware of the increasingly demanding requirements of the competitive global job market. On the whole, there appears to be a lack of cooperation between the corporate world and Saudi universities. College representatives do not engage in meetings with big organizations in order to understand their needs or those of the market in general. With regard to the question about the main skills acquired during the university education years, many respondents, somewhat surprisingly, claimed that university education taught them the basic skills of writing, reading, and speaking, especially in English, but in some cases also in Arabic. Reading is mostly understood as extensive perusal for knowledge acquisition. These skills are followed by researching, comprehension (rather than memorization) of study material, communication skills, and public speaking. Moreover, managing time, respecting people's minds, self-organization, marketing oneself, referencing and presenting scholarly information, and professional networking were also listed as useful in the future professional context.

One of the (male) respondents recollected the painful process of learning the specialist skills "on the job":

> I graduated from university in 1994 as computer engineer. At that time the local market wasn't ready for such skills as we don't manufacture or design computers in Saudi. So I had to start from scratch to become [a] system analyst/administrator. From [a] management perspective, the skills required were very poorly taught at university and I learnt it all from work experience or through courses I took at work.

With reference to primary and secondary education and their necessary reforms, the responses are summarized in Table 7.1.

Table 7.1 Pros and cons of Saudi pre-university education

Pros	Cons
School day organization and timing	Subjects and teaching methods do not prepare for higher education: educational shock. A gap between school and university that requires enormous effort to bridge
Activities held at school for individuals and groups encouraging active participation	Memorization as the main learning strategy
Six-year primary education preparing for the next level Literacy skills	Lack of creative tasks/no attention given to individual creativity Lack of critical thinking tasks
Dedication and commitment (unspecified)	Too local – no international content
	Lack of intensive and extensive foreign language programmes, especially in English, although it is a must at university level
	Deficiencies in terms of teacher qualifications, study material, and facilities
	Average or poor general experience and overall impression
	Extensive reading is not encouraged
	Outdated course materials
	Neglect of scientific subjects

As one can see, the majority of respondents were very critical of the Saudi primary and secondary education system. As one of the (male) respondents put it,

> Education in Saudi desperately needs improvement, whether it is the teachers, the study material, or the facilities. Literally, the whole system needs to change. Children don't learn anything. What you are required to do to be able to pass is memorize the book and write down on the exam paper. There is no space for creativity or giving students a chance to discuss or develop any skills in them. Also, the education itself is too local: there is no international information whatsoever.

Generally, students finish high school without any specific preferences for a given subject that they would like to specialize in. The majority of respondents believe that the teaching methods should undergo a major paradigm shift in order for schools and educational institutions to improve their standards.

Glocalization of tertiary education in the KSA: Recommendations

Glocalization, a blend of "globalization" and "localization", implies that companies and other institutions tailor their offering to suit the interests of local markets across the world. The term refers to those willing and able to "think globally and act locally". It is also a process by which local communities respond differently to global changes. Nguyen, Elliott, Terlouwc, and Pilota (2009) point out rightly that simplistic forms of "transfer" of Western approaches to other contexts may often turn out to be inappropriate, and can potentially undermine existing practice. In the KSA, similarly to Asian contexts, rapid reforms in education may run the risk of "false universalism", involving the relatively uncritical adoption of various Western approaches.

To highlight the need for a more contextualized approach, and to illustrate how inappropriate "cross-cultural cloning" (cf. Dimmock & Walker, 1998) can be, I argue that it is simply impossible to incorporate Western higher education mission and vision statements, as well as evaluation criteria, within a specific context of the KSA. I concur with Nguyen et al. (2009) who are concerned that the educational field is dominated by policy-makers who are interested in quick results and seem unable to await the outcome of systematic and lengthy research studies. Educational policies and practices cannot easily be transferred across cultures (cf. Phillips & Ochs, 2003). However, in the view of the large-scale investment in Saudi education, the pressures put on national governments to appear successful educationally, and the ease with which information about educational policy and practices around the globe can be accessed (cf. Crossley & Watson, 2003), the so-called "copy and paste" practice of some Saudi universities can be observed when they are developing their curricula and programmes. As Nguyen et al. (2009) suggest, cross-cultural cloning, increasingly fuelled by Western-oriented globalization, may consequently result in academic ineffectiveness, and serious neglect of cultural assets, weakening of the host culture's own research capacity, and at the same time it may help to perpetuate a sense of dependency on the expatriate workforce and its educational models.

One of the few examples of glocalized universities in the KSA is that of Al-Faisal University, Riyadh. Although its classes are taught in English and modelled on US-style curricula, it remains distinctively Saudi. Its preparatory programme has been designed to walk those students who need assistance through the basics of lab techniques, scientific research, and critical thinking in medicine, engineering, and business for a year before starting their degree programmes. The vision and mission of the school is to provide future leaders for the KSA and the region. Al-Faisal University develops its own infrastructure and curricula. Its college of medicine has collaborated with Harvard Medical International to design programmes and facilities, and to recruit faculty staff, while the engineering school makes use of free course material from the Massachusetts Institute of Technology through the Cambridge school's web-based open-course-ware initiative. This strategy is becoming increasingly common in the KSA and the region. Effat University, a women's institution in Jeddah, has partnered, for instance, with Swarthmore, Duke University's Pratt School of Engineering, Georgetown's School of Business, Mount Holyoke and others.

The establishment of private colleges in the region, looking up to the US model, has continuously been on the rise. Yet the question remains whether they adhere to US standards, and whether they truly implement the US model of liberal higher education, with its emphasis on classroom interaction, teamwork, and research, and its effort to create effective communicators and critical thinkers. US-style universities fall into four categories: local Arabic institutions of higher education; branches of Western institutions with local connections; local institutions with international connections; and local institutions where the language of instruction is English. The third category comprises local institutions that have an international advisory connection with US-based university. However, successful implementation of quality education in these institutions depends on the extent of their commitment to quality and the depth of the affiliation with their Western counterpart. The fourth category consists of public universities that teach both in English and in Arabic, but that require reforms and higher-quality education. These institutions could benefit from outside affiliations. Currently they lag behind for several reasons, such as the absence of faculty co-governance, local regulations on hiring locally, a workload that hampers faculty research and proper course preparation, and limited access to study trips and study-abroad programmes.

As for my tentative recommendation, first of all, university authorities should not assume that potential students are familiar with study skills and learning strategies. To reduce the "tertiary education shock" mentioned above, preparatory courses should be offered in the form of study guidance. Second, entrance exams ought to be introduced as means of preselection. At present, anyone with a high-school leaving certificate can be admitted to study at tertiary level. There is no selection process in force that would ensure that at least the minimum requirements for becoming a university student are fulfilled. Current preparatory year (PYP) programmes, primarily focused on improving English language skills are far from being sufficient.

Furthermore, psychological "pep up" training ought to be offered, especially to female students who notoriously score low in self-esteem and are predominantly introverted and unwilling to express their opinions. This strongly affects their classroom behaviour. Moreover, development of critical thinking skills should become a priority and the expectations placed in students should be lowered considerably. This is an issue faced especially by foreign faculty who are used to lecturing a different calibre of students in countries where higher education is reserved for a small percentage of top secondary-school leavers with A-levels or the equivalent. Consequently, the marking system has to be adjusted as well, eliminating general expectations on the part of the majority of students to receive top marks without fulfilling university grading criteria, which need to be defined too. Simultaneously, grade inflation, a notorious issue, should be dealt with efficiently. Furthermore, reference materials and case studies require local contextualization and application for a better understanding of the concepts and examples introduced, which, ideally, would also reduce the amount of memorization required. Western textbooks also discuss taboo topics and use language that would have to be modified for Arab students. Moreover, all of the assessment and evaluation criteria related to management, faculty, and student evaluation, currently applied in a copy-and paste-manner, using forms developed for Western universities, require thorough cultural/local modification. To give an example, students, including those in their first-semester PYP, are virtually in no position to evaluate (foreign) faculty staff, yet their opinions count considerably toward faculty evaluation.

In the KSA specifically, female management and faculty ought to become empowered in relation to decision-making processes. This would imply becoming more independent from male counterparts in colleges for men. This would, for instance, result in allowing female students to participate in foreign exchange programmes and academic conferences. The local features of Saudi higher education that can be observed are local academic calendars and timetables encompassing, for example, local Saudi holidays and prayer breaks, respectively. Local characteristics also include gender segregation, dress code, and all-Saudi administration and top management. There is also a strong tendency to appoint Muslims in departmental chair positions. Finally, the Arab concept of time prevails, resulting in planning and scheduling problems and poor time management, as well as a lack of carefully considered long-term strategies.

Conclusion and future implications

As Liu (2010) points out, there is a clear need for a new leadership model for the 21st century. The so-called old model is not only "old" but also to a large extent "American", and biased towards the pursuit of a universal model of leadership. The culture-specific nature of leadership has been demonstrated, advocating locally suitable ways of management. The global era poses its own challenges in cross-cultural leadership. In conclusion, one may observe that it is not only that Arab, and Saudi graduates in particular, lack leadership skills and suitable preparation for the challenges of the global executive world, but also there seems to exist a wide gap worldwide in terms of expectations of global executives placed in graduates and the skills and qualifications that they exhibit – hence the necessity for globalization with the assistance of local human resources managers and customized assessment methods.

Despite global homogeneous tendencies in education, there exist strong relationships between societal, cultural, and leadership characteristics and perceptions. Local culture still determines acceptable and unacceptable behaviours. Therefore locally successful managers are well socialized and acculturated. They tend to be good at acceptable behaviours, as Brodbeck and Frese (2007: 190) point out.

Regarding the leadership in the Middle East, there is a definite need for more impartial literature on the subject. Metcalfe and Mimouni (2011) address this deficit. Leadership in this region has never been as vital as in the times of the global financial crisis and the Arab Spring, yet there is a lack of detailed knowledge concerning strategies for developing capacity in leadership, national skills, and knowledge management. The volume edited by Metcalfe and Mimouni is the first text on the subject of leadership development in the Middle East published in English (drawing on both English and Arabic sources).

To sum up, first, ever-evolving hands-on skills ought to be incorporated into educational systems in order to ensure graduate global success. Second, leadership qualities and executive competencies have to be strongly related to cross-cultural issues – that is, be part of global executive development. Third, internalization and globalization of higher education seems an irreversible process, especially when it comes to modern business school programmes. Sustaining quality of higher education in view of international exchange and globalization is also crucial. Moreover, the Saudi education system has to undergo major reforms in order to face global competition, whereby the dilemma of so-called Islamic universities following both Western tradition and Islamic leadership and management styles remains. The issue of glocalization of Western education in the Middle East has also been addressed, supported by the results of two qualitative surveys conducted with students and graduates from German and Saudi Arabian universities.

References

Al-Dabbagh, M., & Assaad, C. (2010). Taking stock and looking forward: Leadership development in the Arab world. Dubai School of Government. Prepared for "Appreciating and Advancing Leadership for Public Well-being", a workshop sponsored by NYU Abu Dhabi Institute. Retrieved from http://wagner.nyu.edu/leadership/reports/files/LeadershipDevelopmentProgramsArabWorld.pdf.

Arnold, V.J. (2009). Leadership Assessment and development in the Mid-East. In W.H. Mobley, Y. Wang, & M. Li (Eds.), *Advances in Global Leadership* (Vol. 5, pp. 273–295). Cheltenham: Emerald Group Publishing.

Bass, B.M. (1990). From transactional to transformational leadership: Learning to share the vision. *Organizational Dynamics*, Winter, 19–31.

Beekun, R.I., & Badawi, J.A. (2005). Balancing ethical responsibility among multiple stakeholders: The Islamic perspective. *Journal of Business Ethics*, 60, 131–145.

Brodbeck, F.C., & Frese, M. (2007). Societal Culture and Leadership in Germany. In J.C. Chhokar, F.C. Brodbeck, & R.J. House (Eds.), *Culture and Leadership Across the World: The GLOBE Book of In-Depth Studies of 25 Societies* (pp. 147–214). Mahwah: Lawrence Erlbaum Associates.

College learning for the new global century – A report for the National Leadership Council for Liberal Education and America's Promise. Washington, DC: Association of American Colleges and Universities. (2009). Retrieved from http://www.aacu.org/leap/documents/GlobalCentury_final.pdf.

Crossley, M., & Watson, K. (2003). *Comparative and International Research in Education: Globalisation, Context and Difference*. London: Routledge Falmer.

Dimmock, C., & Walker, A.. (1998). Comparative educational administration: Developing a cross-cultural conceptual framework. *Educational Administration Quarterly*, 34(4), 558–595.

Fukushige, A., & Spicer, D.P. (2007). Leadership preferences in Japan: An exploratory study. *Leadership and Organizational Development Journal*, 28, 508–530.

Glunk, U., Wilderom, C., & Ogilvie, R. (1997). Finding the key to German-style management. *International Studies of Management and Organisations*, 26, 93–108.

Hammer, T. (1990). Developing global leaders: A European perspective. In W.H. Mobley, M.J. Gessner, & V. Arnold (Eds.), *Advances in Global Leadership* (Vol.1, pp. 99–113). Stanford, CT: JAI.

Harris, S. (2008). Internationalising the University. *Educational Philosophy and Theory*, 40(2) 346–357.

Hasegawa, H., & Noronha, C. (Eds.). (2009). *Asian Business and Management. Theory, Practice and Perspectives*. Basingstoke: Palgrave Macmillan.

Kamal, R.M., & Palmer, T.G. (2009). Arab Education Displays its Discontents. *The Lebanon Daily Star* on April 27, 2009. Retrieved from http://www.dailystar.com.lb/article.asp?edition_id=1&categ_id=5&article_id=101363.

Lenn, M.P. (2000). Higher education and the global marketplace: a practical guide to sustaining quality. *On the Horizon*, 8(5), 7–10.

Liu, L. (2010). *Conversations on Leadership: Wisdom from Global Management Gurus*. Singapore: John Wiley & Sons.

Ma, Y., & Vermaak, M. (2010). *China: Universities Face Internationalisation Dilemma*, 19 September 2010, Issue: 140. Retrieved from http://www.universityworldnews.com/article.php?story=20100918072559169.

Martin, G.S., Keating, M., & Brodbeck, F.C. (2004). Organisational leadership in Germany and Ireland. In M. Keating, & G.S. Martin (Eds.), *Managing Cross-Cultural Business Relations: The Irish-German Case* (pp. 41–69). Blackhall, Ireland: Dublin.

McCall, M.W., Hollenbeck, G.P. (2002). *Developing Global Executives: The Lessons of International Experience*. Harvard Business School Pr.

Metcalfe, B., & Mimouni, F. (2011). Leadership development in the Middle East. Edward Elgar Pub.

Murad, K. (1996). *Islamic Movement Theory and Practice: A Course for those Striving for Islamic Change in the West*. Young Muslims, Talk 9.

Nguyen, P-M, Elliott, J.G., Terlouw, C., & Pilot, A. (2009). Neocolonialism in education: Cooperative Learning in an Asian context. *Comparative Education*, 45(1), 109–130.

Phillips, D., & Ochs, K. (2003). Processes of policy borrowing in education: Some explanatory and analytical devices. *Comparative Education*, 39(4), 451–461.
Reber, G., Jago, A.G., Auer-Rizzi, W., & Szabo, E. (2000). Führungsstile in sieben Ländern Europas – Ein interkultureller Vergleich. In E. Regnet, & L.M. Hofmann (Eds.), *Personalmanagement in Europa* (pp. 154–173). Göttingen: Verlag für Angewandte Psychologie.
Smith, A, Saslow, S., & Thomas, N. (1999). *Developing the Global Executive Challenges and Opportunities in a Changing World. An Institute of Executive Development/DDI Research Report.* Retrieved from http://www.ddiworld.de/pdf/IED_DevGlobalExec_br_ddi.pdf.
Szabo, E., Brodbeck, F.C., den Hartog, D.E., Reber, G., Weibler, J., & Wunderer, R. (2000). The Germanic Europe cluster: Where employees have a voice. *Journal of World Business*, 37, 55–68.
Workman, D. (2008a). *German Culture Leadership Style.* Retrieved from http://www.suite101.com/content/german-culture-leadership-style-a50346.
Workman, D. (2008b). *Middle Eastern Leadership Style.* Retrieved from http://www.suite101.com/content/middle-eastern-leadership-style-a50519.

Appendix 1

Survey: part 1

German universities

1. What makes German universities particularly "German"? Name key local characteristics.
2. Should German universities become more "international"/globalised – in what ways? Please elaborate taking the programmes and degrees offered, language(s) as medium of instruction, etc. into consideration.
3. Do German universities prepare students for managerial/leadership roles? What is your opinion. Specify why/why not.
4. Does a degree from a German university make graduates competitive on the international job market? Provide some arguments for your answer.
5. Have you participated/are you going to participate in any international exchange programmes? If yes, please specify.
6. Have you been working/did you work on the side during your studies? If yes, please specify.

Appendix 2

Survey: part 2

Saudi universities

1. What measures would you suggest to make Saudi education more "local"/Saudi (Arab/Islamic)-like?

2. What do you think about the current model of Saudi (higher) education? What do you like and what do you dislike about it?
3. Do you think Saudi universities are too "American"? If yes, please specify in what ways.
4. Does Saudi university education *prepare the graduates for challenges of the global job market*? Do you acquire the necessary skills to become successful *leaders of the future*? Why yes/no – in what ways? Please be specific.
5. What are the *main skills* that the university education has taught you?
6. What was your *primary/secondary education* like? Name the good and bad experiences. What would you improve?

8

Face's Consequences: The Impact of "Face" on Leadership, Management and Follower Behaviour in Malaysia

Brian T. O'Donoghue

Introduction

As our world continues to "flatten" with growing globalization, managers are increasingly required to adapt to different cultures. It has been argued by many authors that failure to make such adaptations can lead to negative consequences (Hofstede, 1980a; 2001; Hofstede & Hofstede, 2005; House & Aditya, 1997). Statistics suggest that 70% of international ventures fail (Yan & Luo, 2001), often due to cultural misunderstandings (Livermore, 2011). It is not surprising, therefore, that interest in cross-cultural management research continues to grow (Dickson, Den Hartog & Mitchelson, 2003). It has been argued that a significant barrier to adopting Western management practices in Asia is "face" (Abdullah, 1996; Hofstede, 2001). While significant work has been carried out in this area, it has tended to focus more on the impact of face on societal interactions overall (Earley, 1997; Goffman, 1972; Holtgraves, 1997), on negotiations (Ting-Toomey, 1999), and less on specific management behaviour. Given the importance of face in Asia (Abdullah, 2001; Hofstede, 2001), it is important for Westerners to understand how to adapt their behaviour appropriately to manage and lead others effectively. While recent empirical research on face in Asia exists, notably in China (Kwang, 2006; Leung & Chan, 2003), the concept appears to be under-researched in Southeast Asia and Malaysia in particular. A literature search using *Emerald* and *Google Scholar* revealed only one article on Malaysia with "face" in the title which was focused on conflict management (Raduan, Suppiah, Uli & Othman, 2007). This chapter specifically examines how face impacts leadership, management, and follower behaviour in Malaysia, develops a taxonomy of "face behaviours", and provides guidelines on how management approaches should be adapted in the context of face. It also proposes a theoretical model of face as a "force", which impacts leaders, followers, and peers unequally.

Background and literature review

Within Asia, Malaysia has great potential for cultural research because it has a multiracial population with roots in many parts of Asia, including Indonesia, China, and India. Some 67.7% of the population are deemed Bumiputra, the majority being Malay, who would share some cultural heritage and religion (Islam) with many of those in Indonesia; 24.2% of Malaysians are of Chinese descent; 7.3% are of Indian descent (the latter two both being considered "minorities"); and 0.9% are "others" (Department of Statistics Malaysia, 2012). Given the multi-ethnic background of Malaysia, relevant literature was reviewed not only for Malaysia but also for China and India, from where two of the "minority" races originally came.

Culture and face

Culture has been aptly described as "Software of the Mind" (Hofstede & Hofstede, 2005: 3). Abdullah (1996) points out that while Malaysians may come from different ethnic backgrounds, they share similar Asian values, such as respect for elders, collectivism, a desire for harmony relationships, a concern for "face-saving", and a religious orientation. Among these, face is highly important (Hamzah-Sendut, 1991; Raduan et al., 2007). It is also considered important in Chinese culture (Cardon & Scott, 2003; Ho, 1976):

A number of definitions of "face" have been proposed. Two useful and succinct ones are:

> "Face" means maintaining a person's dignity by not embarrassing or humiliating him in front of others.
>
> (Abdullah, 2001: 18)

> "Face" is the respect, pride, and dignity of an individual as a consequence of his/her social achievement.
>
> (Leung, Chan, 2003: 1575)

Goddard (1997) suggests that the Malay concept of *Maruah* ("face") relates both to how others see you and how you see yourself. In Malay culture it is important that leaders *Jaga Maruah* ("maintain the dignity") of subordinates and display humility towards them (Abdullah & Ong, 2001). A number of authors distinguish different elements of face. Goddard (2002) draws a distinction between the associated Malay concepts of *Malu* and *Menghormati* (*Hormat*), which are subsets of *Maruah*. *Malu* is defined by Swift (1965) as being hypersensitive to how others see you. Goddard mentions that

> "*Malu*" is traditionally a strong force for social cohesion in the "*Kampung*" (Malay Village).
>
> (Goddard, 2002: 28)

Menghormati (Hormat) is to show respect or deference that recognizes another person's higher standing (Goddard, 2002). Earley (1997), and Leung and Chan (2003) also distinguish between two types of face: *Lien* (臉) and *Mianzi* (面子) (Chinese concepts). *Lien* is more of a moral code of conduct, while *Mianzi* is more about prestige reflecting your position in society (Leung & Chan, 2003). A CEO might have strong *Mianzi* but a clerk would not (Earley, 1997). Kwang (2006) subsequently and aptly relabelled these in English, calling them "moral face" and "social face", respectively. It appears that *lien* is more like dignity, which is to be protected, while *Mianzi* is more about having others give you high levels of respect based on position. The importance of *Mianzi* and *Hormat* are demonstrated in the respect and importance that is shown to job titles (Fernandez & Underwood, 2006). Face is also connected to promotions in China, where the giving of promotions can cause those not being promoted to lose face (Fernandez & Underwood, 2006).

Factors contributing to "face-related" behaviours

Collectivism

Face management/preservation of face is considered to be more prevalent in collectivist cultures than in individualistic cultures (Ho, 1976). Malaysia is a collectivist society (Hofstede, 2001; Kennedy & Mansor, 2000). China and India (from where many Malaysians originate) is also considered to be collectivist (Chatterjee, 2010; Sinha, 2008). In a collectivist culture, giving individual recognition in public may not always work because the importance of humility could lead to that recognition causing embarrassment to its recipient and also loss of face to others (Abdullah, 1996). It is also important that the praise is not overstated (Abdullah, 1996). In Malay culture this would be connected to

Malu, or great sensitivity to how others view you (Swift, 1965). Humility is considered to be a way of giving face to others, and is a key element of both Malay and Chinese Culture (Abdullah, 1996; Fernandez & Underwood, 2006; Gallo, 2008).

Power distance, humane orientation and "paternalism"

Power distance can be described as how accepting people are of inequalities in society (Hofstede & Hofstede, 2005). It is strongly upheld in Confucian philosophy where respect for age and authority help to maintain stability (Bass, 2008). Malaysia has been ranked as a country with high power distance (Hofstede, 2001; Kennedy & Mansor, 2000). It is likely that power distance significantly influences the great amount of face which is given to the boss. A second relevant dimension in many Asian countries is "humane orientation". Malaysia was found in the GLOBE study to be high on this dimension (Kennedy & Mansor, 2000). This is likely to affect how much face is given by the boss to subordinates. When high power distance and collectivism combine, "paternalistic" management often prevails. Jogulu (2010) describes a paternalistic leadership/management style as follows:

> managers are expected to act as parents of extended family members and protect the wellbeing of their staff. Organisations are managed as families where father is the head of organisation and employees are the children.
>
> (Jogulu, 2010: 715)

Several authors state that this paternalism is a key element of Chinese (Drucker, 1994), Indian (Selvarajah & Meyer, 2008; Sinha, 2008), and Malaysian (Abdullah, 2001; Jogulu, 2010) leadership styles. In such cultures the word of the leader is to be obeyed (Drucker, 1994). The obedience of followers is considered important in Malay culture (Zawawi, 2008). Such obedience is likely to be part of "giving face" to the leader. Paternalism involves mutual obligations between the leader and the follower (Jogulu, 2010). As part of this obligation, underperformers are less likely to be severely admonished or fired, thus saving their face. Another aspect of the reciprocal nature of paternalism is attendance at ritual events/gatherings by the leader. This is a part of Confucian culture (Yu, 2009) and is a way of giving face to subordinates.

Communication styles, emotion, and conflict

Hall (1960) classified communication styles as "high" and "low context". In high-context cultures, people communicate in polite and indirect ways, and this is normally practiced in collectivist cultures. Zawawi (2008) found that politeness and tact were important to all three major cultures in Malaysia: Malay, Chinese, and Indian. The use of high-context, indirect language has been associated with face management (Ting-Toomey, 1999). Such language helps to save the face of others. In low-context cultures, people speak directly and specifically (Hall, 1960). Abdullah and Gallagher (1995) found Malaysia to be a high-context culture. In polite collectivist cultures, to admonish someone with great emotion could result in a great loss of face for the subordinate. In countries such as Malaysia (Goddard, 1997) and China (Humphreys, 2007), to raise one's voice in enthusiasm, anger, or impatience would be considered aggressive and unacceptable. Indeed, Confucian culture discourages the use of overt displays of anger (Edelmann, 1987). Yu (2009) comments that in some instances people handle embarrassment through laughter. I have observed that such behaviour is sometimes adopted in Malaysia to avoid heated arguments. Face affects giving feedback and criticism. Asians will be uncomfortable when critically evaluating subordinates, therefore indirect high-context communication will be the norm (Abdullah, 2001). In Asia, negative feedback is generally given sensitively (Humphreys, 2007), and rarely in public (Abdullah, 2001), to save the face of the recipient. Face is also significant in conflict resolution. Disagreement between parties may be resolved via a third party (Abdullah, 2001; Cardon & Scott, 2003; Gallo, 2008), whereby this allows both of the disagreeing parties to save face and avoids a potentially heated conflict.

Methodology

Tranfield and Starkey (1998) argue that much management research is out of touch with the needs of practitioners, and that academics must rethink how to make their work valuable. This research on face, while aiming to be academically valuable, hopes to provide equal value to practitioners. Due to the exploratory nature of the work, it is qualitative in its approach. Bryman (2011) comments that interviews are by far the most popular qualitative instrument in leadership research. A series of 18 semistructured interviews were carried out. These were recorded in a digital format and subsequently transcribed.

To minimize the impact of "reflexivity" on the interview process, I followed some of King's guidelines (2004a), particularly listening critically to the interviews shortly afterwards to improve interviewer performance. The interviews varied in length from 40 minutes to 90 minutes, with most being around 1 hour. The data were analysed using template analysis (King, 2004b). The semistructured questionnaire contained 14 questions, although the interviews were handled flexibly. The coding was initially carried out using the question/themes as the main codes, with specific quotes which were cross-referenced back to their original script. Later phases included the clustering of the quotes into various other groupings as further themes emerged.

As is usual with qualitative work of this nature (Bryman, 2008; Zikmund, 2003), purposive sampling was used, and many interviewees were chosen because they were in middle-management positions and so could see things both as leader and as follower. Government statistics state that the split of Malaysian managers/senior officials in 2005 was Malaysian Chinese 55.1, Bumiputra 37.1% (mostly of Malay origin), 7.1% Malaysian Indian, and 0.7% others (Department of Statistics Malaysia, 2006), and the estimate for the general population statistics were 67.7% Bumiputra, 24.2% Chinese, 7.3% Indian, and 1.2% others (Department of Statistics Malaysia, 2012). These figures were used as directional guidelines for sampling. In this study, seven Chinese, seven Malays, three Indians and one British national were interviewed. Care was also taken to ensure that interviewees came from different age groups and industries. The profile of interviewees is shown in Table 8.1.

It was originally planned that two more Indian women managers would be interviewed, but scheduling issues prevented this from happening. Hence the sample has fewer women (5) and fewer Malaysian Indians (3) than is desirable.

The purposive sampling was facilitated by my links with the Malaysian Institute of Management and personal contacts from lecturing on various MBA and professional programmes. The use of MBA students is an accepted method of sampling in leadership research (Nana, Jackson & Burch, 2010). This gave ready access to many middle and senior managers/directors. However, the possibility of some selection bias does exist. Due to cost constraints the research was carried out in and around Kuala Lumpur, within a 70 km radius of the capital city and commercial hub.

Findings

Overview

After analysis, the responses tended to cluster around the following areas: the importance of face; humility and praise; promotions and job titles; face and seniority; the reciprocity of the relationship between leader and follower; feedback. indirect language, and disagreement.

Table 8.1 Profile of interviewees

Age	Sex	Ethnic origin	Industry experience	Position
20–30	F	Chinese	entertainment, IT software	manager
31–40	F	Malay	logistics	senior manager
20–30	M	Chinese	ceramics	GM
20–30	M	Chinese	market research	junior exec
31–40	M	Indian	IT manufacturing	senior manager
65+	M	Indian	education	retired
51–64	M	Malay	finance, property	MD
65+	M	Malay	education	director
65+	M	Chinese	construction	retired
51–64	M	Chinese	catering, automobiles, education	director
20–30	M	Malay	aviation	manager
31–40	F	Malay	footwear, exhibitions, education	lecturer
41–50	F	Malay	training, education	manager
20–30	F	Chinese	cosmetics	manager
31–40	M	Indian	manufacturing	senior manager
20–30	M	Malay	consultirg, IT software	manager
51–64	M	UK	civil Service, training	trainer
41–50	M	Chinese	rubber, wellness	sole trader

Table 8.2 provides a quick overview using these headings, giving sample responses. Deeper analysis follows below.

There was general agreement about the importance of face in Malaysia. This was across race, gender, and generation. For example, an older male Malay respondent (R12)[1] commented that it is "core", an older male Malaysian Indian respondent (R10) said it was "very, very important", with all three races, while one of the younger Malaysian Chinese female respondents (R16) commented that

> It is very important, and being a Chinese myself, I think it plays a very big part in our lives in general, not just in work, but in everything... It affects everything.

Its critical importance in Malay culture was stressed. For example, one Malay managing director (R9) commented:

> [It is] [v]ery important in the Asian context, because it guides an Asian's world view... You would rather die than lose face

Table 8.2 Interview responses overview

Topic	Example response
Importance	"it guides an Asian's worldview... You would rather die than lose face"
Humility and praise	"I guess that being uncomfortable being praised is partly our [Malay] culture"
	"I try not to focus on one person when giving praise. They are very sensitive about this"
Promotions and job titles	Your whole credibility and how people look at you is on that card"
Face and seniority	"Sometimes people would prefer to keep quiet in the meeting [rather than disagree with the boss] and then resign"
	"[My boss] does not like to be challenged at meetings due to face"
Reciprocity between leader and follower	"[When the boss invites] to give 'face' subordinates must honour his invitation"
Feedback, indirect language, disagreement	"If you scream and shout you actually lose your face... Scolding in public is two way. It loses their face and downgrades you"
	"If you openly degrade someone, there will be repercussions.... it is just a question of degree"
	"I think being Malaysian before I open my mouth, I would usually think twice whatever I want to say"

Views on whether face was becoming less important were divided. One respondent mentioned that it was equally important today (R11), while one young female Malaysian Chinese manager (R16) commented:

> But now it is being diluted because of the influence from the West

Her view was supported by a Malay managing director and a Malay lecturer:

> I don't think my children and the younger generation would see it as so important (R9)
>
> During my father's time [they[were even more sensitive. When I started working I can see a little change, but not a big change (R4)

Views on whether face was a good thing were also mixed:

> I can understand its value, it is important but it can be a hindrance. In meetings or crucial situations you aren't honest, you don't address the problem because of face (R4)
>
> [giving] too much of face is actually wasting time, but [being] too direct makes you feel disconnected. There is no personal touch or elements of warmth, no humanity (R16)

Humility and praise

The importance of showing humility as a way of giving face was also mentioned (R9, R2). This was particularly relevant to the receiving of praise. One respondent commented that you do not want other people to feel jealous or inferior (R8), and another (R9) that you don't want to come across as somebody looking for praise. One Malay manager expressed her discomfort about being publicly and effusively praised by her European boss:

> [He] keeps on acknowledging me until I feel like I didn't want to be here anymore. There are already people looking at me, like... you know. I guess that being uncomfortable for being praised is partly our [Malay] culture... it is connected to your concern for what other people are thinking (R14)
>
> the receiver [of praise] will try to be quite humble. In his heart he feels very happy but he has to show that he is humble. [This is] a core part of Chinese Culture (R11)
>
> [When reacting to praise] "They tend to push it back [praise], they will be humble, [saying] no no... fulsome US style praise might be seen as fake". (R3)

A young Malaysian Chinese general manager and a Malaysian Indian planning manager mentioned that to praise individuals in front of others could cause problems, because the others might lose face and become demotivated (R2, R13):

> I try not to focus on one person when giving praise, they are very sensitive about this (R2)

A senior Malay director in education (R12) mentioned that it is acceptable to give praise in public, as long as you "manage the face of others". He also stressed that when giving praise you must be careful not to give too much or in an exaggerated manner. He and another respondent (R2) recommended that the way to get round the difficulty with public praise was to praise the group first and only then to praise a particular person.

Promotions and job titles

Care must also be taken when giving promotions, as those not being promoted might lose face. Respondents commented that someone should be promoted only if they were clearly and objectively an outstanding performer (R5, R11, R15, R6). Two respondents reported extreme behaviour by those who had been passed over for promotion, due to loss of face. One (R15) spoke of an employee resorting to unco-operative behaviour, such as direct disobedience and absence without notification. Another (R5) reported tantrums and "chaos" in the office with the person refusing to do any work. This issue becomes even more precarious when you bring in an outsider to manage the team, particularly if they are younger than the team members (R17) as then the whole team loses face. One respondent reflected on the importance of job titles in Malaysian business circles:

> Titles are in a way your face when you are in corporate industry (R5)

(R5) mentioned that his company has recently changed designations of their senior management team from "general manager" and "Assistant general manager" to "vice president and executive vice president" to reflect their seniority. A former director mentioned that while at his previous organization he was under pressure to upgrade every "manager" to "senior manager" for the same reason (R17).

The importance of job titles on business cards as part of face is also apparent:

> Having the good title in the card I think represents what status you are, especially among your friends (R18)

> Your whole credibility and how people look at you is on that card. They want a big title. I don't see a lot of that in the US (R4)

Face and seniority

The reciprocal/paternalistic nature of leadership/management and followership in Malaysia is evident. Part of the manager's role was seen as protecting their staff (R8, R10), and is viewed as a very positive and motivating thing (R9). The other side of the equation is that the followers "obediently follow" (R10). There is evidence that superiors are not contradicted directly (R7), or in meetings (R12, R3), even if the boss is "not right" (R15). In Malaysia the boss expects respect and is given respect:

> [The subordinates are] very respectful... Will try to follow more what the boss wants... They are mere followers (R1)
>
> Sometimes people would prefer to keep quiet in the meeting [rather than disagree with the boss] and then resign. I have friends who leave at 24 hours notice. (R4)
>
> [My boss] does not like to be challenged at meetings due to face (R15)
>
> When dealing with higher management [you] have to give face to them. (R8)

One Malaysian Chinese respondent (R6) mentioned that his lack of giving face (to bosses) had damaged his early career, and he had been passed over for promotion because of it. Some mentioned that they could disagree but would do so politely (R7, R15). One mentioned that he would take it to the boss in private after the meeting (R18):

> They did state their disagreement to the superior, stated in a very nice, softly manner. Not the same as in the west, where you put up a relatively strong argument to try to change the mind of your immediate superior. A lot of the time this was due to face giving (R7)

Nevertheless a few mentioned that discussion in their companies was encouraged and was two way (R5, R15):

In my place it's two-way discussion. The bosses encourage that (R5) One Chinese general manager (R2) stated that he tried to create a constructive 'discussion space' where feedback and input could be given by his subordinates.

However, it appears that more face is given vertically upwards to senior management than horizontally (R1, R2, R6):

> When we are on the same rank, face doesn't count. [It's] every man for himself... A different dynamic... The 'face' is vertical, not horizontal. It is only given up (R14)

Reciprocity of relationship

Some obligations between followers and leaders are mutual. For example, attendance at ritual events by subordinates and leaders is part of this obligation (R4, R1, R6):

> It is your responsibility to attend... [When the boss invites] to give face, subordinates must honour his invitation (R1)

Feedback, indirect language and disagreement

The mutual relationship between leaders and followers also extends to saving the face of subordinates when giving them feedback, which is usually given in private (R4, R6, R7):

> Normally a good supervisor will tell you secretly, not in public... he [the subordinate] will appreciate that you did not let him lose face (R11)
>
> Asian bosses try to give feedback in a very fatherly manner. (He) does not want you to be sad or demotivated. [It is] very gentle, not aggressive at all (R4)

One Malay managing director (R9) described giving negative feedback as a "sandwich", with compliments and positive feedback at the start, the negative feedback (gently given) in the middle, finished with positive feedback. However, some mentioned that they had been, or had seen others, admonished in public (R5, R16, R18).

> With Dutch and American directness you could immediately have people lose respect for you (R4)

Two Malay respondents (male and female; R12, R4) mentioned that if a person was scolded in public they would be extremely unhappy, and there could be very serious consequences, such as a desire for retribution. A young Malay manager (R18) commented after being criticized publicly:

> I feel really bad. I believe that my *maruah* [dignity] has been *tercalar* [scratched/downgraded].

A Malaysian Chinese general manager (R2) commented on the reaction of subordinates to a public scolding:

> they might keep it in [suppress their anger] and then just quit. A second reaction might be reduced productivity or absenteeism (R2)

One respondent (R1) gave an example of a European boss (in Malaysia) who did not give face, and vociferously chastised staff in public. The result was very high turnover. In fact, a number of staff resigned immediately after the public admonishments. Many respondents mentioned that in Malaysia, raising your voice in public is unacceptable.

> If you scream and shout you actually lose your face... Scolding in public is two way, it loses their face and also downgrades you. [Giving] feedback one to one, this is saving their face and saving our face (R2)

> If you openly degrade someone, there will be repercussions... it is just a question of degree,... no matter what,... there will be repercussions (R4)

There were some comments that when mistakes were made, face-saving was done by apologizing to the boss (R5, R6, R15). This was often successful in preventing serious action from being taken against them. This again reflects the paternalistic attitude of some managers and CEOs:

> He won't fire you, he will think of your family (R15)

Face-saving is also facilitated by the use of high-context language:

> I think being Malaysian, before I open my mouth, I would usually think twice whatever that I want to say. (R18)

Interestingly some considered face-saving communication to be a skill (R12, R15). This is particularly important when trying to create an ideas-generating culture:

> those skilled at face will not say "I don't agree with your idea", they say "that's a very interesting idea, but I would like to give another perspective," or "I'd just like to add on to that idea" (R12)

In terms of disagreement and conflict there were differing views, with some stating that at meetings between those at the same level, conflict was often addressed directly (R5, R6, R11) with less face being given. The heat was sometimes taken out of these conversations by the parties smiling and laughing while disagreeing vociferously (R5, R8). Others mentioned that more serious conflicts were often dealt with through avoidance of the other parties (R6, R17) or by using a respected third party to save face for both parties. One former British director commented on one conflict that he tried to resolve in Malaysia. "In true British 'Anglo-Saxon' manner" he thought that it was best to "clear the air", so he got the two protagonists in a room together to deal with it:

> On reflection it was probably a mistake. (R17)

Discussion and recommendations

In my opinion the two most significant practical findings from the research relate to the very significant consequences of publicly chastising subordinates, and the great pressure felt by followers not to challenge the boss in front of others. The importance of giving negative feedback in private, as opposed to in public, has very significant implications for a Western manager who is heading a team of Malaysians. Authors in the area of cultural intelligence stress the need for mindfulness, or a heightened awareness of self and cultural situations (Thomas & Inkson, 2003). This quality would be required and fostered in Western managers, otherwise their natural inclination to give immediate feedback in public could have grave consequences.

Congruent with the assertions of Abdullah (1996), there is evidence that much of the time superiors are not contradicted directly or in meetings. This is rather at odds with the desire of many Western gurus who strongly encourage disagreement to improve the quality of thinking and to test assumptions (Bossidy, Charan, & Burck, 2002; Collins, 2001). In Malaysia the boss expects face, and is given face, through the avoidance of public disagreement. Current views on followership often focus on being courageous or being able to disagree with the leader (Bennis, 2008; Chaleff, 2009). Given the results of this research, taking such action would be very difficult for followers in Malaysia. Also a Westerner who is a follower might find that openly disagreeing with their superior in public could create problems for them in some Malaysian organizations. A third significant finding is that from a theoretical perspective, the pressure to give face seems to be more important when being given by a follower to the leader, than when it is given between follower and follower.

The importance of face in Malaysian and Chinese culture (Abdullah, 1996, 2001; Hofstede, 2001) was generally confirmed, although there was a feeling that its importance was diminishing slightly under the influence of Western culture. Kennedy and Mansour (2000) in their work for the GLOBE project have made similar comments, suggesting that the significant number of Malaysians who study abroad (in the US, the UK, Australia, and New Zealand) come back with a more Western value system. The importance of humility and sensitivity to what others think of you (Abdullah, 2001; Fernandez & Underwood, 2006; Gallo, 2008; Goddard, 1997; Swift, 1965) was generally supported. The importance of praising carefully (Abdullah, 2001; Humphreys, 2007) and the risks of the loss of face of others by giving individual praise (Abdullah, 2001) were strongly confirmed. A number of respondent followers commented on how uncomfortable they felt when receiving public praise, and a number of senior leaders commented that public praise must be handled very carefully and given appropriately. This is somewhat at odds with recommendations of leadership gurus Kouzes and Posner (2003), who stress the importance of regular, fulsome public praise and recognition for individuals. On the other side of the coin is negative feedback. This is clearly an extremely sensitive and explosive topic, which if mishandled could have calamitous results. The risk of loss of face caused by the promotion of staff was consistent with the views of Fernandez and Underwood (2006). The Western concept of meritocracy, while appearing fair to a Western observer, could cause serious problems through losing the face of those who are not promoted. A number of other findings were consistent with the previous literature: the paternalistic style of management which was often mentioned is consistent with the views of Abdullah (2001), Jogulu (2010) and Drucker (1994); the high-context polite communication which enables face-saving is consistent with the research of Abdullah and Gallagher (1995), and Zawawi (2008); the tendency for third parties to be used to resolve disputes and save face is congruent with much of the literature (Abdullah, 2001; Gallo, 2008); and the use of laughter to avoid heated disagreement shows similarity with Edelman's views (1987) about humour being used to avoid embarrassment.

Implications and conclusions: Face's consequences

In article form, this chapter was entitled "Face's Consequences" in honour of Hofstede's influential book, "Culture's Consequences" (1980b, 2001). The *Oxford English Dictionary* defines "consequence" as a "result or effect" (Hawker, 2006: 139). However, while it is more usually used in negative terms, I found both potentially negative and positive consequences to face in Malaysia. Some of the negative consequences of face are that feedback for improved employee performance might be restricted, those worthy of promotion might not be promoted, those worthy of praise might not receive it, and the leader will find it difficult to get feedback. On the positive side there are clearly many benefits to face: all parties are treated with respect, people's feelings are not hurt through aggressive and direct communication, and underperforming employees are not callously discarded by companies as they might be in some cultures.

A theoretical perspective

While theory development was not a core objective of the research, some thoughts do emerge, and it is hoped that these might spark further research and debate. In keeping with the ideas of Earley (1997), it appears that face could be defined as a force which appears to impart varying degrees of pressure on actors to behave in certain ways in certain situations, particularly situations connected to hierarchy. A simple model is hereby proposed.

The extent of the force seems to vary according to the nature of the hierarchical relationship between the actors. For example, the greatest amount of pressure to give face appears to fall upon subordinates who are very strongly obliged to give face. Here I would categorize the force as very strong. I would categorize the pressure to give face, felt by leaders or managers to their subordinates, as medium–high strength. They are obliged through paternalism to avoid public criticism, and to retain less effective employees, but the pressure is significantly less than that felt by subordinates. The pressure for followers to give face to each other is still noticeable in this collectivist culture, evidenced by how uncomfortable people are when receiving praise, and how they sometimes laugh when confronting others at the same level. Nevertheless, I would categorize it as medium. In Figure 8.1 the direction of the arrow signifies the actor to whom face is given, and the size of the arrow signifies the extent of the pressure felt by the person giving face.

I have also made tentative steps towards developing a taxonomy of observable face-related behaviours. These deal with leader to follower, follower to leader, and follower to follower behaviours. While leader to leader behaviours would also be relevant, the nature of the interview content did not shed light on this area but it could be developed through further research.

Practical guidelines

Based on the interviews, some clear practical recommendations emerge:

- *Praise* in Malaysia must be given appropriately. It should be given gently rather than effusively. It can be done in public but the whole group should be praised first before particular individuals are singled out. Such an approach should typically be followed for "employee of the month" awards.
- *Promotions* must be handled very sensitively, particularly if it involves promoting someone from within the team to manage the team. In such cases before a public announcement is made, each member of the team should be counselled to explain the rationale for the promotion, and also to manage their face by giving some positive feedback. In addition, promotions should only be given when a person is clearly acknowledged as a star performer. If the difference between them and others is marginal, it would be safer not to promote but to find an alternate solution.
- Sensitivity should be given to the importance of *job titles*. The "manager" job title should be given more freely. This allows staff to gain more respect and *mianzi* and will be more motivating for them, given that their face is on that business card.
- *Critical feedback* should never be given in public or with a raised voice. To do so could have grave consequences, the least of which is loss of respect for the superior, but more extreme cases would lead to a lack of cooperation, resignation, or retribution. It may also be better for such feedback to be given in an informal setting, and for the "sandwich" to be used: positive feedback, followed by the critical feedback, followed by positive feedback.
- When requesting *feedback* or *ideas* from subordinates, all inputs must be met without obvious rejection. You must make it a "safe" place (in terms of losing face) for such discussions to happen. Constructive high-context language must be used when the boss is disagreeing with a point. Also, a proactive open-door policy should be in operation, as many Malaysians will prefer to share their disagreement with the boss, and also to contribute ideas in private out of respect for the boss, and for fear of losing face.
- When serious conflict arises, the Western method of getting the two parties in a room to clear the air should be avoided at all costs. If possible a respected senior third party should be used to resolve the matter.
- When a manager is invited to attend a ritual event he is obliged to go.

It should be noted that a number of these recommendations are consistent with those made by Abdullah in the excellent book *Managing the*

Malaysian Workforce (2001), most of the research for which was carried out between 1990 and 1992. Particular recommendations are numbers 1, 4, and 6 regarding praise, feedback, and conflict resolution. It is notable that even though that research is 18 years old, much of it is still relevant today.

Limitations/future research

The interview scripts yielded more than 500 pages of material, and it is difficult to capture the full richness of the information within this chapter. Therefore many illuminating quotes have by necessity been left out. In addition it was not possible for the literature review to give due credit to all of the good work done in this area, most notably that of Earley (1997), who has written an excellent book specifically on the topic. Also I encountered difficulty gaining an Indian perspective on face from the literature, as searches for face and *Mariyathay* ("face" in Tamil) did not yield significant literature. Nevertheless, the interviews shed light on the topic, and the perspective appeared similar to that of Malays and Malaysian Chinese. A search using more Hindi terms might have been more useful, although my inability to use the Devangari alphabet would cause problems. Further investigation would be facilitated by working with an Indian scholar.

While only 18 interviews were carried out, this was enough to gain initial insight into face-related behaviour. However, given the low representation of Malaysian Indians, and women in the original research, a larger sample with more Malaysian Indian and female representation would be preferable to avoid the risk of future findings having a male and Malay/Malaysian Chinese bias. In addition the research was carried out in and around Kuala Lumpur, the capital city and commercial hub, so a perspective from the less developed parts of Peninsular Malaysia and East Malaysia is not included. In addition, I am Irish, and while I have lived in Asia for some time I still view the world through a Western lense.

Future research could focus on further exploring the taxonomy, and perhaps adding "leader to leader" behaviours. The taxonomy might assist in the future development of a quantitative scale for measuring face in different organizations and cultures, to gauge whether face behaviour is strong or weak.

Note

1. "R" is used to denote different interviewees.

References

Abdullah, A. (1996). *Going Glocal: Cultural Dimensions in Malaysian Management.* Kuala Lumpur: Malaysian Institute of Management.

Abdullah, A. (2001). Influence of ethnic values at the Malaysian workplace. In A. Abdullah, & A.H.M. Low (Eds.), *Understanding the Malaysian Workforce, Revised Edition* (pp. 1–24). Kuala Lumpur: Malaysian Institute of Management.

Abdullah, A., & Gallagher, E.L. (1995). Managing with cultural differences. *Malaysian Management Review, 30*(2), 1–18.

Abdullah, A., & Ong, E.E. (2001). Counselling on the job. In A. Abdullah, & A.H.M. Low (Eds.), *Understanding the Malaysian Workforce, Revised Edition* (pp. 112–125). Kuala Lumpur: Malaysian Institute of Management.

Bass, B.M. (2008). *The Bass Handbook of Leadership; Theory, Research & Managerial Applications*, 4th edition. New York: Free Press.

Bennis, W. (2008). Introduction. In R.E. Riggio, I. Chaleff, & J. Lipman-Blumen (Eds.), *The Art of Followership; How Great Followers Create Great Leaders and Organisations.* (pp. xxiii–xxviii). San Francisco, CA: Jossey Bass.

Bossidy, L., Charan, R., & Burck, C. (2002). *Execution, The Discipline of Getting Things Done.* London: Random House Business Books.

Bryman, A. (2008). *Social Research Methods*, 3rd edition. Oxford: Oxford University Press.

Bryman, A. (2011). Research methods in the study of leadership. In A. Bryman, D. Collinson, K. Grint, & B. Jackson (Eds.), *The Sage Handbook of Leadership* (pp. 15–28). London: Sage.

Cardon, P.W., & Scott, J.C. (2003). Chinese business face: Communication behaviors and teaching approaches. *Business Communication Quarterly*, 66 (4), 9–22.

Chaleff, I. (2009). *The Courageous Follower: Standing Up to and for Our Leaders*, 3rd edition. San Francisco, CA: Berrett-Koehler Publishers.

Chatterjee, D. (2010). Leading consciously. In L. Liu (Ed.), *Conversations on Leadership: Wisdom from Global Gurus* (pp. 235–253). Singapore: John Wiley & Sons (Asia).

Collins, J. (2001). *Good to Great: Why Some Companies Make The Leap And Others Don't.* New York: Harper Collins.

Department of Statistics Malaysia (2006, 2012). *Population and Vital Statistics*, August 2012, p10. Retrieved from http://www.statistics.gov.my/portal/index.php?option=com_content&view=article&id=1748%3Afree-download-monthly-statistical-bulletin-malaysia-august-2012.

Dickson, M.W., Den Hartog, D.N., & Mitchelson, J.K. (2003). Research on leadership in a cross-cultural context: Making progress, and raising new questions. *The Leadership Quarterly*, 14(6),729–768.

Drucker, P. (1994). The new superpower: The overseas Chinese. In *The Wall Street Journal* (Dec 20):17; cited in Thomas, D. & Inkson, K., (2003). *Cultural Intelligence: People Skills for Global Business* (p. 129). San Francisco, CA: Behrett Koehler.

Earley, C.P. (1997). *Face, Harmony & Social Structures.* Oxford: Oxford UniversityPress.

Edelmann, R.J. (1987). *The Psychology of Embarrassment.* Chichester: Wiley.

Fernandez, J.A., & Underwood, L. (2006). *China CEO*. Singapore: John Wiley & Sons.

Gallo, F.T. (2008). *Business Leadership in China: How to Blend Best Western Practices with Chinese Wisdom*. Singapore: John Wiley & Sons (Asia).

Goddard, G. (1997). Cultural values and "cultural scripts" of Malay (Bahasa Melayu). *Journal of Pragmatics*, 27, 183–201.

Goddard, C. (2002). Overcoming terminological ethnocentrism. *IIAS Newsletter* 27, March, 28.

Goffman, E. (1972). On face-work: An analysis of ritual elements in social interaction. In E. Goffman (Ed.), *Interaction Ritual* (pp. 5–46). The Penguin Press: Allen Lane, Harmondsworth.

Hall, E.T. (1960). The silent language of overseas business. *Harvard Business Review*, 38(3), 87–95.

Hamzah-Sendut (1991). Managing in a multicultural society – The Malaysian experience. *Malaysian Management Review*, 26(1), 61–69.

Hawker S, (2006). *Little Oxford Dictionary*. Oxford: Oxford University Press.

Ho, D.Y.F. (1976). On the concept of face. *American Journal of Sociology*, 81(4), 867–884.

Hofstede, G. (1980a). Motivation, leadership, and organisation: Do American theories apply abroad? *Organisational Dynamics*, Summer, 42–63.

Hofstede, G. (1980b). *Culture's Consequences: International Differences in Work-Related Values*. Beverley Hills, CA: Sage

Hofstede, G. (2001). *Culture's Consequences; Comparing Values, Behaviors, Institutions and Organisations Across Nations*. London: Sage.

Hofstede, G., & Hofstede, G.J. (2005). *Cultures and Organisation: Software of the Mind*. Second edition. New York: McGraw Hill.

Holtgraves, T. (1997). Styles of language use: Individual and cultural variability in conversation indirectness. *Journal of Personality and Social Psychology*, 73, 624–637.

House, R.J., & Aditya, N.R. (1997). The social scientific study of leadership: Quo vadis? *Journal of Management*, 23(3), 409–74.

Humphreys, J. (2007). Adapting the congruent temperament model with culturally specific work motivation elements. *Cross Cultural Management: An International Journal*, 14(3), 202–216.

Jogulu, U.D. (2010). Culturally-linked leadership styles. *Leadership & Organization Development Journal*, 31(8), 705–719.

Kennedy, J., & Mansor, N. (2000). Malaysian culture and the leadership of organizations: A GLOBE study. *Malaysian Management Review*, 2000, 44–53.

King, N. (2004a). Using interviews in qualitative research. In C. Cassell, & G. Symon (Eds.), *Essential Guide to Qualitative Methods in Organizational Research* (pp. 11–22). London: Sage

King, N. (2004b). Using templates in the thematic analysis of text. In C. Cassell, & G. Symon (Eds,), *Essential Guide to Qualitative Methods in Organizational Research* (pp. 256–270). London: Sage.

Kouzes, J.M., & Posner, B.Z. (2003). *Encouraging the Heart: A Leaders' Guide to Rewarding and Recognising others*. San Francisco, CA: Jossey Bass.

Kwang, K.H. (2006). Moral face and social face: Contingent self-esteem in Confucian society. *International Journal of Psychology*, 41(4), 276–281.

Leung, T.K.P, & Chan, R.Y.K. (2003). Face, favour and positioning – a Chinese power game. *European Journal of Marketing*, 37(11/12), 1575–1598.

Livermore, D. (2011). *The Cultural Intelligence Difference: Master the One Skill you can't do without in Today's Global Economy*. New York: AMACOM.

Nana, E., Jackson, B., & Burch, G. (2010). Attributing leadership personality and effectiveness from the leader's face: An exploratory study. *Leadership & Organization Development Journal*, 31(8), 720–742.

Raduan, C.R., Suppiah, W.R.R.V, Uli, J., & Othman, J. (2007). A face concern approach to conflict management – A Malaysian perspective. *Journal of Social Sciences*, 2(4), 121–126.

Selvarajah, C., & Meyer, D. (2008). One nation, three cultures: Exploring dimensions that relate to leadership in Malaysia. *Leadership & Organization Development Journal*, 29(8), 693–712.

Sinha, J.P.B. (2008). *Culture and Organisational Behaviour*. New Delhi: Sage.

Swift, M.G. (1965). *Malay Peasant Society in Jelebu*. London: Athlone Press.

Thomas, D., & Inkson, K (2003). *Cultural Intelligence; People Skills for Global Business*. San Francisco, CA: Berrett-Koehler.

Ting-Toomey, S. (1999). *Communicating Across Cultures*. New York: The Guilford Press.

Tranfield, D., & Starkey, K. (1998). The nature, social organisation and promotion of management research: Towards policy. *British Journal of Management*, 9, 341–353.

Yan, A., & Luo, Y. (2001). *International Joint Ventures: Theory and Practice*. Armonk, New York: ME Sharpe.

Yu, D. (2009). *Confucius from the Heart: Ancient Wisdom for Today's World*. Oxford: MacMillan.

Zawawi, D. (2008). Cultural dimensions among Malaysian employees. *International Journal of Economics and Management*, 2(2), 409–426.

Zikmund, W.G. (2003). *Business Research Methods*, 7th edition. Ohio: South Western.

9
Indian Leadership: Concept and Context

Rajesh Kumar and Madhavi Harshadrai Mehta

Introduction

This chapter is an attempt to understand how the concept of leadership as prevalent in Indian society is affected by the social context. The context of society can be explained as the social, economic or political structure of a society that has a role in formulating the concept of its leaders over the ages. Some of the questions to be examined are as follows. How has this concept of leadership grown through the ages? Which are the factors that have affected its growth and have finally shaped its current status? It is the understanding of context and its impact that will provide us the key to realizing the uniqueness of the concept of leadership in India.

According to Morrison (2008), structures constitute themselves as diverse social fields, which include the economy, political structure, family system and field of law and religion. These social structures tend to impose external limits on actions of individuals and compel them to act in ways which may even override their personal will. A very broad area of investigation in social theory relates to describing the ways in which the values and standards which have existed in the social and historical past have come to act upon us in the present. Marx, Durkheim and Weber showed that these practices and social obligations develop themselves into societies and patterns of actions which often come to override our own personal choices and private discretions (Morrison, 2008).

Russell (1984) suggests that in order to understand an age or a nation, we must understand its philosophy. There is a reciprocal causation. The circumstances of men determine their philosophy but, conversely, their philosophies too determine their circumstances.

Leadership

While talking about leadership we find many definitions but the one widely accepted is given by Stogdill (1950; as cited in Parry & Bryman, 2006): "Leadership may be considered as the process [act] of influencing the activities of an organized group in its efforts towards goal setting and goal achievement" (Parry & Bryman, 2006). They identify three elements in this definition: influence, group and goal. Thus leadership is a process to influence others so as to induce them to behave in a certain way. The influencing process takes place in a group and the leader gives direction to the group in the desired way according to the situation. In addition, leadership can come from any person in the group.

Similarly, according to Pfeffer (1981; as cited in Parry & Bryman, 2006) and Weick (1995; as cited in Parry & Bryman, 2006), leadership is a symbolic action – that is, it engages in "sense-making" on behalf of others and develops a social consensus around the resulting meanings. This means that leadership emerges as a process whereby a leader provides a worldview and gives a sense of direction to his subordinates.

Parry & Bryman (2006) observed that Western theory on leadership has passed through several approaches successively. The Trait Approach tried to emphasize the personal qualities and characteristics of the leaders, dominating up to the 1940s, whereas the Style Approach tried to study the behaviours of the leaders, and this was prevalent until the 1960s. Later, the Contingency Approach tried to place the situational factors towards the centre of any understanding of leadership, which dominated from the 1960s to the 1980s. This was followed by the New Leadership approach, which includes transformational leadership, charismatic leadership and visionary leadership. This defines leaders as those who articulate a vision. This approach emerged during the 1980s and then followed the Post-Charismatic and Post-Transformational leadership approach, which emerged during the 1990s. Each of these approaches signalled a change in emphasis rather than the demise of the previous one.

A later review of research by Sinha (1994; as cited in Chhokar, 2002) identified two broad streams of leadership studies. One dealt with personal characteristics and traits distinguishing leaders from non-leaders, and it did not yield any theoretical formulation. The other dealt directly with effective leadership styles which reflected a mixture of concern for task, for turbulent environment, and for the cultural needs and values.

Thus, till now, most of the leadership theories have tried to view the personality, personal characteristics, qualities of or styles used by successful leaders to control or direct the masses. The point of view missing in this perspective is how the leadership is accepted by the society. Very few scholars have tried to see leadership from the perspective of the masses (Rost, 2011) – that is, how they would like their leaders to be and, if they had a choice, what kind of leaders they would have chosen. This chapter is an attempt to understand the preferences of Indian society, the kinds of leader which have developed over the ages which might explain the kind of leaders they prefer, and why some leaders succeed and others fail in the Indian context.

Methodology

Here we attempt to understand the concept of leadership which is acceptable to and prevalent in society. In this context we will explore the perception of leadership grown through different ages – that is, ancient, medieval and modern. In so doing we will analyse the prevalent norms in the society of those ages which made certain types of leader acceptable to society, which could define the understanding of society about the normative forms of leadership of those ages. Hence we use the concept of kingship for the ancient and middle ages, because in those ages kings were the most prevalent forms of leadership and closest to the concept of leadership, while in the modern era we draw on Gandhi as the best icon we could have who is not only accepted by the people and political leaders but also by the corporate world as an example of an ideal leader. To understand the concept we refer to the historical record available that can explain the situation along with the context of society, in addition to the relevant books and journal articles available.

Leadership in ancient India

To initiate the process of understanding the concept of leadership, let's trace it to the early days of ancient India. The first sign of leadership in the early days of India can be seen in the kings, because it was they who led society in those days and thus any concept of leadership whatsoever present then was in the form of kings.

The earliest picture of the origin of kingship occurs in the *Aitareya Brahmana* (Basham, 1985), one of the later Vedic texts, perhaps of the 8th or 7th century BC. This tells how the gods and demons were at war, and the gods were suffering badly at the hands of their enemies. So they met together and decided that they needed a *raja* (king) to lead them in the battle. They appointed Indra as their king, and the tide soon turned in their favour. This legend suggests that in the earliest times kingship in India was thought to be based upon human need and military necessity, and that the king's first duty was to lead his subjects in war. A little later, *Taittiriya Upnishad*[1] repeats the story, but in a significantly altered form. Here, gods did not elect *Indra* but offered sacrifices to the high God *Prajapati*, who sent his son *Indra* to become their king. At this stage the king was still thought of primarily as a leader in war – "they who have no king cannot fight" (Basham, 1985:81), says the text – but kingship was already given divine sanction.

We can also see the story of origin of kingship from *Mahabharata*:

> On the question of Yudhishthir asking Bhishma about the origin of Kingship, Bhishma answered, "...Neither the kingship nor the king was there in the beginning (*Kritayuga*), neither scepter (*danda*) nor the bearer of the scepter. All the people protected one another by means of righteous conduct" (Embree, 1991: 238). He further explains that "...Then delusion overcame them. Men were thus overpowered by infatuation, O[2] leader of men, on account of the delusion of understanding; (Embree, 1991:238) their sense of righteous conduct was lost. When understanding was lost, all men, O best of the Bharatas, overpowered by infatuation, became victims of greed. Then they sought to acquire what should not be acquired. Thereby...desire, overcame them" and thus "Attachment attacked them...Attached to objects of senses, they did not discriminate between right and wrong action, O Yudhishthira. They did not avoid...what was not worth pursuing, nor, similarly, did they discriminate between the edible and inedible," thus, "all spiritual knowledge (Brahman) perished; and when spiritual knowledge, O king, righteous conduct also perished."
>
> (Embree, 1991: 239)

> "When spiritual knowledge and righteous conduct perished, the gods..., fearfully sought refuge with Brahma, the creator." Thereupon he (Brahma) composed a work consisting...righteous conduct (*dharma*), as well as material gain (*artha*) and enjoyment of sensual pleasure (*kama*)..." and "a fourth objective, spiritual emancipation (*moksha*).
>
> (Embree, 1991: 239)

> "Then the gods approached Vishnu, the lord of creatures, and said: "indicate to us that one person among mortals who alone is worthy of the highest eminence." Then the blessed lord god Narayana

> reflected, and brought forth an illustrious mind-born son, called Virajas (who became the first king)."
>
> (Embree, 1991: 239)

So the very origin of leadership in India was not only to protect people from external aggression but also to preserve the social order. This latter was to make people achieve the ultimate goal of life – that is, to reach spiritual emancipation (*moksha*). As has been explained in *varnashrama-dharma* (the right way of life for all classes and ages),

> The king's function was not conceived in terms of legislation, but of protection, and this involved protection of not only his subjects from invasion, but also of the order of society, the right way of life for all classes and ages (*varnashrama-dharma*) as laid down in the sacred texts.
>
> (Basham, 1985: 87)

This explains the fact that the way of life or the social order had to follow the sacred text, and not any secular path.

Majumdar (1980) explains that Hindu thought always assumes that man must try to achieve salvation and that the social institutions exist to further that aim. Thus the political institutions, too, existed to sustain the social order subsequently to help man to attain the spiritual aim – that is, emancipation. This proposition set the stage for the state to be an integral part of the vast institutional apparatus for the realization of spiritual life, and as a result could not set limits for its functions as to mere police functions, or the administration of justice. It could not be negative but had to adopt a proactive or positive attitude towards all of the main concerns of life – that is, religion, ethics, family, economics, culture and so on. Thus the king's functions can be summed up as protection of the religion, the morality, the customs and the tradition which have been derived from the gods or have evolved in society.

Basham (1985) says that if the king infringed sacred customs too blatantly he incurred the hostility of the *Brahmanas* (the priests), and often the lower orders also. In such cases his fate was pointed out in many a cautionary tale, such as that of the legendry king Vena:

> Vena took his divinity very seriously and as a result forbade all sacrifices except those meant to himself. He also promoted interclass marriages. He continued with this even after being warned by the

> ancient sages. "they (sages) finally beset him I na body and slew him with blades of sacred grass, which miraculously turned to spears in their hands" (Basham, 1985:87). This story has been repeated in numerous sources, which shows a continual warning to the secular minded kings who attempted to flout the sacred law.

This story explains that the *Brahmanas* and the sacred law used to have control over the actions and decisions of the king. All textbooks on statecraft recommended that the king should listen to the counsel of his ministers, who were advised to be fearless in debate, and according to Basham (1985) more than one king was overthrown through the intrigues of his councillors. Another important source of control was public opinion. The Buddhist *jataka* stories, reflecting the situation in northern India, gave more than one instance of kings deposed by mass revolt. In the case of *Ramayana*, the legend of Rama, who was held up as the ideal king to all later Hindu rulers, the hero exiles his beloved wife, Sita, even though he was convinced of her innocence, on knowing that his subjects suspect her chastity and fear that her presence might create problems.

Thus the king's primary function was to protect society, and the state was merely an extension of the king for the furtherance of that end. The ideal set before the king was one of energetic beneficence, as Basham (1985) asserts that Ashoka was not the only king of India to proclaim that all men were his children.

Arthashastra[3] goes to the extent of suggesting a timetable for the king's day, which allows him only four-and-a-half hours sleep and three hours for eating and recreation, the rest of the day being spent in state affairs of one kind or another. However, according to Basham (1985), such a programme was rarely kept in practice, but this shows the ideal at which the king was expected to aim. About income, he further explains, Shukra advised kings that after storing one sixth of their income in his treasury they should allot half to defence, a twelfth for their personal use, a twelfth for charity, a twelfth for payment of civil servants and the last twelfth to *prakritayah* (work for public value).

The most important fact which Basham (1985) explains is that the royal decrees (*Sasana*) were not generally new laws but orders referring to special cases. *Dharma* and established customs were usually looked on as inviolable, and the king's commands were merely applications of the sacred law. Majumdar (1980) too claims that the political writers repeatedly remind the kings of their duty to follow the *dharma* or principles of law laid down by the sages, and warn them against doing things which are likely to incur the wrath or displeasure of their subjects and perhaps even falling victim to a public uprising. This clearly shows the severe limitations within which the kings had to live, where they were merely obeying the already defined rules and regulations.

Though divinity was enshrined in the king, in practice a king was rarely an autocrat and his decisions did not go unchallenged, so in practice his divinity often made little difference to the body politic. To understand this position we should try to understand Hindu society. Basham (1985) explains that divinity was cheap (easy to attain) in ancient India; every *Brahmana* was in a sense a god, as were ascetics[4] or sages with a reputation for sanctity. Householders sponsoring and financing sacrifices, too, were in theory raised to divinity, at least for the duration of the ceremony, while even sticks and stones might be alive with inherent godhead. Moreover, the gods were fallible and capable of sin. If the king was a god on earth he was only one among many, and so his divinity might not always weigh heavily upon his subjects.

Before the days of Buddha, the king was exalted far above ordinary mortals through the magical powers of the great royal sacrifices. The royal consecration (*rajasuya* later replaced by simplified *ahishek*) imbued the king with divine power. The magical power of the king was further strengthened by rites, such as the *vajapeya* and the *ashvamedha*, which also ensured the prosperity and fertility of the kingdom. This clearly shows that kings were more or less dependent upon the *Brahmanas* (the priestly class) to exalt their status to the gods because it was only through rituals conducted by the *Brahmanas* that they could attain such status. Thus *Brahmanas* already had a decisive role in the positioning of the kings, which consequently gave them the upper hand in the power system.

At all times, Basham (1985) says, the priestly class claimed many privileges in law. According to most orthodox sources, the *Brahmanas* were exempt from execution, torture and corporal punishment, and the worst penalty that could be imposed on them was the humiliation of losing their topknot, followed by confiscation of property and banishment. But the *Smriti* of *Katyayana* allows the execution of a *Brahmana* for procuring abortion, the murder of a respectable woman, and the theft of gold, while the Arthashastra admits sedition, and also sanctions the branding of *Brahmanas*.

The Indian sacerdotal caste were the *Brahmanas*, some of whom functioned as priests, preceptors, writers and political advisers. They enjoyed high prestige of birth but were mostly poor (Majumdar, 1980). They were expected to lead austere lives and depended on gifts or offerings from princes and peasants alike. Another caste was the warrior caste, the Kshatriyas, who were also supposed to rule. They had to share social control with the *Brahmanas*, who represented the brain power, and the Vaishyas who represented the economic strength of the community. In this way there was no concentration of the prestige of birth, influence of wealth and political office.

There was rarely presented a scenario of a high degree of centralization. The organization of government consisted of federalism, feudalism and local autonomy. Even then, says Majumdar (1980), it could not exhaust the whole subject of social regulation. There existed parallel organizations, on the basis of function, in the form of village communities, kinship associations and guilds of manufacturers, merchants, bankers and so forth. They enjoyed considerable autonomy and their customs and rules were well recognized by the state and the law-givers.

Thus the organization of state was both vertical and horizontal, and it comprised a number of local and functional jurisdictions and intermediate associations standing in various, more or less ill-defined, relations with the state.

Thus the leadership in this condition was more of a person who could uphold the already defined laws and which were external to his personality. It was not his personal charisma, as in Western society, which provided legitimacy to the leader in the society but rather the observance of the customs and law of the land which provided him with acceptance among the masses. That is why the ideal leader was Ram of Ramayana who could go to the extreme of banishing even his wife if the act was not in accordance with the existing customs or *shastra*. This story of Rama is more an anecdote and tells much more about the society and norms prevalent then.

Leadership in medieval India

Carrying on the discussion of the medieval period which was supposedly dominated by Muslim rulers, especially concentrated in Delhi, we can see a lot of diversity in the type of leadership in a society where the majority of the population did not conform to the norms and customs of the rulers. When the Muslim leadership came to India they found a very different situation. Their customs were very different and they were faced with a situation where the majority of the population did not conform to their religion. Nor were they ready to accept it. They had to take a middle path which conformed neither to the Islamic regulations nor to the law of the land – that is, Hinduism.

According to Majumdar (1984), the Mughal emperor ruled without any effective check on their authority. In theory they were only servants of their Muslim law but they could neither supersede nor modify it. In practice this was true of the personal law of the Muslims alone. The administrative organization was recognized in practice as lying beyond the jurisdiction of Qazis. Even in countries like Persia, Afghanistan and Egypt, rulers had felt it necessary to incorporate pre-Muslim customs into the organization of government. In India, where the preponderant bulk of the population refused to accept Islam, it was all the more difficult to run government according to Muslim law (Majumdar, 1984). As a result, the rulers exercised greater liberty in the organization of government. They acknowledged themselves as the agents of Islam, interested in its spread among the non-Muslims and in securing conformity to orthodox practices among Muslims. In return, the theologians usually left them alone in the organization of government.

Akbar[5] too did not claim the authority to do what he liked; he simply asserted that his innovations should not be condemned unless they were contrary to the Quran. Thus the Quran was recognized in theory at least as the fundamental law of the state. This could have tempered Mughul despotism and rendered a limited monarchy to the Mughuls on the basis of their religious ideology. It failed to do so, however, because there was no institution in the Mughul state capable of effectively containing the Mughul rulers if they ever transgressed the law. A theocracy without an independent religious head is impossible. It is further necessary that the authority of such a theologian should be recognized without dispute by the vast majority of the population, but in India the majority comprised Hindus. Thus the authority of theologians failed to make a limited monarchy of the Mughul government. It remained free of any effective control of any kind of theologians.

The Mughul government was then a despotism but of a peculiar kind. Its absolute authority was never so interpreted by its rulers. Theoretically, and to a large extent in practice, the judiciary was independent. Administration of justice through Hindu Panchayats and Qazis courts owed nothing to the king, though he made provisions for the maintenance of the Qazis. The Mughul rulers made few laws of their own and did not claim the right to do so.

Akbar laid the foundations of the Mughul School of Painting and the Mughul style of architecture. Persian as well as Hindi literature saw a glorious revival under his generous patronage. Akbar's knowledge, acquired via listening, could be neither methodological nor coordinated. He was a man of original ideas and bold conceptions. His administrative and military reforms reveal his constructive ability and organizational power. In his social reforms – the abolition of forced *sati* (immolation of widow), encouragement of widow remarriage and prohibition of child marriage – he anticipated the ideas of modern times. He believed in the divinity of kingship regarding royalty as a "light emanating from monarchy". Few monarchs have come nearer to the ideal of a father of his people. As the apostle of *sulh-i-kull* (universal toleration) he stands unique.

Thus the situation in which the Muslim rulers controlled the state created a condition where they had no customs and norms controlling their behaviour because Muslim theologians were not in a position to control them and the Hindu majority were militarily defeated so they could not enforce their laws upon the rulers. In this condition the Muslim ruler by and large ruled their territory free of any control. They relied primarily on their own intellect and charisma rather than on the basis of any independent rules guiding them, which was a new phenomenon for India in those days. So this was perhaps the first time that India actually witnessed charismatic leaders in the form of their rulers.

One more important factor of Muslim rule was that it never broke the social and cultural fabric of the Hindu majority of India. Hindu society remained intact along with its customs and beliefs. The kings ruled with an assimilation of Muslim and Hindu culture.

Leaders in modern India

As a background to modernization in India before we discuss Gandhi's leadership, we see a totally different period when India found new rulers in the form of the British, whose main purpose was not to rule but to use India as a colony for its products and trade. It was the British colonialism, says Jaitly (1991), during modern times that fundamentally altered the social situation in India. There was not a single aspect of Indian society and economy that remained unaffected by it. The old structure was shaken to its foundation and with it the common culture. The British rulers were not interested in assimilating the local culture like the Muslim rulers. Instead their main aim was to maximize profit for the British Empire. They initiated cultural invasion of India and, in the process, not only deliberately undermined the cultural legacies of the country but also introduced missionary methods and an educational system that would strengthen this cultural invasion.

On top of this the modern Western cultural traits and belief systems were superimposed on Indian, which led to a contact with

Western culture without harmonizing the different categories of culture. Consequently a counterproductive cross-fertilization of cultures took place and proceeded to further transform the cultural fabric of Indian society. The Hindus and Muslims came out with differing and often mutually antagonistic response patterns to the colonial rules.

Once this cultural authority was streamrolled by the newly emergent nation-state authority as represented by the colonial British rule, it inevitably established the primacy of the political arena. The fallout from this was that people, both Hindu and Muslim, became alienated from the foreign rulers as well as from each other. British rule systematically reduced Hindus to a truncated, less confident and closed community. Accordingly, Hindus were preoccupied with defending their reduced position against the cultural onslaught of the British colonizers. According to Jaitly (1991), they resorted to reactionary efforts to depict Ram and Krishna as characters of history, while their inability to substantiate their *Lilas* led them to call them unhistorical and imaginary. They became victims of stagnation and decay while chasing the external criteria of progress and development. They raised the slogan of intellectualism and rationality but succumbed to inconsistencies and stagnation in their manifest behaviour and life pursuits.

In response to British annexation, Muslims (being in power) were first rudely shocked and surprised over their inability to respond. According to Arnold Toynbee (as cited in Jaitly, 1991), "the sudden demonstration of their (Muslims) latter day decadence by the unanswerable logic of defeat in battle was as surprising to them as it was humiliating". According to Jaitly (1991), along with the realization of their inability to acquire control, there grew a sense of insecurity and fear among them about their position in society as an ineffective minority – a minority that had been the rulers till now but was not sure about the response of the majority to its defenceless existence. In addition they were disrespectful of British modern education which led to their lower level of literacy and education, which in turn led to their minimal presence in government jobs in addition to the neglect of the British rule for their interest. Devoid of the past glory and the current socioeconomic miseries, Muslims slid back to scriptural orthodoxy on the one hand and resorted to pan-Islamic rebuilding on the other. These differing responses were considerably conditioned by the British, who consciously pitted them against each other (Jaitly, 1991: 50). During the revolt of 1857 the British felt threatened by the Muslims as they held them responsible for initiating a jihad against the British. In contrast they patronized the Hindus. They replaced Urdu with Hindi as the language to be used in court. Later, when the British were faced with the rise of Indian nationalism, they felt that this was carried out by the Hindu majority. As a result they favoured Muslims over Hindus, so much so that the British formed the Muslim League to act as a consolidated voice of the community at a social as well as a political level. This division ultimately led to the division of the country itself, and Pakistan emerged in 1947.

The coming of a renaissance prompted the Hindu intellectuals to go to their roots. This led to their reinterpretation of their ancient cultural heritage to suit their modern needs. This helped them to bring back their lost identity. It was not exactly the restoration of the past but a reinterpretation which gave them enough strength to talk on equal terms with their British and Muslim counterparts. According to Jaitly (1991), the Hindu renaissance acquired three fundamental qualities: rationalism, cosmopolitanism and a dynamic classicism.

Rationalism provided the unceasing search for constant and universal principles of human nature. Cosmopolitanism provided the ideals of tolerance and understanding between people and culture. While dynamic classicism acted as a link between the past and the present, where though they took help of their ancient knowledge but at the same time they were also aware of the ongoing changes in modern times, thus providing a new lease of life to the decaying cultural world.

The coming of Mahatma Gandhi in this context was the most important event of this period. He was not only a leader of his time but is regarded thus far as the most important and an ideal leader for Indian society. Any leader even today who adopts Gandhi's methods is more readily accepted by society than any other form of leadership. The essence of Gandhi's politics lies, says Jaitly (1991), in his incessant exploration of truth, the sincerity of which can be judged by the title of his autobiography, *The Story of My Experiments with Truth*. According to Gandhi's thoughts, the truth embraced the totality of human endeavours as contained in his thought, speech and actions. Truth for him was both relative and absolute. He strove to come to terms with absolute truth through relative truth. Truth was his ultimate quest: "as long as I have not realized this absolute truth, so long must I hold the relative truth as I have conceived it. That relative truth must, meanwhile be my beacon, my shield, my buckler." (Jaitly, 1991:60). In his quest for truth, Gandhi was a *Sanatani*.[6]

It is *dharma*, which according to him, sustained all the diversities of life and coordinated their interplay. Politics was integrated in *dharm* in the Gandhian framework, for Gandhi specified that "life of a nation like that of individual is an indivisible whole". In this way he again brought forth the ancient principles of state, politics and kingship or leadership because these are the stories told about the state in ancient scriptures:

> The state was conceived as an organic whole and its different constituent as its limbs (on the analogy of a human body), while the king was merely a part of it. The limbs of a state are described as, the king, the minister, the country, the fort, the treasury, the army, and the friend. Manu[7] recognizes that none of the organs is really superior to the others. "Each limb is particularly qualified for the fulfillment of a distinct purpose and hence each is declared to be the most important in reference to that purpose which is fulfilled by its means".
>
> (Majumdar, 1980: 307)

Gandhi thus spoke of the attainment of the ultimate truth as his and his movement's ultimate destination. His entire journey of national movement was a spiritual journey. For him, everything he did was not politics but religion – that is, to reach the ultimate truth. His entire philosophy of *satyagraha, ahimsa* (non-violence), *Anshan* (fasting), being celibate, vegetarianism, his *maunvrat* (keeping of one day in silence) all spoke of his deep faith in Indian spiritualism. Above all, the tendency to offer a sacrifice in personal life for others' welfare, which he also practised n his political life, made him a saint in Indian politics (Prabhu & Rao, 1996). Whether in South Africa or in India, the dwelling space where he lived with his followers was known as an *ashram* (spiritual hermitage). These are all indicators of his political life being spiritual, which also served as a symbol used for leadership. Chakrabarty (2007) explains that the term *Mahatma* became a metaphor which used to inspire the masses into action even under adverse conditions. The evolution of such a metaphor was inspired by the saintly image of Gandhi as well as his ideology of non-violence.

He further elaborates that Gandhi translated the age-old Indian tradition of *ahimsa* into modern nationalist action. He stood out in the nationalist crown simply because his ideology was well articulated in the terms or language of local people. He never spoke of high ideals; rather he always used the metaphors of Ramayana and Gita to convey his message to the masses so that they could understand as well as accept them as their own. Chakrabarty (2007), remembering Subhash Chandra Bose's words, further explains that Gandhi spoke in a language that the common masses could comprehend – that is, in the language of

Bhagwat Gita and Ramayana. While talking about *swaraj* (home rule), he reminded people of the glories of the Ramayana rather than explaining the virtues of provincial autonomy, and the people understood him, and when talking about *ahimsa* (non-violence) he reminded them of Buddha and Mahavira, and the people accepted him (Chakrabarty, 2007:190).

In *Hind Swaraj* (home rule; Gandhi, 1997) he has said that he used the *Atma Shakti* (inner force or force of the soul) in place of the physical force. According to Chakrabarty (2007), his fasting was an intense purification process for his soul force and consequently for his spiritual strength. He also used fasting for atoning for the misdeeds of his followers as he held himself responsible for their deeds as their leader. He always declared himself to be a seeker of the truth, which is the single most subject explored by all the leaders or kings as was instructed by the ancient scriptures of India. According to Murphy (1991), "truth" is an imperfect translation of the word *Satya* used by Gandhi, which means "the ultimate reality", and the ultimate truth is god himself, the force behind everything.

Thus in India we can see that the greatest leader ever born was Gandhi. He followed the path of the ancient scriptures, which incessantly spoke of the attainment of the ultimate truth as the ultimate search of every man, and thus instructed the kings and the state to be so organized to be able to facilitate the attainment of all their subjects to attain the ultimate truth. Never had India known such a popular leader, and in Gandhi we can easily see a person who was also pursuing the path suggested by the ancient scriptures, which ultimately matched with the spiritual soul of the land and brought masses thronging to him.

Today we have Anna Hazare[8] – the crusader against corruption, who emulated Gandhi and achieved unprecedented success. The reason is that even today the majority of India's population lives with its ancient scriptures and follows them in their daily chorus. Still India follows its more than 5000-year-old values and can be found chanting mantras from those days. A very small fraction of the population has accepted the Western lifestyle, but it is the majority of India who count in support of a new leader rather than the fraction of people who follow Western philosophies.

Leadership in Indian management literature

One name that looms large in terms of India's contribution to management theory is that of Dr Jai B.P. Sinha (1980), who attempted to explore which type of leadership most suited the Indian context. He has witnessed and tested the theory in the field, besides interacting extensively with practitioners before developing his theory of leadership. According to Sinha (1980), the sociopsychological makeup of an employee can be traced back to the sociocultural roots of their family and to the social groups they belong to. The reason for this is that before an individual joins an organization, they have already developed a need structure, value system, cognitive maps and habit hierarchy strongly influenced by the family and a close-knit social group.

Sinha, Dayal and De have noted that Indians have a preference for a personalized relationship (Sinha, 1980). Someone in a personal relationship will receive all sorts of favours (time, money, favourable decisions, etc). In addition, rules, regulations and even formal obligations and duties may be ignored in order to accommodate a friend or a relative. Dayal (1976, as cited in Sinha, 1980) has noted that in India "relationship and organizational performance are generally not separated". He also noted that personal relationships makes juniors more involved and hard working.

Sinha (1980) found that it is nurturant task (NT) leadership[9] is applicable in the case of India. This has two components: concern for task and nurturant orientation. The NT leader is responsible for initiating, guiding and directing his subordinates to work hard and maintain a high level of productivity. However, this task orientation has a mixture of nurturance. The leader cares for his subordinates, shows affection, takes a personal interest in their well-being and, above all, is committed to their growth. One may find striking similarities in the roles played by the kings – leaders in ancient and medieval India – and NT leaders. NT leadership is indicative of almost the same elements and sentiments as found in the leaders in ancient and medieval India. Of course, the attainment of the ultimate truth does not get a mention in NT leadership.

In the case of Indian managers, they need hierarchy, assessed by Haire et al. (1966, as cited in Sinha, 1980), and follow the path of security, esteem, social status, autonomy and self-actualization. Thus even among managers this self-actualization part still exists even though these are the segments of society which have generally received a Western style of education.

Conclusion

In India, attainment of the ultimate truth has been the ultimate goal for mankind since the ancient ages, and all of the ancient scriptures endorsed and prescribed this. This went to the extent of organizing the entire state around the idea of facilitating the journey of its subject to the ultimate truth. The leaders of society or the kings were advised to take special care of their subjects, keeping in mind their general welfare and paving their path for their ultimate realization of the truth. This idea has passed through the ages and is still guiding the principles of leadership in India today.

Gandhi made his entire freedom movement a search for truth and led the life of a saint. This made him an unquestionable leader of the masses. First, his search for ultimate truth made him reach the same path which the ancient scriptures always pointed to. Second, he accepted the life of a saint. Saints were those people who renounced the world to obtain the ultimate truth and society always kept the search for ultimate truth as the highest level of pursuit for mankind. For them, therefore, a saint was always someone who was revered the most. Thus Gandhi received the utmost reverence.

Further, Sinha (1980) found that the preference of the masses is for nurturant task leadership, where the leader takes care of his subordinates' well-being and, above all, their personal growth. This also points in the same direction as has been described through the ages by the Indian literature about the ideal leader. Sinha (1980) further applied his argument in the context of the organization, whereas the leadership concept as prevalent in Indian society has always been about grooming people for realization of the ultimate truth, which has remained the ultimate goal of the state, and any other institution.

This realization of the ultimate truth needs a holistic approach of grooming where the entire being of a person is geared towards achieving completeness to the extent that they discover the ultimate reality. The concept came from Indian spiritualism and was accepted in every aspect of Indian society, whether polity or economy. This was the ultimate goal designed for leadership and the person who nurtures this aspect is accepted as a leader in the Indian context.

Notes

1. *Upanishads* are philosophical texts considered to be an early source of Hindu tradition. *Taittiriya Upanishad* is the seventh of the 108 *Upanishads*. It talks about the various degrees of happiness enjoyed by the different beings in creation.
2. "O" is a way to address someone, often with respect. The quote is from an English book containing transliteration from Sanskrit.
3. Arthashastra is an ancient Indian treatise on statecraft, economic policy and military strategy written by Koutilya in the 4th century BC. Koutilya is

identified with Chanakya, the prime minister of Chandragupta Maurya, the founder of the great ancient Indian Mauryan dynasty.

4. Anyone who practises a renunciation of worldly pursuits to achieve higher intellectual and spiritual goals.
5. Akbar (1542–1605) was the third Mughal emperor and one of the greatest rulers of India. He was the grandson of Babur who founded the Mughal Dynasty in India. During his reign the Mughal Empire spread over most of north and central India.
6. Sanatani is one who is looking for the eternal essence of life and the values governing it. It is a follower of *sanatan dharma (eternal path)*, the original form of what is today called the Hindu religion or Hinduism.
7. In Indian tradition, Manu is considered to be the progenitor of mankind and the first king to rule the earth.
8. Anna Hazare is a much acclaimed social activist in India. A former soldier in the Indian army, he is well known and respected for upgrading the ecology and economy of the village of Ralegan Siddhi in Maharashtra, India. Currently he is famous for his campaign against corruption and for suggesting the introduction of a strong position of *Jan Lokpal* (ombudsman) to control corruption in India.
9. Nurturant task leadership is the term coined by Dr J.B.P. Sinha to indicate the type of leadership that suits the Indian context the most.

References

Basham, A.L. (1985). *The Wonder that was India*. London: Sidwick & Jackson.

Chakrabarty, B. (2007). *Mahatma Gandhi a Historical Biography*. New Delhi: Roli Books Pvt. Ltd.

Chhokar, J. (2002). Leadership and culture in India: The GLOBE research project. In R. House, & J. Chhokar (Eds.), *Studies of Managerial Cultures in 12 Countries*. Retrieved from http://www.ucalgary.ca/mg/GLOBE/Public/Links/india.pdf.

Embree, A.T. (1991). *Sources of Indian Tradition* (vol. 1). Delhi: Viking, Penguin.

Gandhi, M.K. (1997). *Hind Swaraj and Other Writings*. A.J. Parel (Ed.). New York: Cambridge University Press.

Jaitly, A. (1991). *India's Political Culture*. Jaipur: Aalekh Publisher.

Majumdar, R.C. (1980). *The History and Culture of Indian People – The Age of Imperial Unity*. Bombay: Bhartiya Vidya Bhavan.

Majumdar, R.C. (1984). *The History and Culture of Indian People – The Mughul Empire*. Bombay: Bhartiya Vidya Bhavan.

Morrison, K. (2008). *Marx Durkheim Weber Formation of Modern Social Thought*. New Delhi: Sage.

Murphy, S. (1991). *Brief Outline of Gandhi's Philosophy*. Retrieved from www.mkgandhi.org/articles/articleindex.htm.

Parry, K.W., & Bryman, A. (2006). Leadership in organisations. In S.R. Clegg, C. Hardy, T.B. Lawrance, & W.R. Nord (Eds.), *The Sage Handbook of Organisation Studies* (pp. 447–468). New Delhi: Sage.

Prabhu, R.K., & Rao, U.R. (1996). *The Mind of Mahatma Gandhi*. Ahmedabad: Navajivan Trust.

Rost, J.C. (2011). Leadership development in the new millennium. In D. Collinson, K. Grint, & B. Jackson (Eds.), *Leadership* (pp. 89–107, vol. II). London: Sage.
Russell, B. (1984). *A History of Western Philosophy*. London: Unwin Hyman.
Sinha, J.B.P. (1980). *The Nurturant-Task Leader*. New Delhi: Concept Publishing Company.

10
Transformational Leadership in the Saudi Arabian Cultural Context: Prospects and Challenges

Sami A. Khan and Deepanjana Varshney

Introduction

Leadership has become the key issue in managing organizations, societies, and entire nations. The emerging business and economic environments have forced organizations to be flexible, adaptive, entrepreneurial, and innovative in order to effectively meet the changing demands of the present-day business environment (Orchard, 1998; Parker & Bradley, 2000; Sarros, Cooper, & Santora, 2008; Valle, 1999). Adopting and sharpening these virtues is not possible without a transformational leader who can fix the jigsaw puzzle and influence others to achieve greater goals. A plethora of literature has investigated leadership issues in recent times, and the importance of leadership has achieved a distinct reference in terms of managing organizations and sustaining the pace of change. Leaders provide vision to achieve goals, and followers feel contentment because they have a vision of a better tomorrow with the help of their leader. Despite so much being written about transformational leadership, there is a dearth of country- and region-specific research, especially in the Middle Eastern and Arab regions. The national leadership dimension is being redefined, and the new meaning of leadership is being developed. Against this background, this chapter is an attempt to understand the dynamics of transformational leadership and its relevance for Saudi managers. The Kingdom of Saudi Arabia (KSA) consented to World Trade Organization in 2005, and it aspires to become one of the world's ten most competitive economies. However, it is not possible to achieve this without having a set of transformational business leaders who can put their energies into achieving that goal.

Emerging views about transformational leadership

The concept of leadership has achieved significant importance, and most business schools are teaching their students to be leaders and not managers. A large volume of literature about leadership that has emerged in recent years is confusing and contradictory (Robbins, 2005). There have been many schools of thought on leadership, from the trait theorists to behavioural, contingency, and charismatic theorists. Ethical leadership and cross-cultural leadership are additional types that add to the confusion. As defined by Boseman (2008), leaders are given the opportunity to lead not because they are appointed by senior managers but because they are perceived and accepted by followers as leaders. Thus the acceptance and readiness of followers is the key leadership attribute. Riaz and Haider (2010) also rightly claim that a leader is responsible for not only leading but also providing followers with the tools that are needed to accomplish the organizational goals. In the event that a leader is unable to provide adequate information or resources, a conflict may arise rooted in distrust and demotivation. They believe that a leader's role is very delicate, and every action or decision must be strategic. Leaders can anticipate future likelihoods and plan alternative strategies to meet uncertainties. Such traits are common in historical leaders. This sense of anticipation is believed to be innate and cannot be learned. A strong leader must have self-confidence and must be able to listen, consult, involve, and explain why and how things should be done. Sheetz-Runkle (2011) claimed that boldness, decisiveness, commitment, authority, conviction, and right decision making are qualities that influence self-confidence.

The behavioural school of leadership advocates that leaders are not only born but also made. Certain behaviours can be learnt and one can be a leader by demonstrating those behaviours. Worldwide organizations train their managers and enrol them in development programmes to master those behavioural dispositions and acquire those leadership attributes. Schwartz, Jones, and McCarthy (2010) found that these organizations build their leadership programmes around competency models, which include a list of core skills that they expect their leaders to cultivate to become effective in this role. Leadership has to be taught and attributes need to be acquired. Organizations need employees who can be moulded into leaders who can influence others to complete tasks and follow the mission of the organization. Leaders are also able to empower followers by "making key behaviours automatic" (Schwartz et al., 2010). They must embrace the importance of change and treat their employees better in order to thrive in a global and competitive society. Kouzes and Posner (2003) believed that in a highly competitive and rapidly changing environment, caring and appreciative leaders are the ones to bet on for long-term success. These attributes allow leaders to relate to employees and encourage them to achieve their goals.

Leadership and vision are synonymous. Leadership in the workplace is about having vision and being able to transform it into action by influencing others to perform at higher levels and promoting the importance of organizational and interpersonal citizenship behaviours. According to Jago (1982), leadership is expressed or displayed through interaction among people and necessarily implies its complement: followership. For one to be able to exert an influence, another must permit themselves to be influenced. In fact, leadership is defined as an ability to influence followers. In the organizational context, managers do that using their authority or legitimate authority, which empowers them to delegate work to others. Managers also do that by influencing their subordinates through rewards. In that respect, transactional leadership styles involve motivating followers through the exchange of rewards, praise, and promises. Ivey and Kline (2010) characterized the transactional leadership by leader–follower exchanges, whereby leaders exchange things of value with followers to advance both the leaders' own and the followers' agendas. Xirasagar (2008) contended that three subscales could be used to assess the transactional leadership. These are contingent reward, management-by-exception (active), and management-by-exception (passive). Vecchio, Justin, and Pearce (2008) have emphasized the importance of transformational leadership over transactional leadership. They believe that Bass and his associates' views about morality relative to transformational and transactional leadership suggest that transactional leaders would be expected to engage in unethical practices more so than transformational leaders. A leader's ethical values may play a particularly strong role in influencing followers' satisfaction with them. It makes transformational leadership more appealing for effective managers.

Transformational leadership, which is also referred to as charismatic leadership, inspires followers to transcend their own self-interest for the good of the organization. These leaders are capable of having a profound and extraordinary effect on their followers (Robbins, 2005). Conger and Kanungo (1998) identified a few key characteristics of these leaders, indicating that they have vision and clearly articulate it, they take personal risk, they are sensitive to the followers' needs and the environment's needs, and they show unconventional behaviour. Jung, Chow, and Wu (2003) argued that transformational leadership could also enhance innovation by engaging employees' personal value systems (Bass, 1985; Gardner & Avolio, 1998) and thereby increasing their levels of motivation by encouraging them to think creatively. Thus transformational leadership appears to be a sure success recipe for business leaders. Rhodes, Walsh, and Lok (2008) stated that while leaders initiate and drive organizational change, they manage change only with the help of other change agents. These operate with different change skills and competencies, depending on the particular requirements and circumstances. Pounder (2008) explained interlinkages of transformational leaders with their followers. He found that the effect of transformational leadership on subordinates rests on three leadership outcomes:

- the ability of the leader to generate extra effort on the part of those being led;
- the subordinates' perception of leader effectiveness;
- the subordinates' satisfaction with the leader.

What factors influence the performance of these transformational leaders? Are the contextual factors as important as the attributes of the leaders? When exploring the conditions under which transformational leadership affects the performance, the findings show that transformational leadership relates to the followers' identification with the work unit and self-efficacy, which interact via efficacy to predict individual performance, thus representing a moderated mediation effect (Walumbwa, Avolio, Gardner, Wernsing & Peterson, 2008). Franken, Edwards, and Lambert (2009) found that business leaders are under constant pressure to comply with their demands while maintaining the organization's competitiveness in increasingly complex markets. In such a situation the effective transformational leaders are able to motivate, empower, and build healthy relationships with their peers throughout an organization. Walumbwa et al. (2008) hold the view that over the last decade a considerable amount of research has been undertaken to understand the processes by which transformational leadership positively relates to followers' attitudes, behaviour, and performance. Vecchio et al. (2008) also found that the proposed association of transformational and transactional leadership has been one of augmentation. The augmentation hypothesis argues that transformational leadership significantly predicts leadership criteria after controlling for transactional leadership. In other research, Podsakoff, MacKenzie, Moorman, and Fetter (1990) propose six factors which are important for transformational leadership. Transformational leaders

- articulate a vision of the future;
- provide an appropriate role model;
- foster the acceptance of the goals;
- set high performance standards;
- provide individual support;
- provide intellectual stimulation.

It is important to differentiate between transformational and transactional leadership (Bass, 1985; Keeley, 1995). Transformational leadership looks forward to followers, and it achieves superior performance by transforming followers' values, their attitudes, and their motives from a lower to a higher plane of arousal and maturity (Bass, 1985). Banerjee and Krishnan (2000) studied the ethical decision making of transformational leaders and did not find support for the commonly held assumption that transformational leaders are necessarily ethical. However, transformational leaders can be very effective ethical leaders (Keeley, 1995). Burns (1978) believed that transformational leadership is more concerned with end values, such as equality, liberty, and justice, than with means values. However, insufficient attention to means can corrupt the ends. In the Saudi context, a high value-based leadership is highly relevant. KSA is an Islamic country and there is no denying that sociocultural factors play a very important role in this respect (Khan, Al-Maimani, & Al-Yafi, 2012). Islam emphasizes leadership and advocates practising value-based leadership to maximize the benefits for society. The Prophet Muhammad is revered as the greatest leader and role model that humanity has seen. The Quran (33: 21) declares: "The messenger of God is an excellent model for those of you who put your hope in God and the last day and remember him often". John Adair (2010), in his book entitled *The Leadership of Muhammad,* evaluates the leadership of the Prophet Muhammad and highlights his extraordinary qualities as one who transformed Arabia and much of the world with his teachings and actions. In the introduction of his book (2010:1–2) he wrote:

> For Muslims, the first and original leader is God, and all are bound by their faiths to obey God's law. Thus, any leader of any

organization – business, political or religious is also first and foremost a follower of God. This fact imposes limit on Islamic leaders, and defines their duties to the people they lead. In Islamic thought, model leaders were [sic: are] simultaneously both exalted and humble, capable of vision and inspiration, yet at the same time dedicated to the service of the people.

Islam teaches an individual to be a responsible human being who is concerned about their society, community, and environment. It also informs them how businesses should be carried out and prohibits certain businesses. Ethics and religion go hand in hand in Islam (Khan et al., 2012). Business leaders in an Islamic context are supposed to adhere to these norms, and their success depends not only on achieving the end but also on the means that they adopt. Thus in the Saudi context, leadership in organizations is a huge challenge in terms of balancing the means and the ends. Therefore ethical leadership issues become dominant. The Saudi business environment and its culture play an important role in shaping the relevant leadership qualities among managers. The following paragraphs discuss three dominant dimensions of leadership that have a profound effect on the leadership attributes of Saudi managers, their value system, and the cultural context, as well as the effect of Islam in shaping managerial attributes.

Leadership and the value dimension: Its relevance for Saudi managers

Western awareness of the Arab world, including the KSA, jumped sharply with the oil boom in the early 1970s, and those who entered the region found a "strange" and "different" world. Several stereotypes of Saudis developed, including the one of persons lacking individuality controlled by fatalism and not concerned with rational economic issues (Czinkota, Rivoli, & Ronkainen, 1989). The cultural milieu shaping the mentality and behaviour of the Saudis is a unique blend of Islam mixed with Arab traditions (Bjerke & Al-Meer, 1993). The Arab culture has tribal, Bedouin, and colonial influences, which shape its cultural context. The tribal culture emphasizes family networks, personal relationships, and connections. Arnold, Palmatier, Grewal, and Sharma (2009) claimed that it is important to understand the values such as shame, avoidance, the importance of image, religion, and Arab cultural pride in order to appreciate how leadership assessment and development are practised in the Middle East (Arnold et al., 2009). Thus we find that these factors have a great effect on understanding the relevance of leadership effectiveness in the KSA as well. The leader must understand the culture milieu and its nuances to let their followers feel comfortable and believe in their dream or vision. As we know, transformational leadership is a style of leadership that transforms followers by stimulating them to go beyond self-interest by altering the followers' morale, values, and ideals, and motivating them to achieve the abovementioned expectation (Bass, 1985; Yukl, 1999).

Most of the value research has been conducted in Western countries with only limited investigation of managerial values in the developing nations. Empirical research and information about managerial practices or the ways in which managers plan, organize, staff, direct, and control in the Arab world are scarce (Murrell, 1979). Most writing about Saudi Arabian values reflects Arab values. Equality and basic human values are central to Islamic teachings, and Islam discourages discrimination based on class and socioeconomic status (Syed & Ali, 2010). The Quran says: "O believers, be your securers of justice, witnesses for God. Let not detestation for a people move you not to be equitable, be equitable – that is nearer to the God-fearing" (Quran, 5: 8). These values are innate, and they are seen as a prerequisite of a good leader in an Islamic context.

Al-Wardi (1951) argued that in the Arabian culture there is a manifestation of two value systems: the ancient values of a sedentary population on the one hand and Bedouin values on the other. Muna (1980) and Polk (1980) suggested that Arabs (modern and traditional) have an inner similarity and share certain values despite the obvious differences in the economic and political attainment of their peoples. However, Ali and Al-Shakis (1985) in their study stressed that value differences do exist even within certain groups (managers) across demographic variables. Thus personal and organizational backgrounds influence working values. Their study also brought forward the finding that Arabian managers are not homogenous in their value systems (Ali & Al-Shakis, 1985). The KSA is an Islamic country with civil and criminal laws based on Shariah law. Saudi values are based primarily on the country's Islamic and nomadic heritage (At-Twaijri, 1989). Ali and Al-Shakhis (1990) reported that Arab managers generally display strong commitment and attachment to work. They also show commitment to the Islamic work ethic and a moderate tendency towards individualism (Ali, 1992). In sum, the Saudi Arabian culture is strongly influenced by Islamic teachings and by the nomadic roots of those teachings (Anastos, Bedos, & Seaman, 1980). Asaf (1983) found that Saudi managers give priority to friendships and personal considerations over organizational goals and performance.

In a study on managers' perception of the significance of the goals of the organization, which they feel should be pursued, it was found that Saudi managers at various levels in an organization share the same values with the exception of marital status (Hunt & At-Twaijri, 1996). Talley (1993) argues that a manager's personal values greatly influence their decisions regarding which organizational goal(s) to pursue. Moreover, these values may include the correct setting of priorities as well. These goals/priorities were chosen because previous researchers had demonstrated them to be directly related to managerial behaviour (see also England, 1967; Posner & Munson, 1981). In their study on the key values and attitudinal area, Hunt and At-Twaijri (1996) considered the detailed demographic profile, such as age, educational level, marital status, work experience in the present organization, and managerial experience. This was done because prior studies have suggested that these demographic factors help to explain belief systems (Buchholz, 1978). Hunt and At-Twaijri (1996) found that Saudi managers generally perceived "quality" as their primary goal. "Profit maximization", "service to the public", and "innovativeness" were rated lowest. All Saudi managers, at all hierarchical levels, tended to weigh the importance of organizational goals as the same. Most Saudi managers emphasized "quality" as the primary goal of the organization, except for those managers who were over the age of 54, who rated "profit maximization" as the main goal. However, managers of all ages weighed the importance of goals, "quality" or "profits", as the same, and the significant difference was only moderate. The results of Multivariate Analysis of Variance (MANOVA) and ANOVA clearly illustrate that most demographic variables did not show highly significant effects on the sampled Saudi managers' value systems. This finding has some support in the literature on Arab managerial values. Badawy (1980) also found that culture affects the hierarchy of needs of Middle-Eastern executives, and the demographic and organizational variables also had a minimal influence on managerial orientations (Ali, 1992).

Organizational culture and leadership effectiveness in the Saudi context

Organizational culture is an important issue in both academic research and management practice because it is the most important factor that can make organizations succeed or fail (McShane & Von Glinow, 2003; Schein, 2004). Culture might be one of the strongest and most stable strengths within the organizational context (Schein, 2004). Hofstede

(1991) noted in his writing that it is important to recognize that national culture and organizational culture differ in nature. His research indicated that national culture considers mostly consistency in values while organizational culture considers mostly consistency in practices. Organizational culture is defined as the basic pattern of shared assumptions, values, and beliefs that are believed to reflect a correct way of thinking about and acting on problems and opportunities facing an organization (McShane & Von Glinow, 2003). Schein (2004: 17) offered the most widely used definition of organizational culture, revealing that organizational culture can be seen as:

> A pattern of shared basic assumptions that the group learned as it solved its problems of external adaptation and internal integration that has worked well enough to be considered valid and, therefore, to be taught to new members as the correct way to perceive, think, and feel in relation to those problems.

For any society and its members, values are important. In the workplace, values play an important role in shaping norms and behaviour. Organizational culture and leadership effectiveness are highly related. To achieve excellence in organizations it is necessary to link leadership with the desired organizational culture. Organizational culture is conceptualized as a mediator of the relationship between transformational leadership and organizational innovation (Amabile, Conti, Coon, Lazanby, & Herron, 1996; Deshpande, Farley, & Webster, 1993; Prather & Turrell, 2002; see also Sarros et al., 2008). Values can affect managers' leadership styles (Schampp, 1978) and determine their personal effectiveness as leaders. Posner and Schmidt (1984) found that work values have a moderately strong correlation with the variable of organizational commitment, and an individual manager's values influence their selection of organizational goals. It is also true that values are difficult to investigate with precision because they are abstract ideas, positive or negative, not tied to any specific object or situation, representing a person's beliefs about modes of conduct and ideal terminal modes (Rokeach, 1968).

The KSA is almost identical to other Arab countries. Their Muslim faith plays a large role in people's lives (Hofstede, 1991). A large power distance and uncertainty avoidance are predominant characteristics of this region. This means that it is expected and accepted that leaders separate themselves from the group and issue complete and specific directives. However, other cultural attributes, including the accumulative nature of Saudi culture, may promote knowledge exchange among members of society (Al-Adaileh & Al-Atawi, 2011). In addition, Arabs live in a high-context world where responsibility lies with the receiver to understand the message. Thus what is to be understood relies heavily on the context that the receiver is expected to understand and interpret correctly. The Arabic language is more connotative, evocative, and less explicit than English. This is visible, for example, in boss–subordinate relationships where bosses may give only general hints as to what is expected, and it is the subordinates' responsibility to figure it out. Leadership flows from centralized authority and leaders are responsible for decisions and taking care of people. Leadership is typically not shared. Even sharing can appear as a sign of weakness, and the leader's power is often quite strong, if not absolute. Those under authority look to the leader for direction and decisions, and they expect their own welfare to be considered. Fairness is important to all, especially in an environment where a Western view of fairness may be in conflict with cultural norms of *wasta*. In the Middle East, where authority is indeed concentrated in the leader, few subordinate leaders are willing to push back on authority or do something they fear their boss might not approve of. Leadership tends to be personal while loyalty is personal, and disloyalty or usurping against authority is taken seriously. At the national level it can be life or death. At the corporate level it can be career life or death (Arnold et al., 2009).

Saudi leaders are high on power distance and uncertainty avoidance. They are also found to be high on collectivism and femininity. To be a successful transformational leader, an individual has to see how they are able to connect with their followers' values. Bjerke & Al-Meer (1993) analysed Saudi culture along the four cultural dimensions defined by Hofstede (1980). They found that Saudi managers scored high on power distance, relatively high on uncertainty avoidance, and high on collectivism, and femininity. They attribute Saudi managers' high scores on collectivism and femininity to the Islamic teachings. Comparing their results with those of Hofstede, they suggest that compared with the US, the KSA scores considerably higher on power distance and uncertainty avoidance, considerably lower on individualism, and relatively lower on masculinity. A second characterization of the Arab managers (see Abdallah & Al-Homoud, 2001) is that they have a strong concern for their interpersonal relationships. However, in collectivist and high power distance contexts, such as those found in the Arab nations (Hofstede, 1980), we may expect concern for interpersonal relations to be expressed in different ways, depending on the more differentiated nature of role relationships (Smith, Bond, & Kagitcibasi, 2006). It is important to behave in procedurally correct and respectful ways towards one's seniors and in nurturing ways toward one's juniors. These dimensions are quire relevant for nurturing transformational leadership in the Saudi context.

Robertson, Al-Khatib, Al-Habib, and Lanoue (2001) surveyed the work values of managers in the KSA, Kuwait, and Oman. Compared with Kuwait and Oman, in the KSA they found stronger endorsement of the belief that work is good in itself and that it bestows dignity on the individual. In an early study, Ali and Al-Shakis (1989) found Saudi managers to be more individualistic, less egalitarian, and less humanistic compared with Iraqi managers at that time. The 62-nation GLOBE survey conducted by House, Hanges, Javidan, Dorfman, and Gupta (2004) also serves as a key point of reference. They collected data from samples of managers in Egypt, Kuwait, Morocco, and Qatar. Effective managers from the Arab cluster were found to score significantly lower compared with those from elsewhere on charismatic, team-oriented, and participative qualities. However, effective Arab managers were reported to score significantly higher on "self-protective" traits – namely, self-centredness, status-consciousness, face-saving, conflict induction, and reliance on procedure. Face-saving and status-consciousness are often said to be important values in traditional Arab culture, especially within tribal cultures (Gregg, 2005).

However, there is continuing debate as to whether the standardizations that were used by the GLOBE researchers were appropriate for nation-level comparisons (Peterson & Castro, 2006). Within one's peer group, it is important to act in informal and collaborative ways. Considering this range of relationships as a whole, there are reasons to expect Arab managers to report relying more strongly on formal rules and procedures, on unwritten rules, and on consulting more frequently with others, such as their co-workers and their subordinates (Smith, Achoui, & Harb, 2007). Achoui (2006) also compared the responses of executives with middle-level managers from both public and private sectors. He reported that responses on the use of sources of guidance for decision making, such as unwritten rules, subordinates, peers, one's own experience, and friends, differed significantly. These differences were attributed to subcultural variations as well as to personal and organizational variables. Further analysis of the Saudi data indicated that reliance on formal rules was substantially greater among Saudi executives than among Saudi middle managers, even though many more middle manager respondents were working in state enterprises. The profile of the

Saudi middle managers came closest to the predicted pattern. Particularly striking was their low reported reliance on superiors, the lowest from any of the 64 nations that have been sampled using these measures. This may seem surprising in view of the frequent portrayals of the KSA as a nation high in power distance. However, as we have argued, leadership in a high power distance context does not necessarily need to entail direct seeking of guidance from one's superiors. It can equally involve anticipating one's superior's wishes, relying on the written rules, and consulting with one's peers and others about how best to satisfy one's superior (Smith et al., 2007).

Transformational leadership consists of charisma/inspirational leadership, which entails appealing to a collective identity and expressing an energizing vision to followers. In the Saudi context the loyalty of followers, a higher degree of acceptance of the leader and their vision, a stronger collectivist approach of leaders and their value system encourage them to take this role easily. The important aspect here is the honesty and integrity of the transformational leader in selling their ideas, dreams, and visions. The value ambience makes it easier to practice transformational leadership in the Saudi context. The second most important aspect of transformational leadership is intellectual stimulation, which is expressed by encouraging followers to see things in a new light. The high collectivist and feminine value system encourages Saudi leaders to reach to their followers. The high degree of interpersonal relationships, as evident among Saudi managers, can surely help them to adopt a transformational leadership role. The third important construct of transformational leadership is the individualized consideration of the followers, which entails understanding their needs and helping them to grow to their full potential, which is also evident among Saudi managers (see also Schippers et al., 2008).

Islamic influences on Saudi leadership

Islam has greatly influenced business practices and business activities in the KSA. All Saudis are Muslims, and in the KSA, Islam is the recognized religion. Islam connotes complete submission and obedience to God (Allah). According to Islam, people worship one God, who is distinguished by his divinity, creatorship, and omnipotence in the full meaning of these words. People derive their conceptions, values and standards, institutions, legislature and laws, orientation, ethics, and morals from him alone (Qutb, 1988, cited in Tripp, 1994). Within Islam there is no separation of mosque, state, personal, and private. Islam influences how most people think – how they view themselves, their work, their family, and their government. To be a good worker and a good leader, one needs to be a good Muslim. These Islamic values are intertwined and permeate life in a way that is difficult to comprehend for those who are not raised with that mindset (Arnold et al., 2009). Thus Islamic values and its belief system play an important role in shaping the values and behaviours of individuals. The leadership values shown by the Prophet Muhammad are highly regarded and revered in the KSA. Adair (2010) evaluated the diverse aspects of the Prophet Muhammad's personality and cultural context to illuminate his leadership qualities. Using metaphors like comparing leaders to shepherds, he said that a good shepherd guides his sheep, unites them, works for their welfare without taking advantage of them, and cares for each individual. Adair found all of these characteristics in the Prophet Muhammad. Great leaders lead from the front and by example. They eschew arrogance, exude humility, are truthful, are prepared to share any hardship with followers, and esteem both vision and dedication to achieve a task. To Adair, success is a function of leadership, and the Prophet Muhammad who transformed Arabia and much of the world could not have achieved this without being a good leader (Khan, 2010).

We found that Islamic teaching and practices greatly influence the values of Saudi leaders and managers. Hunt and At-Twaijri (1996) also reported that Saudi executives derive their values mainly from Islam and show a moderate tendency towards individualism. In general, Arab managers have been shown to strongly endorse the Islamic work ethic (Ali, 1988, 1992; Abu Saad, 1998). Several authors have asserted that Islamic beliefs and the Islamic work ethic (Ali, 1988, 1992) provide a core basis for understanding Arab organizational behaviour and leadership, and studies using a measure of the Islamic work ethic within organizations in the Emirates have also shown significant effects in this regard (Yousef, 2000).

For the devout Muslim, Allah is in control, unknowable, unsearchable, totally other, and totally sovereign. Although humans can and should try to do their best, things will only happen if Allah wills it. The phrase *inshallah* means God's will, and when used at the end of any statement of intent, it recognizes the theological point that this will only happen if God wills it (Arnold et al., 2009). This approach has been badly practised in the Muslim world and Saudi cultural context is not bereft of it. Islam places emphasis on doing and on actions. Thus individuals are responsible for their own actions. However, for the non-doers, *inshallah* has become a scapegoat. Nevertheless, those who are not aware of the Muslim cultural context misunderstand this word. This philosophy is crucial, and if not understood and practised properly it may render a leader vulnerable and helpless, as well as dilute the authority they exercise. The other negative aspect of Islam is the fatalistic streaks found among managers. Saudi managers, as Muslims and Arabs, do not tolerate persons who deviate from Islamic teachings and Arab traditions. They are very loyal to their organization (Muna, 1980). Muna analysed past and present Islamic achievements (which are in harmony with Islamic teachings) demonstrating the use of long-range planning, and a desire to understand and control the environment. Bjerke and Al-Meer (1993) corroborated this view and found that Arab managers are far from fatalistic. They are future-oriented, rational in their planning, and they attempt to prevent adverse results. In all, the present Saudi Arabian cultural context provides many opportunities to develop leadership qualities. The business and economic environment provides opportunities to demonstrate leadership qualities to young and new managers. The business environment, which is becoming global, diverse, and networked, provides a great opportunity for Saudi leaders to demonstrate to the world the core values of Islam, which are based on honesty, integrity, equality, truthfulness, and sincerity, to reflect the true message of Islamic teaching and learning. Adair (2010: 110) sums up:

> within Islamic thought there is a bridge between theology and philosophy...that bridge, of course is the concept of truth. For truth is truth, whether it is found by contemplating the names of God or through the study of human nature and social life....Therefore Islam today is both an inheritor of the world's body of knowledge about leadership and a great contributor to it.

Select case analysis of Saudi leaders

The present study attempts to study transformational leadership in the KSA. Previous sections introduced the pivotal issues that construct Saudi Arabian leadership. They also take into account the deep-rooted values and the nature of the culture in which leadership qualities are embedded. After careful review of the literature available on Saudi leadership, the discussion is reinforced by cases of successful Saudi business leaders. The KSA is rated as the 13th most economically competitive country in the world, according to the IFC-World Bank annual "Doing Business" report issued in 2010. Accordingly, there have been continuous government initiatives to encourage businesses to diversify and achieve competitiveness by channelling available resources. Many Saudi entrepreneurs, business leaders, and corporate managers have shown extraordinary talent in achieving their individual milestones, which is praiseworthy. The following paragraphs showcase nine such cases which throw light on both leadership qualities and achievements. At the end, a framework of leadership is proposed to help an understanding of the leadership development process in the KSA.

Achievement, philanthropy, and Islamic business and work ethic

In this category, five cases are discussed, including Ali Ibrahim Al-Naimi, Sulaiman Al-Rajhi, Prince Alwaleed Bin Talal Al-Saud, Khalid A. Al-Falih, and Dr Abdullah bin Marei bin Mahfouz. As we know, philanthropy is essentially rooted in Islam, and it is quite evident in the Saudi Arabian context. A good leader has to be a philanthropist, humble, and kind. These are the least expected virtues in the Saudi business environment.

Ali Ibrahim Al-Naimi

Ali Al-Naimi has been the minister of petroleum and mineral resources of the KSA since August 1995. His is a great success story and motivating for every Saudi who wants to be successful. He started his career as a foreman in Aramco and went on to become its CEO and president, later becoming the petroleum and mineral resources minister of the kingdom. He was born in 1935 in the Eastern province of the KSA and joined Aramco in 1947 at the age of 12. In 1953, after two years of full time schooling sponsored by the company, he became an assistant geologist in the exploration department. During 1956–1963, with Aramco's sponsorship, he studied at International College, Beirut, and at the American University of Beirut. He earned a BS degree in geology from Lehigh University in 1962 and an MS in geology from Stanford University in 1963. He worked in Aramco's exploration department as a hydrologist and geologist during 1963–1967. He became supervisor of the Abqaiq production department in 1969 (SAGIA-GCF, 2012).

Al-Naimi rose through the rank of the company's oil operation in the Eastern province from foreman to assistant superintendent and from superintendent to manager. He became the vice president of production affairs in 1975, a senior vice president in 1978 and was elected to the board of directors at Aramco in 1980. In 1982 he was made the executive vice president-operations and finally he was named president of the company in 1983. He was the first Saudi citizen to hold this office.

Later, after combining both positions, he was named president and CEO of Saudi Aramco, which he remained until 1995. In August 1995 he became the minister for petroleum and mineral resources. During this time the global economy has gone through many crises, but with his able leadership and vision, he has been able to position Saudi leadership at OPEC and various other forums. He was listed as one of the most influential people in the world by *Time* magazine in 2008 and in 2011 he was ranked as one of the 50 most influential people by Bloomberg Markets (SAGIA-GCF, 2012; *Wikipedia*, 2012).

Sulaiman Al-Rajhi

Sulaiman Al-Rajhi is the founder of the Al-Rajhi Bank. He is from an impoverished background but overcame adversity and experienced a meteoric rise. His is a rag-to-riches story. As of 2011, his wealth was estimated by Forbes to be $7.7 billion, making him the 120th richest person in the world. His flagship SAAR Foundation is a leading charity in the kingdom. The Al-Rajhi family is considered one of the kingdom's wealthiest non-royal families and is among the world's leading philanthropists. Interestingly, he is now both a philanthropist and a financially poor man by choice after he willingly transferred much of his assets to his children and kept the rest for charity and donation-related purposes. In an interview, he expressed his views on wealth: "All wealth belongs to Allah, and we are only those who are entrusted (by God) to take care of them." Overcoming adverse situations and a firm belief in Allah are just two of his traits, which are praiseworthy. For example, there was a fire in one of his factories and his son came to tell him about the incident. He repeated his words in one interview: "Say praise to God. I asked him not to submit any report about the losses to the authorities seeking compensation. In fact, the compensation is from Allah, and it is essential for us to be satisfied with what Allah destined for us." In response to another fire incident he said: "*AlHamdulillah* (praise to God)" (Arab News, 2012). The roots of Islam also pervaded the inception of the Al-Rajhi Bank, which is strictly Islamic. The entrepreneur who has a deep faith in the Islamic principles and their effect on Muslim individuals' banking practices was eventually successful in convincing the Bank of England authorities about the virtues of Islamic banking codes. In his words: "I told them that Muslims and Christians see interest as forbidden (*haram*), and the Muslim and Christian religious people are unwilling to make transactions with banks based on interest and instead prefer to keep their cash and other valuables in boxes at their homes. I tried to convince them that (if we establish Islamic banks) this money would strengthen the world economy. These talks were helpful in convincing them and they agreed to open Islamic banks" (*Arab News*, 2012). His other business venture that has been widely appreciated involved the poultry project Al-Watania Poultry, which was an initiative against the slaughtering of animals based on Islamic ethics. He said: "I saw that slaughtering chicken was not proper. Then I decided to make investments in the field of poultry after considering it a duty to my religion and nation...The company enjoys a 40 percent market share in the Kingdom, and Al-Watania chickens are naturally fed and *halal* slaughtered in accordance with the Shariah principles" (*Arab News*, 2012).

Sulaiman Al-Rajhi displayed an exemplary work ethic, which is an exceptional case to be followed by the followers. He is known to be a strict disciplinarian and a hard worker. Even in his advanced age, he follows a rigorous regime. Al-Rajhi is still active and possesses youthful spirits even in his 80s. He begins his daily work after morning prayers and is active until Isha prayers before going to bed early. He is now fully focused on running the endowment project under his SAAR Foundation and travelling to various regions of the kingdom to manage related activities. He always carries a pocket diary containing his daily programmes and activities, and he likes to stick to the schedule he has prepared well in advance. He clarifies his passion for work as a responsibility for managing Allah's assets entrusted to him with honesty and sincerity. Al-Rajhi achieved excellent performance results in almost all businesses in which he carved out a niche for himself. In addition to establishing the world's largest Islamic bank, he founded the largest poultry farm in the Middle East (*Arab News*, 2012).

Prince Alwaleed bin Talal Al-Saud

Prince Alwaleed Al-Saud has been a very successful executive acknowledged worldwide. He has consistently made donations personally and through his foundations. He is the chairperson of the Kingdom Holding Company and he topped the *Middle East* magazine's 2011 list. As a multibillionaire businessman and philanthropist he was the region's most highly recognizable face in 2011. The Alwaleed Bin Talal Foundation focuses on removing the gaps between communities and religions, reducing poverty, and educating the people of the KSA (*Arab News*, 2011). In an interview, he focused on the emerging Saudi work ethic and conforming to essential ethical practices. As a business leader he had the foresight to introduce proper governance practices in his company long before US companies were shaken by fraud. In his words, "Our corporate governance policies preceded all the scandals and problems that took place in the States and before US companies were forced to reform. For example, I established the relationship with my company, Kingdom Holding, since we had our IPO. So it was important to me early on" (*Leaders Online*, 2012). As a leader, he is tough, straightforward in dealing with things, and tolerant towards mistakes to the extent that his people learn from their mistakes. He emphasizes moral standards expected from his employees on which no compromise can be made. He says: "we have very high standards of ethics – that is very important to me" (*Leaders Online*, 2012). His charisma, concern for quality and attainment of goals, his work ethic, and his humbleness are good examples of attributes of a transformational leader who aims to motivate his followers.

Khalid A. Al-Falih

Khalid Al-Falih is the president and CEO of Saudi Aramco and oversees the company's management of the world's largest proven conventional oil reserves. The transformational approach is aptly highlighted by Al-Falih whose association with Saudi Aramco has been long and fulfilling. He graduated with a bachelor's degree in mechanical engineering in 1982 from Texas A&M University. He did his MBA in 1991 at KFUPM, the KSA. "He places high value on self-initiative in knowledge, collaboration and networking in an increasingly interdependent world and has made social responsibility a personal initiative." Al-Falih's commitments at the local and regional levels to support education, professional development, entrepreneurship and empowerment of women in business, as well as philanthropic activities on behalf of the poor and victims of disaster, has been noted worldwide. He was chosen as outstanding International Alumnus at Texas A&M (TAMU, 2010). Al-Falih's vision and broad intentions are well charted out for his future route to accomplishments. In his words, "We aim to leverage our intellectual capacity, supply chain, scale and expertise in supporting the development of the Kingdom's knowledge-based economy and job creation. So really, it's about both the company and the Kingdom" (Saudi Aramco News, 2011). He is passionate about his jobs: "I love my job and I'm passionate about delivering the transformation our company needs... rather than being content with the status quo, we are challenging ourselves to unleash the full potential of our company – and above all, of our people" (Saudi Aramco, 2012).

Dr Abdullah bin Marei bin Mahfouz

Saudi businessperson Dr Abdullah bin Marei bin Mahfouz donated one-third of his wealth for charitable purposes. In doing so he was advocating disparity among the social classes whereby the wealthy bestow on the lesser who are less privileged to alleviate poverty. Moreover, he was inspired by the US practice where famous billionaires distribute a huge part of their earned wealth. He feels that this had a cascading effect on other affluent people who were motivated to do the same. Dr Mahfouz encouraged the emulation of such a model in the KSA. He said: "I believe the experience of American billionaires could be applicable in the KSA and I don't see why [we should] not adopt a similar initiative" (Al-Arabiya News, 2010).

Women empowerment and leadership

Saudi Arabian society is known for gender segregation rather than gender discrimination. In recent times there have been many reforms and commendable strides taken by the government to empower women in the workforce. The recent reforms highlight a renewed attempt to redefine women's roles in all vital activities. The announcement of the King regarding woman playing a greater role in Saudi society and politics in future has been accepted with unprecedented happiness and expectation of a more empowered future for women. About ten years ago the Saudi monarch said that women should be central to the Saudi economy. In the intervening years the kingdom has been gradually taking steps to reduce segregation and give more respect to women. Allowing women to stand and vote in municipal elections is a big step towards political reform. The right for women to join the all-male Shura Council could turn out to be even more significant since it is the most influential political body in the country. The country would not have realized all of these remarkable achievements without the farsighted vision of its leadership, which supports the role of women in the development process (Gulf Times, 2011). Three cases of successful women are discussed below.

Norah Al-Fayez

The case of the appointment of Norah Al-Fayez to the Saudi Ministry has been a milestone and has given clear indication of the King's keen interest in the genuine empowerment of Saudi women in different areas of male-oriented professional activities. She broke the gender barrier in the oil-rich kingdom when King Abdullah bin Abdul Aziz Al Saud appointed her as the deputy education minister for female education affairs, the most senior position ever granted to a woman in the kingdom. This appears to be the first and only crack in the glass ceiling. Analysts and commentators hailed Norah's appointment as a historic step for the conservative, oil-rich monarchy where women were denied the right to vote in the country's first-ever municipal elections in 2005 despite campaigning heavily for suffrage rights (Al-Arabiya News, 2009).

Suhaila Zain Al-Abedin

Suhaila Al-Abidin is a good example of a successful woman leader who has played an important role in influencing women in the KSA. She is a member of the National Society for Human Rights and serves on the board. She is vice-president of the studies and consultations committee and the scientific committee (*Saudi Gazette*, 2010). She epitomizes a symbol of dignity and grace. She has written 20 books on social, intellectual, literary, media, political, and historical issues. Some of these are being taught at universities today. One of her first books was a two-part study of the progress that women have made in the KSA. Her views and activities regarding women empowerment are strongly inspired by the tenets of Islam. She stated clearly in an interview: "it's a God-given right for qualified women to participate in decision making as they used to do in the days of the Prophet (peace be upon him) when women used to participate in wars and offer their opinion on a variety of issues" (*Saudi Gazette*, 2010).

Maria Mahdaly

Maria is known for her dynamism and for bringing new ideas to the fore for women. She stresses the paradigm transformation of social values and the emerging trend of growing women participation. Her journey has been rapid and overwhelming. In 2007, aged 19, she started Rumman, a media and publishing house in Jeddah, with Enas Hashani and Bayan Abuzinadah. The company runs two ventures: a monthly city magazine with a circulation of 70,000 called *Destination Jeddah* and a social network called *Fainak*. By 2010, Rumman was ranked by the AllWorld Network, which provides rankings of private growth companies in emerging economies around the world, as the KSA's fastest growing start-up, with a growth rate of nearly 600%. Maria feels that she is benefiting from changing attitudes of people in the KSA. She said: "we get a lot of support from other businesses, the media, and individuals in general" (Hoare, 2012).

Leadership among government officials

Prince Khaled Al-Faisal Al-Saud

The government initiatives and efforts to extol officials developing leadership programmes for the general public helps in leadership-building exercises at the grassroots level. In this context the case of Prince Khaled Al-Faisal, the governor of Makkah, will open up new opportunities for an effective understanding of Saudi leadership. His continuous focus on the development of Arab youth's leadership features has made him the best Arab personality in the field of solving issues related to Arab youth. Prince Khaled's role as the president of the Arab Thought Foundation (ATF) is commendable. The ATF aims to empower Arab youth to lead developmental activities in the Arab world. It has succeeded in producing a large number of young ambassadors who are distinguished in the areas of social responsibility, voluntary services, and developmental activities. The prince has taken the initiative to appoint a number of distinguished youths to the board and committees of the foundation and has stressed the need to include young speakers in the annual conferences of the ATF. He also set apart sessions of the foundation for youth leadership projects (Al-Sulami, 2012). After becoming the governor of Makkah province, the prince laid out a strategic plan for increased youth participation in various projects. He also set up a youth committee under the provincial council with the aim of improving young people's welfare. The committee serves as an umbrella organization for the Makkah Youth Development Council, Young Businessmen Committee, Makkah Province Youth Meet, Business Pioneers Committee, Makkah Youth Committee for Social Media and the Makkah Youth Committee for Voluntary Work (Al-Sulami, 2012).

Based on the above discussion, this chapter proposes a framework to increase our understanding of the leadership development process in the KSA. The external environmental factors are important in developing leadership styles. The cultural context, Islamic teachings, and individual values play important roles in practising appropriate leadership styles in the KSA. Government initiatives are seen as very important in the development process, and the role of government in developing leadership lies at the core of the problem. It is also important to understand the current scenario and to arrest those processes which are detrimental to leadership development, while augmenting those that facilitate and support it. Leadership in the KSA can be classified into three strands – namely, entrepreneurial and corporate/business leaders, women empowerment and women leadership, and political

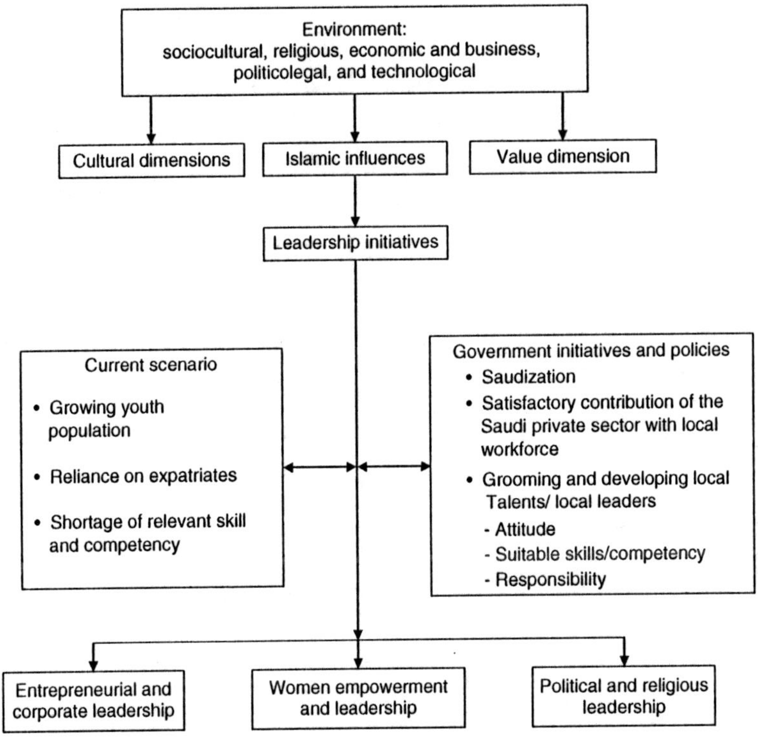

Figure 10.1 A framework: leadership development in Saudi Arabia

and religious leadership. The following framework helps us to understand the Saudi leadership process, which takes into account visible and invisible stakeholders in the process (Figure 10.1).

Conclusion

Leadership is synonymous with success, and it has emerged as the key factor in achieving excellence in organization, which is true for the KSA as well as any other state. Ribelin (2003) argued that leadership not only improves organizational performance but also influences employees' job satisfaction. With its accession to the World Trade Organization in 2005, the quest for leadership drive in the country has been accentuated in recent times. The KSA aims to become one of the world's top ten competitive economies. Considering this background, the transformational leadership paradigm seems highly relevant in the Saudi cultural context. Saudi society is highly networked and collectivist. People show immense regard for their leaders. Managers are found to be high on collectivism and femininity. Leadership tends to be personal, and the loyalty of followers is important in the Saudi cultural context. The interpersonal relationship between leaders and followers is also high. In this cultural context, transformational leadership is highly relevant for Saudi managers who can provide a motivating environment to their followers. Transformational leadership entails appealing to a collective identity and expressing an energizing vision to followers. Transformational leaders can stimulate followers to challenge their current working conditions and, in turn, followers will perform innovatively. Thus transformational leaders are able to innovate with the organization, satisfy followers, and achieve higher organizational performance (Tang, 2006). In the Saudi context, the loyalty of followers, the higher degree of acceptance of the leaders and their vision, and the value system all encourage leaders to pursue transformational leadership goals.

The Islamic perspective on leadership also encourages leaders to adopt the transformational leadership style in the KSA. From the Islamic perspective, the world has not seen a better leader and human being than the Prophet Muhammad, and he is the role model for Muslims in the KSA and elsewhere. His words, actions, and behaviours form the basis of *Sunnah* and *Sharia* laws in Islam. As for Muslims, any leader of any organization, whether business, political, or religious, is first a follower of God, and this imposes limits and defines their duties to the people they lead. Model leaders are supposed to be exalted and humble, capable of vision and inspiration, yet, at the same time, dedicated to the service of the people (Adair, 2010). This Islamic manifestation of leadership is highly relevant for the Saudi context. Although this is an ideal situation, leaders can emulate the effectiveness of a true leader who can be successful in their pursuits. The cases also endorse this view, and we find a coherence of Islamic principles and their supremacy in propelling these leaders to their desired goals in all cases, be it Al-Rajhi's business ethics and humble approach, Prince Alwaleed's adherence to ethics and high performance standard, Prince Khaled Al-Faisal's connectedness with his people and effective interpersonal relationship, or Suhaila Al-Abedin's quest for women's equality and empowerment. Islamic principles and ethics shape the values of society and its leaders in the KSA. At workplaces as well, values play an important role in shaping the norms and behaviour of the people, which relate strongly to organizational culture and leadership effectiveness. To achieve excellence in organizations, it is also mandatory to link transformational leadership with the desired organizational culture. Organizational culture is conceptualized as a mediator of the relationship between transformational leadership and organizational innovation as well. In all, a transformational leadership style with its shared vision – that is, inspirational and charismatic leadership attributes providing individual attention and intellectual stimulation for followers' learning and growth – appears to be a sure recipe for success in the Saudi cultural context, but it needs further empirical probing.

References

Abdallah, I., & Al-Homoud, M. (2001). Exploring the implicit leadership theory in the Arabian Gulf States. *Applied Psychology: An International Review*, 50(4), 506–531.

Abu-Saad, I. (1998). Individualism and Islamic work beliefs. *Journal of Cross-Cultural Psychology*, 29, 377–383.

Achoui, M. (2006). Decision making styles: a Saudi managerial context. *Proceedings of 18th Congress of the International Association for Cross-Cultural Psychology*, Spetses, Greece, 11–15 July.

Adair, J. (2010). *The Leadership of Muhammad*. London: Kogan Page.

Al-Adaileh, A.R.M., & Al-Atawi, M.S. (2011). Organizational culture impact on knowledge exchange: Saudi telecom context. *Journal of Knowledge Management*, 15(2), 212–230.

Al-Arabiya News (2009, February 15). Saudi's first female minister cracks glass ceiling. Retrieved from http://www.alarabiya.net/articles/2009/02/15/66532.html.

Al-Arabiya News (2010, August 19). Saudi businessman promotes wealth donation. Retrieved from http://www.alarabiya.net/articles/2010/08/19/117071.html.

Al-Sulami, M.D. (2012, February 28). Makkah governor named best Arab personality by a forum. *Arab News*. Retrieved from http://www.arabnews.com/node/407505.

Al-Wardi, A. (1951). *The Personality of Iraqi Individuals*. Baghdad: Al-Raipta Press.

Ali, A. (1988). Scaling an Islamic work ethic. *Journal of Social Psychology*, 128(5), 575–583.

Ali, A. (1992). Islamic work ethic in Arabia. *Journal of Psychology*, 126(5), 507–520.

Ali, A., & Al-Shakis, M. (1985). Managerial value systems for working in Saudi Arabia: An empirical investigation. *Group and Organization Studies*, 10(2), 135–152.

Ali, A., & Al-Shakis, M. (1989). Managerial beliefs about work in two Arab states. *Organization Studies*, 10(2), 169–186.

Ali, A., & Al-Shakhis, M. (1990). Multinationals and the host Arab society. *Leadership and Organizational Development*, 11(5), 17–21.

Amabile, T.M., Conti, R., Coon, H., Lazenby, J., & Herron, M. (1996). Assessing the work environment for creativity. *Academy of Management Journal*, 39(5), 1154–1184.

Anastos, D., Bedos, A., & Seaman, B. (1980). The development of modern management practices in Saudi Arabia. *Columbia Journal of World Business*, 15 (2), 81–91.
Arab News (2011, August 6). Prince Al-Waleed tops list of 50 most influential Arabs. Retrieved from http://www.arabnews.com/node/386826.
Arab News (2012, May 29). Sulaiman Al-Rajhi's life, a rag to riches story. Retrieved from http://www.arabnews.com/economy/sulaiman-al-rajhi%E2%80%99s-life-rags-riches-story.
Arnold, T.J., Palmatier, R.W., Grewal, D., & Sharma, A. (2009). Understanding retail managers' role in the sales of products and services. *Journal of Retailing*, 85(2), 129–144.
Asaf, A. (1983). *The Organization's Administration in Saudi Arabia*. Riyadh, Saudi Arabia: Dar Al Alom Publishers.
At-Twaijri, M. (1989). A cross-cultural comparison of American-Saudi managerial values in US-related firms in Saudi Arabia: An empirical investigation. *International Studies in Management of Organizations*, 19(2), 58–73.
Badawy, M.K. (1980). Styles of mid-eastern managers. *California Management Review*, 22(2), 51–58.
Banerjee, P., & Krishnan, V.R. (2000). Ethical preferences of transformational leaders: An empirical investigation. *Leadership and Organization Development Journal*, 21(8), 405–413.
Bass, B.M. (1985). *Leadership and Performance beyond Expectations*. New York: Free Press.
Bjerke, B., & Al-Meer, A. (1993). Culture's consequences: Management in Saudi Arabia. *Leadership & Organization Development Journal*, 14(2), 30–35.
Boseman, G. (2008). Effective leadership in a changing world. *Journal of Financial Service Professionals*, 62(3), 36–38.
Buchholz, R.A. (1978). An empirical study of contemporary beliefs about work in American Society. *Journal of Applied Psychology*, 63(2), 219–227.
Burns, J.M. (1978). *Leadership*. New York: Harper & Row.
Conger, J.A., & Kanungo, R.N. (1998). *Charismatic Leadership Organizations*, Thousand Oaks, CA: Sage Publications.
Czinkota, M.R., Rivoli, P., & Ronkainen, I.A. (1989). *International Business*. New York: The Dryden Press.
Deshpande, R., Farley, J.U., & Webster, F.E. (1993). Corporate culture, customer orientation and innovativeness in Japanese firms: A quadrad analysis. *Journal of Marketing*, 57 (January), 23–27.
England, G. (1967). The personal values of American managers. *Academy of Management Journal*, 10(1), 53–68.
Franken A., Edwards C., & Lambert R. (2009). Executing strategic change: Understanding the critical management elements that lead to success. *California Management Review*, 51(3), 49–73.
Gardner, W.L., & Avolio, B.J. (1998). The charismatic relationship: A dramaturgical perspective. *Academy of Management Review*, 23(1), 32–58.
Gregg, G.S. (2005). *The Middle East: A Cultural Psychology*. Oxford: Oxford University Press.
Gulf Times (2011). Viewpoint: a significant step forward for Saudi women's rights. Retrieved from http://www.gulftimes.com/site/topics/article.asp?cu_no=2&item_no=460266&version=1&template_id=46&parent_id=26.

Hoare, R. (2012). Saudi female entrepreneurs exploit changing attitudes. *CNN*. Retrieved from http://edition.cnn.com/2012/05/30/business/saudi-female-entrepreneurs/index.html.

Hofstede, G. (1980). *Culture's Consequences: International differences in Work Related Values*. Beverly Hills, CA: Sage.

Hofstede, G. (1991). *Cultures and Organizations: Software of the Mind*. Maidenhead: McGraw-Hill.

House, R.J., Hanges, P.J., Javidan, M., Dorfman, P.W., & Gupta, V. (2004). *Leadership, Culture and Organizations: The GLOBE Study of 62 Societies*. Thousand Oaks, CA: Sage Publications.

Hunt, D.M., & At-Twaijri M.I. (1996). Values and the Saudi manager: An empirical investigation. *Journal of Management Development*, 15(5), 48–55.

Ivey, G.W., & Kline, T.J.B. (2010). Transformational and active transactional leadership in the Canadian military. *Leadership & Organizational Development Journal*, 31(3), 246–262.

Jago, A.G. (1982). Leadership: Perspectives in theory and research. *Management Science*, 28(3), 315–336.

Jung, D.I., Chow, C., & Wu, A. (2003). The role of transformational leadership in enhancing organizational innovation: Hypotheses and some preliminary findings. *Leadership Quarterly*, 14(4–5), 525–544.

Keeley, M. (1995). The trouble with transformational leadership: Toward a federalist ethic for organizations. *Business Ethics Quarterly*, 5(1), 67–96.

Khan, M. (2010). Lessons in leadership from the life of the Prophet Muhammad. (Review of the book *The Leadership of Muhammad* by J. Adair). Retrieved from http://knowledge.wharton.upenn.edu/arabic/article.cfm?articleid=2540.

Khan, S.A., Al-Maimani, K., & Al-Yafi, W. (2012). Corporate social responsibility in Saudi Arabia: An exploratory study. *Proceedings of the 19th Annual Conference on International Business & Contemporary Issues in Business*. Deadwood, SD, 4–6 October.

Kouzes, J.M., & Posner, B.Z. (2003). *Encouraging the Heart*. San Francisco, CA: Jossey-Bass.

Leaders Online (2012). Success breeds success. Retrieved from http://www.leadersmag.com/issues/2012.1_Jan/ROB/LEADERS-HRH-Prince-Alwaleed-bin-Talal-Kingdom-Holding-Company.html.

Locke, E.A. (1991). *The Essence of Leadership: The Four Keys to Leading Successfully*. New York: Lexington Books.

McShane, S.L., & Von Glinow, M.A. (2003). *Organizational Behavior*. Columbus, OH: McGraw- Hill/Irwin.

Muna, F.A. (1980). *The Arab Executive*. London: Macmillan.

Murrell, K. (1979). A cultural analysis of the Egyptian management environment. In P.R. Harris, & G. Malin (Eds.), *Innovation in Global Consultation*. Washington, DC: International Consultants Foundation.

Orchard, L. (1998). Managerialism, economic rationalism and public sector reform in Australia: Connections, divergences, alternatives. *Australian Journal of Public Administration*, 57(1), 19–32.

Parker, R., & Bradley, L. (2000). Organizational culture in the public sector: Evidence from six organizations. *International Journal of Public Sector Management*, 13(2), 125–141.

Peterson, M.F., & Castro, S.L. (2006). Measurement metrics at aggregate levels of analysis: Implications for organization culture research and the GLOBE project. *The Leadership Quarterly*, 17, 506-521.
Podsakoff, P.M., MacKenzie, S.B., Moorman, R.H., & Fetter, R. (1990). Transformational leader behaviors and their effects on followers' trust in leader, satisfaction, and organizational citizenship behaviours. *Leadership Quarterly*, 1(2), 107–142.
Polk, W.R. (1980). *The Arab World*. Cambridge, MA: Cambridge University Press.
Posner, B., & Munson, J.M. (1981). Gender differences in managerial values. *Psychological Reports*, 49, 867–881.
Posner, B.Z., & Schmidt, W.H. (1984). Values and the American manager: An update. *California Management Review*, 26(3), 202–216.
Prather, C.W., & Turrell, M.C. (2002). Involve everyone in the innovation process research. *Technology Management*, September–October, 13–16.
Pounder, J. (2008). Transformational leadership: Practicing what we teach in the management classroom. *Journal of Education for Business*, 84(1), 2–6.
Qutb, S. (1988). *Ma'alim fi al-Tariq*. Cairo: Dar al-Shuruq.
Rhodes, J., Walsh, P., & Lok, P. (2008). Convergence and divergence issues in strategic management: Indonesia's experience with the balanced scorecard in HR management. *The International Journal of Human Resources Management*, 19(6), 1170–1185.
Riaz, A., & Haider, M.H. (2010). Role of transformational and transactional leadership on job satisfaction and career satisfaction. *Business Economic Horizon*, 1, 29–38.
Ribelin, P.J. (2003). Retention reflects leadership style. *Nursing Management*, 34(8), 18–19.
Robbins, S.P. (2005). *Essentials of Organizational Behavior*. Upper Saddle River, NJ: Pearson Education.
Robertson, C.J., Al-Khatib, J.A., Al-Habib, M., & Lanoue, D. (2001). Beliefs about work in the Middle East and the convergence versus divergence of values. *Journal of World Business*, 36, 223–244.
Rokeach, M. (1968). *Beliefs, Attitudes, and Values: A Theory of Organization and Change*. San Francisco, CA: Jossey-Bass.
SAGIA-GCF (2012). Ali bin Ibrahim al-Naimi. Retrieved from http://sagiagcf.tmwtest.co.uk/en/Speakers/Ali-Bin-Ibrahim-Al-Naimi.
Sarros, J.C., Cooper, B.K., & Santora, J.C. (2008). Building a climate for innovation through transformational leadership and organizational culture. *Journal of Leadership & Organizational Studies*, 15(2), 145–158.
Saudi Aramco (2012). CEO speaks at Stanford University. Retrieved from http://www.saudiaramco.com/en/home/news/latest-news/2012/ceo-speaks-at-stanford-university.html.
Saudi Aramco News (2011). Saudi Aramco charts a course for the future. Retrieved from http://www.aramcoexpats.com/articles/2011/05/Saudi-Aramco-Charts-a-Course-for-the-Future/
Saudi Gazette (2010, February 21). Story of Success. Retrieved from http://www.saudigazette.com.sa/index.cfm?method=home.regcon&contented=20100221 64078.
Schampp, D. (1978). *A Cross-Cultural Study of Multinational Companies*. New York: Praeger.

Schein, E.H. (2004). *Organizational Culture and Leadership*. San Francisco, CA: Jossey-Bass.

Schippers, M.C., Hartog, D.N.D., Koopman, P.L., and Knippenberg, D.N. (2008), The role of transformational leadership in enhancing team reflexivity. *Human Relations*, 61(11), 1593–1616.

Schwartz, T., Jones, J., & McCarthy, C. (2010). *The Way We're Working Isn't Working*. New York: Free Press.

Sheetz-Runkle, B. (2011). *Sun Tzu for Women: The Art of War for Winning in Business*. Cincinnati, OH: Adams Business.

Smith, P.B., Bond, M.H., & Kagitcibasi, C. (2006). *Understanding Social Psychology Across Cultures: Living and Working in a Changing World*. London: Sage.

Smith, P.B., Achoui, M., & Harb, C. (2007). Unity and diversity in Arab managerial styles. *International Journal of Cross Cultural Management*, 7(3), 275–290.

Syed, J., & Ali, A.J. (2010). Principles of employment relations in Islam: A normative view. *Employee Relations*, 32(5), 454–469.

Talley, W. (1993). Values in action. *Manage*, 44 (1), 25–27.

TAMU (2010). Khalid A. Al-Falih chosen outstanding international alumnus. Retrieved from http://intlcenter.tamu.edu/sites/default/files/KhalidOIA.pdf.

Tang, Y.T. (2006). Transformational leadership, job motivation, and employees' innovational behavior. *Journal of Human Resource Management*, 6(4), 47–66.

Tripp, C. (1994). Sayyid Qutb: The political vision. In A. Rahnema (Ed.), *Pioneers of Islamic Revival* (pp. 154–183). London: Zed Books Ltd.

Valle, M. (1999). Crisis, culture and charisma: The new leader's work in public organizations. *Public Personnel Management*, 28(2), 245–257.

Vecchio, R., Justin, J., & Pearce, C. (2008). The utility of transactional and transformational leadership for predicting performance and satisfaction within a path-goal theory framework. *Journal of Occupational and Organizational Psychology*, 81(1), 71–82.

Walumbwa, F., Avolio, B., Gardner, W., Wernsing, T., & Peterson, S. (2008). Authentic leadership: Development and validation of a theory-based measure. *Journal of Management*, 34(1), 89–126.

Wikipedia (2012). Ali Al-Naimi. Retrieved from http://en.wikipedia.org/wiki/Ali_I._Al-Naimi.

Xirasagar, S. (2008). Transformational, transactional, and laissez-faire leadership among physician executives: The empirical evidence. *Journal of Health Organization and Management*, 22(6), 519–613.

Yousef, D.A. (2000). Organizational commitment: A mediator of the relationships of leadership behavior with job satisfaction and performance in a non-western country. *Journal of Managerial Psychology*, 15(1), 6–29.

Yukl, G. (1999). An evaluation of conceptual weaknesses in transformational and charismatic leadership theories. *The Leadership Quarterly*, 10, 285–305.

11
Expatriate and Omani Workplace Relationships and Individual Performance

Stuart M. Schmidt, Unnikammu Moideenkutty and Adil Al-Busaidi

Introduction

Middle East nations tend to have large expatriate labour forces employed in their private and public sectors while at the same time young people graduating from secondary schools and universities find their employment opportunities limited or non-existent (Daboub, 2008; Herrera, 2009). This situation becomes politically untenable as unemployed local youth agitate for employment. Therefore providing employment opportunities for nationals has become a priority for nations facing possible domestic turmoil from unemployed citizens, especially college graduates.

The Sultanate of Oman, a Middle-East oil-exporting nation on the Strait of Hormuz, is attempting to move from a "low-value" to a "high-value" economy by providing employment for the tens of thousands of young Omanis entering its labour force each year (Al-Hamadi & Budhwar, 2006; Al-Hamdi, Budhwar, & Shipton, 2007). Oman has historically had a substantial, non-Omani, expatriate labour force working in the public and private sectors. As we use the construct, "expatriates" in Oman are foreigners employed in a business or public agency for a contractual period, but they are not Omani citizens. Though numerous, foreigners are unable to become Omani citizens and typically reside in Oman within the context of their employment contracts. Today approximately 28% of Oman's population (Omani Law Blog, 2011) is composed of expatriate workers (Arab, South Asian, Filipino, and African) who have traditionally dominated Oman's labour force at all levels. However, since 1988, the Sultanate of Oman has been actively pursuing the labour nationalization policy known as "Omanization" to bring increasing numbers of Omanis into both the public and the private workplaces as supervisors and subordinates (Budhwar & Mellahi, 2006; Budhwar, Al-Yahmadi, & Debrah, 2002). This effort has resulted in both private and public sector organizations gaining diverse staffing at most organizational levels.

Unfortunately we have scant knowledge about workplace relationships and individual performance in Omani–expatriate workplace supervisor–subordinate dyads. Additionally, do these relationships compare favourably to those of exclusively Omani or expatriate supervisor–subordinate dyads? In this study we attempt to assess Omani and expatriate supervisor–subordinate workplace relationships and their respective individual workplace performance.

Conceptual model

Figure 11.1 illustrates the conceptual model employed in this study for discussing and analysing the relationships between expatriate and Omani workplace supervisor–subordinate relationships and subsequent individual performance.

The implementation of Oman's labour force nationalization policy, over the past 20 years, has resulted in increasing numbers of Omani supervisors and subordinates entering public and private sector workplaces. In our model we assume that the supervisor–subordinate dyad's nationalities will be related to trust in one's supervisor, liking the supervisor, exercising supportive influence, and the quality of

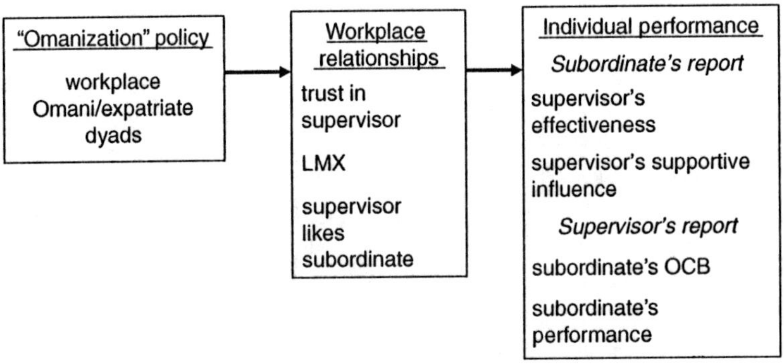

Figure 11.1 Workplace relationships and individual performance

supervisor–subordinate exchange. Furthermore, the individual performance dimensions of supervisor effectiveness, organizational citizenship behaviour, and subordinate performance are also a function of the supervisor–subordinate dyadic relationships.

Displacing expatriates

The modernization of Oman started in 1970 with the current ruler, Sultan Qaboos, and his national unification and modernization drive (Smith, 2004). Historically, Oman has been dependent on foreign workers to fulfil jobs that were either undesirable to Omanis or for which Omani skills were lacking (McElwee & Al-Riyami, 2003). More than 20 years ago, Sultan Qaboos began diversifying Oman's labour force away from dependence on expatriate workers' skills and knowledge. He realized that a modernizing Oman needed to enhance its labour force's expertise, reduce the outflow of foreign remittances (Mujtaba, Khanfar, & Khanfar, 2010), and create employment for increasing numbers of young Omani men and women entering the labour force.

The government's 25-year goal was to achieve employment for Omanis through a policy of nationalizing the labour force. The "Oman 2020" goal was a labour force "Omanization" rate of 95% in the public sector by 2020 compared with 68% in 1995. For the private sector, the conference established that the domestic employment rate of Omanis should grow from 7% in 1995 to 75% by 2020. During the same period the government sought to reduce the total proportion of foreign population in the Sultanate from 25% in 1995 to 15% in 2020 (Valeri, 2005).

Theoretical perspective

We believe that social identity theory and its elaboration, self-categorization theory (Ashforth & Mael, 1989; Simon, 1999; Tajfel & Turner, 1985), provide a perspective for understanding the dynamics of the emerging Omani and expatriate workplace relationships. These theories propose that each person has one or more social identities as well as a self-identity. The self-categorization proposition (Hogg & Terry, 2000; Jackson, Brett, Sessa, Cooper, Julin, & Peyronnin, 1991; Turner, 1987) asserts that a person bases their self-concept on the social categories chosen for association. In the absence of other normative rules, there is a tendency to evaluate one's "in-group" (e.g. being an Omani) positively in comparison with a relevant "out-group" (e.g. being an expatriate).

Alternatively, members of their in-group tend to evaluate negatively members of the out-group (Geddes & Konrad, 2003). Research has supported a consistent in-group bias (Hewstone, Rubin, & Willis, 2002) of positive affect and favouritism toward in-group members.

There are many implications for multicultural employment relationships of self-categorization into groups that make an "us" salient and distinct from "them" (Turner et al., 1987). Thus Omanis share a strong national (citizenship) and, often, tribal identity, and they consider themselves the salient Omani in-group, differentiating themselves from the foreigners/expatriates working in Oman. Alternatively, expatriates share the common, out-group, status of being foreign non-citizen workers in Oman and consequently perceive themselves as sharing a common identity of exclusion from the Omani in-group. A characteristic such as being an expatriate employee becomes a self-categorizing characteristic affecting expectation for workplace relationships and performance (Webster & Hysom, 1998). For example, a non-Omani may not engage in commercial activity without obtaining a special licence. Furthermore, Omani citizenship is nearly impossible to obtain for persons of non-Omani descent, hence permanent out-group status. For the purposes of this study, we categorize supervisors and subordinates according to their in-group or out-group status as "Omani" and "expatriate", respectively.

Needing positive self-identities, people have a preference for and, by suggestion, evaluate positively with those who are similar to themselves. This phenomenon is the similarity-attraction proposition (Jackson et al., 1991; Jackson, May, & Whitney, 1995), which proposes that people are attracted and are sympathetic to others perceived to be similar to them. Hence we expect supervisors and subordinates, either Omanis or expatriates, to have positive, quality relationships with those with whom they share citizenship, language, religion, tribal affiliation, heritage, or other common status (Kuehn & Al-Busaidi, 2000).

Workplace relationships

Trust in supervisor

There is general agreement (Bachmann & Zaheer, 2006) that trust is essential to maintaining effective working relationships between supervisors and their subordinates (Child, 2001; McKnight, Cummings, & Chervany, 1998). Supervisors and subordinates in trusting relationships expect that they can rely on one another's actions and promises (Currall & Judge, 1995; Rotter, 1967). Furthermore, from an employee perspective, trust enhances individual performance and diminishes turnover intentions (Robinson, 1996); these, in turn, contribute to performance. Indeed, trust is essential to productive workplace relationships (Axelrod, 1984).

Likes subordinates

Research in cognitive processing found that affective responses strongly influenced the information processing of supervisors when they conducted subordinate performance appraisals (Srull & Wyer, 1989; Zajonc, 1980). Lefkowitz's (2000) review of the role of affect in supervisory performance appraisals reported that an appraiser's affective regard for a subordinate was frequently associated with positive evaluations. Additional research indicated that a supervisor's positive regard for a subordinate might be a more important determinant of a favourable performance assessment than objective subordinate performance (Alexander & Wilkins, 1982). Additionally, Byrne (1971) and others (Judge & Ferris, 1993; Tsui & O'Reilly, 1989; Wayne & Liden, 1995) demonstrated the effect of perceived personal similarity on liking one another in organizations.

Supportive influence

Kipnis and Schmidt (1985) and others (e.g. Higgins, Judge, & Ferris, 2003; Van Knippenberg & Steensma, 2003) have demonstrated that social influence tactics can be grouped into two or three metacategories, such as hard, soft, and rational styles. Each of these comprises a number of specific interpersonal behaviours (Falbe & Yukl, 1992; Higgins, Judge, & Ferris, 2003; Kipnis, Schmidt, & Wilkinson, 1980). Conceptually, the category of "soft" influence tactics equates with using supportive influence. Supervisors using supportive influence strategies believe that their subordinates voluntarily comply with their requests rather than being forced. Consequently, supervisors attribute subordinates' compliance to their own volition rather than to being forced. Hence supervisors hold these subordinates and their performance in higher regard than if they are perceived to have no choice but to comply (Kipnis, 1976). Yukl and colleagues (Falbe & Yukl, 1992; Yukl & Tracey, 1992; Yukl, Kim, & Falbe, 1996) found that soft influence tactics used by supervisors were positively associated with favourable performance assessments of those subordinates.

Leader–member exchange

Relationships between supervisors and their subordinates have been referred to under leader–member exchange (LMX) theory (Dansereau,

Graen, & Haga, 1975; Graen, 1976; Graen & Cashman, 1975). These relationships are usually viewed from an interactionist perspective (Thibaut & Kelley, 1959) that focuses on the mutually beneficial social exchange with immediate supervisors (Masterson, Lewis, Goldman, & Taylor, 2000; Wayne, Shore, & Liden, 1997). Gerstner & Day (1997) proposed that leaders exhibit very different patterns of behaviour toward different members of work groups. These differences lead to the development of two types of relationship or exchange between organizational leaders and members. High-quality LMX (in-group relations) are friendly exchanges characterized by mutual trust, support (Liden & Graen, 1980), interpersonal attraction (Dansereau, Graen, & Haga, 1975), loyalty, and commitment (Dienesch & Liden, 1986). Alternatively, unidirectional downward influence based on formal organizational authority and contractual relations (Duchon, Green, & Taber, 1986; Deluga, 1994) is characteristic of low-quality LMX. Members of high-quality exchange groups often are the in-group and those of the low-quality exchange are the out-group (Dansereau, Graen, & Haga, 1975).

Individual performance

Supervisor effectiveness

Following from social identity theory, we expect that subordinates who share the same in-group status as their supervisors – for example, common cultural characteristics, values, and attitudes – are likely to evaluate them more favourably than supervisors in an out-group. For instance, Settoon, Bennett, and Liden (1996) found that the more that relationships between supervisors and subordinates are based on mutual trust and loyalty, interpersonal affect, and respect for each other, the better the evaluation of another's performance.

Organizational citizenship behaviour towards supervisor (SOCB)

Organ (1988) described organizational citizenship behaviour (OCB) as discretionary employee behaviour that is not required explicitly or formally rewarded by an organization but at the same time, taken together with other behaviours, contributes to organizational effectiveness. Our focus is on OCB directed towards supervisors that include behaviours such as accepting extra duties and responsibilities at work, working overtime when needed, and helping supervisors with their work.

From the above examples, we conclude that SOCB directed towards supervisors contributes to organizational performance in numerous ways. For instance, Podsakoff and Mackenzie (1997: 135) argue that, in general, SOCB may enhance organizational performance "by 'lubricating' the social machinery of the organization, reducing friction, and/or increasing efficiency". Positive OCB may also contribute to organizational success by enhancing co-workers' and supervisor's productivity by promoting better use of scarce resources, improving coordination, strengthening an organization's ability to attract and retain better employees, reducing variability of performance, and enabling better adaptation to environmental changes.

Subordinate performance

Research indicates that subordinate performance appraisals are affected by aspects of the relationship between supervisors and subordinates (Kipnis, Schmidt, Price, & Stitt, 1981; Schmidt, 1991). While traditionally a supervisor's assessment of subordinates' performance was considered objective, we now know that they are substantially dependent on the quality of the relationship with the supervisor (Heneman & Schwab, 1986; Kipnis, Schmidt, & Stitt, 1981). For instance, Settoon and colleagues (1996) reported that relationships between supervisors and subordinates based on trust, interpersonal affect, and respect for each other result in positive appraisals of subordinates' performance, both on in-role and extra-role behaviours (OCB). Supervisors whose self-identity and self-categorization matches that of their subordinates would be expected to have positive sentiments toward their subordinates. Hence we expect favourable performance evaluations in trusting, affirmative relationships between supervisors and their subordinates.

Hypotheses

Based on the previous discussion of social identity, workplace relationships, and individual performance, we will test the following hypotheses in the current study:

> *Hypothesis 1*: On the basis of social identity theory, exclusively Omani or expatriate supervisor–subordinate dyads will be associated more positively with positive workplace relationships indicated by "trusts supervisor", "likes subordinates", "supportive influence", and "positive LMX" than mixed Omani and expatriate supervisor–subordinate dyads.

> *Hypothesis 2*: On the basis of social identity theory, exclusively Omani or expatriate supervisor–subordinate dyads will be associated more

positively with individual performance indicated by subordinate appraisal, supervisor effectiveness and OCB than mixed Omani and expatriate dyads.

Hypothesis 3: Positive workplace relationships of "trusts supervisor", "likes subordinates", "supportive influence", and "positive LMX" will be associated positively with individual performance indicated by subordinate appraisal, supervisor effectiveness, and OCB for supervisor–subordinate dyads sharing the same national status.

As illustrated in Figure 11.2, we expect more positive supervisor–subordinate relationships in the two matched nationality cells and less positive relationships in the two mixed nationality cells.

Methods

Data collection

We surveyed private and public sector supervisors and their subordinates in Muscat, the largest city and capital of the Sultanate of Oman. By surveying organizations in both sectors, we attempted to discount the possible bias of specific organizational cultures. The surveyed organizations included a government export-promotion agency, a computer services company, an engineering services company, a ceramic tile manufacturer, a bank, a construction company, the staff-training department of a university, and the administrative office of a large hospital. Our anonymous survey instrument consisted of two sections, one completed by subordinates and the other completed by their supervisors. Mostly we administered the survey to groups of employees and immediately collected their completed forms. Then these respondents gave their immediate supervisor the "supervisor" section of the survey to complete.

		Subordinate	
		Omani	Expatriate
Supervisor	Omani	Positive relationship	Less positive relationship
	Expatriate	Less positive relationship	Positive relationship

Figure 11.2 Predicted supervisor–subordinate relationships

After several days, someone in each organization designated by the researchers as the "collector" collected the completed supervisor surveys. Subsequently the two sections of the confidential survey were matched using a unique serial number for each supervisor–subordinate dyad.

In total we were able to analyse 146 out of 168 sets of matched supervisor–subordinate surveys yielding a usable response rate of 86.9%. The 146 subordinates rated 33 different supervisors, producing an average of four ratings per supervisor (range 1–16).

Sample composition

Subordinates

Our subordinate sample consists of 68.2% Omanis and 31.8% expatriates. Women compose 37.6% of subordinates and 62.4% are men. The average length of time respondents had worked for their current organizations was 8.2 years (SD = 5.6). The educational level of 40.8% of the subordinates was a bachelor's or higher degree, and 84.7% of them had worked under their supervisor for at least seven months. Most of the subordinates (83.3%) were between the ages of 21 and 40. Government employees comprised 39.7% of the sample and 33.3% were private sector employees, with the rest reporting their industry as "other." Clerical/administrative employees comprised 37.5% of the sample, sales 10.3%, production/technical 14.1%, and the rest reported their job category as "other."

Supervisors

The supervisory sample consisted of 60.3% Omanis and 38.7% expatriates. These supervisory respondents were 18.7% women and 81.3% men. The educational level of 78.6% of the supervisors was a bachelor's degree or higher and 90.9% of the supervisors were between the ages of 31 and 50. The average period that a supervisor had supervised their subordinate was 34.3 months (SD = 21).

National status

Supervisors and subordinates were coded as either Omani or expatriate (Omani = 1; expatriate = 2). We computed a dummy same national status variable for supervisor–subordinate dyads in which both supervisor and subordinate were both either Omani or expatriate. We recognize that being an expatriate is not a nationality. However, expatriates, regardless of their original political nationality, share experiences, sociopolitical status, and treatment as members of the non-Omani out-group (Webster & Hysom, 1998). Therefore, for this study, we designated Omani non-citizens as expatriates due to their common "outsider" status regardless of their actual political state nationality. Some 32% of the same nationality dyads are either solely Omani or solely expatriate dyads, and 67.8% of the supervisor–subordinate are mixed dyads consisting of an Omani and an expatriate.

Workplace relationships

Supportive influence

Kipnis, Schmidt, and Wilkinson (1980) empirically developed a comprehensive 33-item measure of the tactics that supervisors use when attempting to influence their subordinates. This instrument has been widely used and validated across diverse populations during the past 25 years (Blickle, 2000; Farmer & Maslyn, 1999; Higgins, Judge, & Ferris, 2003; Rao & Hashimoto, 1996; Schriesheim & Hinkin, 1990). Furthermore, its cross-cultural validity has been demonstrated across diverse nationalities (Schmidt & Yeh, 1992). Subordinates, using a modified version of the Profile of Organizational Influence Strategies (POIS, Form-M) reported the influence tactics typically used by their immediate supervisors. The POIS instrument protocol requires indicating actual supervisor influence behaviours used with subordinates in employment contexts rather than desired behaviours or personality dimensions. We modified the wording of the POIS items so that subordinates could report on the influence tactics that their supervisors used with them. For example, the original POIS Form-M item, "I act very humble and polite while making my request," was changed to "My supervisor acts very humble and polite while making his/her request." Responses for the 33 POIS items ranged from "never" (1) to "almost always" (5).

A principal component factor analysis using varimax rotation and specifying three factors (Deluga, 1991; Kipnis & Schmidt, 1985; Somech & Drach-Zahavy, 2002; Van Knippenberg & Steensma, 2003) yielded factors that we interpreted as the following influence strategies: forceful ($\alpha = 0.89$), supportive ($\alpha = 0.81$), and directive rational ($\alpha = 0.75$), accounting for 45.3% of the total item variance.

Leader–member exchange relationship

Subordinates assessed their relationships with their supervisors using a customized version of the LMX scale reported by Scandura and

Graen (1984). For this study we selected four items deemed appropriate to the respondents and their respective contexts that referred to the quality of the working relationships with supervisors (Bauer & Green, 1996). These items are as follows: "I usually know where I stand with my supervisor," "My working relationship with my supervisor is effective," "My supervisor understands my problems and needs," and "My supervisor recognizes my potential." The response options for this scale ranged from "strongly disagree" (1) to "strongly agree" (7) ($\alpha = 0.83$).

Trust

Trust was measured with the three-item scale developed by Roberts and O'Reilly (1974) (e.g. "How free do you feel to discuss with your supervisor the problems and difficulties in your job without jeopardizing your position or having it held against you?"). The response categories ranged from very much (1) to very little (7) ($\alpha = 0.77$).

Likes subordinate

The following three items from Wayne and Ferris (1990) were used to measure how much supervisors like their subordinates: ("I think this employee would make a good friend," "I get along well with this employee," and "I like this employee very much"). Supervisors responded on a seven-point scale ranging from "strongly disagree" (1) to "strongly agree" (7) ($\alpha = 0.84$).

Individual performance

Supervisors rated the organizational citizenship behaviour of their subordinates using the seven-item SOCB-subordinate measure (e.g. "Accepts extra duties and responsibilities at work") reported by Masterson, Lewis, Goldman, and Taylor (2000). We used this scale because the Masterson et al. (2000) study indicates that subordinate social exchange relationships with supervisors are related to behaviours directed towards supervisors. The scale responses obtained from supervisors ranged from "never true" (1) to "always true" (5). A factor analysis indicated that the seven items composed a single SOCB dimension ($\alpha = 0.76$).

Subordinate performance

Supervisors assessed the performance of their subordinates on a six-item scale consisting of items such as "ability to solve problems," "potential for promotion," and "motivation to work hard." Kipnis and Schmidt (1988) reported an earlier version of this scale evaluating subordinate performance across various jobs and organizations. Responses for this scale ranged from "very poor" (1) to "outstanding" (5). A factor analysis of the items indicated a single performance dimension ($\alpha = 0.92$).

Supervisor effectiveness

Subordinates assessed the effectiveness of their supervisors using a one-item measure with response categories ranging from "The least effective supervisor I have known" (1) to "The most effective supervisor I have ever known" (5).

Results

Table 11.1 shows the means and standard deviations for the measures of workplace relationships and individual performance according to the national status (same or dissimilar) of the supervisor–subordinate dyads in this study. Additionally, Table 11.2 displays the descriptive statistics and correlations of all the variables as well as their means and standard deviations.

Hypothesis 1 predicted that the same "national status" (either Omani or expatriate) supervisor–subordinate dyads would be more positively associated with the workplace relationship dimensions of supervisors liking their subordinates, quality supervisor–subordinate

Table 11.1 Descriptive statistics for supervisor–subordinate dyads

	Exclusively Omani or expatriate *M* (SD)	Mixed Omani or expatriate *M* (SD)
Workplace relationships		
trusts supervisor	5.24 (1.27)	4.95 (1.36)
likes subordinate	5.82 (0.85)	6.12[a] (0.95)
supportive influence	3.12 (0.71)	3.00 (0.75)
LMX	5.24 (1.27)	5.91 (1.10)
Individual performance		
supervisor effectiveness	4.09 (0.97)	4.15 (0.86)
SOCB	3.87 (0.77)	4.11 (0.85)
subordinate performance	3.65 (0.68)	3.61 (0.80)

Notes: [a]$p < 0.10$.
Supervisor and subordinate national status (Omani = 1; expatriate = 2).
Same national status = 1; dissimilar national status = 0.

Table 11.2 Descriptive statistics and correlations

Variable	*M* (SD)	Trusts supervisor	Likes subordinates	Supportive influence			
Workplace relationships							
trusts supervisor	5.17 (1.28)						
likes subordinate	5.92 (.89)	0.35**					
supportive influence	3.11 (.73)	0.26**	−0.01				
LMX	5.70 (1.07)	0.68**	0.33**	0.20*			
Variable	***M* (SD)**	**Trusts supervisor**	**Likes subordinates**	**Supportive influence**	**LMX**	**Supervisor effectiveness**	**OCB**
Individual performance							
Supervisor effectiveness	4.08 (0.95)	0.48**	0.26**	0.14	0.53**		
SOCB	3.93 (0.78)	0.16+	0.53**	0.19+	0.25**	0.09	
Subordinate performance	3.62 (0.73)	0.13	0.07	0.11	0.27**	0.24**	0.06
Dyad composition							
subordinate national status	1.26 (0.44)	0.10	−0.09	0.02	0.20*	0.06	0.16
supervisor national status	1.31 (0.46)	−0.07	0.00	0.08	0.04	−0.03	0.05
same national status	0.76 (0.43)	0.10	−0.17+	0.09	−0.09	−0.03	−0.14
Variable	***M* (SD)**	**Subordinate performance**	**Subordinate national status**	**Supervisor national status**			
Dyad composition							
subordinate national status	1.26 (0.44)	0.07					
supervisor national status	1.31 (0.46)	0.01	0.41**				
same national status	0.76 (0.43)	0.03	−0.20*	−0.34**			

Notes: supervisor and subordinate national status (Omani = 1; expatriate = 2).
Same national status = 1; dissimilar national status = 0.
+ $p < 0.1$; *$p < 0.05$**; $p < 0.01$.
Pairwise deletion used for missing data.

exchange relationships, subordinates trusting their supervisors, and supervisors using supportive influence than mixed Omani or expatriate supervisor–subordinate dyads. We tested this hypothesis using Multivariate Analysis of Variance (MANOVA).

There was no statistically significant difference between "same national" status (either Omani or expatriate) supervisor–subordinate dyads and mixed Omani or expatriate supervisor–subordinate dyads on workplace relationships $F\ (4,135) = 1.223$, $p = 0.30$, Wilks' $\lambda = 0.96$, Partial $\varepsilon^2 = 0.03$. This finding is counter to our prediction that supervisors sharing either in-group (Omani) or out-group (expatriate) status with their subordinates would like them more than in dissimilar national status dyads. Hence the results of our analyses do not support our first hypothesis.

Hypothesis 2 posited that the same "national status" (either Omani or expatriate) supervisor–subordinate dyads would be more positively associated with the individual performance dimensions of subordinate performance appraisal, supervisor effectiveness, and SOCB than mixed Omani or expatriate supervisor–subordinate dyads. We expected that supervisors and their subordinates sharing common national status (Omani or expatriate) would be assessed as performing better than supervisors and their subordinates who were not of the same national status. This hypothesis was also tested using MANOVA. Again, we found no statistically significant relationship between "same national" status (either Omani or expatriate) supervisor–subordinate dyads and mixed Omani or expatriate supervisor–subordinate dyads on individual performance $F\ (3,136) = 0.580$, $p = 0.62$, Wilks' $\lambda = 987$, Partial $\varepsilon^2 = 0.01$. Thus the results did not support our second hypothesis.

Hypothesis 3 predicted that supervisors and their subordinates sharing the same national status would be positively associated with the extent to which workplace relationships were related to individual performance. For each performance measure we first tested a regression model containing the workplace relationship measures, subordinate national status, and supervisor national status. Then we tested a second model that added the same national status to the independent variables in the first model. A comparison of the two models for each performance dimension indicated the relative contribution made to explaining the performance dimensions by each workplace relationship dimension or national status. Table 11.3 shows that only the subordinates' national status contributes to supervisory assessment of subordinates' SOCB. However, adding the same national status variable not only did not increase the explanatory power of the models but also reduced the amount of variance explained in each instance. Therefore

Table 11.3 Regression analysis for individual performance

	Supervisor effectiveness		SOCB		Subordinate performance	
	1	2	1	2	1	2
Trusts supervisor	0.20[+]	0.20[+]	−0.20[+]	−0.20[+]	−0.12	−0.15
Likes subordinate	0.09	0.06	0.60***	0.59***	0.01	0.02
Supportive influence	0.02	0.02	0.24*	0.24*	0.08	0.07
LMX	0.37**	0.37**	0.10	0.09	0.34*	0.35*
Subordinate in dyad either Omani or expatriate[a]	−0.03	−0.03	0.24*	0.24*	0.02	0.03
Supervisor in dyad either Omani or expatriate	−0.02	−0.03	0.09	−0.09	−0.02	−0.00
Supervisors and subordinates are both either Omani or expatriate[b]		−0.02		−0.02		0.07
df	6,90	7,89	6,90	7,89	6,90	7,89
Adj. R^2	0.26	0.26	0.34	0.34	0.03	0.02
F	6.73***	5.71***	9.39***	7.97***	1.41	1.26

Notes: standardized beta weights are shown.
$+p < 0.10$; $*p < 0.05$; $**p < 0.01$; $***p < 0.001$.
[a]Supervisor and subordinate national status (Omani = 1; expatriate = 2).
[b]Same national status = 1; dissimilar national status = 0.

our third hypothesis was not supported by our findings, as shown in the hierarchical regression analyses reported in Table 11.3.

As a further step, we conducted correlation and regression analyses to determine if gender or the same gender of supervisors and their subordinates might be confusing our findings (Geddes & Konrad, 2003). However, our results indicated that there was no relationship between gender and performance or workplace relationship measures. An interesting finding, as shown in Table 11.3, is the relationship between dimensions of workplace relationships, supervisors' effectiveness, and subordinates' organizational citizenship behaviour directed towards their supervisors.

Supervisory effectiveness as rated by subordinates is related to the quality of LMX and to a lesser extent subordinates trusting their supervisors. SOCB as illustrated in Table 11.3 is related to supervisors liking their subordinates, using supportive influence with them, and being a different national status from their subordinates. To a slight degree, subordinates who trusted their supervisors had a negative association with SOCB. Finally, our regression models that attempted to account for subordinate performance appraisals explained an insignificant amount of the variance in the performance appraisals. However, LMX is significantly and positively associated with subordinate individual performance. Overall we found that aspects of workplace relationships predicted individual performance in the organizations surveyed, but the same national status of supervisors and their subordinates did not produce the effects that we had hypothesized.

Discussion

The policy of "Omanization" is changing the nationality composition of the Sultanate of Oman's workplaces as Omanis replace expatriates. We examined the relationship between the nationality of supervisor–subordinate dyads and workplace relationships and individual performance in public and private sector organizations. These organizations have diverse workforces composed of both Omanis and expatriates in positions of both supervisors and subordinates. Three hypotheses based on workplace relationships involving social identity and similarity-attraction theories were tested. We expected to find quality workplace relationships and better individual performance when both members of a supervisor–subordinate dyad were of the same nationality status (Omani or expatriate) than when they were dissimilar. Generally we found that specific dimensions of workplace relationships were associated with important dimensions of individual performance. However, we did not find that "nationality" status (Omani or expatriate) similarity between supervisors and their subordinates was associated with quality workplace relationships or dimensions of individual performance. Counter to our expectations based on similarity-attraction theory, subordinates in national status dissimilar dyads seem to be liked more by their supervisors than in same nationality status (Omani or expatriate) dyads. Additionally, expatriates appeared to be more likely to be perceived exhibiting OCB toward their supervisors than did Omanis. Perhaps expatriates engage in more SOCB than Omanis due to their precarious economic and political status. Expatriates are vulnerable since both their in-country families and, often, their extended families are economically dependent on them. Yet expatriates have limited access to Omani protective labour legislation, subsidies, and citizenship. Thus expatriates have a greater incentive than Omanis to work hard in extra-role behaviours and SOCB, to maintain their employment and hence work permits as national pressure increases to displace them with Omanis.

We were intrigued to find that subordinates, Omani or expatriate, who trusted their supervisors tended to rate them as effective. However, we do not know the direction of causality between these variables given that this was a cross-sectional study. Therefore effective supervisors, Omani or expatriate, may elicit trust from their subordinates, or trusting subordinates may contribute to their supervisors' effectiveness.

The negative relationship between subordinates trusting their supervisors and their OCB towards their supervisors (SOCB measure) requires some consideration. One explanation may be that subordinates who do not trust their supervisors to look out for their interests will more probably exhibit extra-role behaviour (SOCB) as a means of creating a favourable impression with their supervisors (Rao, Schmidt, & Murray, 1995; Wayne & Green, 1993; Wayne & Liden, 1995).

However, several researchers have indicated that negative stereotypes (Hilton & Von Hipple, 1996) about indigenous employees are widely prevalent in the Middle East (Mellahi, 2007; Mellahi & Wood, 2001; Rees, Mammen, & Bin Braik, 2007). Indigenous employees are widely believed to be unmotivated, lazy, and without a sufficient work ethic who come and go from their workplace as they please (Rees et al., 2007). Empirical evidence from the United Arab Emirates indicates that both indigenous nationals and expatriates (Al-Waqfi & Forstenlechner, 2010) share these negative stereotypes. Further, the same study found that agreement with the negative stereotype was stronger at the higher levels of the organizational hierarchy independent of nationality. This means that both national and expatriate supervisors may share negative stereotypes of indigenous employees.

Supervisors influenced by negative stereotypes of employees are likely to perceive and respond negatively to these employees. The employees in turn will respond negatively to these negative perceptions and behaviours. In addition, there is evidence that stereotyping may reduce the motivation of the stereotyped (Page, 2007). This results in a vicious cycle of self-fulfilling prophecy (Merton, 1968).

From the perspective of the negative "kernel of truth" stereotype model (McCauley, Stitt, & Segal, 1980), we can expect reports of quality relationships between supervisors and national employees versus expatriate employees, regardless of the nationality of the supervisors, since both supervisors and subordinates may share a cognitive bias regarding Omanis. We can also expect supervisor-rated subordinate performance for national employees to be lower compared with expatriate employees. In fact, our regression results appear to support this perspective in the case of SOCB. We found that nationality of the subordinate (being an expatriate employee) was a positive predictor of SOCB. Looking at workplace relationships and individual performance from the negative stereotype perspective may be a promising avenue for future research in the Arabian Gulf.

Considering these intriguing findings from social identity and self-categorization perspectives permits us to see the fault lines between Omanis and expatriates. In this study we used nationality status – Omani or expatriate – as the basis for determining whether or not supervisors and their subordinates were of the same or different nationality status. "Expatriate" was a proxy for not being an Omani and, therefore, an "outsider." This perspective is in keeping with the Turner (1987) argument that self-identity at one moment (e.g. nationality status) suppresses other possible identities or self-categorizations. By defining nationality status as being Omani or not, we focused on a single demographic category in isolation from other, perhaps more relevant, social identities, such as Omani tribal and/or family affiliations, or even organizational identification (Siegfried, 2000). For instance, Cinnirella (1996) argues that a theory of self is required to account for when two or more social identities are salient. Therefore we propose that future theorizing and research on the effects of similarity and dissimilarity in host national and expatriate dyads consider the specific basis of self-categorization as reported by the participants. Organizational members may consider themselves more or less similar based on cultural values such as individualism, organizational culture, collectivism, and religious practice rather than a political definition of nationality (Singelis & Brown, 1995; Triandis, 1994).

The results of this study indicate that we need to reassess an assumption that the same nationality between supervisors and their subordinates will result in quality workplace relationships and ultimately enhanced individual performance. Whether or not the supervisor–subordinate pairs are exclusively host nationals (Omani) or expatriates (outsiders) does not necessarily determine workforce effectiveness as determined in this study. Rather, organizational members may be developing workplace relationships (trust, liking, and quality exchanges) on the bases of factors other than Omani nationality. Our findings are promising for organizations with nationality and ethnically diverse workforces because performance-enhancing workplace relationships may develop independent of the specific nationality mix of their supervisor–subordinate pairs.

References

Alexander, E.R., & Wilkins, R.D. (1982). Performance rating validity: The relationship between objective and subjective measures of performance, *Group and Organization Studies*, 7, 485–496.

Al-Hamadi, A.D., & Budhwar, P.S. (2006). Human resource management in Oman. In P.S. Budhwar, & K. Mellahi (Eds.), *Managing Human Resource in the Middle-East* (pp. 40–58). Oxford: Routledge.

Al-Hamdi, A.D., Budhwar, P.S., & Shipton, H. (2007). Management of human resource in Oman. *The International Journal of Human Resource Management*, 18, 100–113.

Al-Waqfi, M., & Forstenlechner, I. (2010). Stereotyping of citizens in an expatriate-dominated labour market: Implications for workforce localization policy. *Employee Relations*, 32(4), 364–381.

Ashforth, B.E., & Mael, F. (1989). Social identity theory and the organization, *Academy of Management Review*, 145(1), 20–39.

Axelrod, R. (1984). *The Evolution of Cooperation*. New York: Basic Books.

Bachmann, R. & Zaheer, A. (Eds). (2006). *Handbook of Trust Research*. Cheltenham: Edward Elgar Publishing, Ltd.

Bauer, T.N., & Green, S.G. (1996). Development of leader-member exchange: A longitudinal test. *Academy of Management Journal*, 39, 1538–1567.

Blickle, G. (2000). Influence tactics used by subordinates: An empirical analysis of the Kipnis and Schmidt subscales. *Psychological Reports*, 86(1), 143–155.

Budhwar, P.S., Al-Yahmadi, S., & Debrah, Y. (2002). Human resource development in the Sultanate of Oman. *International Journal of Training and Development*, 6(3), 198–215.

Budhwar, P.S., & Mellahi, K. (2006). Introduction: Managing human resources in the Middle East. In Budhwar, P.S. and Mellahi, K. (Eds). *Managing Human Resource in the Middle-East*. Routledge, Oxford.

Byrne, D. (1971). *The Attraction Paradigm*. New York: Academic Press.

Child, J. (2001). Trust-the fundamental bond in global collaboration. *Organizational Dynamics*, 29(4),274–288.

Cinnirella, M. (1996). Exploring temporal aspects of social identity: The concept of possible social identities, *European Journal of Social Psychology*, 28, 227–248.

Currall, S.C., & Judge, T.A. (1995). Measuring trust between organizational boundary role persons. *Organizational Behavior and Human Decision Processes*, 64, 151–170.

Daboub, J.J. (2008). Middle East economics. *Issues in Science & Technology*, 24, 9–10

Dansereau, F., Graen, G., & Haga, W.J. (1975). A vertical dyad linkage approach to leadership within formal organizations: A longitudinal investigation of the role making process. *Organizational Behavior and Human Performance*, 13, 46–78.

Deluga, R.J. (1991). The relationship of leader and subordinate influencing activity in naval environments. *Military Psychology*, 3(1), 25–40.

Deluga, R.J. (1994). Supervisor trust building, leader-member exchange and organizational citizenship behavior. *Journal of Occupational and Organizational Psychology*, 67, 315–326.

Dienesch, R.M., & Liden, R.L. (1986). Leader-member exchange model of leadership: A critique and further development. *Academy of Management Review*,11, 618–634.

Duchon, D., Green, S.G., & Taber, T.D. (1986). Vertical dyad linkages: A longitudinal assessment of antecedents, measures and consequences. *Journal of Applied Psychology*, 71, 56–60.

Farmer, S.M., & Maslyn, J.M. (1999). Why are styles of upward influence neglected? Making the case for a configurational approach to influences. *Journal of Management*, 25(5), 653–683.

Falbe, C.M., & Yukl, G. (1992). Consequences for managers of using single influence tactics and combinations of tactics. *Academy of Management Journal*, 35, 638–652.

Geddes, D., & Konrad, A. (2003). Demographic differences and reasons to perform feedback. *Human Relations*, 56, 1485–2012.

Gerstner, L.R., & Day, D.V. (1997). Meta-analytic review of leader-member exchange theory: Correlates and construct issues. *Journal of Applied Psychology*, 82, 522–552.

Graen, G. (1976). Role making processes within complex organizations. In M.D. Dunnette (Ed.), *Handbook of Industrial and Organizational Psychology* (pp. 1201–1245). Chicago, IL: Rand McNally.

Graen, G., & Cashman, J. (1975). A role-making model of leadership in formal organizations: A development approach. In J.G. Hunt, & L.L. Larson (Eds.), *Leadership Frontiers* (pp. 143–165). Kent, OH: Kent State University Press.

Heneman, H.G., & Schwab, D.P. (1986). *Perspectives on Personnel/Human Resource Management*. Homewood, IL: Irwin.

Herrera, L. (2009). Is "Youth" being addressed in important and distinctive ways in Middle East Studies? *International Journal of Middle East Studies*, 41, 368–371.

Hewstone, M. Rubin, M., & Willis, H. (2002). Intergroup bias. *Annual Review of Psychology*, 53, 575–604.

Higgins, C.A., Judge, T.A., & Ferris, G.R. (2003). Influence tactics and work outcomes: A meta- analysis. *Journal of Organizational Behavior*, 24, 89–106.

Hilton, J.L., & von Hipple, W. (1996). Stereotypes. *Annual Review of Psychology*, 47, 237–71.

Hogg, M.A., & Terry, D.J. (2000). Social identity and self-categorization processes in organizational contexts. *Academy of Management Review*, 25(1), 121–140.

Jackson, S.E., Brett, J.F., Sessa, V.I., Cooper, D.M., Julin, J.A., & Peyronnin, K.(1991). Some differences make a difference: Individual dissimilarity and group heterogeneity as correlates of recruitment, promotions, and turnover. *Journal of Applied Psychology*, 76, 675–689.

Jackson, S.E., May, K.E., & Whitney, K. (1995). Understanding the dynamics of diversity in decision-making teams. In R.A.Guzzo and E. Salas (Eds.), *Teameffectiveness and Decision Making in Organizations* (pp. 204–261). San Francisco, CA: Jossey-Bass.

Judge, T.A., & Ferris, G.R. (1993). Social context of performance evaluation decisions. *Academy of Management Journal*, 36, 80–105.

Kipnis, D. (1976). *The Powerholders*. Chicago, IL: University of Chicago Press.

Kipnis, D., & Schmidt, S. (1988). Upward-influence styles: Relationship with performance evaluations, salary, and stress. *Administrative Science Quarterly*, 33, 528–542.

Kipnis, D., & Schmidt, S.M. (1985).The language of persuasion. *Psychology Today*, 4, 40–46.

Kipnis, D., Schmidt, S., Price, K., & Stitt, C. (1981). Why do I like thee: Is it your performance or my orders. *Journal of Applied Psychology*, 66, 324–328.

Kipnis, D., Schmidt, S.M., & Wilkinson, I. (1980). Intraorganizational influence tactics: Explorations in getting one's way. *Journal of Applied Psychology*, 65, 440–452.

Kuehn, K.W., & Al-Busaidi, Y. (2000). A difference of perspective: An exploratory study of Omani and expatriate values and attitudes. *International Journal of Commerce & Management*, 10(1), 74–90.

Liden, R.C., & Graen, G. (1980). Generalizability of the vertical dyad linkage model of leadership. *Academy of Management Journal*, 23, 451–465.

Lefkowitz, J. (2000). The role of interpersonal affective regard in supervisory performance ratings. *Journal of Occupational and Organizational Psychology*, 73, 67–85.

Masterson, S.S., Lewis, K., Goldman, B.M., & Taylor, S.M. (2000). Integrating justice and social exchange: The differing effects of fair procedures and treatment on work relationships. *Academy of Management Review*, 43, 738–748.

McCauley, C., Stitt, C.L., & Segal, M. (1980). Stereotyping: From prejudice to prediction. *Psychological Bulletin*, 87, 195–208.

McElwee, G., & Al-Riyami, R. (2003). Women entrepreneurs in Oman: Some barriers to success. *Career Development International*, 8(7), 339–346.

McKnight, D.H., Cummings, L.L., & Chervany, N.L. (1998). Initial trust formation in new organizational relationships. *Academy of Management Review*, 23, 473–490.

Mellahi, K. (2007). The effect of regulation on HRM: Private sector firms in Saudi Arabia. *International Journal of Human Resource Management*, 18(1), 85–99.

Mellahi, K., & Wood, G. (2001). Human resource management in Saudi Arabia. In P. Budhwar, & Y. Debrah (Eds.). *Human Resource Management in Developing Countries* (pp. 135–51). London: Routledge.

Merton, R.K. (1968, 1949) *Social Theory and Social Structure*. New York: The Free Press.

Mujtaba, G.B., Khanfar, N.M., & Khanfar, S.M. (2010). Leadership tendencies of government employees in Oman: A study of task and relationship based on age and gender. *Public Organization Review*, 10, 173–190.

Omani Law Blog (2011). Retrieved from http://omanlawblog.curtis.com/2008/06/oman-law-digest-2008-nationality-and.html.

Organ, D.W. (1988). *Organizational Citizenship Behavior: The Good Soldier Syndrome*. Lexington, MA: Lexington Books.

Page, S.E. (November, 2007). Making the difference: Applying the logic of diversity. *Academy of Management Perspectives*, 21, 6–20.

Podsakoff, P.M., & Mackenzie, S.B. (1997). Impact of organizational citizenship behavior on organizational performance: A review and suggestions for future research. *Human Performance*, 10,133–151.

Rees, C., Mammen, A., & Bin Braik, A. (2007). Emiratization as a strategic HRM change initiative: Case study evidence from UAE petroleum company. *International Journal of Human Resource Management*, 18(1), 33–53.

Rao, A., & Hashimoto, K. (1996). Universal and culturally specific aspects of managerial influence: A study of Japanese managers. *Leadership Quarterly*, 8(3), 295–313.

Rao, A., Schmidt, S.M., & Murray, L. (1995). Upward impression management: Goals, influence strategies, and consequences. *Human Relations*, 48, 147–167.

Roberts, K.H., & O'Reilly, C.A. (1974). Measuring organizational communication. *Journal of Applied Psychology*, 59, 321–326.

Robinson, S. (1996). Trust and the breach of psychological contract. *Administrative Science Quarterly*, 41, 574–599.

Rotter, J. (1967). A new scale for the measurement of interpersonal trust. *Journal of Personality*, 35, 651–665.

Scandura, T.A., & Graen, G.B. (1984). Moderating effects of initial leader-member exchange status on the effects of a leadership intervention. *Journal of Applied Psychology*, 69, 436.

Schmidt, S.M. (1991). Organizational life: There is more to work than working. *Interfaces*, 21, 48–52.

Schmidt, S.M., & Yeh, R.-S. (1992). The structure of leader influence: A cross-national comparison. *Journal of Cross-Cultural Psychology*, 23(2), 251–264.

Schriesheim, C.A., & Hinkin, T.R. (1990). Influence tactics used by subordinates: A theoretical and empirical analysis and refinement of Kipnis, Schmidt and Wilkinson. *Journal of Applied Psychology*, 75(3), 246–268.

Settoon, R., Bennett, N., & Liden, R.C. (1996). Social exchange in organizations: Perceived organizational support, leader-member exchange, and employee reciprocity. *Journal of Applied Psychology*, 81, 219–227.

Siegfried, N. (2000). Legislation and legitimation in Oman: The basic law. *Islamic Law and Society*, 7, 359–397.

Singelis, T.M., & Brown, W.J. (1995). Culture, self, and collectivist communication. *Human Communication Research*, 21, 354–389.

Simon, B. (1999). A place in the world. In T. Tyler, R. Kramer & O. John (Eds.), *The Psychology of the Social Self* (pp. 47–69). Mahwah, NJ: Erlbaum.

Smith, S. (2004). *Britain's Revival and Fall in the Gulf.* London: Routledge-Curzon.

Somech, A., & Drach-Zahavy, A. (2002). Relative Power and influence strategy: The effects of agent/target organizational power on superiors' choices of influence strategies. *Journal of Organizational Behavior*. 23(2), 167–178.

Srull, T.K., & Wyer, R.S. (1989). *Memory and Cognition in its Social Context.* Hillsdale, NJ: Erlbaum.

Tajfel, H., & Turner, J.C. (1985).The social identity theory of intergroup behavior. In S. Worchel, & W.G. Austin (Eds.),*Handbook of Industrial and Organizational Psychology*, 2nd edition (pp. 769–827). Palo Alto, CA: Consulting Psychologists Press.

Thibaut, J.W., & Kelley, H.H. (1959). *The Social Psychology of Groups*. New York: John Wiley & Sons.

Triandis, H.C. (1994).*Culture and Social Behavior*. New York: McGraw-Hill.
Tsui, A.S., & O'Rilly, C.A. (1989). Beyond simple demographic effects: The importance of relational demography in superior-subordinate dyads. *Academy of Management Journal*, 32, 402–423.
Turner, J.C. (1987). *Rediscovering the Social Group: A Self-Categorization Theory*. Oxford: Blackwell.
Turner, J.C., Hogg, M.A., Oakes, P.J., Reicher, S.D., & Wetherell (1987). *Rediscovering the Social Group*. Oxford, England: Basil Blackwell.
Valeri, M. (2005). The Omanisation policy of employment: Omani economic dilemma. *The Gulf Monarchies in Transition, Colloquium*. CERI, 10–11.
Van Knippenberg, B., & Steensma, H. (2003). Future interaction expectation and the use of soft and hard influence tactics. *Applied Psychology: An International Review*, 52, 55–67.
Wayne, S.J., & Ferris, G.R. (1990). Influence tactics, affect, and exchange quality in supervisor-subordinate interactions: A laboratory experiment and field study. *Journal of Applied Psychology*, 75, 487–499.
Wayne, S.J., & Green, S.A. (1993).The effects of employee citizenship on employee citizenship and impression management behavior. *Human Relations*, 46, 1431–1440.
Wayne, S.J., & Liden, R.C. (1995). Effects of impression management on performance ratings: A longitudinal study. *Academy of Management Journal*, 38, 232–260.
Wayne, S.J., Shore, L.M., & Liden, R.L. (1997). Perceived organizational support and leader-member exchange: A social exchange perspective. *Academy of Management Journal*, 10, 82–111.
Webster, M., & Hysom, S.J. (1998). Creating status characteristics. *American Sociological Review*, 63, 351–378.
Yukl, G., Kim, H., & Falbe, C.M. (1996). Antecedents of influence outcomes. *Journal of Applied Psychology*, 81, 309–317.
Yukl, G., & Tracey, J.B. (1992). Consequences of influence tactics used with subordinates. peers, and the boss. *Journal of Applied Psychology*, 77, 525–535.
Zajonc, R.B. (1980). Thinking and feeling. *American Psychologist*, 35, 151–175.

Section III

Gender and Leadership

12
Glass Fence Thicker than Glass Ceiling: The Puzzling Gaps of Women's Leadership in Korea

Hunmin Kim

Introduction

Despite the rapid economic growth and the high level of educational achievement in Korea, the role of women in leadership positions is severely limited. A number of affirmative policies implemented to encourage women's labour market participation, prohibit discrimination in personnel management, improve gender representation and so on seem to have some effect, but this is slow. Nevertheless, Korean women's status is lower than those of many developing countries as seen by various official indices, with women leaders scarce and confined to certain sectors.

The restrictive status of women's leadership in Korea represents an enigma as to why there is such a mismatch between the national economic and educational performances and women's leadership. This study examines the characteristics of women's leadership in Korea focusing on four puzzling gaps: in women's leadership with economic growth, with human development, in women's leadership between government and business sectors, and between women's social leadership and household leadership.

The main contention of this study in explaining these gaps is that the traditional and cultural division of gender roles in Korea is distinguished by the boundary separating the household from society. That is, the most prominent and persistent stereotype of gender roles permeating the Korean culture is that the man's domain is outside the household and the woman's domain is inside the household. Men have very little, if any, housework left to them while women are expected to do all of the domestic work regardless of whether it requires strength or not. Inside the house it is common for Korean women to do dangerous, heavy and demanding tasks because all the housework is supposed to be women's work.

Gender roles in Korea are quite different from Western society where the role division between men and women can be explained by the women deemed as being weak and the men as strong. Men opening doors for women and other "ladies first" customs reflect the perception of women as the weaker sex. Housework requiring strength, such as mowing the lawn, moving and carrying heavy items, and hammering nails are considered men's work. Unlike the Western tradition, Korean women are not deemed to be the weaker sex *per se*.

Gender roles defined along the demarcation between the world inside the house, or the private sphere, and the world outside the house, or the public sphere, are not as prominent in Western societies as in Korea. Such a strong fence between the realms inside the house and outside the house holds back Korean women from actively pursuing social careers and reaching leadership positions. Added to this cultural wall are institutional barriers making it enormously difficult for women to balance both family and a career. For Korean women the glass fence is yet to be hurdled to even perceive a glass ceiling, and in some respects the glass fence is tougher to break than the glass ceiling.

This chapter starts with a discussion of leadership characteristics by gender, then presents a comparison of the status of women's leadership in Korea with some OECD (Organization for Economic Co-operation and Development) countries and Asian countries as reflected by the Gender Empowerment Measure (GEM) and other indices. The status of Korean women's leadership is contrasted with the economic development level and the achievements in human development in Korea. An examination of the divergence between women's leadership in political or government organizations and the business sector is followed by a discussion of the contrasting roles of Korean women in the public sphere from those in the private sphere. In the concluding section, the implications for employment, human development and social policies are discussed.

Leadership characteristics by gender

Discussion of leadership styles by gender usually starts with whether men and women are inherently similar or different (Adler, 1994; Bass, 1990; Hopkins, O'Neil, Passarelli, & Bilimoria, 2008; Lee, 2005;

Powell, 1988; Savage & Witz, 1992). The research literature on gender differences in leadership suggest that women's leadership is more democratic and relationship oriented while men's leadership is characterized as autocratic and task oriented. Women leaders give counsel and care, whereas men leaders control and command. Men's leadership is better suited to hierarchical organizations in contrast to women's leadership, which is more advantageous for teamwork. Men are more likely to be risk takers, making bold and daring decisions, whereas women are more likely to be risk averse, cautious and meticulous in their leadership style (Epstein, Olivares, Bass, Grahen, Schwartz, & Siegel, 1991; Loden, 1985; Muldrow & Bayton, 1979). Women leaders seek cooperation rather than competition, exercising personal power based on expertise rather than position power, relying on intuitive skills rather than analytical skills, and they have been associated with interactive and shared leadership (Kim & Kim, 2000; Loden, 1985; Rosener, 1990; Vinnicombe, 1987).

People have different expectations and perceptions of men leaders and women leaders. There are more negative perceptions regarding women leaders and people do not have high expectations from them even though in actual performance, inferiority in female leadership is unfounded (Eagly, Makhijani, & Klonsky, 1992; Izraeli & Adler, 1994; Powell, 1988).

However, the predominance of male leaders in most societies cannot be attributed fully to the difference in leadership style between men and women, nor for that matter to the similarity between the genders. Neither can it be explained sufficiently by the difference in people's evaluation of male and female leadership (Eagly, Karau, & Makhijani, 1995; Powell, 1988). Even if one assumes that there are significant differences in leadership style by gender, it does not necessarily imply that one is better than the other in absolute terms in all situations. So-called masculine leadership may have advantages in certain contexts and feminine leadership may have advantages in others (Hollander, 1992; Izraeli & Adler, 1994).

Cultural and institutional factors provide better explanations for why women lag so much behind men in reaching leadership positions. Particularly in Korea the Confucian tradition, patriarchal culture and patrilineal family practices have confined women's roles within the home much longer and much more strictly than in many other countries. Consequently Korean women's struggle in reaching top positions in the workplace had a very late start and has a long way to go while facing a multitude of obstacles.

International comparison of women's leadership

One of the most frequently used indices for the international comparison of women's leadership status is the GEM, published annually by the United Nations Development Programme (UNDP) until 2009. As shown in Table 12.1 and Figure 12.1, Korea's GEM ranked 61st out of 109 countries in 2009, much below most of the OECD countries, such as the UK, France and the US, which ranked 15th, 17th, and 18th, respectively. Korea and Singapore were among the "four dragons" in Asia recognized for their exemplary economic development. However, Korean women's empowerment level is much lower than that of Singapore, which had a GEM ranking of 16th in 2009, a notable improvement from 2002 when it was 23rd. Japan is the only country which, like Korea, exhibits

Table 12.1 Gender empowerment measure value and rank of some countries, 2002–2009

	2002	2004	2006	2008	2009
Spain	0.702 (15)	0.716 (15)	0.776 (15)	0.825 (12)	0.835 (11) [15]
UK	0.684 (16)	0.698 (18)	0.755 (16)	0.786 (14)	0.790 (15) [21]
Singapore	0.592 (23)	0.648 (20)	0.707 (18)	0.782 (15)	0.786 (16) [23]
France	–	–	–	0.780 (17)	0.779 (17) [8]
US	0.757 (11)	0.769 (14)	0.808 (12)	0.769 (18)	0.767 (18) [13]
Mexico	0.517 (38)	0.563 (34)	0.597 (35)	0.603 (47)	0.629 (39) [53]
Japan	0.527 (32)	0.531 (38)	0.557 (42)	0.575 (58)	0.567 (57) [10]
Philippines	0.523 (35)	0.542 (37)	0.533 (45)	0.560 (61)	0.560 (59) [105]
Korea, Rep. of	0.378 (61)	0.377 (68)	0.502 (53)	0.540 (68)	0.554 (61) [26]
Malaysia	0.505 (43)	0.519 (44)	0.500 (55)	0.538 (69)	0.542 (68) [66]
China	–	–	–	0.526 (72)	0.533 (72) [92]
Thailand	0.458 (50)	0.461 (57)	0.486 (60)	0.506 (78)	0.514 (76) [87]

Note: GEM rank in parentheses (), HDI rank in brackets [].
Source: UNDP "Human Development Report" (2002, 2004, 2006, 2008, 2009).

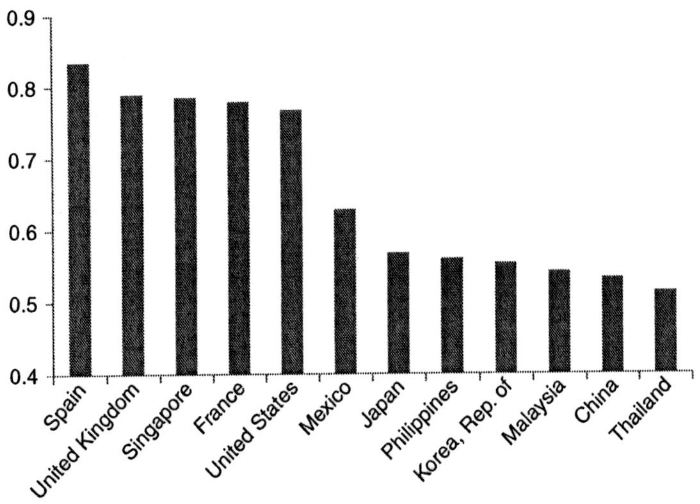

Figure 12.1 Gender empowerment measure value of some countries in 2009
Data source: UNDP "Human Development Report" (2009).

low gender empowerment in contrast to its national economic development. The average GEM value for 33 OECD countries, excluding Luxemburg, in 2009 was 0.742, Turkey having the lowest value of 0.379 and Korea the next lowest of 0.554.

Even more disconcerting about Korea is that the trend in its GEM does not show much improvement over the years, fluctuating from year to year but never reaching above 53rd, which was attained in 2006. Japan and the Philippines show a deteriorating trend in women's empowerment but their GEM scores have always been better than that of Korea in absolute terms. In the early part of the 2000s, Korean women's empowerment status was below that of Malaysia, becoming similar only by 2006 and slightly edging ahead since 2008.

Korea's GEM value is lower than many South American countries, such as Argentina at 24th, Peru at 36th, Ecuador at 41st and Honduras at 54th. Compared with some African countries, such as South Africa at 26th, Namibia at 43rd, Uganda 49th, and Lesotho 50th, Korean women's empowerment is quite low (UNDP, 2009).

Women's leadership can be divided into forerunner, token, substance and ubiquity stages (Kang, 2007). At the forerunner stage with the emergence of women activists trying to break cultural barriers, social movements are launched but have limited impact. In the token stage a handful of women can be found in leadership positions but their roles are only symbolic. It is at the substance stage when the presence of women leaders becomes significantly visible and they are able to exert effective influence. For women leaders to exercise real and substantive power it has been suggested that they should make up a critical mass of about 15% of all leadership positions (Kang, 2007). Women's leadership becomes more extensive at the ubiquity stage, where the proportion of women leaders reaches 30% (Kang, 2007).

Although women leaders in Korea are gradually increasing in proportion and expanding more and more into male-dominated sectors, the status of women leadership still shows a wide gap with other socioeconomic development levels of the Korean society.

Women leadership in Korea

Gap with national economic development

Korea is known for rapid economic growth which it has experienced since the 1960s, and today its economy is one of the top 20 in the world. In terms of the size of its gross domestic product (GDP) it ranked 15th in the world in 2011, 12th when ranked by purchasing power parity (PPP) valuation of GDP, as shown in Table 12.2. A per capita GDP of about US$20,000 puts Korea at the forefront of countries with middle-level incomes. The country has been regarded as a model case in economic development for achieving high growth and relatively low income inequality for quite some time. Although the polarization of income has been worsening recently, the global economic status of Korea has been increasing fast over recent years and it is now ranked as the 12–15th largest national economy in the world.

In contrast the advancement in the status of women's leadership is slow with only a handful of women leaders in most sectors of society. The proportion of women in leadership positions in Korea is less than that of many neighbouring Asian countries with lower levels of economic development, and certainly behind OECD countries. Women leaders fare much better in countries like Mexico and Spain, which have a similar rank to Korea's in terms of GDP. Spain has a very high GEM value ranked at 11th and Mexico, even though its per capita GDP is only about half of Korea's, as shown in Figure 12.2, has a GEM value ranked at 39th – much higher than Korea. Another indication of Korea's lagging women's leadership is the low proportion of women in the legislature. Comparing political leadership one can see from Figure 12.3 that the proportion of seats held by women in national parliaments in 2011 is

Table 12.2 Rank by GDP

Country	2008		2009		2010		2011	
	CP[a]	PPP[b]	CP	PPP	CP	PPP	CP	PPP
US	1	1	1	1	1	1	1	1
China	3	2	3	2	2	2	2	2
Japan	2	3	2	3	3	3	3	4
UK	6	7	6	6	6	7	7	8
France	5	8	5	8	5	9	5	9
Mexico	13	11	14	11	14	11	14	11
Republic of Korea	15	13	15	12	15	12	15	12
Spain	10	12	9	13	12	13	12	13
Thailand	35	24	34	24	30	24	32	24
Malaysia	39	30	41	29	37	29	38	29
Philippines	47	36	46	33	46	32	47	32
Singapore	45	43	44	43	40	40	37	39

Note: [a]current price, [b]purchasing power parity valuation.
Source: International Monetary Fund.

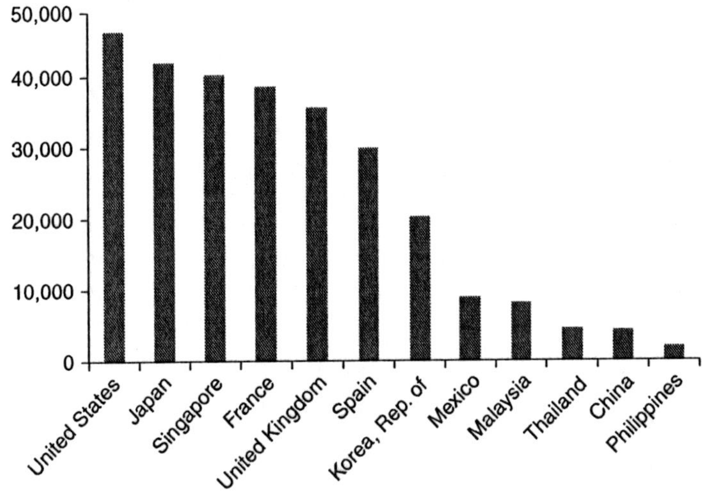

Figure 12.2 GDP per capita, 2010 (current US$)
Data source: World Bank.

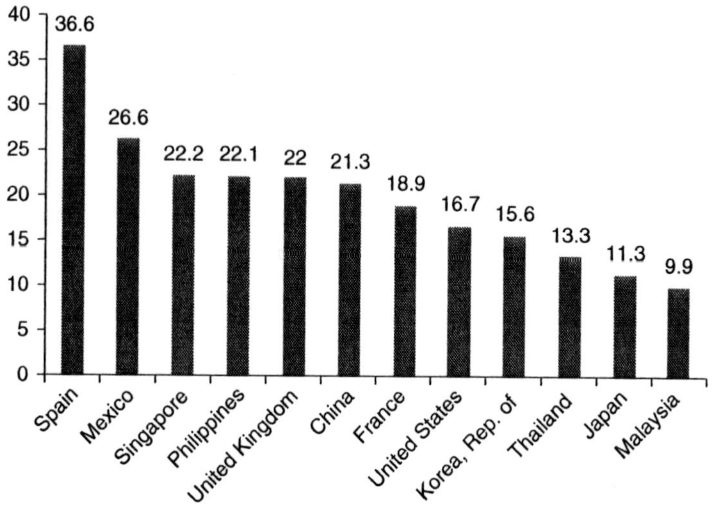

Figure 12.3 Proportion of seats held by women in national parliaments in 2011
Data source: World Bank.

36.6% in Spain, more than 26.2% in Mexico and only about 15.6% in Korea.

In fact, Korea's GEM value is not much better than that of countries like Malaysia, China, Thailand and the Philippines, which have considerably lower per capita income. Korean women's empowerment level has been consistently worse than that of the Philippines, which ranks at 47th in terms of GDP and 32nd in terms of purchasing power parity valuation of GDP, far below those of Korea, as can be seen in Table 12.2. In 2002 and 2004, Korea's GEM value was lower than that of Malaysia and Thailand, stepping up slightly above these countries only since 2006.

Gap with the level of human development

Koreans are known worldwide for their unusually high educational motivations. Advancement into tertiary education in Korea is one of the highest in the world. Unlike the olden days, Korean women now have almost equal access to college education as men. This is attributable to increased incomes along with a diminishing preference for sons induced by the composite effects of a range of anti-discrimination legislation and affirmative action policies, an increase in women with jobs, and high-quality performance among female students.

The entry rate or advancement rate of college education in Korea is among the highest in the world and it is not so different between male and female students. Figure 12.4 shows that the entry rate into tertiary education in Korea is higher than that of the US and the UK, and much higher than the OECD average. Looking at women only, the rates for the US and Korea are the highest, and substantially higher than Spain or Mexico, which had higher GEM values than Korea. Table 12.3 shows that there used to be some disparity between male and female access to tertiary education in Korea, but since the 2000s, women have quickly caught up with men, with hardly any gender difference today. In fact in 2010 the college entry rate was higher for women, at 80.5%, than for men, at 77.6%.

With top rates of access to higher education for both men and women, added to strong health and longevity in Korea, the country's Human Development Index (HDI) is 26th in international standing, which is much higher than the GEM ranking. Korea belongs to the group of countries with very high HDI values but its GEM value is one of the

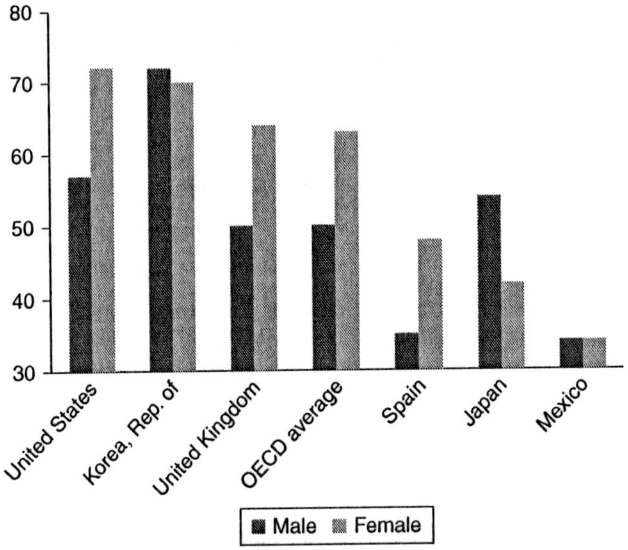

Figure 12.4 Net entry rates of tertiary education: male and female
Notes: International students are included.
For tertiary-type A education. For explanation of tertiary-type A and calculation of net entry rates see the source of these data.
Data source: Education at a Glance 2010: OECD Indicators.

Table 12.3 Access to tertiary education

Year	Enrollment rate			Entry rate		
	Total	Male	Female	Total	Male	Female
1985	22.6	28.7	16.1	36.4	38.3	34.1
1990	22.9	26.5	19.1	33.2	33.9	32.4
1995	35.9	40.1	31.4	51.4	52.8	49.8
2000	50.2	54.2	46.1	68.0	70.4	65.4
2005	61.8	65.0	58.3	82.1	83.3	80.8
2008	67.6	69.3	65.6	83.8	84.0	83.5
2010	67.4	68.5	66.2	79.0	77.6	80.5

Source: Statistics Korea, (2011).

lowest among them. The "Human Development Report" (UNDP, 2009) categorizes countries of the world into four levels of HDI. Out of the 38 countries in the "very high" group where Korea resides, its GEM value is the lowest next to Malta, with a rank of 74th, and Qatar, with a rank of 88th. Compared with most other countries, the discrepancy between HDI and GEM is particularly big for Korea (see Table 12.1). Considering such a high level of human development for Korean women, immense social cost is being incurred by their contrastingly low representation in leadership positions.

Gap between public and business sectors

As examined above, the general status of women's leadership in Korea is not on a par with the country's level of economic and human development. Progress is being made as more and more women participate in the labour market aided by anti-discrimination and other legislation, enabling women to stay on in their careers, and changing perceptions about women's roles. A notable change in the stature of women's leadership in Korea is the rapid progress in the presence of women in politics and government.

In politics and elected public offices, women's presence has increased dramatically during the past decade. Until recently, women political candidates were severely disadvantaged with regard to getting party endorsement, winning voters' confidence and raising funds (Kim, Min, Kim, & Kim, 2003). Women made up 15.66% of the National Assembly in 2012, a substantial change compared with 1996, when the female proportion was only 0.79%, as shown in Figure 12.5. Similarly, Table 12.4 shows that the proportion of women in local councils

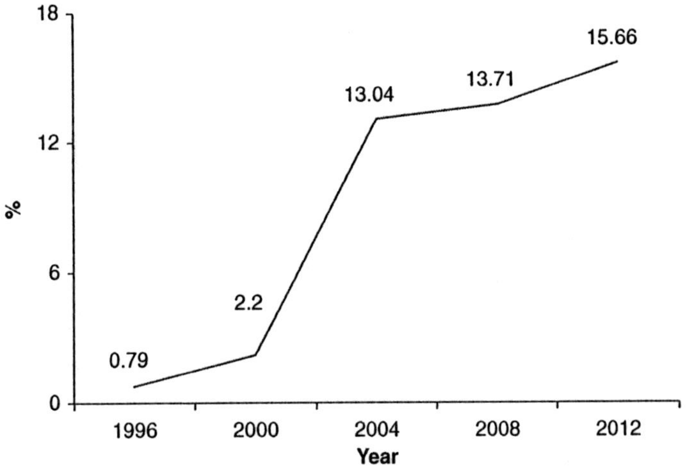

Figure 12.5 Proportion of seats held by women in national parliament in Korea
Data source: National Election Commission.

Table 12.4 Proportion of women in local councils

	Total	Male	Female	Female (%)
1995	5415	5331	84	1.5
1998	4105	4035	70	1.7
2002	4167	4027	140	3.4
2006	4074	3167	907	22.3
2010	3649	2910	739	20.3

Source: National Election Commission.

increased from 1.5% in 1995 to 20.3% in 2010, with accelerated increases since the 2000s. Unlike the legislature, the proportion of women mayors and governors is still negligible at 2.6% in 2010 and the increase over the years has been very slow, as can be seen in Table 12.5.

Overall, the turn around in women's political leadership has been so dramatic as to have the three major political parties headed by women during the 2012 National Assembly election period. The major opposition party leader was the first woman prime minister in the previous administration, rising to the top having been recognized for her experience as a leading women's movement activist. The ruling party leader, Park Geun-Hye, endowed with the legacy of her father who was formerly president, was deemed to be the most promising of the

Table 12.5 Proportion of women mayors and governors

	Total	Male	Female	Female (%)
1995	245	244	1	0.4
1998	248	248	0	0
2002	248	246	2	0.8
2006	246	243	3	1.2
2010	244	238	6	2.6

Source: National Election Commission.

presidential hopefuls in the 2012 presidential election held in December and, indeed, she won.

In male-dominated societies the exceptionally few women who advance into leadership positions in politics or public organizations are mostly beneficiaries of the political legacies of their fathers, husbands, sons or brothers. Particularly in Asia the unexpected incidences of women in top political positions are made possible largely by means of directly or indirectly bequeathing family power. In India, Indonesia, Thailand, Pakistan, Myanmar, the Philippines, Sri Lanka and others, most of the women prime ministers, presidents and opposition leaders reached the top by stepping on the legacies left by their male family members. Of course, most of these women leaders had their own qualifications and made social contributions, and so deserved to be candidates for top political positions, but those credentials alone would not have been sufficient – the powerful influence bestowed by their male next of kin is crucial to their success. The 2012 presidential election resulting in the first woman president in Korea makes the country to join the roster of those where women have become top political leaders under the influence of powerful men in their families.

Entry into government jobs in Korea requires success in a state examination that is notoriously difficult to pass. For a long time hardly any women passed because very few were in a position to challenge it. Consequently women in top managerial positions in government agencies are rare, with only a handful being appointed to ministerial posts, and these are mostly for symbolic purpose. As shown in Table 12.6, the proportion of women government employees in managerial positions has been slowly inching up from 3.6% in 2001 to 11% in 2010. The proportion is lower in local government than in the central government. Because currently there is a very small pool of women in government who are approaching top managerial positions, the growth in the ratio

Table 12.6 Women government employees in managerial position

Year	2001	2003	2005	2007	2009	2010
Total	12,676	13,531	16,282	18,598	19,082	19,412
Female	455	607	1,059	1,571	1,936	2,143
%	3.59	4.49	6.50	8.45	10.15	11.04

Note: Number of civil servants in general service.
Source: Ministry of Public Administration and Security (2011).

of high-level women managers in public service will continue to be slow for some years.

On the other hand, growth in the number of women newly admitted into government service has been impressive in recent years. Since about a decade ago, increases in women entering government through the state examinations have been significant. Table 12.7 shows a rapid rise in the proportion of women who pass in all three areas of the bar exam, administration exam and foreign service exam. The proportion of women passing the state examinations have more than quadrupled between 1995 and 2009, the number for the foreign service exam in particular increasing by more than eight times. In the next decade or so, as these women move up the ladder, the proportion of women in managerial positions in government agencies can be expected to take a leap forward and eventually we should see many women in high government posts.

The unprecedented acceleration of women's advancement into political and government positions after a long period of extremely slow progress can be attributed to a number of factors making the Korean public sector less biased against women. Since 2002, proportional representation has been implemented in the National Assembly election ,mandating 50% of the candidates for proportional representatives to be women. Since the second half of the 1990s, a number of significant

Table 12.7 Proportion of women passing the state examinations

	1995	2000	2005	2006	2007	2008	2009
Administration	10.4	25.1	41.1	42.8	45.8	45.8	41.2
Bar exam	8.8	18.9	32.3	37.7	35.0	38.0	35.6
Foreign service	5.7	20.0	52.6	36.0	67.7	65.7	48.8

Source: Ministry of Public Administration and Security; Ministry of Justice.

measures have been adopted in the civil service system. In 1995, quotas for women government employees were set as annual targets, which were more ambitiously and extensively pursued in 2000 (Civil Service Commission, 2002). Although the quota of 20% has not been fulfilled in most agencies, this laid the foundations for less bias against women applicants and encouraged more women to take the challenge of entering the civil service. The state examination took measures to eliminate practices discouraging women applicants, such as giving bonus points to men who completed compulsory military service. Previous administrations making bold gestures by appointing women as a minister of justice, as a supreme court judge, and as a prime minister certainly helped to boost the image of women in politics and government.

Unlike the political and government sectors, the business sector has not shown equivalent advances in women's leadership. Excluding subsistence-level proprietresses of petty shops, female heads of business are still scarce, and those few in charge of big businesses are daughters of business tycoons in conglomerates or "chaebols". Similar to their political counterparts, top women leaders in private corporations are likely to be heiresses of their fathers or husbands who founded the business. The business sector in general seems to have more difficulty in producing top women leaders comparable to the public sector and a turn around towards accelerated progress is yet to be seen.

The proportions of women CEOs by industry are shown in Table 12.8. The highest proportion of 11.7% is in the hotel and restaurant industry, followed by health with 9.4%, retail with 8.4% and wholesale with 6.3%. These are relatively more favourable industries for women, as opposed to finance, transport and communications industries, which have the lowest presence of women CEOs.

Whether in Korea or elsewhere, women face many disadvantages in reaching managerial positions, let alone top executive positions. It has been suggested that the disadvantages come from the individual differences in managerial style, and women's personality and behaviour deviating from those of men, which are perceived as the norm. Organizational context and institutionalized discrimination biased for the male culture are other obstacles to women's climb up the organizational ladder (Izraeli & Adler, 1994; Savage & Witz, 1992). In addition, power dynamics in which senior managers exert power and influence to limit women's access to executive ranks protects men's vested interests and confine competition to men (Izraeli & Adler, 1994). Exclusionary pressures also come from subordinates, who tend to prefer male supervisors

Table 12.8 CEOs by industry and gender, 2009

	Male	Female	Female (%)
Manufacturing	9603	395	4.0
Wholesale	5217	353	6.3
Construction	2888	147	4.8
Service	2563	95	3.6
Transport and communication	531	15	2.8
Retail	425	39	8.4
Real estate	365	18	4.7
Finance	321	8	2.4
Health	144	15	9.4
Hotel and restaurant	113	15	11.7
Fishing	83	6	6.7
Electricity	65	2	3.0
Mining	34	4	10.5

Note: Survey of 22,203 corporations with revenue of KRW10 billion or more in 2008.
Source: National Tax Service (2010).

and have unreasonably low evaluations of women supervisors (Eagly et al., 1992; Kim & Kim, 2000). In addition to these factors, other even more profound cultural factors keep Korean women from reaching top positions in the business sector.

In general, the economic participation rate of women in Korea has been low and growing only slowly. As shown in Figure 12.6, women's employment rates have been consistently below the OECD average. Although women with jobs are growing in number, still the majority are in small self-employed businesses or in menial work. Participation in the labour market of women who are not economically pressured to earn an income has been very low for a long time, women pursuing professional careers remaining a small minority until recently. The ratio of female to male earnings is one of the lowest among OECD countries and *de facto* discrimination is still rampant in the workplace (see Economic Intelligence Unit, 2012 for an international comparison of women's economic opportunities). When women's general status in the labour market has been lagging behind other industrialized countries, women leaders in the business sector are even harder to come by.

Recognizing that the low economic participation rate of educated women means a substantial waste in human resources, Korea

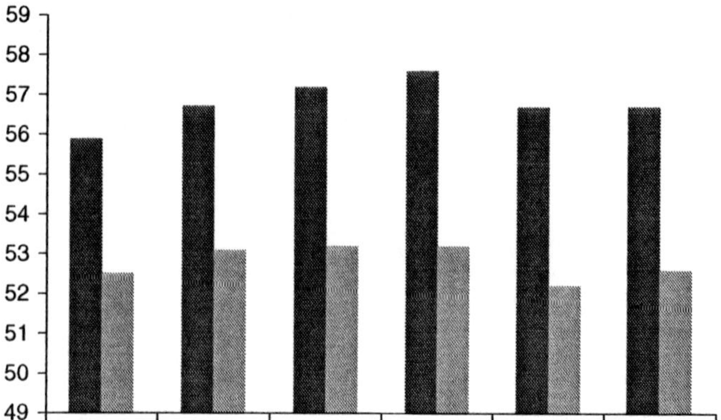

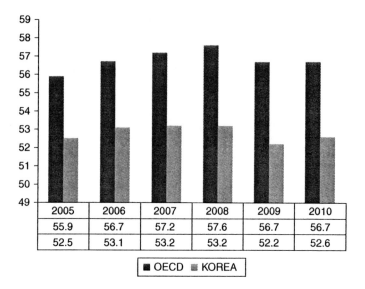

2005	2006	2007	2008	2009	2010
55.9	56.7	57.2	57.6	56.7	56.7
52.5	53.1	53.2	53.2	52.2	52.6

■ OECD ▒ KOREA

Figure 12.6 Women's employment rate in OECD countries
Source: OECD (age 15–64).

has instituted a range of equal opportunity legislation to address discriminatory practices in the labour market and to encourage women to be economically active. A number of maternity protection laws were introduced in an attempt to enable women to better balance both family and work. In 2006 the Equal Employment Act was amended to include affirmative action measures to strengthen the legal support for women workers (Ministry of Employment and Labor, 2010). These measures do seem to have had some influence in encouraging more women to seek careers and stay on in their jobs. As can be seen in Table 12.9, the proportion of women managers in workplaces subject to the affirmative action measures increased from about 10% in 2006 to about 13% in 2009. However, it still needs more time to take full effect and even longer to see as many women business chiefs as women political leaders in Korea.

With changing perceptions about women's leadership ability, rapid growth in the number of women political leaders in a relatively short period of time could be realized through elections and political appointments in Korea. In contrast, women have to climb up the corporate ladder by persevering and overcoming all kinds of barriers for a long time to reach the executive level. In Korea, voters' perception of women's leadership has been changing in a positive direction faster than workers' and supervisors' perceptions about women's corporate leadership.

Table 12.9 Proportion of women managers in corporations

	2006	2007	2008		2009	
			over 1000 employees	500–999	over 1000 employees	500–999
Executives	3.31%	4.35%	5.66%	6.45%	6.05%	6.56%
Managers and above	10.04%	11.07%	12.56%	11.56%	13.30%	13.34%

Source: Ministry of Employment and Labor (2010).

Gap between roles inside and outside the house

Even in modern Korean families, women are expected to do most of the housework. Unlike their Western counterparts, Korean women are not seen as the weaker sex. In fact, they are expected to be strong mentally, physically and emotionally in their roles not only as mothers but also as wives, taking on all kinds of work that is strenuous for both the mind and the body. It is not unusual to see a husband walking empty handed followed by his wife carrying a child on her back and loads of household items in each hand.

Men on the other hand have very little responsibility at home other than being the primary breadwinners, which implicitly exonerates them from all household chores. Korean fathers are figurative heads of the household with limited interaction with family members. In general, children exchange very few words with their father, consulting in almost all matters with their mother. Fathers may seem authoritative but they have very little opportunity to exercise real authority (Cho, 1994; Choe, 1994; Lee, 1994).

The tradition of assigning all of the roles in the private sphere to women and all of those in the public sphere to men is still deeply embedded in Korean society. The Korean word for wife literally means "inside person" and the word for husband means "outside person". The stark disparity in the household workload between men and women is only slightly reduced for women who are earning. Women with jobs therefore have to carry the double burden and the more fortunate ones rely on their mothers or mothers-in-law to help them with domestic work (Byeon, Baek, Kim, 2000; Yoo & Lee, 1990). In families of the younger generation, men are more likely to do some domestic work (Byeon et al., 2000) but the general pattern of most domestic work falling to women is still prevalent.

Ironically this dichotomy of gender roles where women take care of all the matters inside the house and men those outside the house has given much power to women in the home. Women take part in most of the important decisions regarding the family often being the sole decision maker (Choe, 1994; Byeon et al., 2000). The most distinguishing aspect about women's power in the family is that women are usually in charge of managing the family finance. It is a common practice for husbands to pass their earnings to their wives and get allowances from them. Women are perceived to be better managers of family finance than men.

In all societies there differences between the role and status of women in the public sphere and in the private sphere, but the two are interrelated (Bradley & Khor, 1993). However, in Korea there is a gap between women's status in the public sphere and that in the private sphere. Women in leadership positions in most sectors of the public sphere are still under-represented, barely making up 15%, which is thought to be the threshold at which a substantive influence starts to be exerted. In contrast, Korean women exercise considerably more leadership than men regarding family matters, taking charge of managing important household affairs. While Korean women's leadership stature in the public sphere falls well behind that of other countries with similar levels of socioeconomic development, their leadership and power inside the home probably surpasses what women in most other countries wield.

Conclusion and policy implications

This study examines the issue of incongruity of women's leadership in Korea with its level of socioeconomic development. While Korea can boast of impressive achievements in national economic and human development, its progress with regard to the status of women's empowerment and leadership has been very slow. Compared with OECD countries or others with similar economic development, women's leadership lags behind considerably. The gap can be explained by the long and deeply running tradition of separating gender roles into work outside the house for men and work inside the house for women.

Only since the 2000s have some notable and significant advances begun. New legislation, changing perceptions and values, and the high performances of women have reinforced each other in encouraging more women to take jobs and to aspire to leadership positions in many sectors of society.

To step up the progress in women's leadership stature befitting Korea's economic and human development levels, more extensive and systematic policy measures are required. These relate to employment policy to enhance affirmative actions, human development policy to provide effective leadership training for women, and social policy to address deeply embedded social bias and to mitigate women's double burden.

For employment policy, anti-discrimination and affirmative action measures should be improved to have greater effectiveness. Larger incentives should be provided in the workplace to practise and disseminate equal opportunities, and to reduce male-oriented organizational factors not only at the entry or lower levels but also at the executive level. There is a need for more measures directly aimed at bringing about better gender representation in the upper ranks of management in both the public and the private sectors.

Regarding human development policy, assistance should be provided in creating effective educational programmes tailored to enhance women's leadership and these should be made available to more women. In particular, Hopkins et al. (2008) suggest development practices in assessment, training and education, coaching, mentoring, networking, experiential learning and career planning. Similarly, others suggest leadership training that incorporates vision setting and a better understanding of organizational culture. Developing negotiation skills, building credentials, acquiring further qualifications, attaining certified licences and diplomas and so forth should enhance women's leadership abilities.

Employment and human development policy measures are not enough to boost women's leadership in the public sphere or outside the glass fence. Social policy programmes should aim to transform the social and cultural environment that has been pulling back women's resources inside the glass fence and thus deterring career women from challenging for executive positions. Lifestyles, values and family customs have to change to generate more women leaders, and the changes that have started only recently need to be continued and escalated. Social policy measures that can lighten the burden of women's household duties can bring about faster transformation of the social environment so that it can be more conducive for generating women leaders. The difficulty of working women who have to bear the double burden of working in both the private sphere and the public sphere partly explains Korea's fertility rate, which is the lowest in the world. This implies that balancing family and work is particularly difficult for Korean women, prohibiting them from excelling and reaching the upper echelons of the public sphere.

The tradition of segregating gender roles along the fence that divides the public and the private spheres shapes and prolongs the social perception of women as the "inside" persons. For the majority of Korean women the glass fence blocking them from taking a more active role outside the house is still the largest obstacle to their becoming leaders. Having the first woman president for Korea in the 2012 presidential election is an achievement representing the highest glass ceiling being broken. However, for the majority of Korean women they still need to break through the glass fence to show that they are no longer "inside" persons. In Korea, the glass fence seems to be thicker than the glass ceiling.

References

Adler, N.J. (1994). Competitive frontiers: Women managing across borders. In N.J. Adler, & D.N. Izraeli (Eds.), *Competitive Frontiers: Women Managers in a Global Economy* (pp. 22–40). Cambridge: Blackwell.

Bass, B.M. (1990). Women and leadership . In B. M. Bass & R. M. Stogdill (Eds.), *Bass and Stogdill's Handbook of Leadership: Theory, Research, and Managerial Applications*, 3rd edition (pp. 707–737). New York: The Free Press.

Bradley, K. & Khor, D. (1993). Toward an integration of theory and research on the status of women. *Gender & Society*, 7(3), September.

Byeon, H., Baek, K., & Kim, H. (2000). 한국 가족 변화와 여성의 역할 및 지위에 관한 연구. (*Study on Changes in Family and Women's Role and Status in Korea*). Seoul: Korean Women's Development Institute. Retrieved from http://www.kwdi.re.kr/reportView.kw?sgrp=S01&siteCmsCd=CM0001&topCmsCd=CM0002&cmsCd=CM0004&pnum=1&cnum=0&rptCdSel=&sbjCdSel=&src=TITLE&srcTemp=%EC%A7%80%EC%9C%84&x=0&y=0&ntNo=309&currtPg=1&pageSize=10.

Cho, H. (1994). Household economy and gender division of labor. In H. Cho, & P. Chang (Eds.), *Gender Division of Labor in Korea* (pp. 169–198). Seoul: Ewha Womans University Press.

Choe, S. (1994). Sex role socialization in the Korean family. In H. Cho, & P. Chang (Eds.), *Gender Division of Labor in Korea* (pp. 256–271). Seoul: Ewha Womans University Press.

Civil Service Commission. (2002). *Public Human Resources Reform*. Seoul: Civil Service Commission.

Eagly, A.H., Karau, S.J., & Makhijani, M.G. (1995). Gender and the effectiveness of leader: A Meta-analysis. *Psychological Bulletin*, 117(1), 125–145. doi: 10.1037/0033-2909.117.1.125.

Eagly, A.H., Makhijani, M.G., & Klonsky, B.G. (1992). Gender and the evaluation of leaders: A meta-analysis. *Psychological Bulletin*, 111(1), 3–22. doi: 10.1037/0033-2909.111.1.3.

Economist Intelligence Unit. (2012). Women's economic opportunity index. Retrieved from http://www.eiu.com/public/thankyou_download.aspx?activity=download&campaignid=weoindex2012.

Epstein, C.F., Olivares, F., Bass, B., Grahen, P., Schwartz F.N., Siegel M.R. . . . Cohen, A.R. (1991). Ways men and women lead. *Harvard Business Review*, 69(1), 150–160.

Hollander, E.P. (1992). The essential interdependence of leadership and followership. *Current Direction in Psychological Science*, 1, 71–75.

Hopkins, M.M., O'Neil, D. A, Passarelli, A., & Bilimoria, D. (2008). Women's leadership development strategic practices for women and organizations. *Consulting Psychology Journal: Practice and Research*, 60(4), 348–365. doi: 10.1037/a0014093.

International Monetary Fund. (2011). Gross domestic product, current price 2008 to 2011. Retrieved from World Economic Outlook database.

International Monetary Fund. (2011). Gross domestic product based on purchasing-power-parity (PPP) valuation of country GDP 2008 to 2011. Retrieved from World Economic Outlook database.

Izraeli, D.N., & Adler, N.J. (1994). Competitive frontiers: Women managers in a global economy. In N.J. Adler, & D.N. Izraeli (Eds.), *Competitive Frontiers: Women Managers in a Global Economy* (pp. 3–21). Cambridge: Blackwell.

Kang, W. (2007). *Rise of Female Leaders and Prospect*. Seoul: Samsung Economic Research Institute. Retrieved from http://www.seri.org/db/dbReptV.html?g_menu= 02&s_menu= 0202&pubkey= db20070307001

Kim, W., Min, M., Kim, H., & Kim, Y. (2003). Policy-making challenges for increasing female professional resources: Focusing on political field. *The Women' Studies*, 64, 1–48.

Kim, Y., & Kim, H. (2000). 기업내 남녀 관리자의 리더십 비교연구. (A Comparative Study of Male and Female Managers' Leaderships in a Firm). Seoul: Korean Women's Development Institute. Retrieved from http://www.kwdi.re.kr/reportView.kw?sgrp=S01&siteCmsCd=CM0001&topCmsCd=CM0002&cmsCd=CM0004&pnum=1&cnum=0&rptCdSel=&sbjCdSel=&src=TITLE&srcTemp=%EB%A6%AC%EB%8D%94%EC%8B%AD&x=0&y=0&ntNo=272&currtPg=1&pageSize=10.

Lee, H. (1994). Gender division of labor and the authoritarian developmental state: Korean experience. In H. Cho, & P. Chang (Eds.), *Gender Division of Labor in Korea* (pp. 292–323). Seoul: Ewha Womans University Press.

Lee, S. (2005). Feminist reconceptualization of leadership and power. *Women's Studies Review*, 22(1), 3–22.

Loden, M. (1985). *Feminine Leadership or How to Succeed in Business without Being One of the Boys*. New York: Times Books.

Ministry of Employment and Labor. (2010). 여성과 취업. (Women and Employment). Retrieved from http://www.moel.go.kr/download.jsp?type=/bbs/&file=2010 년_여성과취업(편집).pdf.

Ministry of Justice. (2009) **사법시험 통계** (Bar Exam Statistics). Retrieved from http://www.moj.go.kr/HP/BAR/index.do?strOrgGbnCd=103000.

Ministry of Public Administration and Security. (2011). 2011 행정안전 통계연보. (Annual Statistics of Administration and Security). Retrieved from http://www.mopas.go.kr/gpms/ns/mogaha/user/userlayout/bulletin/userBtView.action?userBtBean.bbsSeq=1021240&userBtBean.ctxCd=1290&userBtBean.ctxType=21010002&currentPage=1.

Muldrow, T.W., & Bayton, J.A. (1979). Men and women executives and processes related to decision accuracy. *Journal of Applied Psychology*, 64, 99–106.

National Election Commission. (2010). 역대 지방선거 당선인 각종 통계. (Statistics of winners in local elections). 06/27/1995 to 06/02/2010. Retrieved from 선거통계시스템 (Election statistics system) database.

National Election Commission. (2010). 역대 국회의원 선거 당선인 각종 통계. (Statistics of winners in National Assembly elections). 04/11/1996 to 04/11/2012. Retrieved from 선거통계시스템 (Election statistics system) database.

National Tax Service. (2010). 국세통계로 본 한국의 CEO. (CEO of Korea as Seen Through National Tax Statistics). Retrieved from http://www.nts.go.kr/news/news_03_01.asp?minfoKey=MINF8420080211204826&top_code=&sub_code=&IsSearch=0&type=V&mbsinfoKey=MBS20100414153657630.

Organization for Economic Cooperation and Development. (2010). How many students finish secondary education and access tertiary education. Retrieved from Education at a Glance 2010: OECD Indicators database.

Powell, G.N. (1988). *Women and Men in Management*. Newbury Park: Sage.

Rosener, J.B. (1990). *Ways Women Lead. Harvard Business Review*, Nov/Dec.

Savage, M., & Witz, A. (Eds.) (1992). *Gender and Bureaucracy*. Oxford: Blackwell.

Statistics Korea. (2011). 한국의 사회동향 2011 (Korean Social Trends 2011). Retrieved from http://kostat.go.kr/portal/korea/kor_nw/2/1/index.board?bmode=read&bSeq=&aSeq=253180&pageNo=1&rowNum=10&navCount=10&currPg=&sTarget=title&sTxt=%EC%82%AC%ED%9A%8C%EB%8F%99%ED%96%A5.

United Nations Development Programme. (2002). *Human Development Report 2002*. Retrieved from http://hdr.undp.org/en/reports/

United Nations Development Programme. (2004). *Human Development Report 2004*. Retrieved from http://hdr.undp.org/en/reports/

United Nations Development Programme. (2006). *Human Development Report 2006*. Retrieved from http://hdr.undp.org/en/reports/

United Nations Development Programme. (2008). *Human Development Report 2008*. Retrieved from http://hdr.undp.org/en/reports/

United Nations Development Programme. (2009). *Human Development Report 2009*. Retrieved from http://hdr.undp.org/en/reports/

Vinnicombe, S. (1987). What exactly are the differences in male and female working styles? *Women in Management Review*, 3(1), 13–21.

Yoo, H., & Lee, J. (1990). Work and life of academic women in Korea. *Women's Studies Review*, 7, 159–179.

13

Why Women Are Missing: Women's Leadership in Afghanistan's Education Policy and Practice

Susan Wardak and Edna Mitchell

Introduction

The constitution of the Islamic Republic of Afghanistan proclaims the principle of equity for women as full participants in the national government and the life of the nation. Currently, women leaders are still mostly missing. A critical mass needed to shape policy is not yet evident (Aikman & Unterhalter, 2005). The recent Ministry of Education National Interim Plan (2011:56) states:

> The . . . goal is to eliminate discrimination against women, develop their human capital, and ensure their leadership in order to guarantee their full and equal participation in all aspects of life. In support of this objective, the MoE, by 2014, aims to (a) close the gender gap in education, (b) provide and enforce universal access to primary education for girls, (c) increase the number of female teachers by 50 percent to reflect the social demographic by gender, (d) increase female enrollment to 60 percent, (e) have facilities for girls' education in 75 percent of schools, (f) significantly reduce gender disparities by province, and (g) achieve significant improvement in female literacy from 15 percent in 1389 (2010) to 43 percent in 1393 (2014).

However laudable and ambitious these stated goals, the same report adds a note of irony in predicting the actual outcomes that may be realized:

> The government lacks the capacity to mainstream gender. Government agencies concerned with gender issues lack awareness of the

> importance of a gender responsive approach towards policymaking. They have insufficient institutional management and human resource capacities to mainstream gender into all aspects of their work. There is no accountability mechanism to evaluate performance on gender issues. In *addition, political will to accelerate reforms is often absent.*
>
> (Ministry of Education, 2011: 56, emphasis added)

Despite those declarations of law, women are barely visible in positions of leadership in the public arena. This chapter discusses the conditions and traditions that create obstacles for women to be prepared to exercise leadership, especially related to educational leadership. Education is the major focus since it provides the foundation for all advancement and policy participation for women.

Beginning with a brief discussion of theories of leadership from a historical and cultural perspective as applied to women in Afghanistan, the chapter moves to a description of the current limitations on Afghan women's leadership related to a lack of education, a lack of opportunity and cultural traditions. However, it is important to inform the reader that "women's leadership" as a subject for study and theorizing is largely a Western-dominated concept. Much has been made in the Western press in recent years about the repression of Afghan women and the need to liberate them. Afghan women dislike and reject the image of themselves perpetrated in the media as helpless victims of brutal male oppressors. They also seek to clarify misconceptions about Islam and the idea that it stipulates female subordination.

These generalized Western attitudes focus more on what the Afghan woman wears, the veil or the burqa, rather than what she does or what she stands for. In reviewing efforts of recent foreign occupiers or international assistance groups to liberate women from "old-fashioned" restrictions, it is evident that the subsequent backlash against those foreign ideas has done more harm to women than it has helped. Mistakes made by the Soviet Communists are frequently repeated by other internationals who would "help" to modernize the nation. The goals and ideas are not bad or wrong; many are important and useful. However, the attack on basic values and traditions – stemming in part from ideas about liberating women and enforcing coeducation, and encouraging clothing styles offensive to the community – has turned the whole country against those introducing change and led to the destruction of the nation.

Although many political philosophers believe that revolution is essential for change, we believe that lasting and meaningful change in Afghanistan will occur more slowly over time and must go through a process of natural maturation. It begins at the grassroots level, in the family and community, rather than coming solely from the top. As more girls go to school, for example, there will be a progression of acceptance of the changing roles of females from childhood through adulthood.

Afghanistan has a national culture with a proud tradition that is committed to conserving its Islamic traditions. The population has often confused "Westernization" with modernization. Women's leadership is not anti-Islamic, but the term carries a "western tone", a kind of hegemony that is rejected when viewed as a Western imposition. The emphasis placed by outsiders, when they judge the strength and influence of Afghan women, too commonly emphasizes clothes and Western manners (for both men and women) rather than intelligence, capacity and vision for national progress. An overview of women as Afghan leaders – past and present – is given here to put the present context into perspective. This brief review provides a historical basis in Afghanistan to support the constitutional civil rights of women's equity in society. Information about current social and economic, as well as cultural, conditions that restrict girls' education, and conditions that inhibit women from being mentored as leaders, are presented. We are concerned that instead of moving women forward through education into positions of influence and leadership, the backlash against the outside imposition of change and superficial measurements of change in such things as the removal of the burqa, tearing off the "veil", the popularity of jeans and Western dress has actually inhibited the progress of women. The chapter concludes by summarizing the status today and offering hope for the future.

Theoretical background on leadership and the limits of women's leadership theory

Culture and leadership

In the wave of cross-cultural interactions through a global economy, the importance of understanding dissonances in cultural behaviours, particularly behaviours of business leaders, has created a major body of research literature on how culture affects leadership. Most of this is based on Western male perspectives with very little that is relevant to women's leadership, especially that of women in the non-Western world and specifically women in Central Asia.

Typical studies of leadership have shifted from traits, personal characteristics and behaviours to dimensional scales and measurements of complex interactions across the cultural dimensions.

The work of Hofstede (1980; 2001) has provided impetus for a large body of research on the impact of culture on leadership. His work was inspired by the difficulties experienced in business negotiations across cultures. His original study in 1980 was based on a survey of IBM managers and employees in more than 40 countries. He originally produced a cross-cultural scale for analysis based on four culture dimensions (individualism–collectivism; masculinity–femininity; uncertainty avoidance; and power distance), and in later work a fifth dimension (future orientation) was added.

Using Hofstede's work, Den Hartog (2004) and others in the GLOBE study identified another aspect for analysis. The question was as follows. How do societal norms affect whether emotions are shown in public? For instance, in the GLOBE study, Javidan and House (2001) found that the appreciation of leader attributes, such as 'subdued" and "enthusiastic", varies across cultures depending upon differences in cultural rules regarding the appropriate expression of emotion. In affective cultures, people typically show their emotions. Effective leaders communicate through a vivid and temperamental expression of emotion. In more neutral cultures, people keep their emotions in check. The norm is to present oneself in a composed and subdued manner. Other research confirms that displaying emotion may be interpreted as a lack of self-control, or a weakness (Trompenaars & Hampden-Turner, 1997). In many Western societies, a leader shedding tears is seen as feminine behaviour, thus a weakness normally to be avoided. The subtext is that characteristics associated with female behaviour must be avoided by leaders, even women leaders.

Ardichvili (2001) analysed transformational leadership and cultural values related to work in a sample of managers and employees in the post-Communist and former USSR countries of Russia, Georgia, Kazakhstan and Kyrgystan. Because these countries are geographically close to Afghanistan, and because of the recent Soviet influence on the culture of Afghanistan, this study seemed particularly relevant. More importantly, in the Ardichvili study, additional dimensions of fatalism and paternalism were considered alongside Hofstede's cultural values. Fatalism was the main predictor of most leadership dimensions in Georgia, Kazakhstan and Kyrgyz Republic. Both fatalism and paternalism are characteristics that one would expect in male leaders in Afghanistan. However, the missing factor is the issue of women's leadership. Of course, since women are missing, the problem is that of a closed loop. Without women leaders to study, the research sample is largely restricted to leaders who are male.

Is leadership qualitatively different based on gender, or is culture the greater influence? How intertwined are these two factors? These discussions are missing from the leadership literature. They are barely touched upon in the sparse literature on women's leadership although studies and rhetoric are beginning to appear.

Gender and leadership

When studying leadership, gender makes a world of difference. Women's leadership characteristics, behaviours and values cannot be considered separately from cultural context any more than can men's leadership. Within each society, men's culture differs greatly from women's culture. Although men and women may be qualified for the same jobs, the way in which they perceive and perform their jobs may be quite different. The way in which one gender responds to the assigned leadership role may be completely unacceptable to the other sex. The degree of gender differentiation in a country depends primarily on the culture within that nation and its history.

Training Afghan women for leadership

A dilemma in Afghanistan is the lack of appropriate contemporary female leadership role models. As Western nations, after 9/11, became concerned about women's rights in Afghanistan many well-intentioned groups attempted to develop women's leadership skills using Western leadership models. Seeing Afghan women as intelligent and eager to learn, too often training overlooked the cultural milieu in which those women lived and would work. Future training for leadership for Afghan women must do a better job of incorporating and accommodating the customs of the culture. Future training for Afghan women as leaders must start with Afghan women themselves rather than being imposed from outside.

The possibility of training for leadership is popular in the Western world. Within feminist scholarship, attention to women's leadership is a growing research and training interest. Controversies over studies of gender differences focused a spotlight on women leaders, the diversity in their leadership styles, and the differences in strategies and outcomes between men and women leaders. In recent decades the discussion about women as leaders has moved beyond the duality of gender, in which the arguments were limited to men versus women, and has now expanded to cultural differences in leadership for both men and women. One size, or one style, does not fit all women or all cultures.

Perhaps some basic characteristics of women's leadership are shared by women globally. Listening skills, reflecting, collaborating, egalitarian decision making and shared leadership roles may be characteristics attributed to women in some general way. However, it is clear that women leaders in countries of the East have not been cut from a single, simple, global gender pattern. This is certainly true of Muslim women as leaders in Afghanistan, past and present. Their differences from one another call for respect, just as do their differences from women of other cultures. Their frequently negative responses to the term "women's leadership", as well as the types of women's leadership they admire, need explication and appreciation. To many women of Asia, the translations of the word "leadership" often convey a meaning of dominance, control and even aggression.

Discussions of women's leadership, women's ways of leading and preparation for leadership are taking place in women's associations and through training packages delivered in non-governmental organization (NGO) workshops in Afghanistan, often reflecting leadership theories of non-Afghan women's groups. The application of these skills must be carefully processed and filtered through a cultural screen. Some of the training is being created by local women, or at the very least modified by local women. Culturally sensitive examples are found in the Women's Learning Partnership (WLP, 2010) and UNIFEM (2010). Both programmes require local women to create or adapt training materials for their own society and ethnic group. These training materials include manuals for women's organizational leadership, political participation and legal rights within their nations.

Greater awareness of cultural differences in leadership, and cultural differences in how women express their leadership, is important in understanding the apparent gender gap in women's participation in governance and leadership in Afghanistan. Generalizations about cultural differences often breed cultural stereotypes that can be misleading and embarrassing at best and explosively offensive at worst.

Chinese, Indian and most other Asian cultures are reportedly highly collectivistic (House, 1999), with relationships governed by high "power distance" – a sharp awareness of difference in status. On the other hand, the Western leader is more likely to be individualistic, defining work relationships in terms of objectivity, impersonality and organizational goals.

To understand the missing leadership of women on a national level, it is useful to consider Hofstede's dimensions of cultural values as they provide a framework for leadership in Afghanistan. Although no studies using these dimensions have been reported for Afghanistan, it is possible to make some assumptions based on other studies and knowledge of the culture. Collectivism is valued above individualism. The *shura* is deeply embedded in the culture, using community discussion to arrive at the appearance of consensus.

According to Hofstede (1980), masculinity implies dominant values in a society that stresses assertiveness and being tough, acquisition of money and material objects and not caring for others or for their quality of life. In feminine cultures, according to Hofstede, values such as warm social relationships, quality of life and care of the weak are stressed. Male Afghans would score high on the masculinity dimension valuing assertiveness, strength and honour, but this scale oversimplifies and ignores the warm social relationships, care for the weak, strong family values and male friendships that are shared by Afghan men. To typify societies as masculine or feminine may be convenient but it disregards the subtleties that are significant contradictions in the theory.

Another dimension examined in creating a national profile that characterizes successful leadership is the question of how a culture handles living daily with uncertainty and ambiguity. The assumption is that Afghan tolerance for uncertainty is low. Issues tend to be solved quickly, and controversy and disputes are handled on the spot. A "wait-and-see" approach is uncommon; the general response for an Afghan when facing a problem is to refer the outcome to the hands of God: "Inshah'Allah" is the common phrase. Although the *shura* encourages equity in discussion, and gives everyone an equal voice, there is no question about respect for power and the awareness of the distance between the powerful and the powerless. Women are generally categorized among the powerless. However, there are daily examples of exceptions to this generalization.

If being a leader pushes a woman to a place that is inappropriate for her role, and sets her above her peers (in contrast with male leadership that almost requires a status differentiation as a necessity for power), the accompanying lack of support may deplete her potential as a leader.

Clearly, the analysis of leadership has moved far from the old view that one is born to lead, yet the remnants remain of beliefs that leadership skills, however developed, are universal. In practice, all too often the same training packages and expectations for leadership are applied without reference to culture and gender. Concepts and judgements about women's leadership must take into account the historical, social, economic, political, religious, ethnic, age and gender contexts in which leadership is demonstrated. Perspectives on women in Afghanistan, and their modes of leadership both public and private, can be better understood by knowing about women of past generations who influenced the attitudes of their day. When and how have Afghan women, without Western leadership training, performed as leaders who are admired and remembered for their courage? Perhaps they adopted male strategies; perhaps they used the element of innovation and did the unexpected. Leaving theory behind, it is important to understand the history of Afghanistan and how women especially were affected. Why are women missing today as leaders?

Afghan women leaders were present in the past

Have Afghan women leaders always been missing as they appear to be today? Have Afghan women's voices always been a soft sound in a minor key with no public influence, or were women's voices heard in the leadership dialogues of previous generations? To examine this question, a brief historical review of highlights of Afghan women's leadership will be useful. It is also an inspiring history.

Women leaders in the past

While women played important and influential roles in history, rarely were their contributions documented and it is even rarer to find them in education texts in today's schools. Historically and globally, the influence of women in both the private and the public spheres was often quietly exerted with credit for a woman's idea or deed given to a male family member. If one searches it is possible to find records of outstanding and astonishingly accomplished Afghan women. However, this chapter is limited to brief sketches to illustrate the point that women's leadership in Afghanistan is not a new or revolutionary concept. Yet despite hundreds of stories of courageous women, the dominant cultural attitude towards women then and now is that female roles are subservient to male authority. A woman fulfils her destiny in the private sphere out of the public view.

Nevertheless, some courageous women in Afghan history are remembered by men as well as women. For example, the courage and martyrdom of Malalai in an 1880 battle against the British made her admired by boys and girls alike for grabbing up the fallen flag and leading men into a battle which they were on the verge of losing. Even earlier, Queen Gohar Shad Begum, the 15th-century wife of Shah Rukh, took the throne upon his death and ruled efficiently and wisely for many years. She relocated the capital of the kingdom from Samarkand to Herat. Known for her interests in the arts and supporting the education of women, she initiated an intellectual and cultural renaissance in the Timurid court. (Saeed, n.d.) The names and achievements of these two women of previous centuries may be more familiar than others, but an Afghan women's hall of fame could be filled with many women in many categories of achievement, including authors, poets, philosophers, politicians, rebels, reformers, rulers, warriors and scientists. Some worked behind the scenes through powerful husbands or sons, some actually took the throne in the absence or death of the acknowledged ruler, some dared to speak with their own voices through writing, and some earned their places in history through courageous action in defence of family or community or, as in the case of Queen Soraya in the early 20th century, daring to serve as a model for social change (Rahimi, 1986).

Women leaders in the modern era

The birth of modern Afghanistan is marked by the rule of Abdur Rahman Khan from 1880 to 1901. Although not a believer in women's equality, he did introduce laws that were less restrictive for women. His liberal and educated wife, affectionately called Bobo Jan, undoubtedly had a strong influence on him. She was interested in politics as social progress. Habibullah, her son, continued the path of modernization for a decade, even opening a school for girls with an English curriculum and introducing numerous technical, social, economic and international initiatives. These activities did not necessarily endear Habibullah to tribal leaders and groups holding fast to traditional customs. However, his assassination did not slow the modernization movement because he was followed on the throne by his son, Amanullah, who continued the modernization effort relentlessly.

Habibullah's wife, Queen Soraya, took a public leadership role, spoke out for the emancipation of women and their full participation in society, and founded the first magazine for women, *Ershad-E-Niswan* ("Guidance for Women"). It was too much, too fast. Amanullah had to pull back on some of his policies, most notably those affecting women. In 1929 he was forced to abdicate and leave the country (Trembley, 2004).

During the 1940s and 1950s, with some temerity on the part of rulers and male politicians, women's issues were moved forward again, slowly. The constitution of 1964 gave women the right to vote and to be candidates for election. Four women were elected to parliament, including one who had been the first minister of health. Women were entering professions as educated nurses, doctors, teachers and university instructors (Dupree, 1986).

Many organizations led by women, focusing on improvement in women's lives, were created during the decades of the 1950s, 1960s and 1970s. NGOs with international ties were active, but local NGOs and projects were started as well. Women headed and worked in these organizations that provided education, job training, opportunities for private entrepreneurship for widows, and education and homes for orphans.

Scholarly histories of gender roles in Afghanistan point to the movement towards modernization in urban centres at the turn of the 20th century during which, by 1958, many women in urban centres were professionals, technicians and administrators employed by the government. The majority worked in health and education, the two sectors considered to be most appropriate for women as they are extensions of traditional women's roles (Lewis, 1997).

Even before the Taliban came to power, Afghanistan had high maternal and child mortality rates and a very low literacy rate among women. However, many women participated economically, socially and politically in the life of their societies. They helped to draft the 1964 constitution. In the 1970s there were at least three women legislators in the parliament. Up to the early 1990s, women were teachers, government workers and medical doctors. They also worked as professors, lawyers, judges, journalists, writers and poets.

Women leaders in Afghanistan today

The wheel of progress for women leaders grinds slowly backwards

After decades of war, destruction and the increased dominance of conservative traditions, the wheel has turned again away from liberation and equity for women to male control and ownership over female lives:

> The current revival of conservative attitudes toward appropriate extra domestic roles for women and the criticism of women's visibility in public have largely impacted these professional women. Islamic texts do not delineate roles for women. What they imply is open to interpretation. What they command is equality and justice guaranteeing that women be treated in no way lesser than men. Educated Afghan women are standing fast in their determination to find ways in which they may participate in the nation's reconstruction according to their interpretations of Islam's tenets. This is a powerful challenge now facing the society.
>
> (Lewis, 1997)

In Afghanistan, as in most nations, the measure of women's leadership and influence is not found in government or public positions of power. More often women's voices come from non-public places where they have wielded influence in much less obvious ways. However, government positions, even if seen as a minor accession and a token to women, play an important and symbolic role in encouraging women as leaders. In Afghanistan the new constitution mandates the election of two women to parliament from each of the 34 provinces in the nation. Consequently, 68 seats out of the 249 in the lower house are reserved for women, and 23 of 102 in the upper house are held by women (Wordsworth, 2007).

Dr Massouda Jalal was the only woman presidential candidate in the 2004 election. She lost the presidency but was appointed as the first minister for women's affairs. She later resigned from this post because of differences and disillusionment with President Karzai. She chose not to run again in 2009 (CEDPA, 2010).

In 2010, three women served as government ministers: Dr Husn Banu Ghazanfar as minister of women's affairs, Amina Afzali as minister of public affairs, and Dr Suraya Dalil as minister of public health. Former head of women's affairs Habiba Sorabi was appointed Governor of Bamiyan Province in 2005. This made her the first and only female governor of an Afghan province. Azra Jafari became the first female city mayor in Afghanistan when appointed by President Karzai in December 2008. She was appointed as mayor of the town of Nili in Daikundi province. Both of these women have been subject to criticism for taking positions in what are viewed as roles only appropriate for men, if taken seriously.

Women make up less than 10% of employees in 16 of the 25 ministries. In 2008, 18.4% of all government workers were women, a decrease from 25.9% in 2005 (CSO, 2008). The number of female regular government employees decreased from 31.2% in 2005 to 22% in 2007 (NHDR, 2007). Therefore progress may be seen as "a step forwards with two steps backwards".

Being a candidate for political office is a risky decision for any Afghan woman. Women candidates and women in politics have been assassinated by the Taliban in recent years. Holding office, whether by election or by appointment, also carries a risk to a woman's reputation, which is always a concern to her family. Even serving as an administrator in an organization or government department is problematic for the Afghan professional woman because of jealousies, gossip, and the possibility of quick dismissal or demotion, where decisions are made by men with greater authority. How do women become leaders in education, a vocation considered acceptable as women's work?

Women's leadership in education remains a vacuum

Teaching became one of the fields acceptable for women in Afghanistan in the 20th century. Even though women held the majority of teaching jobs at all levels before the Taliban came to power, these positions were not considered serious leadership roles. Administrators, department heads, supervisors and decision makers were predominantly men.

The new government is now challenged to rebuild education, to recruit and train teachers, and to use women's talents at every level, even in non-traditional leadership roles. The devastation of decades of war not only destroyed schools and eliminated a potential pool of educators, but also drastically reduced the male population, leaving millions of widows without protection or income. Teachers in the past were predominantly men, but as schools were reopened in 2002, women were needed to step in and fill the gap left by the loss of men as teachers. Many women who returned from international refuge were motivated to use their knowledge to restore schools and other educational institutions. The low-paid classroom teaching jobs did not capitalize on the energized and educated women who could have been a source of educational leadership.

Positions for women in government leadership would seem to be a logical use of intelligent, articulate women. Even today, no woman has been appointed minister of education or minister of higher education. Only one woman now holds a position of leadership at or above the level of general director in the Ministry of Education. However, the recent effort to create equity is beginning to show some results. A small increase in the number of women in educational leadership positions in the provinces as provincial administrators and school heads is reported. These women take their jobs seriously, but ultimately men hold the power as provincial education directors.

Overview of past policies and practices of women's education in Afghanistan

Destruction of Afghanistan

The facts are well known. Decades of warfare have drained the educational energy from Afghanistan. Soviet occupation, followed by civil conflict culminating in repressive Taliban rule, destroyed the infrastructure of a fragile but evolving modern education system in Afghanistan. Universities throughout the country were the scenes of uprisings, resistance and open conflict. Students and faculty were targeted and attacked, buildings looted and destroyed. The premier institution of higher education, Kabul University, became a killing field during the years of Soviet conflict and internal warfare – the campus was a warzone. Faculty sought safe places to hide, many fled and many were killed. Students, along with faculty, took sides in the resistance. Many were hunted down, disappeared, were imprisoned and were never heard from again. Students who managed to escape took refuge in other countries. There is not a person today in Afghanistan who does not have personal stories of horror and grief from those days, including the Soviet Occupation, the Civil War and the subsequent rule of the Taliban. The burden of the wars affected all families; however, women in particular suffered in the background as men fought the battles. Women were left as widows to provide for families in a society that gave them no agency and few rights. Among those without literacy or skills to earn a living, women form the overwhelming majority.

Now, more than two decades after the departure of Soviet troops, the end of the Civil war and the overthrow of the Taliban, efforts to rebuild education from the ground up still face enormous challenges, although dramatic progress is being made. Clearly the destruction of the education of girls and women is one of the tragic consequences of the years of conflict.

Gender equity in education – A new challenge

As the debris of war is cleared away, amid continuing unpredictable bombings, insecurity and insurgency, a clearer picture of national education's strengths and weaknesses is emerging. Although the number of students enrolled in school has increased exponentially since the defeat of the Taliban, a continuing critical weak link is the dramatic gender inequity, female absence, at every level of education and where educational policy is made. Girls' attendance at school falls far short of any equity goal. Women teachers are missing from classrooms, particularly in rural provincial regions, and women as administrators or policy leaders are almost non-existent. Strategies to address these issues have been promoted by the government, and the Teacher Education Directorate (TED) of the Ministry of Education is especially active in advocating more women in educational leadership roles (Ministry of Education, 2006).

The missing women leaders

The constitution and official statements from the Islamic government of Afghanistan give high priority to education for all. The need to advance women's roles in the nation is clearly articulated. The dilemma is complex; solutions are not simple. If girls cannot attend school for multiple reasons, among the most serious being cultural tradition that girls must not be taught by men, then the production of educated women citizens to be teachers, professionals and leaders is obviously constricted. The pipeline allows for a mere trickle of female students to make it beyond grade four.

There are many educated, brave women in Afghanistan – many of them teachers – who have the potential to be powerful leaders, but there are not enough with public voices in visible places. Women need supporting cohorts, a critical mass of other capable women, if they are to brave the barriers to shared leadership that confront them daily. Young girls need new female role models if they are to develop as the voices of a new generation of leaders. Currently, women as leaders are mostly missing. This statement is not to disparage the efforts of those tireless, courageous women of vision who have, in both the past and the present, worked to restore civil society in their country.

National policies and paper solutions designed to reconstruct institutions and to modify age-old customs have slowly been introduced. Desperately needed is informed and competent leadership from both men and women to make and implement policy decisions. Leadership is needed for the development of programmes and curricula, for teacher education and deployment, for school construction and management, and a myriad of issues from the provinces to the capital.

Women's participation in decision making and the implementation of educational goals is also desperately needed but is in short supply. Even when given seats at the policy table, women are rarely heard, drowned out by the overwhelming cacophony of male opinion, power and leadership. The problem is a combination of insufficient numbers of qualified women along with the cultural traditions that prevent women from holding positions of power. The appearance of power is an essential element for any Afghan leader. With power comes respect. Real respect for women outside the walls of the home is a remote possibility. To have an influence in policy in a male-dominated discussion, a woman leader in Afghanistan must walk the line and find her balance between assertion with exercise of power and the cultural expectation that she should be soft-spoken, retiring and acquiescent in public.

Women make up more than half of the population in Afghan recovery. Why are so few found in leadership roles? The educational pipeline for girls has been too narrow for significant numbers to progress from elementary school through college or university. Incentives and models of many different kinds, addressing many different barriers, must be offered to girls, and to families and communities.

Post-Taliban progress in education

Girls missing in schools – Broken pipeline for producing female teachers

Under the Taliban's short but strict control, no girls were registered in schools, although secret classes were conducted for girls in homes where women clandestinely taught, braving the consequences of being exposed. In some rural areas the Taliban were more cooperative with local community leaders and permitted some schools with classes for girls to continue. The reasons for this rigidity are not as simple and misogynist as commonly depicted. The disapproval of Taliban governing tactics was also not as universal as is commonly assumed.

With the defeat of the Taliban, school enrolment dramatically increased from 900,000 students with 20,000 teachers in 2001 to over 6.3 million with 170,000 teachers in 2011. The urgent effort to restore the education structure required finding people to teach classes. Hundreds of thousands of new students were trying to enroll, often without classrooms, teachers or textbooks. In remote rural areas, and in provinces far from the capital, some teachers were hired who were barely literate and were either too young or too old to meet the demands of teaching. Most of them were men (Spink, 2005).

After the fall of the Taliban, with all pre-service teacher-training institutions damaged or destroyed, there was no pool of female students from which to recruit teachers. At that time, two teacher-training colleges were operating. However, by 2012, there were 42, at least one in each of the 34 provinces, and 89 satellite teacher development centre affiliated to the provincial teacher-training colleges.

Approximately one-third of students enrolled in pre-collegiate education today are girls. This does not reflect the number of eligible school-age girls who are not on enrolment lists. A dramatic drop in girls' enrolment occurs at the end of grade four. The line of decline continues from that point, making girls' enrolment in secondary schools statistically low. Reasons for this dropout rate are easy to understand but difficult to remedy. A major reason is the lack of female teachers. Although teaching is one of the more acceptable jobs for a woman, it is still predominantly a man's job. In many families, any job outside the home is unacceptable for a woman. This attitude is slowly changing based on economic need, exposure to other models and as a result of seeing girls' achievement as they attend schools in increasing numbers.

Many factors limit the school attendance of girls, including distance from school, security and responsibilities at home. However, cultural traditions and the lack of female teachers are perhaps the most powerful deterrents. Traditional families will not send their pre-adolescent and adolescent daughters to classes taught by male teachers, especially young men. Yet the supply of educated women who could be teachers is obviously severely limited, except in urban areas such as Kabul. The majority of female teachers are concentrated in major urban centres. Some 51% of all female teachers and 70% of female high-school teachers are based in five big cities: Kabul, Balkh, Herat, Baghlan and Jawzjan. Some 90% of the 364 districts have no girls' high school and 13% of them (48 of 364) have no female teachers at all.

The Ministry of Education is making a major effort to find and train prospective teachers and to recruit women as teachers. Of the 170,000 teachers who were employed in 2011 from elementary through secondary grades, fewer than a third were female: 71% were male, 29% female. Of equal concern was the fact that almost three-quarters (74%) of all teachers were not even high-school graduates, a government requirement for being hired as a teacher. The implications for educational quality and strong student achievement are obvious.

By 2011 the two-year teacher-training colleges graduated 20,000 new teachers, of which 40% were female (Ministry of Education, 2011). This trend shows the promise of continuing because of several innovative programmes planned by the TED and supported by international donors. While the numbers of women teachers is an indicator of movement towards parity, and is of vital importance to the expanded educational opportunities for girls, the leadership dimension has yet to be boldly addressed.

Challenges in restoring education infrastructure

The leaders: Afghan ownership or international intervention?

The challenges facing the nation in 2002 were dependent upon a quick recovery of the education sector. In addition to rebuilding the infrastructure for education and the actual schools in which learning could take place, the government had to develop new curricula, print new textbooks, recruit new teachers, and provide learning not only for children but for those adults who had for two generations lost the opportunity to become literate. The literacy rate for men was low, but for women it was almost non-existent according to these statistics (UNDP, 2007):

- Only 12.6% of adult women in Afghanistan are literate, compared with 32.4% of men.
- Almost 50% of children are not in school.
- There is tremendous gender disparity: 60% of girls are not in school and girls represent less than 15% of total enrolment in nine provinces in the east and south.
- Among the 70% of students enrolled in urban areas, only 5% are girls.
- Dropout rates are 74% for girls compared with 56% for boys (grades 1–5).
- Some 80% of school buildings have been damaged or destroyed.

Not only were education and basic literacy needed for the existing population but also returning to their Afghan homeland were waves of hundreds of thousands of refugees creating new demands for education. After the 2001 defeat of the Taliban, scores of refugee families saw no option but to return to the ruins of what used to be their villages, where no basic facilities or services, such as schools, existed.

The international community is greatly interested in supporting opportunities for girls' education and literacy for women. The international community stepped in to assist in rebuilding the nation with an unprecedented commitment to education. Contributions of financial aid as well as international educational consultants flooded the country, providing expertise in all areas. While necessary and helpful, this support did not come without a "price". Although appreciated and needed, the international assistance overwhelmed Afghan initiative, pride and confidence in many instances. The number of international NGOs working in the education and social services sectors contributed to chaos and confusion even though they were working frantically to rebuild the education system and the nation. Frequently they competed rather than collaborated with one another; often they worked independently of the government or of ministry supervision. At issue was the practice of bypassing the government as money paid for contracted services and salaries for project personnel were inflated exorbitantly compared with government civil service standards.

Often the international NGOs competed with the government by employing the best-educated citizens who could have provided leadership in government posts. The NGOs, of course, paid well compared with the government, which hardly paid at all. Some women benefited by, and became visible as leaders through, the jobs available with the international NGOs. However, the benefit to girls and women, as voices to be heard in policy-making, was negligible.

To nourish and support the leadership of women, especially in the education arena, it is important to know how their leadership is exerted, what styles of leadership are characteristic of Afghan women and how they describe their own ways of leading.

Women's ways of leading

In government and education, a small but significant number of women do hold posts that are considered appropriate for women – some as department heads, some as school heads and some as directors of teacher-training colleges, but almost none as heads of ministries or in the president's cabinet. Women in government, women in the media and women in sports remain tainted activities and are viewed by many as inappropriate for women.

Despite the barriers of tradition and limited access, women are providing educational, political and social leadership in many ways, and in their own ways. Often unrecognized, women's leadership in Afghanistan, contained and circumscribed by life conditions, is beginning to permeate every area of life. The ways in which Afghan women lead depends greatly on their individual life experiences.

Women and girls who have lived in refugee camps outside the country or who have lived in modern nations in the West or in the East tend to have a more assertive, independent approach to leadership with less concern for social criticism, male rejection and even family disapproval. Often, however, their lives are at risk and the consequences are fatal.

The women entering politics or accepting government appointments seem to share characteristics of independent thinking, self-confidence and a willingness to be authoritarian as if they have absorbed a male model. They have great concern for the status of other women and girls in their country, but often express impatience with progress and at times blame their own gender, other women, for a lack of courage and assertiveness. Women heads of NGOs, while varying widely in personal leadership characteristics and background experience, and while remaining goal oriented, seem to share a more consensual and inclusive style of leadership that reflects the traditional *shura* approach to problem-solving.

Women and educational leadership

Women educators in their diverse roles of leadership in education present a mixed group, making style analysis or broad generalizations difficult. Status and hierarchy appear to count more here than in either of the two above categories. Position level and perceived power make a difference in approaches to leadership for women administrators or education experts. Yet, as a whole, women educators appear to wield less power individually and to blaze fewer trails towards reform than do the women in government or in organizational leadership. This may be attributed to the fact that there are many more women in education with relatively weak leadership positions based on multiple factors, including relationships and networking, not necessarily on merit. Networking strategies, cronyism and relying on close relations is even more true for the male leaders with whom these women must work. However, increasingly, women are part of training shared with male colleagues, intended to upgrade their skills and knowledge; and increasingly the voices of women in this training are heard, and their ideas are acknowledged and used. The strength of numbers, and the appearance of support in a critical but small cluster, gives women courage. Respect and subordinance towards male colleagues, at least in public, are practised as custom dictates, yet women in these training and planning sessions frequently challenge the *status quo*.

A few women, along with men, are learning techniques of Western organizational management (as contrasted with leadership) in training sessions offered by international consultants, including short- and long-term planning, evaluation skills, record-keeping and budgeting, and other school-management strategies. However, application of this knowledge by women in their daily work as administrators or leaders is shaped by their perception of what is appropriate within Islamic culture, appropriate for their gender, feasible within the specific institution, and personally comfortable within their individual personality structure.

Although Afghanistan is an Islamic republic, and Islamic beliefs are almost seamlessly integrated with centuries of custom and traditions, there are different interpretations of the Holy Quran across Muslim communities worldwide as well as those in Central Asia (Haw, 1998; USAID, 2003; Frogh, 2010). Afghan views about what is acceptable for women's education and involvement in society vary widely.

In this chapter the discussion of women's leadership in Afghanistan, while not discounting the significance of Islam in every aspect of life, does not focus on religion *per se* but rather on how social conditions have shifted and changed, thus impacting women's contributions as leaders. Religion has been important, of course, but tradition and tragedy, repeated destruction and recovery, have been the main threads of this discussion.

Challenges to men as equal partners

Theories of leadership mirror past behaviours. Theories serve us as challenging academic exercises that may be useful in explaining or predicting success and failure in organizations or social movements. The theories discussed at the outset provide interesting categories for analysis but fall short of providing a template for understanding or guiding Afghan women leaders. The women of Afghanistan do not easily conform to theoretical patterns. The theories do not easily apply to a fluid society in which women's behaviour and roles continue to evolve – evolving within a context bound by tradition, yet shaped by conditions that demand women's engagement.

Western ways and male-derived theories do not provide relevant answers to the diverse leadership challenges facing the women of Afghanistan. Only with time – if stabilization of some sort occurs – consistent, reliable and culturally relevant theories of leadership may be hypothesized and tested for Afghan women in the future.

Conclusion

The women leaders who do speak out with courage, demanding more women in the offices of power at the school level as well as in the highest government ranks, take great risks. They must be strident, because being gentle and congenial means being overlooked and unheard. They must be courageous because if they do speak out they are labelled as "hating men". A vocal woman with ideas and independent opinions may be viewed as difficult, bitter, irrational and uncooperative, and may soon lose her job to a man. She must be a model of justice, fairness and incorruptibility. To support another educator, simply because she is a woman, violates criteria of equity; yet not supporting another woman when she is obviously unsuited to the task assigned to her will bring accusations of hypocrisy regarding women's rights.

The strong woman educational leader in Afghanistan must maintain a sense of humour, without which there is no sanity and there can be no victory. Taking the job seriously, without taking oneself too seriously, is a balancing act that comes with the life of leadership, not from being trained to lead. A new and fresh generation of girls and young women is emerging, and they may be leaders in the near future. As the next generation advances, if society does not slide backwards, they can fill the places for the women who are currently missing. Their struggle will be hard, but the path is painfully being paved to make room for them to come in large numbers.

The memories of war must be left behind and not allowed to hold them back. The preservation of cultural values, a respect for tradition and a sensitivity about the deep divide of gender difference are the burdens borne by the next women leaders in the face of predictable social opposition. It is a challenge and responsibility for the fathers, brothers, husbands and friends of the emerging generation of girls to encourage their aspirations and to support the development of their potential.

Shadows of ignorance, oppression and conservative extremism linger on to darken the path towards equity for women as leaders. Yet there is opportunity, hope and promise that future women in Afghanistan will not be found missing. They must construct their own culturally appropriate and powerfully effective leadership models giving rise to new theories.

References

Aikman, S., & Unterhalter, E. (2005). Introduction. In S. *Aikman*, & E. Unterhalter (Eds.), *Beyond Access. Transforming Policy and Practice for Fender Equality in Education*. London: Oxfam.

Ardichvili, A. (2001). Leadership styles and work-related values of managers and employees of manufacturing enterprises in post-communist countries. *Human Resource Development Quarterly*, 12(4), 363–383.

CEDPA. (2010). When women move forward, the world moves with them. Massouda Jalal. Afghanistan. Retrieved from http://www.cedpa.org/section/training/empowering_women/gallery/massouda_jalal.

CSO. (2008). *The Central Statistics Organization, Afghanistan. Women and Men in Afghanistan: Baseline Statistics on Gender*. United Nations Development Fund for Women. (UNIFEM) and Ministry of Women's Affairs (MOWA). Kabul, Islamic Republic of Afghanistan.

Den Hartog, D.N. (2004). Assertiveness. In R.J. House, P.J. Hanges, M. Javidan, P.W. Dorfman, & V. Gupta (Eds.), *Leadership, Culture, and Organizations: The GLOBE Study of 62 Societies*. Thousand Oaks, CA: Sage.

Dupree, N.H. (1986). *Women of Afghanistan*. Germany: Stiftung-Foundation.

Frogh, W. (2010) *The Myths of Women's Empowerment in the Development of Afghanistan* Boloji.com Nov. 22, 2010. Retrieved from http://www.boloji.com/analysis2/0293.htm.

Haw, K. (1998) *Educating Muslim Girls: Shifting Discourses*. Buckingham: Open University Press.

Lewis, J.J. (1997) "Afghanistan – Gender Roles". *Encyclopedia of Women's History*. Washington, DC: Federal Research Division of the Library of Congress. Retrieved from http://womenshistory.about.com/library/ency/blwh_afghanistan_gender_roles.htm.

Hofstede, G. (1980). *Culture's Consequences: International Differences in Work-Related Values* (Abridged ed.) Newbury Park, CA: Sage.

Hofstede, G. (2001). *Culture's Consequences: Comparing Values, Behaviors, Institutions, and Organizations Across Nations*, 2nd edition. Newbury Park, CA: Sage.
House, R.J., Wright, N.S., & Aditya, R.N. (1997). Cross-cultural research on organizational leadership: A critical analysis and a proposed theory. In P.C. Earley, & M. Erez (Eds.), *New Perspectives on International Industrial/Organizational Psychology* (pp. 535–625). San Francisco, CA: Jossey-Bass.
House, R.J., et al. (1999). Cultural influences on leadership and organizations: Project GLOBE. In W.H. Mobley, M.J. Gessner, & V.Arnold (Eds.), *Advances in global leadership* (Vol. 1, pp. 171–233). Stamford, CT: JAI Press.
Javidan, M., & House, R.J. (2001). Cultural acumen for the global manager: Lessons from Project GLOBE. *Organizational Dynamics*, 29(4), 289–305.
Ministry of Education. (2006) *The National Strategic Plan for Education in Afghanistan-2006-2010*. Kabul: Ministry of Education.
Ministry of Education. (2011) *National Education Interim Plan: 2011–2013*. Kabul: Ministry of Education.
NHDR. (2007) National Human Development Report. *Bridging Modernity and Tradition in Afghanistan*. New York: United Nations Development Programme.
Rahimi, F. (1986) *Women in Afghanistan*. Switzerland: Liestal.
Saeed, M. (n.d.) *Women in Afghan History*. Retrieved from http://www.scribd.com/doc/30234527/Women-in-Afghan-History.
Spink, J. (2005) *Teacher Education. Situation Analysis*. Kabul: AREU.
Trembley, D. (2004) "Women in Afghanistan: A tumultuous twentieth century" UCLA: *The Quaestio UCLA Undergraduate History Research Journal*. Retrieved from http://www.sscnet.ucla.edu/history/undergrad/pat/Journal2004/trembly.pdf.
Trompenaars, F. & Hampden-Turner, C. (1997). *Riding The Waves of Culture: Understanding Diversity in Global Business*. Chicago, IL: McGraw-Hill.
UNIFEM. (2010) *Afghan Women in Politics*. Retrieved from http://afghanistan.unifem.org/prog/GJ/politics/.
UNDP. (2007) *Afghanistan Human Development Report*. Retrieved from http://hdr.undp.org.
USAID. (2003) *Strengthening Education in the Muslim World*. Issue Paper Number 2. Washington, DC: Agency for International Development.
Women's Learning Partnership. (2010). Retrieved from http://www.learningpartnership.org/training-manuals.
Wordsworth, A. (2007). *A Matter of Interests: Gender and the Politics of Presence in Afghanistan's Wolesi Jirga*. Afghanistan Research and Evaluation Unit Issues Paper Series. Kabul: AREU.

14
The Development of Arab Women Leaders: An Emirati Perspective

Sara Alhaj and Constance Van Horne

Introduction

As women become an increasingly powerful force in the Arabian Gulf, increased attention needs to be focused on their leadership development. This chapter looks at the role that lived experience plays in developing these leaders, as opposed to formal interventions, and this study seeks to explore the underlying factors that enable women to learn how to lead. The findings are illustrated in a leader apprenticeship framework, which consists of experiencing influential encounters, dealing and learning from difficult events, and transforming directly following a formal training programme. The findings support claims to treat leadership learning as a form of apprenticeship where learning is embedded in the social fabric in which it transpires, calling for contextualizing leader development as supported by situational learning theory.

This chapter contributes to the undertheorized area of leader development and to the near dearth of works on the development of leaders and women leaders in the Emirati context. Individuals who are developing themselves as leaders were used as the unit of analysis. Data derived from in-depth, semistructured interviews were analysed using grounded-theory methodology in a substantive context to account for this gap. The methodology enables the surfacing of contextually embedded factors which impact individuals, whose perceptions are renditions of a socially constructed reality. The findings rely on interviews with four young female Emiratis from different organizations, in both the government and the semigovernment sectors, who were drawn from a leader-development programme, LEAD.

In general, women's leadership in the Gulf region and in the United Arab Emirates (UAE) has not been the focus of much scholarly investigation (Marmenout, 2009), even though women are regarded as a great resource in the Arab world that has not been tapped to its greatest potential. The UAE is currently seen as a leader in the Middle East and North Africa region in women's empowerment (UNDP, 2007). Although significant progress had been made in empowering women – they currently represent 59% of the total workforce in the government – much progress can still be made to promote women's leadership in the public and private sectors. Moreover, as more than 60% of Emirati university students, there will be a greater supply of skilled women to take up the challenge of leadership in the public and private workforce and through entrepreneurial activity (Van Horne, Huang &Al Awad, 2012).

However, as there is a lack of tradition of women's leadership in the workplace, leadership development within and transorganizational can be seen as a key tool to promote and encourage young Emirati women to take on leadership positions. Dramatic changes in the marketplace and workforce (Conger, 1993) contribute to the hypercompetitive environments and turbulence that organizations around the globe operate in.

Organizations of different sizes and shapes are responding by seeking enduring competitive advantage in the form of "leaderful" organizations by developing leaders at all levels (Raelin, 2004) to maintain their leadership pipeline (Charan, Drotter &Noel, 2011). Gardner (1990) contends that opportunities and challenges could be offered as developmental experiences but readiness and motivational attributes are intrinsic factors dependant on the person, and he reminds us that the emergence of leaders remains an enigma.

Moreover, the "business" of making leaders is an area of exponential growth and an annual global spend of an estimated £34 billion is committed by organizations for leader/leadership-development interventions (Reade & Thomas, 2004). However, there are concerns regarding whether these efforts actually contribute to leadership effectiveness and enhanced organizational performance, or that, indeed, learning transfer occurs back into the concerned organization (Cunningham, 2010; Foster, Angus & Rahinel, 2008; Lim & Morris, 2006).

The ways in which leaders develop are based on taken-for-granted assumptions, yet the underlying mechanisms and factors that contribute to development need to be exposed and understood. Given the dearth of research in this area, a grounded-theory methodology is adopted to surface the enabling and constraining factors that facilitate developing a leader's practice. Kempster (2009) argues that leadership is an act of apprenticeship embroiled within social settings. As such, the methodology is suitable for exploring participants' socially constructed realities by focusing on their perspectives.

This chapter is organized as follows. First, we undertake a brief review of the literature on leadership and the leadership development process. Then, as this chapter is based on a grounded theory study, the methodology section will be followed by the results section, which will also present the developed leader apprenticeship framework and additional literature which was used to guide the iterative development of the framework. Then the results within an Emirati context will be discussed. Finally, the conclusion provides a summation of the findings and some avenues for future research.

Leadership development

Organizations develop their leaders according to their own uptake of leadership, resulting in inconsistent practices specific to each organization (Buus, 2005; Lowe & Gardner, 2000). Paradoxically, for an activity that has attracted huge investment, there is a dearth of research in the area of leader development (Day, Harrison & Halpin, 2009; Kempster, 2009; Olivares, Peterson &Hess, 2007) indicating that such interventions are faith-based (Allio, 2005; Cook, 2006; Reade & Thomas, 2004).

Black and Earnest (2009:188) contend that as of yet "There are no known well-developed theories of leadership-development that are grounded in what is being learnt through program evaluation." Day et al. (2009) further argue that leader development encompasses the entire adult lifespan, and as such any theorizing about the process needs to take into consideration the underlying as well as ongoing aspects of human development. Lord and Hall (2005) affirm that development is a slow process by its nature which takes months to years, and, as such, there is a lack of leadership theory and empirical research regarding the qualities that develop within such a timeframe. Hence they (2005:591) call for shedding light on how behaviour and abstract thinking can be changed to drive skill development, thus concluding that "There are no general models for the development of leadership skills."

Training and education

There are wide inconsistencies reported in the literature regarding what constitutes development, training and/or education (Burke & Collins, 2005; Kempster, 2009), resulting in their being used interchangeably, albeit being derived from different theoretical origins (Mabey & Finch-Lees, 2008). Day (2001) argues that leader development focuses on developing human capital, namely interpersonal skills, knowledge and behaviours, whereas leadership development builds social capital, namely relationships and shared sense-making. McCauley and Van Velsor (2004: 2, 18) define leader development as "the expansion of a person's capacity to be effective in leadership roles and processes... those that facilitate setting direction, creating alignment, and maintaining commitment in groups of people who share common work", whereas leadership development is defined as the "expansion of the organization's capacity to enact the basic leadership tasks needed for collective work".

There is a realization that leadership needs to be institutionalized as Groves (2007: 990) states: "institutional leadership-development can be defined as planned and systematic efforts to improve the quality of leadership [within the organisation]".

The in-depth examination of leader versus leadership is beyond the scope of this study but, given the pervasiveness of the interchangeable use of the terms "leader" and "leadership" in the extant literature, the terms "leader/leadership development interventions" is used when generically quoting the literature. It is also used to reflect planned efforts on the organization's side. The term "developmental experience" is used to capture both formal and informal activities targeted at individuals.

Emirati women leadership

In contrast to other Gulf nations, in particular Saudi Arabia, women in the UAE work side by side with their Emirati male counterparts (Marmenout, 2009). They have also been encouraged to attend higher education, and this encouragement has resulted in more women than men in post-secondary and postgraduate education. This formal education has been found to be of great influence in female participation and progress in the workplace (Kemp, 2012). Great attention has been given as well to Emirati women leaders in the political sphere, with 4 female cabinet members, 8 members of the Federal National Council, 65 women diplomats and 3 women ambassadors (Kemp, 2012).

In a recently published study on Emirati women business leaders, Moore (2012) describes the inherent understanding of Emirati women leaders as Muslim women leaders and her findings show that these leaders used a participative and consultative management style. Additionally, the concept of giving back to society and contributing to the development of the UAE was an important motivating factor in the desire to achieve success.

Another recent work on Middle Eastern women's leadership development (Metcalfe & Mutlaq, 2012) presents a framework based on partnerships of key stakeholders who are seen to support women's empowerment: national government organizations, private institutions, international development agencies and the women themselves, through life-long learning supported by non-governmental organizations and women's groups. Challenges in researching leadership development have been cited (Madsen, 2010b) as resulting from a lack of leadership experiences of young Emirati women and a lack of Emirati women leaders in the business and political arena to study. Metcalfe (2011) presents a framework based on human resource development to support women and the development of their own identity in the workplace as there are few women in senior leadership positions for them to emulate.

Madsen (2010b) found that the women leaders in her study held strong beliefs with regard to their Islamic faith, the importance of family, modesty and tradition. Fathers also played an important influential role in their development as leaders and the women referred to their fathers as open-minded and successful, and who supported them in their education and work. Another key influence for these women was access to books and an importance placed on reading in the house, which in turn was expressed with a love of learning.

Influential people were also seen as having a strong influence on the women leaders (Madsen, 2010b) – these could be from the community, school or family. Madsen (2010a) suggests that leadership development, at least in college-aged Emirati women, needs to take into account the important influences, struggles and challenges, and the internal processes used to process the influences and challenges.

While there are many positive aspects, especially when compared with the wider Arab world, Emirati women still face unique challenges to their development into leaders and obtaining leadership positions in the workplace. Women are still the largest demographic of unemployed and many still prefer to remain out of the traditional workforce due to familial and societal pressures, and seemed to be especially reluctant to seek non-traditional occupations in engineering (Lau, Alhasani, Williams & Lau, 2011).

The next section presents the grounded theory methodology which was used in this study to investigate the leadership-development process of Emirati women.

Methodology

As this chapter seeks to investigate ways in which individuals, and in our case Emirati young women, learn to lead, it is necessary to penetrate a socially constructed reality where multiple meanings exist, at least between researcher and participants, and participants with their environment. As such, grounded-theory becomes a suitable methodology, especially in this area where limited empirical studies are available.

Grounded theory is founded on the paradigm of symbolic interactionism where individuals are social actors who contribute to the enactment of reality by engaging in a world of reflexive interactions (Morgan & Smircich, 1980). Given the lack of "scientific rigour" that ailed earlier methodologies, Glaser and Strauss (2010) developed and refined grounded theory as a research method where theory emerges from the data themselves, hence it is grounded, as one that could "track and validate the process of theory building" (Goulding, 2005: 295). It is a systematic and painstakingly reiterative process of data collection, data analysis and conceptualizing/theorizing (Glaser & Strauss, 2010).

In contrast with traditional data sampling techniques that are well defined, grounded theory first scans the environment to find an area of interest. Essentially, grounded theory seeks to explicate a theory in a substantive context and hence follows a purposeful sampling technique. Study participants were invited from LEAD, a leadership-development programme. I had chosen LEAD due to my familiarity with the providers as I was also enrolled in it, which gave me easy access and the full support of resources.

Interviews

Four women were interviewed: two managers and two professionals, working across industries. The interviews varied significantly in terms of how much the participant was ready to share, how much they were aware of to begin with and how much reflection they had gone through on a personal level. The quality of sharing was variable, with some possessing an easy storytelling style while others were abrupt, used short sentences and did not want to discuss the "obvious" further.

I developed a list of potential questions to assist the flow of the interview and to limit any inconsistency that might arise from using a semistructured format. Some prospective interviewees asked for the questions beforehand, so I shared the template to establish trust and rapport, which is an essential ingredient in the local culture.

All interviews lasted around 90 minutes, were conducted face to face, and were tape-recorded and transcribed to preserve data integrity. Following each interview I immediately captured my own feedback. Given grounded theory's spontaneity of approach, emphasis is placed on the interviewer's ability to improvise and act "in the moment", and the notion of piloting the instrument is not common. In any case, I conducted a rehearsal interview with two of my colleagues who are not from this programme.

One participant objected to being tape-recorded but upon further clarification she consented as I reassured her that all data would be deleted. Finally, all interviews were conducted in English to prevent misinterpretation but whenever necessary they could revert to their native Arabic language whereby I immediately translated back their thoughts.

Coding

The open-coding process of the first data set collected allows patterns and themes to emerge which trigger the onset of the iterative process of collecting more data (Glaser & Strauss, 2010). Memos and field notes are copiously generated alongside the coding process (Bryman, 2008). The support software, NVivo9, was crucial in aiding the analysis phase.

The emerging codes from the initial coding process undergoes heavy refinements in light of emerging themes and revisions to adequately reflect a generalized, abstracted notion of the underlying process(es). The ensuing codes are compared and contrasted with each other – that is, axial-coding (Corbin & Strauss, 2008) – to appreciate their dynamic interrelationship and further explicate their properties. This step furthers the abstraction level and expands the basic concepts to an overarching, generalized theory. It must be noted here that the infraction described above between the originators of grounded theory resulted in conflict regarding forcing data into prepared categories (Corbin & Strauss, 2008) as opposed to sticking to the emerging patterns from the data only (Glaser, 1999). In either case the codes and concepts in grounded theory are flexible in that they are neither mutually inclusive nor exclusive, while allowing the possibility of having meaning cut across numerous cases (Goulding, 1998).

The application of grounded-theory principles in this study was limited to time and resource availability. While I relied on a single software package, which arguably could skew the data, my goal was to explore how Emiratis, and women in particular, learned the practice of leadership in an area of sparse published research.

Results and the leadership apprentice framework

All participants shared a similar zest and can-do attitude with grand social objectives for the betterment of society. Success was causally attributed to a leadership capability within a context in all the cases. Consequently, participants pursued the path of becoming leaders to enable success in their organizations and ultimately to serve the country. Moreover, while two cases identified themselves as leaders and pursued their own development plans, such as attending LEAD, the rest were "spotted" and groomed as protégés by an organizational figure, either the CEO or a line manager (CEO/LM), which paved the way for them to see themselves as leaders.

Constructing and negotiating a leader identity

Both leaders and leadership were conflated, with leadership being a person, or a role taken by a person, who exhibits typical leadership attributes, such as vision, decisiveness and motivation. Consequently, leadership was seen as a property of an individual. A distinction arose with females describing leadership with transformational attributes:

> Leadership is...taking people with you through the journey...you can manage people...but once you trust someone, and you believe in him [sic], and you know this person believes in you, you just follow the orders [the task]. Because you will know that this person won't let you down...[or] this project...[or] the organisation down....Building trust is very important.

Moreover, being born a leader was tied to exhibiting authenticity as some argued against the possibility of "making" leaders, as the following explains:

> Even in the art, it has to be a gift. If you draw something and it's not real...if it is not in you, and you're not acting on your natural ways, you cannot be a leader.

The term "follower" was not well accepted as participants expressed concern regarding the passive role that it invoked. There was consensus regarding a leader's role in serving their community's well-being and putting their needs above all others. The term "community" was used interchangeably with "organization". Vision, as a proprietorship of the leader, further indicated the notion of one-to-many, hierarchal notion to leadership. However, there was consensus that a leader's role is to influence in a positive manner – to be a servant of the follower's needs. As being a leader is validated by others, all participants reported that it was their surrounding people who actually give them the "power" to be leaders.

As such, constructing and negotiating a leader identity is at the forefront as well as the background of the participants' minds as they interact and learn from experiencing influential encounters, experiencing difficulties and attending formal training as captured by the proposed leader apprenticeship framework (Figure 14.1).

Engaging in a learning environment

Protégés, in particular, relied heavily on practical experiences, which indicated prevalence on learning resulting from stretching assignments, as well as observing their environment which helps in forming the leader identity by gaining practical experience through role enactment.

Protégés cited organizational figures as instrumental role models in facilitating their development. However, observational learning remains an elusive endeavour locked in tacit knowledge that participants were

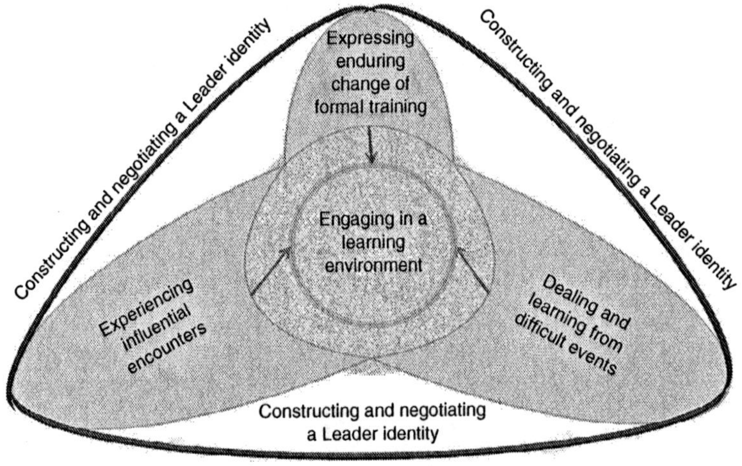

Figure 14.1 Leader apprenticeship framework

not always able to pinpoint sources of learning as the following discloses:

> I think I saw it somewhere but cannot remember where it is and that stuck in my head. Maybe I was in one of the meetings and I saw someone else supporting that person... it's something from my unconscious!!!

Observational learning was noted by its absence too as participants stated that they could benefit from having mentors, especially in their organizations, as the following excerpt shows:

> I'll get the experience from them... be similar to what they are doing, how they plan... discuss different topics... we [can discuss] challenge[s] to start a project...

The impact of observational learning was crystallized where participants were able to handle stretching assignments and the role enactment of leader episodes.

Protégés attributed delivering on assignments as developmental exercises far from any theoretical teachings where the actual practice was vital in explicating their identities as leaders. The following excerpt reflects a newly appointed manager's new conceptualization of leadership:

> I had to understand through the practical experience the definition of leadership rather than the theoretical part. Responsibility- being in a leadership position, you have to be assertive... visionary... your role [is] very strategic... Reading about it will get the knowledge and ideas. But the practical experience- sometimes you make a decision far away from the theoretical inkling.... You're squeezed with time constrains, therefore you need to be intuitive, and have the initiative to decide.

Participants who were privy to such attention noted their awareness of the distinction bestowed on them, which enabled them to see themselves as leaders. However, participants stressed that their active role in the organization, and a proven record of hard work as well as using initiative, set them apart from their peers. Moreover, it was this attention that gave them legitimacy in being leaders among their peers, who clearly took notice of this "special treatment", as the following shows:

> she brought me in these meetings... that gave me power in the team... then it was simple things like they [peers] wanted to go to meetings and they [noted] this girl [herself] would know what the director wants... because I worked a lot with her... I know [how] she thinks so I can comment on them...

In the above scenario, the unavailability of the director prompted the participant's colleagues to re-appraise her abilities and include her in meetings.

Role enactment was strongly emphasized in some cases where participants shared a detailed description of critical incidents, such as absence of the director, which enabled them to put their learnt knowledge into action and handle the consequences. For example, one participant acted on behalf of the director, who was away on emergency leave, without having official authority to do so and took the risk of signing sensitive documents. Incidentally, in all cases, no one got into trouble. The attention to detail, learning about what is acceptable to an organization, and being resourceful in garnering support to pull together an event or an assignment are all tacitly assimilated and implicitly denoted in these interviews.

Finally, most participants reported that LEAD could be enhanced by adding applied learning to the curriculum, as the following participant shared:

> You actually go to organisations and see how the decision making is made... learn how the process of making the financial documents as part of the financial management.

The main components of lived experiences shared by participants are reported under the following themes: experiencing influential encounters, dealing and learning from difficulties, and transforming directly following of formal training, as summarized in Table 14.1.

Experiencing influential encounters

An emerging theme across all cases revealed the presence of notable people in the lives of the participants, including organizational figures such as a CEO/LM, and personal contacts, such as family, friends and colleagues. Protégés referred mostly to people within an organizational context, particularly the CEO, as enablers for further growth, learning and development. However, the salience and degree of support varied widely among the cases.

Table 14.1 Breakdown of leader apprenticeship framework components

Constructing and negotiating a leader's identity		
Conflating leaders/leadership		
Espoused and enacted attributes of a leader		
Describing leadership dilemmas (definitional, born/made, Western influence, leaders/managers, male/female)		
Engaging in a learning environment		
Observing notable people's practices (observational learning)		
Embracing stretching assignments and role enactment (situated learning)		
Experiencing influential encounters	**Dealing and learning from difficult events**	**Expressing enduring changes of formal training**
Describing impact of role models	Struggling to find one's path	Enhancing learning of subjects and skills
Noting supportive organizational environment	Dealing with personal hardships	Expressing need for localization
Being influenced by historical figures and management gurus	Confronting organization realities	Enduring changes in self-conception and self-awareness
		Describing and refining aspirations and objectives
		Learning from each other (peers)

Foremost, notable people provided emotional support and feedback that reinforced self-esteem. Some notable people, acknowledged as role-models or mentors, offered guidance and projected a range of possibilities that a participant could aspire to, particularly in an organizational setting, as illustrated below:

> She [director] was very hard working. She was a mother, she had kids, she was married, [yet] she was all over the place…when she's in meetings, she's better than 10 men! [S]he's young…when you see that, you say 'yes I can do that, I can be that'…she speaks to Shaikhs…to media…to staff…[It] made me [say] 'I really want to be like her'.

Historical figures and management gurus were cited as learning resources in most cases. Reading books was seen as a source of knowledge to keep up with world affairs and as a source of influence by famous figures, particularly with biographies, including local (Shaikh Zayed,

Shaikh Mohammed bin Rashid), regional (Ghazi Al-Ghosaibi) and international (Lady Diana, Barrack Obama, Oprah Winfrey, Jack Welch) figures.

Dealing with and learning from difficult events

Another main theme that emerged was dealing with and learning from difficulties in almost all cases where a mentality of "surviving by persevering" clarified and reinforced one's self-identity as a leader. Difficulties varied across the cases where both personal experiences as well as incidents from work were relayed, resulting in three main categories: struggling to find one's path, dealing with personal hardships and confronting organizational realities.

The majority of cases revealed that young Emiratis changed their careers after graduating from their undergraduate degrees and were on a journey of trying to find who they really are, as the following participant puts it:

> for me, I was one of the people, I'm sure many of the people, maybe the majority in UAE even, they don't know what they want. They don't have the vision.

Participants, particularly the younger ones, revealed that the gap between being a full-time student and a full-time employee prompted them to actively seek ways to "occupy" themselves with exposing the lack of hands-on opportunities at work to channel these energies. It appears that this active search for meaning had put them on a path of self-discovery that led them to LEAD.

Expressing enduring changes of formal-training

This theme revolves around the enduring changes that impacted participants as a result of attending LEAD, which was the majority's first formal leadership training. Keeping in mind that participants are early in their careers, the general content of the curriculum, which closely resembles an MBA, was appraised as relevant and extensive, giving them a full appreciation of the wider organizational activities. Certain tools, such as mind mapping, were reported as influential as they helped in organizing their thinking patterns. Of significance was the realization of the importance of knowledge and skills to a leader, such as finance, as the following shows:

> I was wondering why we're taking financial management... you can get someone who knows how to deal with money!! [But] it's not

> just about leading them to where, any organisation have to have an income sheet... I realised I have to know this skill... it is part of the knowledge in the leader.

While the majority agreed that the case studies, tools and theories used in the programme were relevant to their organizations, upon further reflection some indicated that due to cultural reasons, not everything was appropriate. A struggle appeared in contemplating full adoption of "Westernized" theories in the face of local norms. For instance, a participant expressed his admiration and endorsement of the transformational leadership style and later noted that the hierarchy in the organization must be respected and abided by. Another participant fully supported the taught decision-making tools, such as Covey's time-management matrix (urgent/important), but then noted that decision-making style in the UAE/Arabian context could be described as discontinuous, ambiguous and rushed as figures of authorities can change suddenly, as opposed to "other" cultures. Moreover, everyone expressed that the cases were too generic and noted the need for local customization to reflect the Emirati context.

It was unanimously agreed that the most valuable opportunity that the formal training presented was the chance to learn from peers. All participants noted that this form of learning was crucial to understanding the topics at hand – it grounded the abstract and theoretical notions into practical terms. Nonetheless, the information from an expert – that is, a professor – was still important. The lively discussion in the classroom where experiences are swapped and industry knowledge is shared is seen as a competitive advantage that the programme offered as attendees were from diverse backgrounds. Furthermore, participants were keen on the positioning and offerings by their organizations vis-à-vis the rest to formulate an understanding of how the business environment operates.

Emirati context

For a concept as vague as leadership (Yukl, 1989), there was convergence on viewing leadership as a process of influence, which is consistent with the widely accepted definition (Northouse, 2007). However, all participants equated leadership with servantship, whereby leaders are entrusted messengers whose sole role is to "take care" of their people's needs. This finding confirms the collectivist fabric of the society (Hofestede, 2009) that derives its teachings directly from the Islamic religion, which shapes its conduct in life (Abdallah & Al-Homoud, 2001). Furthermore, the idea that leadership is causally attributed to success was discussed earlier.

While the participants explicitly showed that they do embrace modernity and the imported notions about leadership, implicitly their actions and behaviours revealed a struggle between the applicability of these teachings and the reality of their world, a finding that is in common with Abdallah and Al-Homoud's (2001) work. The commonality arises despite generational and regional differences, possibly because they share ideological convictions where Western-based leadership research, which stems mostly from the US (Yukl, 2002), embraces individualism and profit-seeking means in a free market, whereas the Emirati culture preserves societal ties through collectivist endeavours and conformance to familial obligations in a regulated market where profits are not explicitly sought (Anderson, 2010).

Nonetheless, given both the UAE's multicultural diversity and its endeavour to seek internationality, holding to collectivist notions is a struggle which the participants are exposed to. The inherited nature of a transitional, emerging economy is also evident as participants reveal their struggle to cope with the rigidness of systems, bureaucracy and resistance to change at the ground level. The UAE's aspirations to transform into a knowledge economy will rest on overcoming these traditional obstacles while trying to retain its heritage and identity.

The reliance on distant figures as role models is in contrast with the extant literature where the proximity of role models is prevalent. This finding could be a reflection of the limited range of notables that Emirati women specifically are exposed to, given the lopsided workforce makeup, where 82% are foreign workers. The participants could be compensating for this important source of learning by depending on printed material. Also, it is possible that being a junior member of the organization is also a factor that limits interaction with notables from across the organization. Furthermore, the reliance on distant role models from a multitude of backgrounds and cultures is indicative of the Emirati culture's openness to embracing imported Westernized ideals. This is unsurprising given that all management education and higher education of Emiratis is delivered using Western-based practices (Madsen, 2010a; Wilkins, 2001).

A unique finding in the Emirati context is a preoccupation with finding a career path after graduation and the first years of work. Again, this could be attributed to a lack of role models for Emiratis, possibly because of the UAE's relative youth as a nation (around 40 years). Participants reveal a struggle with abiding to family obligations and societal constraints that make certain occupations more favourable. In the long run, however, they find a way to break the mould and grow into their authentic self (Kouzes & Posner, 2002), which again could be described as a crucible given the strength required to go against the tide.

Moreover, the hands-on role of the CEO/LM stood out as a specific finding in the Emirati culture when compared with Western literature. This role was equally prevalent in all cases irrespective of organization industry, size or maturity. The findings are in line with the patriarchal structure of the society (Abdallah & Al-Homoud, 2001) where a CEO takes it as a personal responsibility to nurture younger talents.

Additionally, there was a sense of using peers as benchmarks to gauge one's developmental needs, which indicates their role as notable people. As mentioned earlier, assessment was not evident and this could be a compensatory reaction by the participants to fill the void, which only underscores its importance.

Conclusion and discussion

In conclusion, this study seeks to explicate the factors that enable young women who are in the workforce to become leaders in the Emirati context. The findings are based on data collected in semistructured interviews from four Emiratis from various backgrounds/industries using grounded-theory methodology where little previous research has been published. The findings shed light on previously taken-for-granted assumptions regarding leader development by revealing the developmental aspects of lived experiences. These were found to include experiencing influential encounters, and experiencing and learning from difficulties, which highlights the importance of processual and relational daily interactions for learning the practice of leadership. The study also highlights the significant role of formal training for young, emerging women leaders who strive to fit in by learning the basic knowledge and skills pertinent to leadership as well as forming bonding experiences with peers at their level.

The study also reveals particularities of the Emirati culture where CEOs are more involved than usual in developing younger talent. While, explicitly, leadership concepts/teachings were accepted "as is", implicitly there is a struggle to reconcile them with cultural beliefs because the concept of leadership is equated with servantship. Moreover, the study shows a lack of feedback and assessment to aid the development process. In particular, human resource management governance was largely missing, thus exposing development to happenstance.

The study has implications for individuals seeking to become leaders and organizations alike in regarding leadership learning processes as an apprenticeship. While there are generic knowledge and skills, learning to lead is context specific and requires individuals to be vigilant about their contexts in which leadership is socially embedded. Individuals need to be aware of notable people in their vicinity, and organizations need to make notable people available as well as increase their frequency of meetings with budding leaders. Hence organizations must be attuned to their cultures and legacies that are tacitly imbibed and replicated. Organizations need to create risk-free and safe environments where individuals can seek out role enactment opportunities and challenging assignments, while providing adequate support and feedback mechanisms to encourage experimentation with provisional selves and reinforce self-efficacy.

The findings of this study could be used as a springboard for future studies in the Emirati context, and they need to be further investigated in various contexts, such as female-dominated versus male-dominated industries, public versus private sectors, employed managers versus owner-managers (i.e. entrepreneurs), and large versus small/medium enterprises. Finally, the study offers an alternative route to development that transcends the dominant functionalist discourse of training and education, and allows participants to take advantage of naturalistic experiences.

References

Abdalla, I.A., & Al-Homoud, M.O. (2001). Exploring the implicit leadership theory in the Arabian Gulf States. *Applied Psychology an International Review*, 50(4), 506–531.

Allio, R.J. (2005). Leadership development: teaching versus learning. *Management Decision*, 43(7/8), 1071–1076.

Anderson, P. (2010). Ten tips for doing Mideast business. *Arabian Business*. Retrieved from http://www.arabianbusiness.com/ten-tips-for-doing-mideast-business-272188.html.

Black, A., & Earnest, G. (2009). Measuring the outcomes of leadership development programs. *Journal of Leadership & Organizational Studies*, 16, 184–196.

Bryman, A. (2008). *Social Research Methods*, 3rd edition. Oxford: Oxford University Press.

Burke, V., & Collins D. (2005). Optimising the effects of leadership development programmes: a framework for analysing the learning and transfer of leadership skills. *Management Decision*, 43(7/8), 975–987.

Buus, I. (2005). The evolution of leadership development: challenges and best practice. *Industrial and Commercial Training*, 37(4/5), 185–188.

Charan, R., Drotter, S., & Noel, J. (2011). *The Leadership Pipeline: How to Build the Leadership Powered Company*, 2nd edition. San Francisco, CA: Jossey-Bass.

Conger, J.A. (1993). The brave new world of leadership training. *Organisational Dynamics*, 21(3), 46–59.

Cook, P. (2006). Management and leadership development: Making it work. *Industrial and Commercial Training*, 38(1), 49–52.

Corbin, J., & Strauss, A. (2008). *Basics of Qualitative Research*, 3rd edition. London: Sage Publications.

Cunningham, I. (2010). Leadership development in crisis: Leadership development hasn't made much difference to organizations. *Development and Learning in Organizations*, 24(5), 5–7.

Day, D.V. (2001). Leadership development: a review in context. *Leadership Quarterly*, 11(4), 581-613.

Day, D., Harrison, M., & Halpin, S. (2009). *An Integrative Approach to Leader Development: Connecting Adult Development, Identity, and Expertise*. London: Routledge.

Foster, M.K., Angus, B., & Rahinel, R. (2008), "All in the hall" or "sage on the stage": learning in leadership development programmes. *Leadership & Organization* Leadership development in crisis: Leadership development hasn't made much difference to organizations *Development Journal*, 29(6), 504–521.

Gardner, J.W. (1990). *On Leadership*. New York: The Free Press.

Glaser, B., & Strauss, A. (2010). *The Discovery of Grounded Theory: Strategies for Qualitative Research*, 5th edition. London: Aldine Transaction.

Glaser, B. (1999). The future of grounded theory. *Qualitative Health Research*, 9, 836–845.

Goulding, C. (1998). Grounded theory: The missing methodology on the interpretivist agenda. *Qualitative Market Research*, 1(1), 50–57.

Goulding, C. (2005). Grounded theory, ethnography and phenomenology: a comparative analysis of three qualitative strategies for marketing research. *European Journal of Marketing*, 39(3/4), 294–308.

Groves, K. (2007). Integrating leadership development and succession planning best practices. *The Journal of Management Development*, 26(3), 239–260.

Hofestede, G. (2009). *Geert Hofestede Cultural Dimensions*. Retrieved from http://www.geert-hofstede.com/hofstede_arab_world.shtml.

Kemp, L. (2012). Change in business dynamics: Female participation and progress in the workforce of the United Arab Emirates. *International Conference on Excellence in Business*, Sharjah, UAE, 9–10 May 2012.

Kempster, S. (2009). *How Managers have Learnt to Lead*. Hampshire: Palgrave Macmillan.

Kouzes, J.M., & Posner, B. (2002). *The Leadership Challenge*, 3rd edition. San Francisco, CA: Jossey-Bass.

Lau, R., Alhasani, N., Williams, J., & Lau, L. (2011). Drilling into Diversity... Developing the Reservoir of Talent. In *SPE Annual Technical Conference and Exhibition*. October.

Lim, D., & Morris, M. (2006). Influence of training characteristics, instructional satisfaction, and organisational climate on perceived learning and training transfer *Human Resources Development Quarterly*, 17(1), 85–115.

Lord, R., & Hall, R. (2005). Identity, deep structure and the development of leadership skill. *Leadership Quarterly*, 16(4), 591–615.

Lowe, K., & Gardner, W. (2000). Ten years of The Leadership Quarterly: Contributions and challenges for the future. *The Leadership Quarterly*, 11(4), 459–514.

Mabey, C., & Finch-Lees, T. (2008). *Management and leadership development.* London: Sage.

Madsen, S.R. (2010a). Leadership development in the United Arab Emirates: The transformational learning experiences of women. *Journal of Leadership & Organizational Studies*, 17(1), 100–110.

Madsen, S.R. (2010b). The experiences of UAE women leaders in developing leadership early in life. *Feminist Formations*, 22(3), 75–95.

Marmenout, K.. (2009). Women-focused leadership development in the Middle East: Generating local knowledge (June 30, 2009). *INSEAD Working Paper No.* 2009/25/IGLC. Available at SSRN: http://ssrn.com/abstract= 1427729 or http://dx.doi.org/10.2139/ssrn.14277

McCauley, C., & Van Velsor, E. (2004). Introduction: Our view of leadership development. In C.D. McCauley, & E. Van Velsor (Eds.), *The Centre for Creative Leadership Handbook of Leadership Development*, 2nd edition. San Francisco, CA: Jossey-Bass.

Metcalfe, B.D. (2011). Women, empowerment and development in Arab Gulf States: A critical appraisal of governance, culture and national human resource development (HRD) frameworks. *Human Resource Development International*, 14(2), 131–148.

Metcalfe, B.D., & Mutlaq, L. (2012). Women, leadership and development: reappraising the value of the feminine in leadership theorizing in the Middle East. *Leadership Development in the Middle East*, 328–370.

Moore, L. (2012). Worldly leadership through local knowledge: Discovering voices of Emirati women business leaders. *Worldly Leadership: Alternative Wisdoms for a Complex World*, 171–191.

Morgan, G., & Smircich, L. (1980). The case for qualitative research. *The Academy Management Review*, 5, 491–500.

Northouse, P. (2007). *Leadership: Theory and Practice*, 4th edition. London: Sage.

Olivares, O., Peterson, G., & Hess, K. (2007). An existential-phenomenological framework for understanding leadership development experiences. *Leadership & Organisation Development Journal*, 28(1), 76–91.

Raelin, J.A. (2004). Don't bother putting leadership into people. *Academy of Management Executive*, 18(3), 131–135.

Reade, Q., & Thomas, D. (2004). Critics question the value of leadership training. *Personnel Today*, 12 October. Retrieved from: http://www.personneltoday.com/articles/2004/10/12/26034/critics-question-value-of-leadership-training.html.

United Nations Development Programme. (2007). *Millennium Development Goals United Arab Emirates Report* (March 2007).

Van Horne, C., Huang, V., & Al Awad, M. (2012). *GEM UAE Report* 2011. Zayed University, UAE.

Wilkins, S. (2001). Management development in the Arab Gulf states: the influence of language and culture. *Industrial and Commercial Training*, 33(6/7), 260–265.

Yukl, G. (1989). Managerial leadership: A review of theory and research. *Journal of Management*, 15(2), 251–289.

Yukl, G. (2002). *Leadership in organisations*, 5th edn, Prentice-Hall, New Jersey.

Index

Note: Locators followed by 'f' and 't' refer to figures and tables respectively.

Printed and bound in the United States of America